The Edinburgh Encyclopedia

The statue of Sir Walter Scott meditates beneath the arch of his monument in Princes Street, with the tower of St Giles High Kirk in the background. (City of Edinburgh Council)

THE
EDINBURGH ENCYCLOPEDIA

SANDY MULLAY

MAINSTREAM PUBLISHING

EDINBURGH AND LONDON

First published in Great Britain in 1996 by
MAINSTREAM PUBLISHING COMPANY (EDINBURGH) LTD
7 Albany Street
Edinburgh EH1 3UG

ISBN 1 85158 762 4

A catalogue record for this book is available from the British Library

Designed by Jenny Haig
Typeset in Bembo
Printed and bound in Great Britain by Butler and Tanner Ltd, Frome

·EDINBVRGH·

THE CITY OF EDINBURGH COUNCIL

The Right Honourable
Eric Milligan
Lord Provost

July 1996

This new book by Sandy Mullay is set to become an essential reference book for all those with an interest in Scotland's capital city. For me personally, it has been published at exactly the right time, following my appointment as Lord Provost in April this year. As I prepare the many speeches I am required to give on all manner of subjects relating to the City of Edinburgh, I will have no further to look than 'The Edinburgh Encyclopedia' to find something of the history as well as a modern day perspective on every aspect of Edinburgh life.

The book makes an excellent read from start to finish. Whilst it gives an invaluable insight into the city's fascinating history, it also depicts the essence of Edinburgh showing how she became the beautiful, successful, dynamic, modern European capital city that she is in the 1990's.

ERIC MILLIGAN
Lord Provost

Acknowledgments

My thanks for information and advice in preparing this encyclopedia go to; Kevin Wilbraham, Alison Scott, and Richard Hunter of Edinburgh City Archives; John Higgins of Lothian Region Press and Marketing Department; Mike Thomson of Lothian Region Water and Drainage Department; Colin Dalrymple of Lothian Region Education Department; and Richard Church-Michael of Lothian and Borders Fire Brigade.

To Graham Duncan and David Jamieson of the District Council Planning Department; Shenaz Bahadur of the District Council Race Relations Department; Philip Saville of the Lothian Biological Records Centre; Kevin McAuley of the Royal Observatory Edinburgh; Chris Sydes of Scottish Natural Heritage; Paul Burgess of the Scottish Prisons Service; Andy Reid of Scottish Office Agriculture and Fisheries Department; Gill Parker of the Royal Scottish Country Dance Society; Elaine Ewing of British Gas Supply; John Frame of Heart of Midlothian F.C.; Jane Ferguson of Historic Scotland; Ian Murray of The Sports Business (on behalf of the Scottish Rugby Union); Bill Brady of *The Scotsman*; Jacqueline Allan of Edinburgh City Council Public Relations Department; and Ann Manfries of the Edinburgh International Festival.

Also, to the staffs of the Scottish Record Office, National Library of Scotland, Edinburgh City Libraries (particularly the Reference, Scottish, and Edinburgh Departments), Edinburgh Tourist Board, Scottish Tourist Board, Scottish Natural Heritage Library, Scottish Agricultural College Library (Edinburgh), Scottish Education Department, Meteorological Office, British Geological Survey, Royal Caledonian Curling Club, Royal Mail.

Editorial supervision of this volume was undertaken by John Beaton, to whom I extend my thanks. Photographs herein were supplied by the author, except where indicated.

Particular acknowledgment goes to Frank Reid for writing the article on RACING, and to George McMurdo for his piece on GOLF. My thanks for the assistance rendered by the following individuals is also willingly acknowledged: Elizabeth Reid, Margaret Ferguson, Stuart Sellar, Ethel Tweedie, Jim Suddon, Councillor Mike Pringle, and last but not exactly least, my wife Marilyn.

Contents

Foreword

A visiting English writer once remarked that the Forth Railway Bridge has 'an unconscious beauty, typical of so many Victorian structures'. Perhaps 'unconscious beauty' is an exactly apt phrase with which to describe Edinburgh.

For the fact is that Edinburgh, despite its attractiveness, is, and always has been, a working city. It traditionally has had a mixed economy, more service-orientated than product-related, and much more industrial than, say, Florence or Venice, with which it has been compared. On the other hand, the city is probably more attractive to visit than most British cities nurtured in the now exhausted Industrial Revolution, all of which are struggling to readjust their economies to a more service-related base, particularly through tourism. Some of these communities are now turning their eyes enviously to Edinburgh's status as a tourist centre of international renown, all too well aware that one city's tourist attractions can rapidly become another's. In other words, many of Edinburgh's tourist attractions could easily be moved – unless they happen to be embedded in solid rock!

A newspaper contributor alleged in 1995, for example, that the Royal Botanic Garden did not 'belong' to Edinburgh, but is a national treasure funded by British taxpayers, and could just as well be located elsewhere. This overlooked the fact that the Garden grew out of Edinburgh University's need for botanical sources of medicines, and has simply expanded to its existing pre-eminence despite the existence of other academically-fostered gardens elsewhere.

Equally, the suggestion of a National Gallery of Scottish Art *not* being located in Scotland's capital city seems self-contradictory, but the principal argument for moving it elsewhere appears to be governed by the economic problems facing another city, and has nothing to do with a national arts policy viewed from a professional or historical viewpoint. Edinburgh's elected representatives should be prepared to fight to retain all such attractions which are indigenous to Edinburgh and its status as a historic capital.

This book is aimed very much at the citizen who sees Edinburgh in all its moods and seasons, although, hopefully, there is much here to interest the visitor as well. The editor makes no apology for featuring the workaday aspects of the city – there is less here about castle and cathedral, about palace and tattoo, than there is on housing, industry, education, transport, and sport. The bibliography will indicate where additional reading can be pursued, but any visit to a city bookshop will reveal plenty of guidebooks and other tourist-orientated literature.

This introduction opened with a comment about the unconscious beauty of Victorian architecture, and it is worth returning our attention to that historical period to discover why and how Edinburgh looks the way it does today. Walking along any city street, the pedestrian sees shops empty or turned into charity bazaars, vacant bank buildings, and churches with their doors locked and barred.

The simple truth is that the Victorians dictated the way our city has looked since their time. Not only did they expand Edinburgh up to and beyond its boundaries, they hesitated not one second in tearing down antiquities and venerable buildings if these stood in the way of Victorian progress. Then they built too many churches – evidence of the extraordinary splintering of the Church of Scotland after 1843 – too many shops – 'fall out' from the shopkeepers versus hawkers war which the former group emphatically won – and too many pubs. Now the wheel has come half-circle; now we seem to preserve too much and don't tear down nearly enough! And while the shops have hit hard times, vacant buildings are being converted into stall markets!

Finally, as this book was going to press, it was learned that Edinburgh has been designated a World Heritage site by the United Nations Education, Scientific, and Cultural Organisation (UNESCO). The city is only Scotland's second site to be designated, after St Kilda, and only the third British city to be so honoured. The award is particularly valuable for being made by an organisation which does not enjoy the United Kingdom's support, and so can hardly be accused of bias!

Abbeys

Holyrood Abbey is the most historic religious site in the city, despite having ceased to be a working abbey around 1610. Reduced to ruins by English predation in the first half of the 16th century, and following a disastrous attempt at re-roofing with stone slabs in the 18th, the abbey is now no more than an open-air annexe to the tourist trap which is the Palace of Holyroodhouse. The whole Holyrood site is one of the city's most important visitors' attractions, situated at the foot of the Royal Mile (High Street) stretching down from the castle. A description of the Palace can be found under ROYAL RESIDENCES.

The principal part of the Abbey remaining is the roofless nave with aisle walls showing Romanesque arcading decoration. The west front is massively impressive, although much altered in 1633 for the coronation visit of Charles I, and the choir has been ruined since the 1570s. Restoration schemes were rejected in 1906 and 1945 on the grounds that too much stonework would need to be replaced, although it can be argued that the lack of archival plans could ease the work of the restorer, since only an approximation to period authenticity need be achieved. At least, the ruins were mystical enough in 1829 to inspire the visiting Felix Mendelssohn to write his Scottish Symphony.

History
Holyrood Abbey was founded on its present site in 1128 after David I's legendary encounter with a stag with a holy rood (cross) in its antlers. He interpreted this to

The ruins of Holyrood Abbey as pictured in an early commercial postcard, looking north-eastwards. (Edinburgh City Libraries)

mean that he must build an abbey for the Augustinian order on this site. Unfortunately it was outside the walls of the city, and was frequently sacked and damaged, never more so than in the 16th century.

The 12th century Augustinians are believed to have based the design of their new abbey on their planned structure at Merton in Surrey. The dimensions have been described as 'surprisingly modest' by the Buildings of Scotland volume for Edinburgh, and this source should be consulted for a detailed architectural description (see BIBLIOGRAPHY). Scholars researching the building of the Abbey have been frustrated by a lack of documentation.

After the pillaging by the English invader in 1544 and 1547, no major reconstruction was attempted, while James V preferred to build up the palatial aspects of the site. Only 21 canons remained by 1560, although it was to be another 50 years before the palace was completely secularised. Later Stewart attempts to restore a Catholic chapel at Holyrood, and the casting out of the Canongate congregation which had used the Abbey Church (see CHURCHES), led to the buildings being damaged by a mob in 1688, and the royal tombs desecrated (see CEMETERIES AND CREMATORIA). The congregation stayed away, using their new church which is still the parish church of the Canongate (opposite Huntly House).

Holyrood's sanctuary refuge stretched from the Girth Cross, near the foot of the Canongate, as far as Duddingston village, and lasted well into Victorian times, when imprisonment for civil debt ceased in 1880. It had previously resulted in Edinburgh debtors (known colloquially as 'Abbey Lairds') improvising a new life for themselves in and around Holyrood, without fear of arrest from the civic authorities or pursuit by creditors, provided they did not leave the sanctuary on any weekday. In these curious circumstances much of the seminal second edition of the *Encyclopaedia Britannica* came to be written by the impoverished James Tytler (see INDUSTRY).

One aspect of the work of the Holyrood Augustinians which has proved to be immortal is the process of education. Holyrood was one of the two earliest schools in Edinburgh, and the Royal High School has traditionally claimed that its origins can be traced back to Holyrood when it was a working abbey, before the Town Council became involved in the school's funding and administration (see SCHOOLS).

Another former abbey site can be found on the outskirts of Edinburgh at Newbattle, near Dalkeith. There were important ecclesiastical institutions in Edinburgh at various times at Blackfriars, in the south-east of the city (from 1230), and at Greyfriars, founded south of the Grassmarket in the 15th century. Collegiate churches also existed at Leith, St Giles's at Corstorphine, and at Restalrig, and a nunnery dedicated to St Catherine of Sienna gave its name to the Sciennes district in which it was situated.

Agriculture

Edinburgh has played a major role in the development of Scottish agriculture. As

Scotland's most populous city for a major part of the nation's history, it created a consumer demand which much of the surrounding countryside has traditionally served (*see also* MARKETS), as well as making a vital contribution to the study of agricultural science.

As late as 1957 there were no fewer than 52 farms within the city boundaries, along with 120 market gardens, 37 piggeries, and 17 small holdings, giving a total of 226 main holdings. In contrast, in June 1994, Scottish Office statistics showed 108 agricultural sites comprising one or more hectare (2.47 acres), and 190 of less than that area. Twenty-one sites are laid out as allotments administered by the City Council.

It is doubly difficult to compare these figures; Edinburgh city boundaries now extend much farther west than they did in 1957, but the spread of peripheral housing schemes has undoubtedly reduced the number of the larger agricultural holdings. For example, as compared to 52 farms in Edinburgh in 1957, there were 31 listed in 1995, and in a larger area, and including the City Farm at Gorgie, which is largely recreational. Suffice to say that Edinburgh has by no means turned its back on the land.

Academically, Edinburgh has made a major contribution to the study of agriculture, the city's university breaking new ground in 1790 with the setting up of Britain's first professorship in agriculture. Today, with Scotland's most important

The countryside intrudes into the city at the Braids and Blackford hills, part of a salient from the Green Belt. In this picture, Edinburgh's equine inhabitants have a view of the Royal Observatory all to themselves. (City of Edinburgh Council)

agricultural college based in Edinburgh, along with a major veterinary college and the headquarters of the Scottish Office's agriculture department and its specialist agencies, Edinburgh's integral position in the nation's food production industry can hardly be overemphasised. The city is also the home of the Scottish Agricultural Museum based a few miles outside the city centre. The City Farm at Gorgie is also an established part of the Edinburgh scene.

SCOTTISH AGRICULTURAL COLLEGE

Also known as the Edinburgh School of Agriculture, this is one of the oldest academically-based centres teaching agriculture in Scotland. With its headquarters at King's Buildings, having removed there from George Square in 1960, the college is one of three centres, the other two campuses being located in Aberdeen and Auchincruive (Ayrshire). The college receives funds from the Scottish Office, in addition to earning income from advisory and research contracting. The college houses Edinburgh University's agricultural teaching staff, and it has outstations at the Bush Estate, near Penicuik, and at St Boswells, Perth, Forfar, and Cupar. The college's advisory and consultancy services have helped the college become sturdily self-financing over the last few years.

History

Edinburgh University's Chair of Agriculture was unusual in 1790 in being founded by a private individual, Sir William Pulteney (William Johnstone of Dumfriesshire before he changed his name when marrying the heiress of the Bath estates). Pulteney had a vision of making agricultural research and teaching more academically respectable, and he must have been well pleased with the first incumbent of the new post, Andrew Coventry, professor for no less than 40 years.

ROYAL (DICK) VETERINARY COLLEGE

Scotland's first college dedicated to veterinary studies is situated at Summerhall, in a Grecian-style building facing the Meadows. An extension has overflowed into nearby Summerhall Square, where the statue of a horse can be seen, moved from the college's original premises at Clyde Street (near the present bus station). There is also a college field station at the Bush Estate, south of the city.

History

The establishment of the 'Dick Vet' was something of a triumph for the Dick family, originally from Aberdeen, who believed that Edinburgh should follow London's example in formalising the proper treatment of animal ailments. After qualifying in London, William Dick began lecturing in Edinburgh in 1823, initially to very few students. His perseverance paid dividends, a Veterinary College being established in Clyde Street in 1833, with the co-operation of the Highland and Agricultural Society, but with the bulk of the costs paid by Dick himself.

The ensuing years produced many reversals of fortune for the new college, particularly after Dick died in 1866, and a rival college sprang up at Gayfield House in East London Street. Matters improved with the College becoming incorporated by Act of Parliament in 1906 and with Edinburgh University involvement from 1911. The present building was opened in 1916, gradually extending round the corner as the 'Dick Vet' has taken on a prominent role in British veterinary science.

ROYAL HIGHLAND AND AGRICULTURAL SOCIETY

Founded in 1784 with its headquarters in Edinburgh, the organisers of the well-known Highland Show held their first such event on a one-acre site just off the Canongate in 1822, but this popular annual show has been held at Ingliston since 1960. The Society has also been active in promoting agricultural science, publishing its own periodicals and conducting veterinary scholastic examinations, at one time in conjunction with what is now the Royal (Dick) Veterinary College.

CITY FARM

With so many green spaces in Edinburgh's 100 square miles, Gorgie Road is perhaps the last place that a visitor would expect to find the capital's City Farm. Established as a charity in 1982, and presently containing 150 animals, this is a highly-popular visitor attraction, but is hardly representative of the modern industrialised nature of farming today.

SCOTTISH AGRICULTURAL MUSEUM

Situated at Ingliston, this collection of artefacts and illustrations is now administered by the National Museums of Scotland. It includes the oldest threshing machine, and the world's first reaping machine, the latter

invented by Robert Bell in 1828. Entry is free, except when the Royal Highland Show is taking place, when an entry fee to the showground has to be paid.

see also MARKETS.

Airports

Edinburgh Airport is situated seven miles due west from the centre of the city some 135 feet (40 metres) above mean sea level, north of the A8 Glasgow road from which access to the terminal building is gained. Operational from 1976, the Airport's main runway (designated 07/25) was formally opened by H.M. The Queen on 27 May 1977. It is 2,560 metres long (2,636 yards) by 46 metres (47.3 yards), running east-west, and almost at right-angles to the earlier 13/31 runway, 1,829 metres long (1,883 yards) by 46 metres (47.3 yards), which has always been susceptible to crosswinds.

Owned by Edinburgh Airport Ltd, the terminal is Scotland's second busiest, after Glasgow, with 2.5 million passengers passing through in 1993, and nearly 60,000 aircraft movements, an approximate 50% traffic increase in only five years. There are regular shuttle flights to London, heavy charter traffic in summer, a limited number of flights to European destinations, but none, at the time of writing, to North America on a regularly timetabled basis. The airport is home to two flying clubs – Edinburgh and Turnhouse.

History

The area was first used for aviation in May 1916 when the Royal Flying Corps opened a runway near Turnhouse village, and for many years this place name was synonymous with both civil and military aviation before the former activity was reallocated to the new terminal a short distance westwards in 1976. Home to 603 Squadron in the Second World War, Turnhouse was in the forefront of Britain's air defences when German aircraft targeted the Forth (rail) Bridge and the industries of Central Scotland (*see* MILITARY HISTORY).

One of the highlights of Turnhouse's history between the wars occurred on 15 June 1928 when Imperial Airways staged a demonstration 'race' between one of their Argosy aircraft flying from Croydon, and the famous 'Flying Scotsman' express running non-stop in just over eight hours from London (King's Cross) to Waverley Station. Aesop's fable of tortoises and hares was never proved more true when pilot Gordon Olley, who had diverted across Norfolk en route, to wave to relatives holidaying on a houseboat, found that he had allowed insufficient time for his passengers to reach Waverley by road from Turnhouse, causing them to arrive in the city centre *after* the train!

Edinburgh has had four airfields altogether. Military landing strips existed for a short time from 1916 in the Colinton and Gilmerton areas, used by 77 Squadron of the Royal Flying Corps, but have been disused since the end of the First World War.

Leith also had its own airport. In 1929 the Air Ministry designated the port as one of two national airports (along with Harwich) on the east coast of Britain for flying boat traffic. Leith Dock Commission had embraced air travel with enthusiasm after being requested at short notice to allow pioneering air ace Sir Alan Cobham to touch down in the Western Harbour in his flying boat on a round-Britain flight in the previous year, but found that the Ministry requirements for insurance cover and safety were too expensive to contemplate putting Leith on the map of regular air travel at that time.

However, in 1950, the Western Harbour was once again designated for flying boat takeoffs and landings, with an Air Ministry licence being acquired at the cost of thirty shillings (£1.50) and one guinea (£1.10) annually thereafter. Within a month of a ceremonial opening by Lord Provost Sir Andrew Murray, the air company concerned, Aquila Airways, admitted that they had been unable to even begin to make the Greenock-Leith-Southampton service viable. The Leith Dock Commission renewed the licence every year until 1959, when it was pointed out to the Commission that there were no commercial flying boats left in the United Kingdom.

Architects

From the traditional Scottish building styles of what remains of the Old Town, through the self-conscious classicism of the New, to the bewildering style assortment of the present day, Edinburgh displays an unequalled variety of architecture in its buildings.

Unlike Bath, its fellow UNESCO World Heritage site, Edinburgh cannot be summed up by a single image of one architectural style – as can Bath with its

Georgian crescents – the Scottish capital being more multi-faceted. With its earliest extant building dating from the 12th century (Queen Margaret's Chapel in the Castle, although Duddingston and Dalmeny kirks are contemporaneous), it is impossible to define any one architectural style as being typically Edinburgh's.

Despite that, the construction of the New Town over 60 years from 1776 is the highlight of planned development in Edinburgh, if not Britain, and is dealt with under NEW TOWN. Other architectural matters are considered under relevant subject headings – e.g. BRIDGES, CHURCHES, CINEMAS, HOUSING, and THEATRES. Individual architects responsible for the present-day cityscape are indexed at the rear of the volume, and more details of their work can be found in the 'Index of Artists' in the appropriate *Buildings of Scotland* volume (*see* BIBLIOGRAPHY).

All four of the Adam family of architects were active in Edinburgh to a greater or lesser degree, with Robert Adam (1728-92) the most productive. Born in Kirkcaldy, but educated in the capital, Robert drew on the world of antiquity for his inspiration. His principal monuments in the city are Register House, Charlotte Square, and the exterior of the university's Old Quad. His brothers John (1721-92) and James (1732-94) were also active in the city, the former being involved in laying out the New Town and in advising on the selection of James Craig as its architect (*see* NEW TOWN), while James Adam designed a number of buildings in York Place. Their father William (1689-1748) was responsible for the Infirmary building of 1738 (demolished

1882) and the design of the Exchange building which became the City Chambers.

William Playfair (1790-1857) was responsible, more than any other architect, for the most striking 19th century buildings in central Edinburgh. Educated in the city, Playfair won a contract to complete Adam's Old Quad at the age of 27, and went on to design such landmarks as the National Monument ('Scotland's Disgrace') on Calton Hill, the two gallery buildings on the Mound, and the New College building overlooking them.

David Bryce (1803-1876) and William Burn (1789-1870) worked in partnership for almost all of the 1840s, but were highly industrious as individuals as well. The former is responsible for much of Queen Street and George Street, while Burn was active on a host of projects throughout the New Town, his unfortunate mishandling of the rebuilding of St Giles apparently no barrier to success in his career (*see* CHURCHES).

Edinburgh has been blessed with official municipal architects who designed public buildings which are far more attractive than they needed to be. Robert Morham (1839-1912) was responsible for the impressive Fire Station at Lauriston (*see* FIRE FIGHTING) and the intriguing baths building at Portobello, its interior unfortunately now much altered (*see* SWIMMING).

Edinburgh's best-known modern architect until his death in 1976 was Sir Basil Spence. Born in the city in 1907, and a student at the city's School of Art, Spence is best remembered nationally for his inspiring rebuilding of Coventry Cathedral from its wartime ruins, but has also left his mark in his own city. While his University Library in George Square has been uncharitably compared to a pile of gigantic stacked trays, his earlier work in the Art Deco style is more satisfying. One particular gem is his 1933 garage in Causewayside, all the more intriguing for its cramped terraced location.

Archives

A city as historic as Edinburgh is inevitably rich in archives, those building blocks of the historian's trade. The main centres are the Scottish Record Office, National Registrar's Office, and National Library of Scotland for national records, the City Council Archives for city records, as well as historic collections at Edinburgh University, the medical colleges and other learned institutions.

One loss to the city in recent years has been the transfer away from Edinburgh of the Royal Scottish Geographical Society's records from Randolph Crescent, including those recording the Scottish National Antarctic Expedition in Edwardian times, while the recent establishment of a brewing industry archive in Glasgow seems inappropriate considering Edinburgh's traditional status as Scotland's leading brewing centre.

REGISTRAR GENERAL'S OFFICE

By its very nature, the Registrar General's Office at New Register House is a major archival centre, being dedicated to the preservation of birth, marriage, and death certificates from registry offices all over Scotland. Situated on Register Place and West Register Street, almost opposite the top of Waverley Steps, this is a small complex of buildings dedicated to recording details of the nation's population. It is from here that the nation's censuses are launched, with detailed preparation and analysis being undertaken at Ladywell House on the west side of the city, just outside Corstorphine village (*see also* POPULATION).

The main registry building is well worth visiting, but should not be confused with Register House which houses the Scottish Record Office directly opposite North Bridge. The building, including the impressive Back Dome, was designed by Robert Matheson in Italianate style in 1869.

SCOTTISH RECORD OFFICE

Once the location of Multrie's Hill farm, the building containing the headquarters of the Scottish Record Office is notable for having housed, when incomplete, Britain's first airborne balloon! (*see* BALLOONING). But this is to deviate from a description of the SRO's principal function which is to 'preserve and provide access to our national archival heritage'. Here are lodged written records dating back to the 12th century, including the archives of government, both Scottish and British, of Scottish churches and of the law courts, as well as estate and family records.

West Register House in Charlotte Square houses more modern archives of government departments, as well as records of a more commercial nature, particularly those pertaining to industry and transport. Unfortunately, the sheer volume of records necessitates the use of a separate depository, so the SRO's literature emphasises that the enquirer should phone ahead to ensure that the required materials can be examined on the date of the visit. (This is a strong argument in favour of a unitary-sited Record Office, even if it means the SRO moving to a green-field location from its present impressive centrally-sited facilities). Researchers should remember to take a pencil with them; a pen will be firmly banned!

Land ownership records are held at the Office of Sasines at Meadowbank House, and commercial records at Companies House in George Street.

NATIONAL LIBRARY OF SCOTLAND (NLS)

Although the National Library did not establish a Department of Manuscripts until 1927, two years after the Library itself was set up, it inherited the manuscripts collection of the Advocates' Library begun in the 1680s (*see also* LIBRARIES). This is a fund of archival material relating to such past and present institutions as the Church of Scotland and the Darien Company, along with literary manuscripts and documents relating to Gaelic and Icelandic culture.

Since its inception, the National's Manuscripts Department has pursued an active and imaginative acquisitions policy, specialising in family papers and the archives of such writers as Scott, Mackenzie, and Carlyle. The collection's curators have not been shy of adverse publicity in acquiring materials they considered important to research workers – the very expensive purchase of Earl

Haig's papers in the early 1980s was bitterly opposed by critics of Edinburgh's own First World War general, but their place in the NLS collection was a logical result of a systematic policy of acquiring Scottish materials whenever they became available.

Recent additions to the archival collections include those of such publishing firms as Blackwood, Chambers, and Oliver & Boyd, as well as such writers as Christopher Grieve, John Buchan, Eric Linklater and Leslie Mitchell.

EDINBURGH CITY ARCHIVES

Deep in the bowels of the City Chambers can be found the City Archives department. A systematic attempt to collect Edinburgh's official records has been undertaken over at least four centuries, the first indexed records of the Town Council dating from 1573, although earlier documents than that have been methodically stored. A Keeper of the Records was not officially appointed until 1836, and it was to be exactly 150 years before a public service policy was introduced to attract and process public requests for information, although staff had pursued an informal, and extremely helpful, process of information dissemination long before 1986.

As can be expected, the principal records kept are those of the meetings of the Town Council and its sub-committees before local government reorganisation in 1975. Since that time, the corresponding material for the District Council are maintained. (For Lothian Region, *see below*). Leith Town Council records for 1833-1920 are also stored, although unfortunately not indexed, unlike their Edinburgh counterparts.

So rich in diversity are the City Archives that only a selection can be mentioned here, and the interested reader is advised to pursue their interest further by contacting the City Chambers. Archives are maintained for the Burgh Courts from 1507, City Improvement Schemes (including the original plans for James Craig's New Town) Dean of Guild records, Ale Accounts, Shore Dues, Police Records from 1828 (when a bobby was still only an inkling in Robert Peel's brain), Leith Police Commissioners' files from even earlier (1771) Canongate Gaol Records 1750-1840, and Workhouse Records from 1739-1844. There is a news cuttings collection and a small selection of films featuring the city. The department is particularly appreciated by enquirers researching building developments. One curious omission is the files of the city's Community Councils – elected bodies, funded by the District Council, but not represented in the collection.

The City Archives staff have no budget and no acquisitions policy, in contrast to other, what one might term rival, organisations which actively seek material worthy of preservation. A little more investment might not go amiss in the maintenance of Edinburgh's archives; surely no more than the Scottish capital might reasonably expect.

Lothian Region stores records of its meetings, although at the time of writing, there is no central archives centre. Each department appears to preserve its correspondence at its own discretion.

EDINBURGH CITY LIBRARIES

The city's public library service is yet another source of manuscripts for the interested historian (*see also* LIBRARIES). The Edinburgh Room, tucked away in its mezzanine above the Scottish Department, contains a number of collections of books and MSS accumulated by such local historians as Charles Boog-Watson and William Cowan. Social history is not forgotten in the library's collection, which contains such primary sources as George Baird's reminiscences and his personal history of the city's entertainments. Also notable are the collections on such Edinburgh literati as Scott and Stevenson, and there are Calotypes (early photographs), created by Thomas Keith and David Octavius Hill (*see* PHOTOGRAPHY).

Art Galleries

NATIONAL

NATIONAL GALLERY OF SCOTLAND

Few of the world's art galleries enjoy such an outstanding situation as Scotland's National Gallery, located on the Mound between the Old and New Towns, itself straddling the railway from Waverley Station to the north and west. Designed by William Playfair, and opened in 1854 on land gifted by the Town Council, the gallery was subtly enlarged in 1978 by the provision of a new basement area above the tunnel bores.

Here can be found Scotland's art treasures – the whole spectrum from Renaissance to

Post-Impressionism, in what is surely one of the most sumptuous collections in Britain. Rembrandt, El Greco, Monet, Vermeer, are only some of the foreign masters whose work is on show, and the best of British art can also be found within these walls. Scottish art is well-represented – Raeburn, Ramsay, Wilkie – while the Vaughan bequest of Turner's paintings being shown every January, means that the summer visitor is failing to see all the best that the gallery can offer. Even with the imaginative extension burrowing into the Mound, the building is still incapable of exhibiting all the nation's treasures.

The Gallery was visited by 358,325 people in 1992, but subsequent years have seen an increase, boosted in 1995 by the display of Canova's sculpture *The Three Graces*. The Gallery's director had been closely involved in the campaign to keep this British-commissioned work in this country, and it is to be 'shuttled' between London and Edinburgh for exhibition on a regular basis.

SCOTTISH GALLERY OF MODERN ART

Since 1984 this collection of modern art – one of Europe's finest – has been housed in the former John Watson's School building, just off Belford Road. The already substantial collection of mainly European artworks was added to in 1995 with the acquisition of the Penrose and Keiller collections of surrealist paintings, considerably enhancing this gallery's importance. Scottish artists are not forgotten; indeed the work of Baird, Bellany, and Howson are prominent. There is an impressive sculpture garden. A

particularly well-stocked shop and excellent restaurant complete the site's attractions.

The gallery moved to its present site in 1984, and it is unlikely to fight off suggestions that it is hardly in the best location for visitors. Bus services to the site are few and far between, and even Edinburgh residents have difficulty in finding it for the first time. The notice at Haymarket Station 'For the Scottish Gallery of Modern Art' is perhaps a little optimistic, since a taxi ride is necessary for all but the fully fit art-lover, who is advised to take a street-map along.

History

A decision was taken by the Scottish Office in 1951 that Scotland should have a national gallery of modern art, but it was some ten years later before it opened, filling Inverleith House in the Royal Botanic Garden with a collection of largely borrowed artworks. The opening ceremony was, according to the *Third Statistical Account*, 'honoured by the extraordinary hats, shaped like beehives or large inverted nests of birds, worn by several ladies'.

SCOTTISH NATIONAL PORTRAIT GALLERY

'Junk art' is not perhaps the verdict one expects to hear about Scotland's treasure house of portraiture, but that is the description applied to this collection by a Glasgow councillor during the recent controversy about the future of Scotland's national art galleries. Not that the Trustees appear to have been very much more reverential about this gallery, being prepared to see it divided and diminished by sending portraits of Scottish monarchs to another city which never hosted a royal court, but presently exhibits a desperate need for a more thriving tourist-driven economy. How unfortunate that Scotland's art treasures should be the object of such contention!

The Gallery itself occupies the western half of the building supplied to the city by one-time *Scotsman* proprietor John Findlay, with the National Museum of Antiquities scheduled to vacate the other half in the very near future. The Portrait Gallery, as well as containing, as one would expect, paintings of royalty and aristocrats in their wigs, gowns, and beauty spots – and that's only the men – also collects pencil sketches and photographs, bringing the nation's story right up to date. In 1990, the Gallery published a *Concise Catalogue*, arranged by the portrait subject, thus making the publication doubly useful as a research tool, as well as simply a list of paintings. The gallery also houses the Scottish National Photographic Archive (*see* PHOTOGRAPHIC HISTORY).

MUNICIPAL CITY ART CENTRE

Opened in 1980 in a former fruit and flower warehouse, the City Art Centre is one of the capital's most modern – and most satisfactory – viewing spaces for the arts. It consists of five floors, connected by stairs, lift, and escalators, overlooking the Waverley Station.

The Royal Scottish Academy as seen from the Mound. Now exclusively used by the Academy, the building used to be known as the Royal Institution, and the Royal Society of Edinburgh was also based here until 1909.

In addition to housing the city's own collection – noted as one might expect, for its Raeburns, Octavius Hills and Cursiters – the Centre has undertaken to house a number of prestigious travelling exhibitions whose attendance figures would make its National rivals envious.

Such exhibitions as 'Gold of the Pharaohs', and 'The Emperor's Warriors' have been of international importance, the latter being the product of Edinburgh's twinned relationship with Xi'an, where the Terracotta 'Army' was discovered. A more recent exhibition of artefacts connected with the TV programme *Star Trek* struck some observers as dangerously frivolous, although it certainly indicated an art gallery not afraid to embrace popular culture. A three-volumed catalogue of the city's paintings is available.

OTHER ART GALLERIES IN EDINBURGH

ROYAL SCOTTISH ACADEMY

Mistaken by many as the National Gallery, the Royal Scottish Academy building occupies the most prestigious address in Princes Street, directly opposite the Hanover Street opening. Designed by William Playfair and opened in 1826, this was originally the Royal Institution, and also housed the Royal Society of Edinburgh until 1909.

The RSA is the counterpart of the better-known Royal Academy in London, and totally eclipses it if the official apparel of the respective Presidents is compared, the Scottish society providing its representative to the 1953 Coronation with wine-coloured robes and velvet Rembrandt-styled hat, while his English equivalent had to make do with frock coat and top hat! The RSA's annual exhibition attracts artists from all over the United Kingdom, and touring exhibitions are increasingly using this distinguished venue.

TALBOT RICE GALLERY

Situated in the University's Old Quad off South Bridge, the Talbot Rice Gallery represents an excellent environment for the enjoyment of mainly modern art. Although firmly under the University's wing, the gallery is open to the public. It is divided into 'red' and 'white' galleries, the mezzanine providing a particularly useful vantage point for viewing three-dimensional pieces.

FRUITMARKET GALLERY

Originally situated in Rose Street, this independent gallery moved to its present site opposite the City Art Centre in the early 1980s. It occupies a former fruit and vegetable warehouse on two levels above the Waverley Station, and enjoys a national reputation for the avant-garde.

LOST GALLERIES

An art gallery which Edinburgh people are probably not even aware that they have lost is the Burrell Collection. Now ensconced in Glasgow, the world-famous collection of paintings, sculpture, textiles, and silverware, was originally to be left to the Scottish nation – and that meant Edinburgh. However, according to Burrell's biographer, Dr Richard Marks, the collector changed his mind during the Second World War, incensed by the removal of railings for salvage from around his house, Hutton Castle in Berwickshire. Inexplicably, Burrell blamed Edinburgh for this loss, possibly because he received an understandable 'don't you know there's a war on?' response when he complained to the Scottish Office in Edinburgh. Vowing vengeance on the city, Burrell immediately offered his collection to Glasgow – an unfortunate decision, given that city's inability to display the collection for nearly 40 years because of atmospheric pollution and municipal dithering.

Athletics

Edinburgh is the base for the governing body for Scottish athletics, the Scottish Athletics Federation (SAF), formed from a number of like-minded organisations, including the former Scottish Amateur Athletics Association (SAAA), in October 1992. Based at Caledonia House in the South Gyle area of the city, it administers all track and field events in Scotland. There are currently 17 athletics and running clubs in Edinburgh affiliated to the SAF.

History
Scottish athletics formed its first national association, the SAAA, in February 1883, although its constitution had to be reformed within 18 months, when a conflict developed with athletics clubs in the West of Scotland who insisted on setting up their own association. The new national body worked diligently in the interests of a sport which has never quite achieved the measure of public appreciation it deserves, and the onset of professionalism and the need for a more unified voice for athletics led to the establishment of the SAF in 1992.

Edinburgh's Meadowbank area has figured very largely as the home of Scotland's athletic meets, even before the construction of the present stadium, opened in 1970 (see also SPORTS). Previously, New Meadowbank was the principal athletics centre in Edinburgh, located approximately on the western half of the present stadium site, hosting the SAAA Championships every year between 1952 and 1966. The facility, opened for athletics by Edinburgh Corporation in 1934, lacked covered spectator accommodation and had limited changing facilities. Before 1934, there had been tracks at Northfield and Hawkhill.

Powderhall stadium was also used for athletic meets, the cinder track there being the location for the first Scottish championships in 1883, staged there a total of 16 times before greyhound racing took centre stage in 1922. The stadium gave its name to the Powderhall Sprint, only recently renamed the New Year Sprint. This is a professional short-distance race which, since 1871, has traditionally attracted sprinters from all over the world, tempted by the impressive financial prizes. Handicapping is used, this New Year holiday event now being run at Meadowbank (see also SPORTS). Powderhall closed on 6 October 1995.

Edinburgh's athletics history will always be associated with a certain E.H. (Eric) Liddell whose hold on the 100 and 220 yard events in Scotland in the first half of the 1920s has only been eclipsed by his capture of Olympic Gold for the 400

CLUB	COLOURS
Edinburgh Athletic Club (AC)	White, 2 black diagonal stripes
Edinburgh Southern Harriers	White, 2 blue hoops, red shorts
Edinburgh University AC	Green & white quarters
Edinburgh University Hare & Hounds	Green with white side panel
Edinburgh Woollen Mill	White, 2 blue stripes
Ferranti Amateur AC	Yellow, black letters
Harmeny (sic) AC	Red, green diagonal, red shorts
Heriot-Watt University Harriers	Sky blue, gold trim, blue shorts
Hewlett Packard Marathon/Joggers	(No club colours)
Hunters Bog Trotters	Brown vest
Leslie Deans Racing Club	Blue, turquoise/black side panels
Lothian & Borders Police AC	Blue with crest
Merchiston Castle School AC	Navy
Portobello Running Club	White, navy/gold band, navy shorts
Sri Chinmoy AC (Scotland)	White vest, purple band
Standard Life AC	Blue with gold lining
TSB Corstorphine Amateur AC	White, black trim, black shorts

metres in the Paris Olympiad of 1924 when he memorably refused to run a heat on a Sunday. His story was told in the Oscar-winning 1981 film *Chariots of Fire*, with Liddell played by city actor Ian Charleson, now unfortunately deceased (*see* FILMS). In postwar years, Edinburgh's outstanding track athlete has been Alan Wells, a sprinter who won gold at the 1980 Moscow Olympics, and who dominated British short-distance athletics for a number of years.

Ballooning

Edinburgh was the location of the first manned flight on the British mainland. On 27 August 1784, local journalist and polymath James Tytler took off from the Comely Garden (in the Abbeyhill area, not Comely Bank as sometimes reported) using a hot air balloon to carry him in a basket to a height of 350 feet (105 metres), before making an uneventful landing at Restalrig nearby. Tytler had been inspired by the Italian Vincenti Lunardi, who had just made one of the first flights, and who more fully caught the imagination when he visited Scotland in October the following year.

Tytler's feat should not be underestimated however – indeed, Lunardi himself was full of admiration for the Scot's enterprise and courage – and Tytler beat the better-known balloon ascent at Oxford by James Sadler by five weeks. Unfortunately, Tytler had made something of a spectacle of himself before the flight took place. The public had grown tired of the novelty of seeing 'The Great Edinburgh Fire Balloon' inflated inside the shell of Register House, and rapidly grew unsympathetic to Tytler's technical problems in inflating the linen

Edinburgh was the site of the first balloon flight on the British mainland, from Abbeyhill to Restalrig on 27 August 1784. Exactly 200 years later a balloon rally was held over the city, producing this unusual silhouette shot. (The Scotsman)

envelope 40 feet (12 metres) high by 30 feet (9 metres) wide. Fortunately, the intrepid aeronaut accomplished his intention, but not before the word 'balloon' acquired a derisive dialectic currency, never to be lost.

Historians place more value on Tytler's editing of the second edition of the *Encyclopaedia Britannica* (*see* INDUSTRY: PUBLISHING) than on his ballooning accomplishments, but he proved himself a brave adventurer, his first flight recalled by a bicentennial rally of hot air balloons over the city in August 1984. Tytler is the subject of an excellent biography by the late Sir James Fergusson, *Balloon Tytler*, 1972, to which the interested reader is referred.

Lunardi himself made the first of five successful flights in Scotland in October 1785, ascending from a site in the grounds of Heriot's Hospital (school) and voyaging across the Forth without incident to Ceres in Fife. The flight earned Lunardi the award of the Freedom of the City on 12 October.

in testimony . . . of the undaunted courage of Vincent Lunardi, Esquire of Lucca, in ascending in a Balloon, and passing the Frith (sic) of Forth to Fife . . .

What poor James Tytler must have thought of this award is not known.

Banks

Edinburgh is home to the headquarters of two of Scotland's national banks, the Bank of Scotland, and the Royal Bank of Scotland. It is also the location of Scotland's principal financial centre, many of whose constituent companies have traditionally centred on Charlotte Square, but which have now moved to new custom-built accommodation in the West End or at South Gyle.

As recently as 1969, there were five Scottish banks operating in Edinburgh – the two mentioned above, along with the Clydesdale, the National Commercial, and the British Linen. All but the Clydesdale had their headquarters in the capital city (and the British Linen remains as a merchant bank).

In 1965 the city had no fewer than 175 branches owned by the five Scottish banks. In 1993 this had reduced to 96, owned by three banks, and the number may well have declined even since then, judging by the number of street corners where once-bustling bank branches now stand empty. Indeed, such edifices as the former headquarters of the National Commercial at 14 George Street, and the branch building at the corner of the High Street and South Bridge, are examples of considerable change in the banking business. This has changed in other ways in the last 30 years, with a significant number of English and foreign banks opening offices in the city, and the increase in customer preference for dealing with building societies.

BANK OF SCOTLAND

It is perhaps appropriate that one of the most dominating buildings on the Old Town ridge overlooking the Waverley Station and the New Town, is the headquarters of the Bank of Scotland. Formed in 1695, just one year after the Bank of England, Scotland's first bank originally enjoyed monopoly status but was not permitted to lend to government, and did well to survive its early years when the Darien colonial scheme threatened to bring financial disaster to so many Scottish investors.

The bank's first headquarters were temporarily housed in Mylne Square, before being moved to the east side of Parliament Close for four years until 1700. Old Bank Close, just off the Lawnmarket, became the Bank's base for the next 106 years, on a site now occupied by George IV Bridge's approach to the High Street. The Close's name may have been changed from Bank Close early in the 18th century to differentiate the bank from its new rival established in 1727 (*see* overleaf).

Surprisingly, when the decision was taken to remove the bank from the fetid smells of its restricted location, it was to a site above the Earthen Mound, overlooking the New Town, and not in the later extension to the city. The new building was designed by Robert Reid and Richard Crichton and completed in 1806, although much rebuilt by David Bryce in the 1860s. It is now floodlit at night and makes the best of its imperious site.

The Bank itself enjoyed monopoly conditions until the formation of the Royal Bank, and came to be associated, rightly or wrongly, with Tory interests in Scotland at that time. It has maintained its prominent position in British banking, its right to produce notes confirmed by Parliament in 1845. The Bank shows a taste for innovation – installing Scotland's first 'drive-in' bank facility at Corstorphine in 1964, and is in the forefront of developing remote banking from home.

ROYAL BANK OF SCOTLAND

Founded in 1727 to offer an alternative to the Bank of Scotland. Originally identified with the Whigs, the Royal was seen as more London-connected than the Bank of Scotland in its early years, being required to pay a levy to the invading Jacobite army in 1745, although it hedged its bets by also payrolling the Government forces.

In more peaceful times, the Royal (the 'New Bank'), moved from the Old Town, where it was located firstly in New Bank Close, (possibly Fortune's Close, near where Cockburn Street is now), then from 1753 in the Royal Exchange, now the City Chambers, moving to the New Town in 1819. There it acquired the first house to be built in St Andrew's Square before succeeding to its present headquarters, the mansion once owned by Sir Laurence Dundas, MP for the city from 1768-81. Built in 1772, this looks straight across the Square and along George Street. The bank's Telling Room has a notable blue-painted dome studded with stars.

FORMER EDINBURGH BANKS

The **British Linen Company**, which is now a merchant bank, began serving the public from Halkerston's Wynd in 1746, before moving to the Canongate in 1753, where it became known as the Bank of the Canongate, but in 1791 moved westwards to Tweeddale House, just inside the city of Edinburgh. This was a particularly congested area, so it was no surprise when the Bank moved to the New Town in 1808, occupying the Dalhousie mansion, which it considerably rebuilt in the 1860s. It still stands at the south-eastern corner of St Andrew's Square. Taken over by the Bank of Scotland in 1971, the British Linen has since been relaunched to serve the financial community exclusively, and presently trades from Melville Street.

The **National Commercial Bank** came into being in 1959 as the product of an amalgamation between the Commercial and National Bank of Scotland. The Commercial had begun trading in 1810 from the former Highland Society Hall in the High Street, before building its own, highly impressive, headquarters in George Street, while the National started life in St Andrew's Square in 1825.

The combined company had a short but active existence, pioneering hire-purchase financing and opening a 'women only' branch in Princes Street in 1964. In the following year it had 48 branches in Edinburgh, compared to the Bank of Scotland's 42, the Royal's 34, and the Clydesdale's 18, but merged with the Royal Bank in 1969. As observed above, its impressive headquarters building in George Street is standing empty at the time of writing.

The **Edinburgh and Leith Bank** was formed in 1838 and initially enjoyed considerable popularity with middle-class investors. In 1844 it joined with the Glasgow Joint-Stock Bank to form the **Edinburgh and Glasgow Bank**, thereby doubling its capital, but the directors in each city refused to co-operate with those in the other, and this, coupled with the losses following the end of the Railway Mania, contributed to its end. The **Edinburgh Savings Bank** was founded in 1814, one of the first of its kind. By the 1930s it had 13 branches in Edinburgh in addition to its headquarters in North Bank Street.

Botanic Gardens

Edinburgh is the home of Scotland's Royal Botanic Garden (RBG), the second oldest in the United Kingdom. It is in fact four gardens in one, the Edinburgh centre having 'satellite' gardens at Benmore in Argyll, Dawyck near Peebles, and Logan near Stranraer. In 1994 the four represented a collection of nearly 14,000 plant species, and the Edinburgh garden was the second most-visited in the United Kingdom, after Kew.

Encompassing 75 acres (30 hectares) in the north of Edinburgh, just off Inverleith Row and stretching westwards towards Inverleith Park, the RBG is of course much more than just a place of refuge for busy citizens wishing to spend an hour wandering in tranquil sylvan surroundings. A major centre for botanical and taxonomic research, it employs 230 staff, and contains specimens representing 308 plant families and (including the three outstation gardens)

2,800 genera. The RBG is also home to Britain's oldest botanical library (100,000 volumes) and herbarium (2 million dried plant specimens). Since 1986, the Garden has been designated as a Non-Departmental Public Body, sponsored by the Scottish Office, and with trustees appointed by the Secretary of State for Scotland. The Garden's official purpose is 'to explore and explain the plant kingdom – past, present and future – and its importance to humanity'.

The Garden's strong interest in Oriental plants is founded on the specimens brought back by such collectors as Forrest and Sherriff, and there are 400 species of rhododendrons alone. This Oriental tradition is being continued at the time of writing by a considerable replanting and landscaping programme supported by commercial sponsorship. The main features of the Garden are the tree collection, woodland garden (including a grove dedicated to pioneering Scottish conservationist John Muir), demonstration and peat gardens. The rock garden contains approximately 4,000 alpine plants, with an extensive heath garden close by. An attractive pond makes up the total of outdoor attractions, but the ten greenhouses are worth a visit on their own.

In addition to the two planthouses dating from 1834 and 1858 respectively – one of them is the tallest of its type in Britain – there are eight new glasshouses designed with suspended roofs to maximise space inside for plants and visitors. These houses simulate varying climatic conditions from tropical rainforest to arid desert, and include underwater viewing panels in the aquatic houses.

The Royal Botanic Garden glasshouses were in danger of being rendered redundant during the halcyon summer of 1995. This photograph clearly shows the external skeleton of the building which enhances the internal appearance of these buildings, replicating differing natural environments from the arid to the tropical.

In 1992, 662,459 people visited Edinburgh's Royal Botanic Garden (showing a major increase since the 401,480 visitors in 1970, although entry figures were even higher in the mid-1980s), making it second only in the city to Edinburgh Castle in popularity. At the time of writing, entry to the Garden is free, as one would expect of a centuries-old feature of the city scene, although a voluntary contribution is requested from visitors to the new glasshouses. Unfortunately the Garden's three outstations charge visitors, and this charge doubled in 1995 in the case of Dawyck. This seems strange, given that visitors have to make special journeys to reach these attractions, particularly in the case of Logan which is almost literally at the end of a terminal road, while Edinburgh citizens can enjoy 'their' Garden freely on a daily basis.

History

Medicine was the spur for the creation of the Botanic Garden (originally known as the Physic Garden) in 1670, some 49 years after Oxford's, but nearly 90 before the establishment of the Royal Botanic Garden at Kew. In the 17th century, Edinburgh's burgeoning medical community based in the 'tounis schule' or university, required a supply of herbs and other plants for therapeutic purposes, so an area 40 feet square was secured for this purpose just east of St Anne's Yards near Holyrood.

The garden's founders were Andrew Balfour (1630-94) and Sir Robert Sibbald (1641-1715), both medical practitioners and teachers with private collections of natural history specimens. A royal charter was awarded in 1699. Within five years of the garden's establishment a second site was found next to Trinity Hospital, where the Waverley Station is now situated (a commemorative plaque can be seen on station buildings facing platform 11). This garden was much larger – approximately one acre in extent, although it was damaged during the siege of the city in 1689 and again ten years later, less dramatically, by an invasion of sheep. Historian Charles McKean observes of the Garden at that time:

> It proved a noble asset to the capital: a place where George Hume MP would go for a stroll after dinner, or send to, from the country, for cuttings of herbs and flowers. The English chaplain Thomas Morer admired its 2,700 plants when he visited it in 1689, but regretted the absence of beauty or walks.

The pharmacoepia continued to have first call on the Garden's resources, an 18th century plan showing that rhubarb, much prized for its purgatorial qualities, formed a major part of the collection. In 1763, the Garden moved into more commodious accommodation (5 acres/2.02 hectares) at Leith Walk, where a pond was established and a 140 feet-long (42 metres) glasshouse built. By 1812, the collection comprised 4,000 species in 1,000 genera and a larger location was once again being sought.

Ten years later a 15 acre (6 hectare) site became available at Inverleith, with neighbouring gardens being taken over around Inverleith House until the present 75 acres (30.35 hectares) was accumulated.

It took fully two years to move the collection, with special transport arrangements being devised to transport trees up to 40 feet (12 metres) in height. A West Indian fan palm in the Tropical Palm House is now more than 200 years old, surviving the trip across northern Edinburgh from Leith Walk to Inverleith.

Government support for the collection began in 1833, and the Garden's opening hours were extended to include Sundays from 1889, although only after the matter had been debated in Parliament. By then the palm houses dominated the skyline, and a rock garden added in 1871. Inverleith House was acquired in 1876, originally intended as the Regius Keeper's home, but used for the Scottish Gallery of Modern Art from 1960 to 1984, and now utilised by the Garden as an exhibition space, as is the former Royal Caledonian Horticultural Society show hall, opposite the rock garden.

New glasshouses were added in the 1890s, the 600 feet-long (180 metres) herbaceous border laid out in 1903, and the rock garden rebuilt in a more natural configuration from 1908 to 1914. But the largest addition came in the 1960s with the construction of a new herbarium and library block off Inverleith Place, and the new glasshouses. The external frames and tensional cable supports of the latter maximise the space for those specimens requiring warmth and protection, while offering a fascinating undercover walk for the public.

In 1929 the Younger Botanic Garden at Benmore, north of Dunoon, was added to the establishment, and now constitutes 100 acres (24.7 hectares), with its most striking feature an avenue of sequoias. Forty years later the Logan estate was acquired in the Rhinns of Galloway, and now comprises the Logan Botanic Garden, whose main characteristic is its mild winter climate which permits the growth of chusan palms and tree ferns outdoors. The gunnera colony is particularly notable. The latest outstation (in 1978) is Dawyck Botanic Garden, near Stobo, south-west of Peebles, and comprises 60 acres (25 hectares) of remarkable tree specimens in a beautiful setting.

Edinburgh's Royal Botanic Garden is a credit to the capital city. *The Good Gardens Guide* recently said of the RBG that it is:

maintained to the very highest degree. The overall standard of the horticulture is superb. The specimen trees are among the finest in Britain.

With such a long history behind it, who would expect anything else?

Boxing

Edinburgh has made its mark in the history of British boxing, particularly in the 20 years between the wars in the first half of the 20th century, when it rapidly became known as one of the leading centres of the fight game. In addition, the city has produced the finest British professional boxer of modern times – Ken Buchanan.

Glasgow has tended to portray itself as the centre of Scottish boxing, but that is only true of the postwar years, the city's authorities previously regarding prize fights as a likely incitement to public violence at a time of political unrest. As a result, boxers from the west of Scotland often travelled to Edinburgh to further their fight careers, and such promoters as Leith's Nat Dresner prospered in the capital, hiring such venues as the Industrial Hall in Annandale Street (later remodelled as the Lothian Regional Transport bus garage).

One of the most historic boxing clubs in Britain is the city's Sparta establishment in McDonald Road, which can claim some of boxing's major names among its alumni. Featherweight Bobby Neil, although born in Glasgow, trained at Sparta and won the British championship in 1959, although he was unable to establish himself at world level.

Neil was a popular champion who moved on to London, but he was succeeded by the greatest British boxer of them all. Born in Edinburgh in 1945, Kenny Buchanan was world lightweight champion in 1970-72, and twice undefeated European champion, as well as unbeaten British lightweight champion. In 1970 Buchanan was voted best boxer in the world by no less than the New York boxing media; five years later the British press adjudged him the best British boxer to emerge in 30 years. His life-story is the subject of the play *Buchanan* by Tom McGrath, premiered at the Traverse Theatre in 1993.

Buchanan was unable to fight professionally in front of his own city fans, which makes his achievements all the more remarkable, particularly in comparison with Glasgow's Jim Watt, who enjoyed home advantage for four of his world championship fights, and who came away second-best in his only professional meeting with Buchanan.

Edinburgh hosted no professional fights between 1958 and 1984, and it appears that the capital is turning away from supporting a sport which is regarded by many as ritualised violence, involving a high degree of risk of serious and fatal damage to its participants.

Bridges

Edinburgh bridges are unusual in that comparatively few of them were constructed to span water-crossings. Most of the city's best-known bridges, such as South Bridge or George IV Bridge, are the products of early highway planning, intended to take traffic well away from densely inhabited areas in the Old Town.

Two exceptions to the above description are the Forth Bridges. With their southern landfalls located just within the Edinburgh City Council area at South Queensferry, both road and rail bridges are too important to omit from this chapter. A brief description of these structures, and their history, is therefore in order.

FORTH RAIL BRIDGE

Opened to traffic in 1890, the Forth railway bridge is regarded by many as the world's finest. Consisting of three main cantilevers carrying a seamed viaduct a distance of approximately 2,765 yards (2,528 metres) across the Queensferry Narrows and straddling the island of Inchgarvie, the bridge took seven years to complete. It is only too easy to reel off a list of its statistical details – two-thirds of a million cubic feet of Aberdeen granite, 54,000 tons of steel, 62,000 cubic feet of rubble masonry.

Perhaps more apposite is the comment by the late C. Hamilton Ellis who said of the bridge 'its beauty is unconscious, as in so many Victorian structures'.

The Forth Bridge was designed by Benjamin Baker and John Fowler for the Forth Bridge Railway Company, their philosophy being that the successful engineer is the one who makes the fewest mistakes. No mistakes at all were made in their design for the bridge, which reputedly is based on an Himalayan concept, and was constructed in steel. One of the toughest of the design criteria faced by Baker and Fowler was the clearance required by the Admiralty, who insisted that the Narrows must be treated as open sea. As a result, trains cross at a height of no less than 150 feet (45.6 metres) above high water, and the channel is therefore permanently open to all but the world's biggest ships. Tunnelling had not been an option because of the existence of two channels each around 200 feet (61 metres) in depth.

History

The Forth Bridge Railway Company got off to the most inauspicious of starts, the first meeting of its directors in Edinburgh being declared inquorate, in 1873. When financially supported by four different railway companies, the new concern commissioned Thomas Bouch to design the new structure and he planned a suspension bridge, with two railway lines hanging in tubes from towers no less than 500 feet (150 metres) in height. Preparatory work had already begun on Inchgarvie, and massive chains had been ordered from Vickers Ltd, when the collapse of the Tay Bridge, with terrible loss of life, forced the

The Forth Rail Bridge, as seen from the south-east. This magnificent structure has been described as having an unconscious beauty, and has proved a vital tranport link for over a century.

Forth Bridge directors to call a halt to further construction. The two projects shared a common designer – the newly-knighted Sir Thomas Bouch – and his reputation was seriously damaged by the Tay Bridge enquiry. He died shortly afterwards.

The directors of the Forth Bridge company cancelled their order for chains – which were ready and had to be paid for – and decided to postpone the question of crossing the Forth in the near future. This incensed the English rail companies, who did not appear to be properly represented on the Bridge board at that time, and the cancellation decision was reversed, with Baker and Fowler's design being accepted. The Board of Trade understandably increased its scrutiny of the enterprise and insisted on inspecting the new works on an unprecedented quarterly frequency.

The Bridge has survived more than a century's winds, as well as two world wars. Its four sponsoring railways were grouped into two super-companies in 1923, both of them represented on the Bridge board, at which time it was found that the structure was being administered illegally, without proper adherence to company law – and apparently continued to be so until nationalisation in 1948. The structure is now owned by Railtrack, and there has been considerable controversy in recent years about the level of painting it receives, following changes in working practices in line with new safety legislation.

The Forth Road Bridge is less distinctive than its rail neighbour, being similar to so many other suspension bridges throughout the world. Here it looms in the sea mist behind boats drawn out of the water at South Queensferry's harbour.

FORTH ROAD BRIDGE

Less of a pioneer than its rail counterpart to the east, the Forth Road Bridge is a suspension bridge, whose two main towers, one on each shore and rising to over 500 feet (150 metres), suspend double dual carriageways across the estuary from web-like supports. At the time of writing, its main span is the tenth longest in the world, and second longest (after the Humber Bridge) in the United Kingdom.

The design was prepared with the intention of reducing the new structure's wind resistant profile. Work began in 1958 and was completed in 1964, being opened by HM The Queen on 4 September. To the viewer from the shore, the carriageway is the bridge's strongest visual factor, in contrast to the rail bridge, where the viaduct is hidden by girders for most of its length.

The bridge's very success has spawned the demand for a second bridge to relieve the volume of traffic crossing. In its first year of service the bridge carried fewer than 5 million vehicles, but was never expected to carry more than 60,000 vehicles in a single day. In 1993, that target was passed 15 times, and there is a strong body of opinion in favour of bridging the Forth once again.

NORTH BRIDGE

Recently repainted and floodlit after dark, the North Bridge is less taken for granted than it was until its recent sprucing-up. For

North Bridge, looking south in 1912. Note the tram lines include a middle 'rail'; in fact, a conduit housing a traction cable which quite literally pulled cars around the city. (Edinburgh City Libraries)

this is the second bridge to occupy the site, connecting the Old Town with the New by creating a north-south road at right angles to the High Street at the Tron. The first bridge on the site, completed in 1772, was part of the city's pioneering exploration towards the north, to the site of the planned New Town, and to Leith.

Like the present structure, the first bridge also had three arches, but was narrower than the present bridge, and the railway below had to thread its way round the supports as best it could. (It seems a peculiarly Edinburgh problem for a bridge to be built first, and then a railway have to find its way under it.) A tramline crossed the old bridge by 1872, but the structure was too narrow for the increasing volume of road traffic, and when Waverley Station was remodelled in the 1890s, the opportunity was taken to rebuild North Bridge, redesigned by the Waverley's architects, Cunningham, Blyth, and Westland in 1894. 525 feet (160 metres) in length, the newer structure has ironwork by William Arrol, of Forth Bridge fame, and was opened in 1897.

SOUTH BRIDGE

Even Edinburgh residents might be surprised to learn that South Bridge is a 19-arch viaduct, only one arch of which is left open, to accommodate the Cowgate. It was completed in 1788 after three years' work, and allowed traffic from the south to 'fly over' the dwellings of the Old Town and cross North Bridge to the New. The architect was Robert Kay. The structure was widened in 1929.

GEORGE IV BRIDGE

Running parallel to South Bridge, but with two open arches to the older bridge's one, George IV Bridge was designed by Thomas Hamilton and opened in 1834 as a major route into the city from the south. The roads crossed are the Cowgate and Merchant

Street, the latter now providing vehicular access to the new Sheriff Court buildings.

REGENT BRIDGE (WATERLOO PLACE)

Like South Bridge, Regent Bridge, better known simply as part of Waterloo Place, can be seen as an early variety of flyover, traversing Calton Road. What was basically an extension eastwards of Princes Street involved the destruction of part of the Calton burying ground, and crossing a street linking Leith Street with the Palace, but was viewed as important in connecting up with the planned development of Calton Hill. Completed in 1819, the only open arch of this 'bridge' is decorated with columns by Archibald Elliot, an architect much involved in the construction of the New Town. The colonnades celebrate the victory at Waterloo a few years earlier.

KING'S BRIDGE (WEST END OF JOHNSTON TERRACE)

A product of the 1827 Improvement Act which also produced George IV Bridge, the King's Bridge is usually thought of as part of Johnston Terrace spanning King's Stables Road. Architecture enthusiasts can enjoy viewing Thomas Hamilton's wide tunnel-vault, its portals being reproduced by William Playfair in his Mound railway tunnel, except that here each arch has two obelisks mounted on pedestals.

WAVERLEY BRIDGE

Connecting the Old Town and the New between Market Street and Princes Street, is the Waverley Bridge, providing vehicular access down to Waverley Station. The third bridge on this site, the present structure was built in 1894-6 by Cunningham Blyth and Westland, the same engineeers responsible for North Bridge. Its pierced iron parapets, dating from the 1870s bridge, have been replaced in the 1980s by modern aluminium panels, no doubt because of the danger of the electric catenary below.

DEAN BRIDGE

Designed by Thomas Telford in 1829-31, in a style similar to his viaduct at Pathhead, this is a graceful four-arch bridge carrying the Queensferry Road over the Water of Leith. The road is carried for a distance of 410 feet (123 metres) almost 100 feet (30 metres) above the bed of the river, making this the city's most impressive, as well as its most gracious, structure. The parapet walls were heightened in 1912 for safety's sake. The bridge's construction was a co-operative effort between a Road Trust and a property speculator, John Learmonth, the latter hoping to establish a further colony of the New Town on the north side of the river. That development came much later, although Learmonth Terrace commemorates this former Lord Provost responsible for one of Scotland's finest bridges.

BELFORD BRIDGE

Half a mile to the west of the Dean Bridge, the Belford Bridge connects Palmerston Place with Ravelston Dykes across the Water of Leith. It is lower and less graceful than the Dean Bridge, as well as more recent, built by Blyth and Cunningham in 1885-7. Its single arch is presided over by the city arms.

CRAMOND BRIG

Erected some distance from Cramond village in 1619, on a site where a bridge had already existed for 200 years, this three-arch structure no longer carries the road to Queensferry, succeeded by a rather featureless bridge to the south.

ROSEBURN BRIDGES

At Roseburn Terrace the Water of Leith is crossed by two bridges in close proximity. The older is an 18th century structure now confined to pedestrian use, and crossing the river at an acute angle compared to its modern successor. Carrying the busy A8, the new bridge was built in 1841 and enlarged in 1930.

RAILWAY BRIDGES

Probably the oldest and most interesting railway bridges in the city are the Warriston and Coltbridge viaducts. The former is a three-arch structure crossing the Water of Leith and Warriston Road, built during 1841-3 to carry trains from Canal Street to Granton or Leith via Scotland Street. It now carries a walkway. Coltbridge viaduct is an impressive multi-arch structure erected by the Caledonian Railway in 1861, and also now given over to carrying walkers and cyclists.

A 14-arch viaduct carries electric trains over the Water of Leith, Inglis Green Road and an industrial estate just west of Slateford station. Built in 1847, it runs parallel to the canal aquaduct, which predates it by almost 30 years. For canal bridges and aquaducts, *see* CANAL TRANSPORT.

Broadcasting

Scotland is one of the few developed countries in the world with no national broadcasting centre in its capital city. While the BBC and Scottish Television still maintain small television studios in Edinburgh, both are outstations of these organisations' main Scottish centres in Glasgow. In the case of the BBC, there were 72 employees working in TV and radio in the city in 1992/3; Glasgow had more than ten times as many BBC posts.

In 1991 the Independent Television Commission conceded that the cities of Sheffield, Liverpool, Nottingham, and Edinburgh existed in a TV 'shadow' cast by a regional station in a neighbouring city, a problem made all the more acute by Edinburgh's capital status being ignored. Also, at the time of writing, Edinburgh still has no stereo television broadcasting.

Independent radio (Radio Forth) first established itself in Edinburgh in 1974, with a new network, Scot FM, opening in 1994. Unfortunately, it was announced by the Radio Authority in 1995 that the city was not to become the site of an urban radio station.

History

On 4 May 1922 the House of Commons was told that radio stations could be established in either Glasgow or Edinburgh, but not both. Commercial pressures ensured that the former city would be Scotland's first broadcasting centre, with its concentrated population likely to result in greater sales of radio receivers for commercial suppliers, but such a technical limitation can hardly be used to explain Glasgow's consequent stranglehold on the media as more powerful transmitter technology became available. Edinburgh became a 200 watt radio relay station from 1 May 1924, without generating its own programmes, and although the city began to receive improved radio reception from the new Westerglen transmitter at Falkirk from 1932, this second division status in the broadcasting league has become permanent.

From 1924, the BBC established a presence in Queen Street, taking over the former Queen's Hall. As late as the early 1990s this was transformed into Studio 1, only to be scheduled for closure (since rescinded) in 1995, but nevertheless hardly a gesture indicating the Corporation's commitment to Scotland's capital. Radio programmes are the centre's staple output, with the station's radio drama establishing an enviable reputation nationally. An ambitious plan to establish a major BBC studio at Greenside in the 1970s, just round the Calton Hill from the planned Scottish Assembly, came to nothing, and the site has now been redeveloped.

BBC Television came to Scotland as late as 1952, enabling Edinburgh citizens to see the following year's Coronation in shop windows and in a very few homes. Independent television broadcasting, in the form of Scottish Television, followed in 1956, with the company's first proprietor, Lord Thomson, describing his franchise as 'a licence to print money', and the station's heavy diet of games shows and American potboilers proved a refreshing relief from the BBC's patronising fare.

With few home-generated programmes, as historian Christopher Harvie has pointed out, the great film-maker John Grierson was allowed to present documentaries in his *Wonderful World* programme on STV, but not make his own – STV initially proved to be as heavily Glasgow-biased as the BBC, although in recent years it has made a largely successful effort to improve its news-gathering in the East of Scotland. Even so, its base at the former Gateway Theatre in Elm Row has been reduced in size, part of the building now being leased from Queen Margaret College.

Independent radio came to the capital in 1974, with the opening of Radio Forth, whose studios are appropriately located in Forth Street, just off Broughton Place. The station is now commercially-linked with Radio Clyde, and broadcasts on both Medium Wave and FM (formerly VHF) under the title of Max AM and FM. Its output is largely music-based. A new company, Scot FM, began transmitting from a studio next to the Albert Dock at Leith from 1994.

Buses

Edinburgh's bus services were deregulated in 1986, a measure intended to introduce greater competition into the operation of public transport services on the roads. This has resulted in a large number of companies operating in and around the city, in addition to the traditional carriers, the maroon-liveried 'Corporation' buses (now Lothian Region Transport), and green and/or cream-liveried SMT (Scottish Motor Traction, or Eastern Scottish Omnibuses).

These are the two best-known bus

companies in the area, but the number of carriers has multiplied considerably since deregulation. In mid-1994, 20 companies were offering no fewer than 114 bus services in Edinburgh, not including airport buses, sightseeing tours, and long-distance National Express services. There were also 19 night services offered by four companies.

Although criticised at the time, deregulation has had the positive effects of tying such satellite towns as Dalkeith and Penicuik into what used to be the municipal bus network, and the 'Sprinter' buses introduced by Eastern Scottish on city routes proved highly popular. On the other hand, peripheral city routes (i.e. those not radiating into or from the city centre) went through a very difficult time immediately after deregulation as inexperienced contractors struggled to find their way (sometimes literally, using crews based from outside the city who were often guided by helpful passengers), and the public have found the chopping and changing of operators and timetables on all routes to be unsettling. In theory, anyone can now offer a bus service provided they give six weeks' notice to the Traffic Commissioner and receive a licence from the Commissioner after proving that they have the necessary resources to run a service.

Lothian Region Tranport PLC, the operator of the familiar maroon buses, is now a commercial company independent of Lothian Region, although the Council owns the shares and appoints the directors. There are 12 of these, including eight non-executive directors (one an employee), a non-executive chairman, and three executive directors. The company has to compete with other commercial firms, and

has no statutory privileges, nor does it receive a subsidy. The Region itself offers a Travel Concession scheme for the handicapped. Its Highways Department is responsible, at the time of writing, for the positioning of bus stops after taking advice from the Bus Stop Working Party, comprising the Region, the bus operators, and the police.

SMT is something of a household name throughout Scotland. It is best known in Edinburgh by its Eastern Scottish brand-name, although the ownership of the company has undergone a number of changes since the deregulation of the industry.

History of bus services

A horse-drawn coach service between Edinburgh and Leith was available as early as 1610, operated by one Henri Anderson, about whom little is known, except that he was from Pomerania (now in Germany). It is believed that no more than six passengers were carried at once, and there was no continuity of service. The opening of the North Bridge in 1772 saw regular services being introduced between the Tron and the Shore, Leith. Transport historian D.L.G. Hunter (see BIBLIOGRAPHY) records that stage-coaches in 1826 ran on a 30-minute frequency between the Union Canal at Port Hopetoun (Lothian Road) and Leith, and by the 1840s such areas as Morningside, Newington, and Stockbridge enjoyed some form of public road transport.

However, in the later 19th century, with the growth of railways inculcating a greater public expectancy of transport opportunities, the principle of horse-drawn coach lent itself more to railed transport than to road.

An LRT Leyland Olympian bus on Service 17 prepares to turn eastwards on to Junction Street from Ferry Road in this 1995 shot which shows an imaginative mural illustrating life in Leith. (Frank Reid)

Horses could move a tram more easily than a road vehicle, and in 1871 the Edinburgh public encountered its first tram service, running from Haymarket to Bernard Street in Leith (*see* TRAMS).

Although there was some experimentation with steam-powered buses – Portobello residents could travel on the steam road vehicle Pioneer in 1870 – horses were the mainstay of road vehicles until the petrol engine was introduced. Horse buses were licensed for use in Edinburgh as late as 1910, although the last services operated by genuine horsepower may have been on the Leith-Stockbridge route in 1907. Leith's horse bus operations, continued until October 1909 between Seafield and King's Road (Portobello), with five of the town's

12 horses then being sold to the Fire Service, and one to the Cleansing Department.

Although buses, whether horse-drawn or motorised, originally took on the role of a feeder service to the tram network of Edinburgh and Leith, they were eventually to surpass it.

In 1899, the Edinburgh Autocar Company inaugurated a Daimler waggonette service between the GPO and Haymarket from 19 May, less than a fortnight before Edinburgh began its (already slightly anachronistic) municipal cable car system. Six years later a famous name began to be seen on the city's roads as Scottish Motor Traction (SMT) commenced operations between the Mound and Corstorphine. This eventually was the basis for the Scottish Bus Group, undergoing major metamorphoses at the time of the 1948 Transport Act, and again when reorganised in response to market forces in the 1990s.

The first Corporation bus did not operate until 3 August 1914, the day before the beginning of the First World War. The city's Tramways Department took over direct operation of trams and buses from 1 July 1919, and on 29 December the first continuous ECT bus service began running between Ardmillan and Abbeyhill.

A curious alternative to petrol in wartime was the gas-operated bus. In 1917, 35 SMT buses were adapted to run on coal-gas which was stored in a balloon on the vehicle roof. However grotesque this may have appeared, it proved to be cheaper to operate than conventionally-fuelled vehicles at that time. Another wartime innovation was the introduction of women conductresses – who somehow seemed to suit the nickname of 'clippies' more than their male counterparts – in 1915, their arrival initially opposed by the male staff.

Scottish Motor Traction consolidated their position after the First World War, building on an already excellent trading reputation. In 1929 the company was recapitalised, with the London & North Eastern and London Midland & Scottish railway companies, both locally represented in Edinburgh, heavily investing in the company, presumably on a 'if you can't beat them, join them' principle. Not surprisingly, a number of branch lines in the Lothians closed almost immediately (e.g. Gullane, Gifford, Glencorse). In 1948, with the nationalisation of most British transport undertakings, SMT shed its motor and engineering division, becoming, on 8 April 1949, an exclusively bus operating undertaking called Scottish Omnibuses.

Buses allowed Edinburgh Corporation to extend public transport links into the suburbs, reaching such areas as Craigmillar in 1925, Pilton ten years later, and Sighthill in 1937. Night services began in 1925, originally two routes being operated in winter only; five were run all year round from 1947. Edinburgh's biggest bus garage, the Central Garage in Annandale Street, was built as an exhibition hall in 1922, and converted for buses 12 years later. Depots also existed off Leith Walk at Shrubhill, near Smith's Place, and at King's Road, Portobello. These were all for Edinburgh Corporation vehicles; SMT buses were based at New Street, the garage there now a commercial car-parking area.

Trams outnumbered municipal buses until as late as 1952 – yet within five years there were no trams left. After the decision had been taken to concentrate urban transport on buses, ECT (Edinburgh Corporation Transport since 1928) ordered 370 new vehicles in the 1953-7 period, plus a further 77 refurbished. The mainstay of the new fleet was the double-deck Leyland Titan, which served the city well for more than 20 years, surviving into the age of front-loading buses, which Edinburgh did much to pioneer from 1957 onwards, and one-man operation from 1969.

Edinburgh's Bus Station was opened in April 1957, at the north-east corner of St Andrew's Square, and used by SMT and a few out-of-town companies. Originally unroofed, the station replaced the Square itself as a stance for bus services to destinations furth of Edinburgh. The Bus

Station was roofed about 1969 by commercial premises, and has been the subject of intense speculation in recent years, with the suggestion that it might be completely replaced by offices, with buses once again using the Square.

Local government reorganisation in 1975 saw Edinburgh's municipal bus undertaking becoming Lothian Region Transport, although there was no noticeable 'regional' element discernable at that time. Maroon buses did not pass beyond the city boundaries, not even to Musselburgh, barely two miles beyond the existing routes. Similarly, SMT or their successors, Scottish Omnibuses, or Eastern Scottish, were not expected to cater for passengers between the Bus Station and the suburbs, and much ill-feeling was engendered as a result. 'Out of towners' could use Edinburgh's swimming pools and other municipal facilities, but it was not unknown for city passengers, tired of waiting for a maroon bus, to be ejected by the conductor when trying to board a green one from Musselburgh or Dalkeith. Deregulation put paid to this, with companies vying to attract passengers.

Canal Transport

Edinburgh's only artifical waterway is the Union Canal, more properly called the Edinburgh and Glasgow Union Canal, although it never reached farther west than Camelon, near Falkirk, affording a junction with the Forth & Clyde Canal.

Thirty-one miles (49.6 kilometres) in length and an average of five feet (1.5 metres) deep, the Union Canal is a contour canal, that is, built on one level and avoiding the use of locks, except at its western end, where there were 11 locks to gain entry to the Forth & Clyde. From Port Downie at Camelon its course stretches east to Edinburgh, where its eastern terminal basin was situated at Port Hopetoun off Lothian Road. A 'branch' terminus called Port Hamilton was located near Morrison Street just a little to the north of, and at right-angles to, the main terminal basin. The latter (Port Hopetoun) was closed in 1922, eventually being replaced in 1935-6 by Lothian House, which includes the present MGM (formerly Regal) cinema. The canal has been cut back, presently terminating in West Fountainbridge, close to the Mecca (formerly Palais De Dance) hall.

Owned by British Waterways, the Union no longer carries commercial traffic and has ceased to perform its postwar function of acting as a water conduit for local industry, particularly rubber making (see INDUSTRY). The Union's course is interrupted by culverting in the Kingsknowe area, although its usefulness for leisure traffic was recognised by having a new aquaduct accorded it to bridge the A720 City By-pass west of the Wester Hailes area in the 1980s.

An amenity society dedicated to the waterway's welfare, the Edinburgh Canal Society, has a boathouse at Harrison Park. Otherwise, it has to be said that Edinburgh has not so far realised the tourist and leisure potential of the Union Canal in the manner of a number of English cities which have glorified their waterway heritage. There is however a scheme currently being

Port Hopetoun no longer mirrors the unlovely skyline of slaughterhouses as demolition crews prepare the site for redevelopment, probably around 1922. The streets in the foreground comprise the junction of Lothian Road and West Fountainbridge, and the corner site is presently occupied by Woolworths. Ironically, the area of the Union Canal's western basin lay undeveloped until well into the 1930s, when Lothian House was built on the site. (Historic Scotland)

considered called the 'Millennium Link' which proposes reopening the Forth & Clyde and Union canals as a cross-Scotland waterway for leisure purposes.

History

Intended to improve the capital's supply of coal in the early 19th century, the canal was the first transport undertaking to be built in the Edinburgh area, employing innumerable navvies to 'navigate' its course westwards. These included in their number Irish immigrants Burke and Hare, who soon forsook their digging talents in order to enter the cadaver supply business (*see* CRIME).

Opened in 1822, the canal offered a mode of transport to and from Glasgow via Falkirk, which was greatly superior to that offered by road, seven hours being required for the waterborne journey (14 to or from Glasgow) in 1830. Fares varied from five shillings (25p) 'steerage' to seven shillings (35p) cabin class, and there was even a night boat, known colloquially as the 'Hoolet'. A historian writing in the 1820s records that construction materials for the buildings of the New Town, and the bridges of the Old, were as important an incoming commodity as coal, while the principal 'exports' from the city were 'merchant goods and dung'. One canal historian, Guthrie Hutton, believes that canalside fields in the Ratho area were particularly productive after a century or more of being fertilised with the city's horse-droppings.

Within 20 years the railway offered a speedier means of passenger travel, although bulk freight was still carried for many decades afterwards, ceasing some time before the waterway's official closure in 1965. In 1849 the Union had been taken over by the Edinburgh & Glasgow Railway, which was then absorbed by the North British in 1865, and nationalisation followed, along with the railway system, in 1948. One tragic footnote about the canal was that George Meikle Kemp, designer of the Scott Monument, drowned in its waters in 1844.

Engineering features

The Union Canal boasts three impressive aquaducts, one of them inside the city in the Slateford area, and comprising eight arches carrying the waterway across the Water of Leith, parallel to the railway, as well as across road and industrial properties. Immediately to the east at this point the canal crosses the A70 on an impressive 1937 concrete bridge, sometimes known as Charlie's Bridge, as the Young Pretender had camped near here before taking the city in 1745. A fascinating 30 feet (9 metres) high lifting bridge, which originally carried West Fountainbridge across the canal, and is now preserved, can be found spanning the canal almost at water level at Leamington Road. Lothian House in Lothian Road bears a mural by Pilkington Jackson denoting the former existence of Port Hopetoun on the site.

Castles and Towers

EDINBURGH CASTLE

So well-known is Edinburgh Castle that local residents, to say nothing of a near-million tourists who visit it each year, might not realise that it is only one of a number in Edinburgh surviving from Scotland's troubled past. In 1994 there were 992,078 visitors, making it the most popular attraction in Scotland in the 'paid admission' category, but this was a 5 per cent decrease on 1993.

Built solidly on a 435 feet (130 metres) geological crag and tail formation, the product of Ice Age action on rocks of volcanic origin, (described in detail under GEOLOGY), the Castle Rock has been under continuous human occupation since at least the 9th century BC.

Prehistoric occupation of the rock is not very well-documented, but may date back as much as 7,000 years. There is evidence that the site was held during Roman times by the Votadini, whose major fortification was at Traprain Law in East Lothian. Although Roman artefacts have been found on the rock in recent excavations, the Romans themselves do not appear to figure largely in the history of the site, despite having established military ports at the mouths of the nearby Esk and Almond rivers. This may be because the Roman presence pre-dated the creation of two wells penetrating down to the rock's water table, one of them all of 110 feet deep (33 metres) (see WATER SUPPLY).

The history of the Castle Rock gains firmer ground in the 7th century, when we know that the Angles captured the rock in 638, when it was already known as Din Eidyn, usually taken to be Gaelic for a hill fort on a sloping ridge. At this time the rock and its fortification appears to have been the major settlement for the area, and the rock remained in Northumbrian hands until

Edinburgh has a number of castles, but there is no argument about which is the most famous. This shot shows the National Gallery building on the Mound, with East Princes Street Gardens in the foreground. (City of Edinburgh Council)

1018 when Malcolm II won Lothian for the newly-conceived Kingdom of Scotland, by victory at the Battle of Carham.

A vestige of the history of that time can still be seen at the summit of the Rock in the form of St Margaret's Chapel, built in the 1130s or 1140s to commemorate Malcolm III's Saxon queen who reputedly died of grief on hearing of the deaths of her husband and eldest son at Alnwick in 1093. The chapel was ordered by David I and is generally regarded as the oldest extant building in Edinburgh, having been restored in the 1850s following its use as a gunpowder magazine. The remodelled

doorway and stained-glass window are 20th century features.

Around the time of David's reign, Edinburgh was given royal burgh status, and castle and burgh embarked on a stormy journey through the coming centuries. During the Wars of Independence the castle changed hands four times in 45 years from 1296, and was largely dismantled by Robert the Bruce following Thomas Randolph (Earl of Moray's) capture of it in 1313, the year before Bannockburn. Following the release of David II from English captivity in 1356, the castle underwent an almost continuous building and rebuilding programme for 200 years. This included the strengthening of the defences and the construction of a royal residence. Little of the medieval fortifications are still visible, David's Tower of 1368 having been incorporated into the later Half Moon Battery, while the royal apartments were later remodelled, although on the existing site.

One artefact which does survive from the 15th century is Mons Meg. This is a hugely impressive bombard, or cannon, capable of propelling a gunstone or cannonball nearly two miles. One fired from the castle in celebration in 1558 was recovered from Wardie Muir, near present-day Granton. Meg was given to James II by the Duke of Burgundy at the time of James's marriage to Mary of Gueldres. James's interest in ballistics proved fatal, when he stood too close to a cannon which exploded during the siege of Roxburgh, and Mons Meg also proved unsafe, bursting its barrel when fired in 1681. Never fired again, the bombard was taken south to the Tower of London, before Sir Walter Scott convinced George

IV that its rightful place was in Edinburgh. It is now to be seen in the castle vaults, after many years of standing in the open air near St Margaret's Chapel.

Of all the castle fortifications, the most impressive is the Half Moon Battery, which looms out over Johnston Terrace, on the rock's south-east shoulder. Built in the 1570s, the battery incorporates the ruins of David's Tower, and has been restored after damage sustained in the sieges of 1650 and 1689.

The section of the castle known as the Palace is sited in Crown Square, and the Great Hall, with its magnificent ceiling, is the principal vestige of royal residence on the rock. It was in the royal apartments that

Mary Stewart, Queen of Scots, gave birth in 1566 to James, the king who united the realms of Scotland and England in 1603. Holyrood became the main focus for royal activity by the middle of the 16th century, and much of the royal accommodation became used for storage in later decades (*see* ROYAL RESIDENCES).

The most important royal artefacts connected with the history of the castle is the collection of regalia known as the Honours of Scotland. Comprising the crown made for James V in 1540, embellished with gold from upper Clydesdale, a sword presented to James IV by Pope Julius II in 1507, and sceptre, dating probably from the 15th century.

Edinburgh Castle on a quiet day, with the winter sunshine failing to warm the ancient stones, and with comparatively few tourists seen here visiting Scotland's top visitor attraction in the category for paid entry.

Locked away when the Union of the Parliaments was signed in 1707, the regalia was recovered 111 years later, when Sir Walter Scott obtained royal permission to have the locks of the storage chest broken open and the treasures therein – the oldest in the United Kingdom – once again take pride of place in the castle. One of the most important 20th century additions to the castle is the Scottish National War Memorial (see MILITARY HISTORY). Also worth visiting on the rock is the Scottish United Services Museum.

The castle's prison capacity may not run to the traditional dungeons so beloved of present-day tourists – the rock reduced the amount of excavations that could be undertaken – and a famous escape took place in 1497 when James III's brother, the Duke of Albany, escaped down the rock and helped an injured companion to reach Leith safely. But the castle was used extensively as a prison in the 18th and 19th centuries, particularly during the Napeolonic conflict up until 1815. There was even a mass break-out in 1811.

Edinburgh Castle no longer serves as the principal barracks for the area, such a function being taken over by Redford from 1915. The Army School of Piping is still based on the rock, and it is wholly appropriate that the Edinburgh Military Tattoo should take place on the Castle Esplanade, and has done so every August since 1950. The castle also makes an eye-catching landmark after dark; it was first floodlit in 1932, although regular illumination only began in 1959, and then only on 'weekends and special occasions' frequency, in case Edinburgh people had too much of a good thing!

One feature of the castle which imposes itself on visitors and residents alike is the One o'clock Gun. Every weekday at 1300 hours precisely a 25-pounder artillery piece is fired on the Mills Mount Battery. This practice was introduced in 1861 to supplement a visual time-signal to Forth shipping of a time ball dropping on the mast of Nelson's Monument on the Calton Hill. It is probably an anachronism nowadays, with the widespread availability of precision watches, but is a custom which Edinburgh people would be lost without. Its effect on tourists can however be traumatic.

In recent years a tunnel has been constructed into the castle from the Esplanade to ease tourist access; otherwise the visitor will find striking statues of Wallace and Bruce guarding the (comparatively modern) gatehouse and its ditch dating from Cromwell's time. A few feet from the moat bridge is a plaque commemorating the granting to Scottish citizens of 64 baronetcies of Nova Scotia between 1625 and 1649 by the Earl of Stirling. Since the process of sasine then involved a token transfer of soil from the site being sold, the Scottish parliament gave permission for this part of the then Castle Rock, now the Esplanade, to be considered part of Nova Scotia, and its soil used. It remains part of Nova Scotia to this day, the plaque being erected in 1953.

The castle's earliest builders could hardly have anticipated that the castle would one day be attacked from the air, but exactly that happened on 2 April 1916, during a Zeppelin raid. A plaque high above the path between King's Stables Road and Johnston Terrace records what must have a near-miss (see MILITARY HISTORY).

CRAIGMILLAR CASTLE

Edinburgh's second castle is to be found at Craigmillar, about three miles (4.8 kilometres) south-east of the city centre, on a ridge affording views in all directions. Preserved as an ancient monument by Historic Scotland, it well repays a visit.

Constructed by the Preston family from the 15th century onwards, the castle is basically an L-shaped tower, around which a succession of enclosing walls has been built, creating inner and outer courtyards. The castle was damaged by English troops during the 'Rough Wooing' in the 1540s, but was sufficiently rebuilt by Sir Simon Preston (see also LORD PROVOSTS) for him to host visits from Mary Stewart, Queen of Scots. Here she received the English ambassador, who advised Mary to seek a husband if she wished to count her cousin Elizabeth I of England as a friend. By 1660 the castle and neighbouring estate had passed to the Gilmour family.

For further information, see the HMSO pamphlet written by Denys Pringle.

LAURISTON CASTLE

One of the most attractive fortified houses in Scotland, Lauriston Castle is located in the Davidson's Mains area, three miles north-west of the centre of Edinburgh. It is now in the care of the City Council, having been left to the nation in 1926.

Lauriston Castle's plush stately-home interior should not be allowed to deceive the visitor into dismissing this as a 19th century 'make believe' castle. Although rebuilt and extended in the 1820s, the castle was substantial enough in the 16th century to be worth the trouble of being sacked by the Earl of Hertford during the 'Rough

Wooing' in 1544. The oldest extant part of the castle dates therefore from the later part of that century, the estate falling into the hands of the Napier family around 1590. A four-storey main block was constructed by Archibald Napier, father of the inventor of logarithms, who insisted on the installation of a secret staircase from the first-floor hall, complete with a spy-hole from which the room could be viewed.

At the end of the 16th century, the castle came to be owned by John Law, Comptroller-General of France, and financial adviser to the Scots Parliament. It was owned by another banker in Victorian times, when the castle reached its present size and appearance, and was last privately owned by William Reid, proprietor of an Edinburgh firm of cabinetmakers. An enthusiastic antiques collector, Reid used Lauriston to set off his extensive collections, generously willing both castle and collections for the enjoyment of the public after his death. The guidebooks describe it as a unique snapshot of what an Edwardian country house was like, although Lauriston was of course so much more than that.

Surrounded by 30 acres (12.3 hectares) of gardens and parkland, Lauriston Castle has become a weekend venue for special events, such as vintage car rallies, recitals, and childrens' attractions.

LIBERTON TOWER

One of the privileges enjoyed by the staff and students alike at Edinburgh University's King's Buildings campus is an uninterrupted view southwards up the hillside to Liberton Tower. Dating from around 1500, this four-storey edifice

Lauriston Castle dates from the 15th century, and now doubles as one of the city's most interesting museums. (City of Edinburgh Council)

appears to have been built by the Dalmahoy family, who constructed three winding staircases from the first floor upwards and downwards, all within the walls themselves. Entry was gained by a timber staircase to the first floor, and this could be withdrawn as required for defence. Any invaders gaining entry by the basement door could be seen from a spyhole in the east wall as soon as they entered the hall to gain one of the upward staircases.

Purchased by Provost William Little in 1587, the Tower proved too spartan for the propertied class of the time, and residence was transferred to Liberton House nearby, fortunately without the character of the older building being lost.

LIBERTON HOUSE
Situated some 300 yards (90 metres) from Liberton Tower, Liberton House is neither a castle nor tower but has fortified details in the form of gun-loops. Built by William Little around 1605, this is an L-planned building with three storeys in the main part of the house, four in the wing, and a stair-tower in the angle of the two. Presently undergoing restoration, this interesting building is visible from the main road, Liberton Drive, its lectern-shaped doocot drawing attention to the site.

MERCHISTON TOWER
Ancestral home of the Napier family, Merchiston Tower is now incorporated into the principal campus of Napier University. Records show that the building stood before 1495, and was home to the famous John Napier (1550-1617), inventor of logarithms, builder of a calculating machine and an armoured vehicle. His family castle, although substantially preserved, has

received the addition of a concrete staircase, and has a modern university corridor running through part of it.

PORTOBELLO TOWER

While of no great vintage, (probably built in 1785), the octagonal tower at the foot of Beach Lane is a monument to the late 18th century's preoccupation with antiquity. It is made up of stone and dressings from demolished buildings, including, according to Baird's *Annals of Duddingston and Portobello*, the Edinburgh Market Cross, St Andrews Cathedral, and the former university buildings replaced by the Old Quad. Its associated building is an amusement arcade, and the tower has given its name to the school nearby, Towerbank.

BONALY TOWER

Designed by William Playfair in 1836 for the Cockburn family, of whom the historian and pioneering conservationist Henry, Lord Cockburn (*Memorials of his Time*) was the most illustrious. The house has since been added to, and recently divided into apartments. Attending a commanders' course during the Second World War, Evelyn Waugh recognised the Cockburn coat of arms, realising that this was the home of his great-great-grandfather – the one who disappointed Waugh by not being the kind of 'useless lord' that the novelist would have liked to have been descended from!

CRAIGENTINNY HOUSE

Tucked away in Loaning Road, on the fringe of what was once Restalrig village but now surrounded by council housing, Craigentinny is a 16th century villa built for the Nisbet family. Victorian alterations on behalf of the eccentric William Miller (he of the ornate mausoleum not far away, (*see* CEMETERIES AND CREMATORIA) have reduced its interest, and the Social Work department have an office appended to it, but this is still a building which would be highly prized if located in a less architecturally-rich community than Edinburgh.

LOCHEND HOUSE

Perched on a crag above the loch of the same name (*see* LOCHS), Lochend House has its origins in the 16th century as a home for the Logans of Restalrig, although it was largely destroyed at that time, and living-quarters were added in the 18th century. The detached doocot, now set in the public park nearby, is a 16th century survivor.

BRUNSTANE HOUSE

Now surrounded by a modern housing development, Brunstane House and farm were, until comparatively recently, part of the countryside scene south of Portobello. Parts of the house date from 1565, and it was twice partly rebuilt in 1639 and 1672, and was home to the Duke of Lauderdale in the 17th century, for whom this was a perfect country house, less than a mile from the sea.

Cathedrals

Edinburgh has two cathedrals, both named for Saint Mary. The older is the Roman Catholic St Mary's Metropolitan Cathedral at Picardy Place, the younger (and more architecturally impressive) being St Mary's Episcopalian Cathedral, standing in the city's West End between Palmerston Place and Manor Place. Both of Edinburgh's cathedrals are comparatively modern, although this can partly be explained by the destruction of Holyrood as a place of worship by the 17th century, the abbey there failing to survive as a focal point for religious activity in the city in the manner of Westminster Abbey in London.

Readers expecting to find a description of St Giles in this category, apart from the summary given below, should look under CHURCHES. By definition, a cathedral is the seat of a bishop, so a presbyterian church technically cannot be considered a cathedral.

ST MARY'S ROMAN CATHOLIC CATHEDRAL

Overlooking the traffic island at the junction of Leith Street and Picardy Place (although with its postal address in Broughton Street), this is one of Britain's smaller cathedrals, having only attained that status in 1878. It is the seat of the Archbishop of Edinburgh and St Andrews.

The architectural guidebooks describe it as comprising a gabled facade fronting a wide nave running into an aisled choir, but the building is unusual in lacking a spire or tower to emphasise its importance to the Roman Catholic community in the city. It currently has a congregation of around 2,000, a substantial decrease on the 1960 figure of 5,700, no doubt due to the loss of so much tenemental housing in the Leith Street area.

Edinburgh's High Kirk, St Giles, as seen from the west, with the Signet Library in shadow on the right of the picture and Salisbury Crags beyond. (City of Edinburgh Council)

ST MARY'S EPISCOPAL CATHEDRAL

'The finest church to have been built in Scotland since the Reformation'. This superlative was coined about St Mary's Episcopalian Cathedral in Palmerston Place, by the long-serving minister of St Giles, Dr Charles Warr.

Few would argue with him; built over a period from 1874 up to 1917, this Gothic masterpiece is the work of Gilbert Scott. This is Scotland's second largest ecclesiastical building, excelled in size only by Glasgow Cathedral. Its three spires are its strongest feature, leading to comparisons with Lichfield Cathedral in Staffordshire, and are a landmark on the city skyline from as far away as Fife, while its nave emphasises the building's traditional atmosphere. Its neighbouring Music School is well-known throughout the country.

ST GILES CATHEDRAL

St Giles was redesignated a cathedral, following the Reformation which transferred it to the protestant faith, in 1633. This was when the Episcopal religion was being imposed from London, and led to Jenny Geddes hurling her stool at the pulpit in protest. Presbyterianism re-asserted itself in 1638, but there was a further period of Episcopacy from 1661 to 1689. So run-down did the building become, that no congregation could reoccupy the church until the 1880s, following two rebuildings, and it was of course a presbyterian congregation, rendering St Giles, strictly speaking, a church, not a cathedral.

Cemeteries and Crematoria

Edinburgh has a considerable number of cemeteries and prescribed burial places, despite being one of the leading centres in Britain for the disposal of the dead by cremation. This latter method of disposal accounts for 75 per cent of funeral arrangements nowadays, and the city has three crematoria, one municipally-owned, the others run commercially. In 1979 a survey found that Edinburgh was ranked fourth in Britain for the number of cremations carried out, despite a comparatively small ethnic population for whom cremation is the approved manner for disposal of their dead (*see also* POPULATION).

At the time of writing, Edinburgh District Council is responsible for the maintenance of 40 cemeteries and burial grounds, including the following public cemeteries, totalling 222 acres (90 hectares), and costing approximately £657,600 to maintain in 1993-4:

Public Cemeteries

Causewayside, Corstorphine Hill, Comely Bank, Currie, Dalry, Grange, Kirkliston, Liberton, Morningside, Mortonhall, New Calton, Newington, Old Calton, Portobello, Preston Street, Rosebank, Saughton, South Queensferry, Warriston, Wauchope, West Merchiston.

Churchyards maintained by EDC

Buccleuch Street, Canongate, Colinton, Corstorphine, Cramond, Currie, Dalmeny,

Rosebank cemetery, Pilrig, is administered by the local authority, and is the final resting place for so many of the great and the good from the town of Leith. It also includes the mass graves of those Royal Scots killed in the 1915 railway disaster at Quintinshill.

Duddingston, Gogar, Greyfriars, Kirkliston, Liberton, North Leith, Ratho, Restalrig, St Cuthbert's, South Leith, South Queensferry.

Two graveyards, at Piershill and a site near Easter Road, are maintained by the Edinburgh Eastern Cemetery Company, and accommodate an average total of three new burials per week at the two sites. The Piershill cemetery is the principal Jewish burial ground in the east of Scotland. Roman Catholic burials take place at the Mount Vernon cemetery in the Liberton area.

Edinburgh was something of a pioneer in the provision of commercial burials (*see*

History *opposite*). In 1992, however, the District Council purchased such historic burial sites as Dalry and Morningside cemeteries from a London property company to ensure that no development took place on them, following the public disquiet caused by the building of houses on the Morningside cemetery in 1981.

The Council also operates the Mortonhall crematorium facility, as well as the City Mortuary. In 1994, after four years of consultation and preparation, the two chapels at Mortonhall, seating 250 and 50 mourners, were redecorated to make them equally suitable for atheistic or ethnic funerals involving the Hindu, San, Sikh, and

Tao faiths. Also in 1994, the local authorities addressed the need for members of the Hindu and Sikh communities to allow the ashes of loved ones to be river-borne to the sea. In August of that year a site on the Almond was designated as Gangaghat, so that this rite could be carried out officially.

Historians will find most interest in the illustrious names buried in Greyfriars and Canongate churchyards in the Old Town, and in Calton Burial Ground on the fringe of the New, on Regent Road. However, even suburban cemeteries contain the eminent and the unknown side by side, as in Morningside burial ground, where a Nobel Laureate (Sir Edward Appleton) can be found commemorated among the forgotten.

Perhaps the city's most extraordinary funerary decoration is the Craigentinny Marbles. This is an impressive Roman-style mausoleum a few yards from the A1140 Edinburgh-Portobello road, and is well worth viewing. It was built in 1848-56 over a 20 foot deep pit in which lie the remains of William Henry Christie Miller, a local landowner. Two sides of the construction carry panels illustrating Biblical incidents, carved by Alfred Gatley. It is ironic that Edinburgh's most impressive funerary monument commemorates a man who was almost completely unknown.

Animal burial has been available in the city at the commercially-run Piershill cemetery for a number of years, and the cemetery for soldiers' dogs at Edinburgh Castle is well-known to tourists.

History

The oldest human remains in the city are those in the royal burial vault at Holyrood, including those of David II, who died in

Edinburgh's most impressive funerary monument is to be found among the suburban bungalows of Craigentinny, far from any churchyard site. The mausoleum, known as the Craigentinny Marbles, contains the remains of William Miller, a local landowner.

1371. Unfortunately, his, and other royal remains, including such later monarchs as James II and James V, were scattered by a mob protesting about the consecration of a Catholic chapel at Holyrood in 1688, and their mortal residue had to be collected from a number of different lairs to be reinterred in their present resting place.

Historians have commented on the lack of funerary monuments in Edinburgh before 1600, and the city's principal church, St Giles, has been surrounded by secular buildings for centuries. Pressure on building space forced the closure of its burial ground from the 16th century, and even St Giles itself was used as a burial site, several tons of human remains being removed from the church as late as 1879.

In 1566 Queen Mary donated the monastery gardens at Greyfriars to the city for use as a cemetery. Greyfriars is probably best-known to the wider world as the burial place of Greyfriars Bobby and its master John Gray, and this often obscures the importance of the site, containing an outstanding collection of 17th century monuments, the final resting place of many Covenanters, and a historic location which should not have required lottery money to refurbish it in 1995.

The Resurrectionists were the most sensational feature in the history of the disposal of the city's dead. At one time, the capital's graveyards were seen as reservoirs of specimens for the university's dissection tables, and the city's cemeteries had to be watched at night to prevent the plundering of new graves. The most impressive architectural legacy of this period is the two-storey cylindrical watchtower at St Cuthbert's churchyard, at the corner of Lothian Road and King's Stables Road, completed in 1827. The tower's construction did nothing, however, to stem the activities of the notorious Burke and Hare (see CRIME).

An early example of a commercial company offering internment was the Edinburgh Cemetery Company, founded in 1840. It owned seven cemeteries at Warriston, Dalry and New Dalry (also known as North Merchiston), Saughton, Newington, Comely Bank, and Corstorphine Hill. Investing in cemetery companies was consistently lucrative until cremation started in Edinburgh in 1929, and as late as the outbreak of the Second World War one of the companies was paying a six per cent dividend to its investors.

The concept of privately-owned burial grounds became somewhat tarnished in the early 1990s however, when a London-based firm appeared to harbour development plans for some of the city's graveyards, but the District Council acquired these to ensure their continuance and to placate hostile public opinion. Longer-established cemetery companies have given the city a network of final resting places, such as Piershill cemetery, maintained with care and dignity since 1887.

The first record of a Jewish burial in Edinburgh is recorded in the Town Council Minutes of 6 May 1795, in a natural cave, whose location is now unknown, in the Calton Hill. Scotland's first cemetery for those of the Jewish faith was opened at Braid Place (now Sciennes House Place) in 1816, and this catered for families from as far away as Glasgow. Later burials took place at Echo Bank before the present allocation of space was made possible at Piershill.

Cremation first became available in Edinburgh in 1929, when the city's first crematorium was opened at Warriston, some 34 years after Glasgow had begun to dispose of its dead in this way. The Seafield Crematorium opened in 1939, and a second chapel at Warriston followed in 1957. A municipally-owned facility was opened at Mortonhall in February 1967 by the then Edinburgh Corporation.

Cremation is now the most popular means of disposing of the dead, accounting for around three-quarters of the city's deceased, except where there are religious objections to such a practice. One change in funeral custom brought about by the growing popularity of cremation is the attendance of female mourners at the service itself. The *Third Statistical Account* records that, as late as the 1960s, female relatives would not otherwise attend a funeral service, but would await the return of the male mourners to the bereaved's home. 'In fact', records the Account, 'women nowadays form a large proportion of the mourners at each of Edinburgh's crematoria'.

Chambers of Commerce

Scotland's capital has two Chambers of Commerce – Edinburgh's, dating from 1785, and Leith's, founded in 1864. The two share a building in Randolph Crescent, in the city's west end, and are associated with, but independent of, each other.

Edinburgh Chamber of Commerce has approximately 1,100 corporate members; Leith Chamber of Commerce, 180. The latter moved into the present accommodation, shared with the Edinburgh Chamber, in 1975.

In 1995 the Edinburgh Chamber announced a working partnership, unique in the United Kingdom, with the Capital Enterprise Trust, to create a merged organisation to offer practical support for city businesses. The new Edinburgh Chamber of Commerce and Enterprise is planned to show particular interest in the capital's retail trade, while not forgetting the electrical, tourist, and travel industries.

History
What we would nowadays call a 'steering committee' met on 23 December 1785 to discuss the setting up of an Edinburgh Chamber of Commerce to promote and enhance trade conditions in the capital. The first meeting proper took place in the first week of 1786, the earliest members including printers, bankers, and general merchants.

One of their first acts was to express concern about the lack of a lighthouse-keeper on the Isle of May, at the mouth of the Forth. As the keeper's salary was insufficient to allow him to keep his family comfortably, he was forced to engage in fishing, when he could easily have been isolated from the island by bad weather at the very time when there was most need for his services. As it happens, Scottish lighthouses were regularised in that very year, but the Chamber went on to make its mark in other concerns, not least in suggesting the firing of the One o'clock Gun, beginning in 1861.

Churches

(see also CATHEDRALS)

Edinburgh is the administrative heart of the Church of Scotland, numerically the nation's largest church. The capital is also home to the headquarters of the Free Church of Scotland, the Free Presbyterian Church of Scotland, the Reformed Presbyterian Church, the Scottish Episcopal Church, and the Religious Society of Friends, while the Roman Catholic Church has a strong presence in the capital.

Non-Christian religious groups represented in the city include Jews, Hindus, Sikhs, Muslims, and Buddhists.

CHURCH OF SCOTLAND

The Kirk, as it is familiarly known, has its heart firmly based in Edinburgh. St Giles' is the locus for services on national occasions, part of a tradition of worship, albeit not continuous, going back to the 12th century (*see* History *on page 64*). The Kirk's ultimate governing body, the General Assembly, used to meet in St Giles, but now congegrates every May in the Assembly Hall on the Mound. There are administrative offices in George Street, on the Mound and in Palmerston Place, the last-named being the home of the Edinburgh Presbytery office. The Presbytery, numbered 1 out of 49 (3 outside Scotland in England, Europe, and Jersualem), contains the following charges (1994):

CHARGE	NO. OF COMMUNICANTS, 1993
Abercorn/Dalmeny	322
Albany Deaf Church	176
Balerno	1,070
Barclay	596
Blackhall, St Columba	1,397
Bristo Memorial, Craigmillar	211
Broughton St Mary's	488
Canongate	470
Carrick Knowe	985
Cluny	853
Colinton	1,444
Colinton Mains	431
Corstorphine – Craigsbank	1,182
– Old	910
– St Anne's	587
– St Ninian's	1,445
Craigentinny, St Christopher's	215
Craiglockhart	671
Craigmillar Park	386
Cramond	1,505
Currie	1,623
Davidson's Mains	1,028
Dean	305
Drylaw	334
Duddingston	907
Fairmilehead	1,351
Gilmerton	318
Gorgie	664
Granton	551
Greenbank	1,074
Greenside	410
Greyfriars Tolbooth/Highland	490
Holyrood Abbey	415
Holy Trinity	288
Inverleith	581
Juniper Green	620
Kaimes, Lockhart Memorial	239
Kirkliston	513
Kirk o'Field	403
Leith – North	599
– St Andrew's	478
– St Paul's	328
– St Serf's	399
– St Thomas's, Junction Road	502
– South	1,045
– Wardie	784
Liberton	1,244
Liberton, Northfield	425
London Road	594
Marchmont, St Giles	435
Mayfield Salisbury	1,144
Morningside Braid	611
Morningside United	318
Muirhouse	205
Murrayfield	763
Newhaven	360
New Restalrig	661
Old Kirk	288
Palmerston Place	814
Pilrig/Dalmeny Street	412

Polwarth	598	St Cuthbert's	879
Portobello – Old/Windsor Place	617	St David's, Broomhouse	254
– St James's	502	St George's West	440
– St Philip's, Joppa	973	St Giles High	784
Priestfield	302	St John's, Oxgangs	448
Queensferry	1,010	St Margaret's	507
Ratho	310	St Martin's	329
Reid Memorial	545	St Michael's	790
Richmond Craigmillar	179	St Nicholas, Sighthill	892
Stenhouse St Aidan's	(Not known)	St Stephen's, Comely Bank	664
St Andrew's & St George's	470	Slateford/Longstone	500
St Andrew's, Clermiston	477	Stockbridge	685
St Catherine's, Argyle	428	Tron Kirk/Moredun	228
St Colm's	341	Viewforth	387

FREE CHURCH OF SCOTLAND

With its headquarters also on the Mound, the Free Church divides Scotland into three synods, the Edinburgh and Perth Presbytery being grouped in the South Synod. It contains 13 churches, three of them in Edinburgh – Buccleuch and Greyfriars, St Columba's, and Leith Elder Memorial.

This church split from the Church of Scotland in 1843 in the historic 'Disruption', in the belief that the kirk had allowed too much decision-making to be taken away from congregations, particularly their right to chose their own minister. This was one of the most serious events in Scottish ecclesiastical history since the Reformation. The first meeting of the new breakaway church was held in Edinburgh's Tanfield Hall (*see* page 68), and 500 new churches were built within two years.

The United Free Church of Scotland has its offices in Glasgow. Its Presbytery of Lothians and Borders contains six congregations in the city – Blackhall, Corstorphine, Leith (2), Portobello, and West Edinburgh. This church was formally set up in 1900 from the United Presbyterian Church, but most of its members were prepared to accept union with the Church of Scotland in 1929.

SCOTTISH EPISCOPAL CHURCH

This Church, closest in its style of worship to the Anglican faith, is well represented in the city by the triple spires of St Mary's Cathedral (*see also* CATHEDRALS), seat of the Bishop of Edinburgh. The present bishop was elected Primus of the Scottish Episcopal Church in June 1992. His diocese of Edinburgh presently contains 28 charges and churches, and is particularly well represented in ministering to the city's hospitals.

History

The Scottish Episcopal Church claims its origins as far back as the days of Saints Ninian and Columba, although its matrix was the troubled 17th century. While the Presbyterian faith turned away from a hierarchical structure, the anglicised Stuart monarchs, now ruling from London, attempted to impose Episcopalianism on their Scottish subjects. The led to the famous riot led by Jenny Geddes at St Giles in 1637, and the National Covenant was signed at Greyfriars the following year, but Charles II continued the imposition.

A dark age of persecution followed, the names of those Covenanters martyred being displayed in the Grassmarket to this day (*see* EXECUTIONS). Two-thirds of Scottish people had accepted the imposed religion by 1688, but two years later, following the 'Glorious Revolution' which brought a Protestant king to the throne, William Carstares, later Principal at Edinburgh University, brokered a solution effectively creating separate Episcopalian and Presbyterian faiths. The former's identification with the Stuart dynasty led to the imposition of punitive laws on the Church during nearly all of the second half of the 18th century, and it was only during the calmer years of the 19th that the Scottish Episcopalian Church became an integral part of the Scottish spiritual scene.

ROMAN CATHOLIC CHURCH

The Roman Catholic Church has a strong presence in Edinburgh, which is the administrative centre of the Archdiocese of St Andrews and Edinburgh, making up the Province of St Andrews and Edinburgh along with four suffragan sees (Aberdeen, Argyll and the Isles, Dunkeld, and Galloway). Its spiritual centre is St Mary's Cathedral, sometimes known as St Mary's Metropolitan (*see* CATHEDRALS).

The archdiocese is divided into three deaneries, as listed below, containing 28 parishes. There are also five parishes outside the old city boundaries, but which are now part of the local government area (for example, South Queensferry). There is still an educational presence (Gillis Centre) in the city for Catholic clergy, although it is understood that much of this work is soon to be concentrated in the West of Scotland.

DEANERY	CHURCH
St Thomas of Aquin	St Mary's Cathedral
	Holy Cross
	St Patrick
	St Columba
	Sacred Heart
	St Peter
	St Mark
	University Chaplaincy
	Gilmore Place
	Ukranian Community
	Polish Community
Holy Rood	St Ninian
	Star of the Sea
	St Teresa
	St John Vianney
	St Catherine
	St Mary Magdalene
	St Gregory
	St John the Evangelist
St Augustine	St Cuthbert
	St Joseph (Currie)
	St John the Baptist
	St John Ogilvie
	St Margaret Mary
	St Margaret and St Andrew (South Queensferry)
	Scottish Command
	St Paul (Ratho)
	St Kentigern

History

For many years the Roman Catholic Church was politically and socially marginalised in the spiritual life of Edinburgh. With no major counter-Reformation in Scotland, and with anti-Catholic feeling fanned by the Stewarts' rebuilding of a Catholic chapel at Holyrood in 1687, and their attempts to regain the throne in 1715 and 1745, Catholicism in Scotland only began a sustained recovery with the intake of immigrants from Ireland, Italy, and the Highlands in the 19th century. The Hierarchy was re-established in 1878, and the right of separate schooling won in 1918.

In 1878 there were only five congregations in Edinburgh led by nine members of clergy. By 1960 this had grown to 20 congregations and 66 clergy, and there has been a further increase since then. Probably the best-known Catholic in Edinburgh in the present century was the late Cardinal Gray. Born Gordon Gray in Leith in 1910, he became archbishop in 1951, and went on to become one of the youngest cardinals in recent history in 1969. Retired in 1985, he passed away on 19 July 1993, one of the most highly respected churchmen this nation has ever produced.

St Giles and the Tron as seen on a busy autumn day in 1995. St Giles is the High Kirk of the Church of Scotland and was the meeting place of the General Assembly until the Assembly Hall was opened in 1859. The Tron was built in the mid-17th century to house St Giles's congregation when the larger church was designated a cathedral under the Episopalian faith. St Giles has been a working Church of Scotland kirk since 1883, while the Tron's congregation moved to Moredun in 1952.

SCOTTISH BAPTIST UNION

The headquarters are in Glasgow, with 11 churches in Edinburgh. Perhaps the best-known and most architecturally striking of these is the Bristo Baptist Church, with its Dutch colonial appearance, at the junction of Queensferry Road, Buckingham Terrace, and Dean Path.

METHODISTS

They have had a presence in Edinburgh since John Wesley visited in 1751, although it was to be another 14 years before a meeting house was opened. Nowadays their Edinburgh and Forth district has five ministers appointed, and the Methodist Central Hall at Tollcross is a city landmark, often used on secular occasions.

RELIGIOUS SOCIETY OF FRIENDS

Familiarly known as Quakers, the Society's Edinburgh members have meeting places in Victoria Terrace and in Morningside. There are eight meetings annually in addition to Sunday services, and the south-east of Scotland had a Quaker population of 229 in 1994.

The **Church of Jesus Christ of Latter Day Saints** has a church in Colinton Road. The **Christian Science** movement is also represented in the capital, with a reading room in Waterloo Place.

NON-CHRISTIAN RELIGIONS REPRESENTED IN EDINBURGH

JUDAISM

The main centre religious and meeting centre for the Jewish faith in Edinburgh is the synagogue in Salisbury Road. This opened for worship in November 1932, and in 1981 was modified to accommodate classroom and leisure functions.

Jews first arrived in Edinburgh in numbers during the 1800s, but no synagogue was established in the city until 1816, when Scotland's first Jewish burial ground was also laid out at Braid Place (now Sciennes House Place, *see also* CEMETERIES AND CREMATORIA).

ISLAM

Probably the newest place of worship to be specially built in Edinburgh is the Great Mosque in Potterrow on land purchased in 1981. Topped by a dome, and a minaret 120 feet in height, the mosque was scheduled to open fully in 1995, with accommodation for 1,000 worshippers.

The **Hindu** and **Sikh** religions have both established places of worship in Leith. The Sikh Gurduwara was established in Mill Lane in 1989, and the Hindu Mandir was located at Academy Street in the same year.

BUDDHISM

There are four meeting places for Buddhists living in Edinburgh, but the capital lacks a Buddhist Centre of the kind established in central Glasgow to further understanding of the philosophy and contemplative nature of Buddhism.

HISTORY OF CHRISTIAN WORSHIP IN EDINBURGH

Edinburgh's first place of worship appears to have been founded as far back as AD 854, although whether this was on the present site of St Giles, or a church known as St Cuthbert's (in the present-day West End area), is now unclear.

The oldest existing places of worship in the Edinburgh area are St Cuthbert's at Dalmeny, Kirkliston parish church, and Duddingston Kirk, all of whose origins go back to the 12th century. Vying with them in antiquity is St Margaret's Chapel, built within Edinburgh Castle in the 1130s or 1140s to commemorate Malcolm III's Saxon queen who died, reputedly of grief, in 1093. The chapel was ordered by David I and is generally regarded as the oldest extant building, of any kind, in the city of Edinburgh, both Dalmeny and Duddingston's kirks having been enlarged or added to in subsequent centuries. Kirkliston's church is less well-preserved but still shows its 12th century origins.

At least Duddingston, St Cuthbert's (Abercorn/Dalmeny), and Kirkliston's churches can claim to have been the site of continuous worship – and public worship at that – as St Margaret's Chapel had to be restored in the 1850s following its use as a gunpowder magazine. The last named's remodelled doorway and stained-glass window are 20th century (*see also* CASTLES).

There are records of a church existing in the city by 1150, by which time David I had decided to establish an abbey for Augustinian monks at Holyrood. This location was of course outside the city itself, a matter of more than academic interest in an age when unfortified buildings were frequently put to the torch. So it was with Holyrood, the site being secularised by the beginning of the 17th century (*see also* ABBEYS), although even as late as 1688, the Chapel Royal there was ransacked, by local protestants on this occasion, not by invading English.

St Giles became the centre of Edinburgh's – as opposed to Canongate's – spiritual life from the 12th century onwards, a grange (farm) being established to sustain it in what is now the district of that name. The church was dedicated in 1243, in a form now unknown, although some of the stonework has survived both the rebuilding necessary after destruction by the English in 1384, and two rebuildings in the 19th century. (Other stonework from that time can be found in garden rockeries across the city when contractors disposed of it).

The Reformation in Scotland was a storm with Edinburgh very much at its heart. John Knox preached in a Reformed service at St Giles in 1560, but the arrival of a Catholic queen (Mary Stewart) from France set off a counter-movement which saw the church violently recaptured for the Catholic cause within a few years. Even the Town Council's decision in 1584 (not effective until 1598) to divide the city into four parishes, in line with a reorganisation of civil administration, did not lessen the importance of St Giles, two of the parishes having quarters of the church. The parish system was developed further in 1641, two more parishes being created at that time.

St Giles is no longer a cathedral, as the latter term denotes the seat of a bishop, although the building did in fact fulfil such a function for two periods during the 17th century, when Episcopacy was being imposed from London. Indeed, the St Giles congregation was required to leave the building when it was designated as a cathedral in 1633 (until 1638, and again for a further 28 years from 1661), and this

St Cuthbert's church at Dalmeny dates from Norman times, but with its imposing west tower added as recently as 1937. Since 1975, Dalmeny has been included in the Edinburgh area, and now rivals Duddingston's kirk in its antiquity.

resulted in the construction of the Tron Church a couple of hundred yards to the east. The subsequent loss of so much of the city-centre population to the city's outskirts over the decades, coupled with the restoration of St Giles to the presbyterian faith, (and as a place of worship from 1883), left the Tron Kirk with empty pews. Its steeple was badly damaged by fire in 1824 (*see* FIRE FIGHTING), and it closed its doors to worshippers in 1952, its remaining congregation 'transported' to Moredun.

Meanwhile, St Giles has survived the tumult and counter-tumult of Reformation, although by the 18th century it had fallen from grace, with visitor Samuel Johnson commenting on its dirtiness; divided into four churches, it even

contained a police office and a fire station! A determined effort was made to restore the building to its proper grandeur in 1822 at the time of George IV's visit. Unfortunately, restorative work undertaken at that time by William Burn is now regarded as having been iconoclastic in its insensitive attempt to 'modernise' the building. Burn created three churches within one, with accommodation intended to be more suitable for the General Assembly, something which it was signally unable to provide within a year of reopening in 1833.

William Chambers, of publishing fame and Lord Provost in 1865-69, was so appalled by the results that he moved the Town Council to undertake further restoration, in which he personally invested £30,000, employing architect William Hay. The result was a more sensitive reconstruction, replacing some of the century's earlier 'improvements' and removing the wall between Nave and Choir. By the work's conclusion on 23 May 1883, St Giles became a place of worship for the first time since the Reformation. Two days later the funeral of William Chambers took place there.

Later additions to St Giles include the Thistle Chapel on its south-east corner, designed by Sir Robert Lorimer and completed in 1910. Extensive repairs in 1981 allowed the installation of a shop and basement cafe to make the building more 'visitor friendly', and a scarlet Modernist-Gothic organ was installed in 1992.

Trinity College Church was another important centre of worship in Edinburgh. Constructed in the second half of the 15th century, its subsequent history is made all the more tragic by the insensitive way that the building was dismantled in the 1840s to make way for the station which later became the Waverley. Although an attempt was made to rebuild it in 1872, only the main choir and apse were reconstructed, owing to the loss (to pilfering) of so many of the stones while in store. Even so, its remains just off Jeffrey Street, represents, according to architect-historian Charles McKean, 'a splendid graceful volume even in its reduced state'.

Greyfriars church dates from the beginning of the 16th century, when a building was required as a centre for the then-new South West Parish, although there was a monastery, the Friary of the Observantine Franciscans, situated here for

around 150 years. The monastery grounds were given to the town by Queen Mary to replace St Giles as a burial site, and the location was regarded as perfect for the construction of a new church. Begun in 1602, the building was used for military purposes for a time, and was badly damaged in an explosion in 1718 and by fire in the 19th century. Despite its importance, Greyfriars church always seems to be less well-known than its graveyard (see CEMETERIES).

The same might be said of the Canongate Church which is unfortunate, since it is historically and architecturally interesting in its own right. When James VII decided in 1687 that the nave of Holyrood Abbey would be dedicated as a chapel for the Order of the Thistle, the parishioners of the Canongate were required to go elsewhere. The resulting church was opened in the Canongate in 1691, with a unique cruciate layout, flanked by aisles and with an unusual circular window facing the High Street. At one time the building contained galleries with seating reserved for the magistrates and officials of the Canongate community, independent of Edinburgh until 1856.

This church will always be associated in local citizens' memories with its long-serving minister, the Very Reverend Dr R. Selby Wright, who died on 24 October 1995. Dr Selby Wright was famous throughout the city for his caring ministrations to a congregation which remained commendably large despite mass relocation of local people to housing schemes on the city's outskirts, and he was responsible for instituting the May Morning service on top of Arthur's Seat (see also FAIRS).

Located in the Cowgate at the foot of Candlemaker Row, the Magdalen Chapel was an almshouse chapel built in 1541, although the tower was not completed until 80 years later. The building was probably the earliest centre for higher education in the city, being used for lectures on canon law and Greek, commissioned by Mary of Guise around 1557. The chapel was later secularised to the extent of becoming the headquarters of the Incorporation of Hammermen, and its frontage spoiled by the addition of a Victorian facade. The interior is still worth seeing, containing what is believed to be the only pre-Reformation Scottish stained-glass still in its original location.

One of the most beautifully-situated churches in Britain, Duddingston's kirk stands on a knoll above the loch of the same name. With its origins back in the 12th century, it can claim to be one of the oldest churches in Scotland with a continuous history of worship. It was originally a two-cell building, but has been added to over the centuries, and underwent a considerable rebuilding in 1889.

Farther afield than Duddingston is St Cuthbert's, Dalmeny, described by the *Buildings of Scotland* series as 'the best preserved Norman church in the country'. It appears to date from the mid-12th century, and is noted for the richness of its internal ornamentation, although its west tower was built in 1937.

Another church, formerly in West Lothian, which has a venerable history is Kirkliston Parish Church. Prominently positioned in the village, the building is Norman in origin, and a bigger church than Dalmeny's, but not so well preserved.

It was designated by the Bishop of St Andrews in September 1244, but has its origins in the previous century. It is now Church of Scotland, and still in regular use.

The existence of Tanfield Hall has only recently been revealed to the passer-by in Canonmills, after decades of being hidden behind a now demolished printing works. Originally housing a gas company, the hall's significance lies in its use for the first Free Church Assembly during the Disruption of 1843. This breakaway from the Church of Scotland was made by those ministers who believed in the freedom of congregations to choose their own ministers. The first assembly was recorded in a composite painting by David Octavius Hill using photographs, even at that early time, to provide the artist with a visual aid (*see* PHOTOGRAPHY).

The Scottish Records Society has produced a detailed account of Edinburgh's churches up to 1984 and this source should certainly be consulted for more information, particularly on the history of the congregations and ministers concerned. The *Buildings of Scotland* series has always devoted considerable attention to church architecture, and its two volumes dealing with Edinburgh and the Lothians also represent a useful source of information (*see* BIBLIOGRAPHY *under* Buildings).

Cinemas

Edinburgh cinema audiences have the opportunity of seeing more than 400 films annually on a total of 28 screens at six city locations (*see* list overleaf). The number of

Cinema-going is still popular in Edinburgh, although queues are less common that they were when this picture of Poole's Roxy cinema was taken in the late 1940s. The Roxy closed in 1963, leaving the Poole family with the Synod Hall in Castle Terrace, which closed shortly afterwards. (The Scotsman)

admissions currently runs at 3.4 million annually, the equivalent of eight visits a year for every man, woman, and child in the city. In 1994 the British Film Institute estimated that Lothian Region had 14.8 cinema seats per thousand of the population, nearly twice that of Strathclyde at that time.

Local people also have the opportunity of enjoying films shown by the Film Festival (*see* FESTIVALS) and the pioneering Edinburgh Film Guild. The Guild was formed in 1930, one of the first of its kind in the world, dedicated to the showing of less commercial films by hiring cinemas on Sunday evenings, when cinemas were normally closed. Information about the EFG can be obtained at the Filmhouse in Lothian Road.

There are no fewer than 45 companies in the city working in some aspect of the film or television industry, employing 300 people. Despite all this, audiences have little opportunity to see Edinburgh in feature films (*see* FILMS).

History

The city's first film shows probably took place at a booth in Iona Street in 1893, when a Mr Swallow showed astonished Leithers flickering pictures of a moving train. The equipment is thought to have been a pirated version of Edison's Kinetoscope, where the viewer (probably only one at a time) looked towards the light source where a film was illuminated, rather on the 'What the butler saw' peepshow principle. The first projection of a moving image in Scotland took place at the Empire Palace Theatre (now the Festival Theatre) on 14 April 1896.

The city went on to boast dozens of proper cinemas in later years, the 1909 Cinematograph Act laying down safety requirements, such as having the projection room separate from the auditorium, which forced cinema operators to invest in their premises. Many of them were converted theatres or places of worship, although Edinburgh was lucky enough in the 1930s to enjoy distinctive cinema architecture in the work of T. Bowhill Gibson, whose finest landmark in the city was his Art Deco design for the George, Portobello, now unfortunately much altered. The Dominion still offers a fine example of Gibson's work as originally built, and continues under the same family ownership. The capital's biggest cinema was the Playhouse, Scotland's second largest, seating 3,400, and now given over exclusively to live entertainment since 1987.

One curious aspect of the city's cinema history was the failure of cinemas to permanently colonise Princes Street. Nowadays, there are no cinemas in Scotland's most famous street, but once there were four, at least two of them highly successful. It seems, however, that they were unable to generate sufficient revenue per square foot to prevent shops taking over almost the entire throughfare, this fate befalling the Palace (where Waterstone's is now located at the east end of the street), the New Picture House (Marks & Spencer's), the Picture House (John Menzies), and the Princes/Monseigneur/Jacey, now an audio shop (see also SHOPS). With the current recession in retail trading,

perhaps history has turned a half-circle, and a cinema in Princes Street would nowadays do very well.

Edinburgh's cinema history has been well chronicled in the late Brendon Thomas's book The Last Picture Shows – Edinburgh, first published in 1984. The list below is abstracted from that volume, with information since 1984 added. Since that year, the principal events in the capital's cinema history have been the reopening of the Cameo cinema in 1986 and the appearance of a 12-screen cinema at Newcraighall.

The Cameo, originally the King's Cinema owned by the well-known Poole family, has made a Phoenix-like reappearance in Edinburgh's entertainment scene under new management. Now equipped with three screens, and with a policy of showing first-run films, the Cameo has re-established itself as a place of quality entertainment. Less welcome to cinemagoers has been the loss of the historic La Scala (latterly known as the Metro or simply The Cinema), while the Caley and Playhouse cinemas have proved too large to adapt to multi-screen configurations, the former being converted into a night club, the latter into Edinburgh's biggest theatre.

In contrast, the Odeon currently has five screens, and the MGM and Dominion three. The Filmhouse in Lothian Road continues to offer a varied fare of films, many of them foreign-language, and is the nucleus of Edinburgh's annual film festival, which boasts a longer pedigree than Cannes'. As a result, the capital's cinema scene is projecting itself a little more brightly than ten years ago.

EDINBURGH CINEMAS PAST AND PRESENT

(Arranged by name last used.)

CINEMA	LOCATION	OPENED	CLOSED
ABC (*see* MGM)			
ABBEY	30-32 N. Richmond St.	c1920	c1933
ALBERT HALL	Shandwick Place	c1908	1932
ALHAMBRA	200-204 Leith Walk	1914	1958
ALISON	6 Laurie St, Leith	1911	1946
ASTORIA	Manse Rd, Corstorphine	1930	1974
ATMOSPHERIC (*see* GATEWAY)			
BEVERLEY	3 Lauriston Street	1930	1959
BLUE HALLS (*see* BEVERLEY)			
BROADWAY (*see* GATEWAY)			
BUNGALOW (*see* VICTORY)			
CALEY	31 Lothian Road	1923	1984
CALTON STUDIOS	Calton Road	1977	1984
CAMEO	38 Home Street	1914	
CANNON (*see* MGM)			
CAPITOL	Manderston Street	1928	1961
CARLTON	Piershill	1935	1959
CENTRAL	Casselbank Street	1920	c1929
CENTRAL	281 Portobello High Street	1915	1961
CINE PLAYHOUSE (*see* SPRINGVALLEY)			
THE CINEMA (*see* LA SCALA)			
CINEMA HOUSE	18 Nicolson Street	1903	1930
CINEMA HOUSE (*see also* EMPIRE, Leith)			
CLASSIC (*see* LA SCALA)			
COLISEUM	125 West Fountainbridge	1911	1942
COUNTY	16 Wauchope Ave, Craigmillar	1936	1963
COUNTY (*see also* GEORGE, PORTOBELLO)			
DEAN	26 Dean Street	1917	c1935
DOMINION	Newbattle Terr, Morningside	1938	
EASTWAY	12 Easter Road	1912	1961
EMBASSY	Boswall Parkway	1937	1964
EMPIRE (Leith)	Tolbooth Wynd/Henderson St	1913	c1930
EVANS PICTURE HOUSE (*see* SPRINGVALLEY)			
FILMHOUSE	88 Lothian Road	1978	
GAIETY (*see* OPERETTA HOUSE)			
GAIETY	Kirkgate, Leith	1913	1944

CINEMA	LOCATION	OPENED	CLOSED
GATEWAY	41 Elm Row	1908	c1959
GAUMONT	4-8 Rutland Street	1930	1963
GEORGE	14 Bath St, Portobello	1939	1974
GRAND	99 St Stephen's Street	1920	1960
HAYMARKET (see SCOTIA)			
IMPERIAL CINEMA (see CINEMA HOUSE, Nicolson Street)			
IMPERIAL PICTURE HOUSE	Storries Alley, Leith	1911	?
JACEY	131 Princes Street	1912	1973
KING'S CINEMA (see CAMEO)			
LA SCALA	50 Nicolson Street	1912	1987
LAURIE or LAURIE STREET CINEMA (see ALISON)			
LYCEUM	Slateford Road	1926	1963
LYRIC	30 Nicolson Square	1913	1931
MAGNET	Parliament Street, Leith	1912	c1915
MARCO'S DRAUGHT HOUSE CINEMA	Grove Street	1986	1988
METRO (see LA SCALA)			
MGM	Lothian Road	1938	
MONSEIGNEUR NEWS THEATRE (see JACEY)			
NEW COLISEUM (see COLISEUM)			
NEW ELECTRIC CINEMA (see PETIT PARIS)			
NEW PALACE	18-22 High Street	1929	1956
NEW PICTURE HOUSE (see CENTRAL, Portobello)			
NEW PICTURE HOUSE	56 Princes Street	1913	1951
NEW TIVOLI	Gorgie Road	1913	1973
NEW TOLLCROSS	140 Lauriston Place	1912	1947
NEW VICTORIA (see ODEON)			
NORTH BRITISH ELECTRIC THEATRE (see CINEMA HOUSE, Nicolson St)			
ODEON	Nicolson Street	1930	
OLYMPIA	54 Annandale Street	1912	c1915
OPERETTA HOUSE	3 Chambers Street	1906	1939
PALACE	183 Constitution Street	1913	1966
PALACE	15 Princes Street	1913	1955
PALACE (see SAVOY, St Bernard's Row)			
PALLADIUM	East Fountainbridge	1911	1932
PAVILION (see DEAN)			
PETIT PARIS	Shrubhill, Leith Walk	1908	c1912

CINEMA	LOCATION	OPENED	CLOSED
PICTUREDROME (see EASTWAY)			
PICTURE HOUSE	111 Princes Street		
PLAYHOUSE	Greenside	1929	1987
POOLE'S ROXY	430 Gorgie Road	1937	1963
POOLE'S SYNOD HALL	Castle Terrace	c1920s	1965
PRINCES (see JACEY)			
PRINGLE'S PICTURE PALACE (see also GATEWAY)			
PRINGLE'S PICTURE PALACE	71-75 Grove Street	1906	1917
QUEEN'S HALL	5 Queen Street	c1901	1915
REGAL (see MGM)			
REGENT	Abbeymount	1927	1970
RIO (see COUNTY, Craigmillar)			
RITZ	Rodney Street	1929	1981
RITZ KINEMA (see SPRINGVALLEY)			
ROXBURGH	Drummond Street	1920	c1930
ROXY (see POOLE'S ROXY)			
ROYAL CINEMA (see TRON)			
RUTLAND (see GAUMONT)			
ST ANDREW'S SQUARE CINEMA	Clyde Street	1923	1952
ST BERNARD'S PICTURE PALACE (see TUDOR)			
SALISBURY	38 South Clerk Street	1925	1943
SALON	5 Baxter's Place	1913	1974
SAVOY (see TUDOR)			
SCOTIA	90 Dalry Road	1912	1964
SILVER CINEMA (see LYRIC)			
SPRINGVALLEY	Springvalley Gardens	c1910	1938
STAR	16 St Mary's	1914	c1925
STATE	North Junction Street	1938	1972
TIVOLI (see NEW TIVOLI)			
TOLLCROSS (see NEW TOLLCROSS)			
TRON	235 High Street	1913	1928
TUDOR	St Bernard's Row	1911	1966
UCI	Kinnaird Park, Newcraighall	1990	
VICTORY	Bath Street, Portobello	c1914	1956
WAVERLEY	6 Infirmary Street	c1911	c1920
WEST END CINEMA (see ALBERT HALL)			

City Walls

Edinburgh was never completely surrounded by walls, since the castle and Nor' Loch presented natural defences to the north and north-west. There were, however, a succession of generations of wall-building, although little is now known about those carried out before the 15th century.

Edinburgh's earliest walls appear to have been constructed more for the control of commerce than for the defence of the town's inhabitants. Burgh status was based on the administration of trade, and there are records of ports (i.e. gates) existing from around 1175, where customs could be levied. The oldest of these was the West Gate, with a South Gate built by 1214, and the Netherbow Port in 1369. The walls linking them probably replaced a crude wooden palisade. Architect-historian Charles McKean has argued that, even if and when the gates were breached, the streets of the medieval city were so narrow as to discourage an invading army from entering an area where an ambush could be easily sprung. This might explain why the town managed to survive no fewer than 17 invasions and attempted pillagings in its history, in contrast to, for example, the now-vanished community of Roxburgh.

From the middle of the 15th century three eras of wall building can be identified. In 1450 James II authorised the citizens 'to bulwark, wall, turret, and otherwise strengthen the burgh', specifically against English aggression. The result was the King's Wall, five feet (1.5 metres) high and built over a 25 year period of large pink stone blocks enclosing what to the modern eye is a surprisingly limited area. From the southern ramparts of the Castle Rock, the line stretched eastwards parallel with, but lower down than, what is now Johnston Terrace and the High Street to a point south-east of the Tron, near where Blackfriars Street is now. It then ran northwards to the most eastern stretch of the Nor' Loch, whose waters, by all accounts, would be noxious enough to repel any invader! (*see* LOCHS, NEW TOWN).

In 1513 the disaster of Flodden spurred Edinburgh into a frenzy of defence building – or so tradition has it. In fact, the Flodden Wall, parts of which can be seen to this day, took some 47 years to complete, suggesting that the Wall's existence was again more commercial than military. When completed, it limited the shape of the burgh for some 250 years.

Running south from the Castle Rock, across the West Port and up the Vennel beside the present-day College of Art, the Flodden Wall then followed an indirect course eastwards, enclosing Greyfriars Church and what is now Chambers Street, on to the eastern end of Drummond Street. From here it stretched northwards to a point east of the Nor' Loch, and west to meet its waters. The total area enclosed was 140 acres (57.4 hectares), and Scotland's capital could be traversed on foot in only ten minutes from east to west, and in less from north to south. The path running outside the wall was not known as Thief Row for nothing.

The last walling of Edinburgh took place in 1628-36 when ten acres around Heriot's school were enclosed as far south as the present site of Lauriston Place. This was known as Telfer's wall, after the mason responsible, John Tailefer.

GATES
Known as Ports, these were six openings in the Flodden Wall to control the passage of trade and travellers. They were, in clockwise order from the south: Bristo Port, West Port, New Port, Netherbow Port, Cowgate Port, and Potterrow Port.

Bristo Port was located at the present-day junction of Forrest Road and Bristo Place. Its name is a corruption of 'brewster' or brewer. West Port was situated at the south-west corner of the Grassmarket; this was the entry used to welcome ceremonial visitors such as Mary Stewart in 1561 or her son James VI in 1579 (see KEYS TO THE CITY). The reason for this choice was because it was diametrically opposite the Netherbow, the gate nearest the traditional enemy, England.

New Port was situated alongside the Nor' Loch, approximately where the Market Street/Jeffrey Street junction is now. Netherbow Port opened for traffic passing between the High Street and the independent burgh of Canongate, not formally part of Edinburgh until 1856. The gate here was blown open by the Earl of Hertford during the 'Rough Wooing', being renewed in 1603, complete with a gatehouse crowned by spire and turret. In 1736 the Government demanded the destruction of this gate as a punishment for the Porteous Riot, and although this was not carried out, the gatehouse finally succumbed as a traffic obstacle in 1764. Its clock and weather-vane were donated to the Orphans Hospital and are now to be seen on the Dean Education Centre in Belford Road.

The Cowgate Port was used for cattle being sent out to the fields in the morning, and returning to the city at night. Potterrow Port is the most difficult to envisage in terms of its present site, approximately at South College Street.

Remains
The most visible stretch of defensive wall is the latest, the Telfer Wall, a length of which makes an impressive sight running north-wards from Lauriston Place to the top of the Vennel. The wall's bastions in this locality were demolished in 1762 to improve traffic flow in Lauriston Place. In the Vennel itself a bastion of the Flodden Wall still stands, minus its north side, composed of purple rubble from Bruntsfield Links. Its preservation must be credited to Dr Patrick Neill, who published a pamphlet in 1829 opposing the Town Council's philistine intention to demolish it.

More of the wall, some five feet (1.5 metres) in height, can be seen incorporated into a higher structure in Drummond Street. Decorated setts at the Netherbow indicate the former existence of the Flodden Wall at this site. A good illustrated guide to the City Walls, by William Cullen, is available at the time of writing from the Cockburn Association.

Cleansing

Each Edinburgh resident is estimated to generate half a ton of domestic waste every year. Of this total, 30 per cent is organic and garden waste. Four per cent is disposable nappies!

Edinburgh District Council was responsible at the time of writing for street cleansing, refuse collection and disposal, waste management, and recycling initiatives. Under current legislation, these activities are required to be carried out in a regime of competitive tendering, but the Council's own Direct Services Organisation was successful in submitting an 'in house' tender. Cleansing vehicles were hired from the Council's own Fleet Management Division. Edinburgh City Council is now responsible for street cleansing.

The city has 850 miles (1,360 kilometres) of streets, each one of which is cleaned weekly, according to Council figures (the Regional authority estimated 914 miles/1,462 kilometres), and the city's 3,350 litter bins are checked on a daily basis. If these frequencies appear a little too good to be true, the public seems to be reasonably satisfied – of the 86 complaints received by the Environmental Services Department in an average week in 1994, more than half referred to dumping problems, and only two per cent concerned overflowing litter bins.

Refuse collections are made from approximately 215,000 homes and businesses every week, with tenemental dwellers receiving twice-weekly collections. Bulk refuse collections – 800 in a single quarter in 1994 – are made by arrangement, and recycling facilities are provided by the Council at 58 sites in the Council area. The Council currently offers advice on the disposal of potentially dangerous items such as refrigerators, and has publicised its intention of recycling 25 per cent of household waste.

Edinburgh's major site for refuse processing is at Powderhall, where compaction of waste takes place before being sent by train on a daily basis round the South Suburban line for disposal at Kaimes Quarry, south-west of the city. The city was the fourth authority in Britain to use rail transport for bulk disposal, the journey from Powderhall to Kaimes currently the shortest in Britain for this kind of traffic; negotiations are currently under way to obtain the use of additional quarries on the city's environs, for dumping purposes.

The District Council also permitted the disposal of larger waste items at special sites, such as Craigmillar, the only Council site, at the time of writing, which also accepts steel and aluminium cans for recycling.

Perhaps not one of Edinburgh's more beautiful buildings, but an essential one nevertheless, the Powderhall Refuse Works compacts waste material for transport by rail to former quarry sites for disposal by burying.

History

Edinburgh's method of waste disposal was effectively as non-existent as its sewerage system, despite efforts made by the Town Council in 1505 and 1619 – the latter by the express order of the Privy Council – to cleanse the city's streets. One historian, David Robertson, believes that the actual level of the streets themselves was physically raised by new setts being laid down on layers of accumulated rubbish which had not been cleared away.

No systematic refuse-clearing began until 1805, when the newly established Police Commissioners included cleansing in their remit. In 1856, the Town Council took over from the Police Commissioners the responsibility of cleaning the streets when Edinburgh finally absorbed Canongate. In practice, the police had contented themselves with removing horse droppings from the streets, the detritus being sold for fertiliser, dumped on the shore below the high water mark, or exported through Port Hopetoun to West Lothian, much to the benefit of that county's agricultural output! (see CANAL TRANSPORT).

The city's first large-scale destructor was installed at Powderhall in 1893, and has since been supplemented by plants at Russell Road and Seafield. Hailes and Blackford Quarries have been used as infill sites (now both totally infilled, see QUARRIES), along with dump areas at Braehead near Turnhouse, and at Craigmillar.

see also SEWERAGE.

Cockburn Association

Edinburgh's civic society is named after Henry, Lord Cockburn (1779-1854), a High Court judge who could truly be described as a pioneering conservationist. The society was formed in 1875, when a public meeting was held in the Masonic Hall on 15 June, addressed by Lord Moncrieff, who stressed that the new association would be 'a means of rapid and effective communication of public opinion' on the work of the Town Council, while dedicating it to 'the improvement of Edinburgh and the neighbourhood'.

From the start, there was a strong link with the Council, the earliest calling of a public meeting to establish the Association taking the form of an address to the Lord Provost, and for some time, the Provost was expected to chair the meetings. After the Second World War, this practice lapsed, considerably freeing the Association to view objectively the works and plans of local as well as national government. The Cockburn was particularly involved in opposing some of the more irrevocably damaging plans for inner-city highways (see ROADS), and has proved to be a strong supporter of public transport.

Currently based at Trunk's Close, just off the High Street, the Association meets regularly, publishes an attractive and informative newsletter, and organises site visits, tours, and social occasions. The Cockburn Association is a success story, much copied elsewhere. Glasgow set up its own Civic Society in 1926, the Association for the Protection of Rural Scotland was formed in 1927, and the Civic Trust was established in London 30 years after that. Since 1968 the Cockburn's sub-title has been the 'Edinburgh Civic Trust', and its continued success is a matter of which the city can be proud.

Lord Cockburn had been dead for over 20 years before the formation of the

Association which bears his name. Its success is a tribute to his tireless campaigning against what he viewed as developments lacking in aesthetic value, or involving the removal or destruction of a building or natural attractions worth preserving. He was particularly agitated by the construction of the Edinburgh and Glasgow railway line through Princes Street Gardens, publishing a pamphlet on the subject memorably entitled *Letter to the Lord Provost on the best ways of spoiling the beauty of Edinburgh*. While he did not succeed in that particular campaign, his example lives on, and not just in Edinburgh.

Courts of Law

For centuries, Edinburgh has been the centre of the legal profession in Scotland, and is the site of the nation's highest civil and criminal courts, as well as having its own Sheriff and District courts.

THE COURT OF SESSION

The Court of Session is based at Parliament House, just off the High Street, and is the nation's supreme court in civil matters, its judgements overturnable only by the House of Lords. It consists of the Inner House, comprising the first and second divisions, and the Outer House, the latter occupied by Lords of Session, also known as Senators of the College of Justice. The principal judge is the Lord President, leader of the first division, while the Lord Justice Clerk leads the second.

THE HIGH COURT OF THE JUSTICIARY

The High Court of the Justiciary is the senior criminal court in Scotland, also sitting at Parliament House as well as on circuit round the country. This court consists of the Lord Justice General (who is also Lord President), Lord Justice Clerk, and the Lords Commissionary of Justiciary. It is this court which tries the nation's most serious crimes, many of them moved to Edinburgh for trial from other courts because of localised factors, such as ensuring the recruitment of an unbiased jury. The Court includes a court of criminal appeal.

SHERIFF COURTS

There are Sheriff Courts in many major towns and cities in Scotland, and Edinburgh is no exception. Housed in a new building in Chambers Street, with vehicular access from Merchant Street, the capital's Sheriff Court has both criminal and civil jurisdictions, the former being the busier, dealing with lesser crimes of violence and theft as well as motoring offences. Appeal against a Sheriff court verdict is to the Court of Criminal Appeal.

DISTRICT COURT

Edinburgh also has a District Court dealing with minor criminal matters, presided over by a lay magistrate sitting with an assessor or stipendiary magistrate.

History of Edinburgh's Courts

Scotland's supreme court, the Court of Session, was set up in 1532 during the reign of James V, and has absorbed the functions of the former Scottish Courts of the Exchequer and of Admiralty. Since

1707 the Court of Session and High Court of the Justiciary have occupied Parliament Hall, the building relinquished by the Scottish Parliament when it migrated to Westminster (*see* PARLIAMENTARY REPRESENTATION). The complex of courtrooms has been greatly increased in size since those days, and a tradition has sprung up of advocates being briefed when walking in the Hall itself. The warren of courts and corridors is both confusing and intimidating to the visitor, and no doubt is intended to have such an effect on the accused!

The Sheriff Court only moved into its Chambers Street building, on the former site of Heriot-Watt College, in 1995. For the previous 58 years, the Court had occupied the detached courthouse building at the junction of the High Street and Bridge Street, opened in 1937. It had an 'abandon hope all ye who enter here' air to it, and many a defending solicitor would hope their cases would be tried in the more modern annexes in Spittal Street or Jeffrey Street. At the time of writing, the building is being adapted for further use by the Scottish Courts Administration.

The building used by the Sheriff Court before moving to the High Street was a more impressing edifice in George IV Bridge, demolished to allow the construction of the National Library of Scotland, a project delayed by the Second World War.

Defunct courts in Edinburgh included the ***Burgh Police Court***, located within the former Police HQ in the High Street opposite the City Chambers. This dealt with minor offences within the pre-1975 city boundaries, and in the 1960s was capable of imposing a fine of £10 or a 60 day term of imprisonment; hardly equable terms, even by currency values of the day.

The ***Justice of the Peace Court*** sat to consider the same kind of offence as considered by the Burgh Court, but constituted a quorum of two J.P.s from the pre-1975 county of Midlothian. Decisions in both this, and the Burgh Police Court, could be taken to the High Court on appeal.

The ***Dean of Guild Court*** was abolished during the reorganisation of local government in 1975. It enjoyed legal powers in relation to planning matters now undertaken by the local authority's planning department. Unlike the newer authority, the Dean of Guild Court appeared to hold effective retrospective powers, ensuring that a planning wrong could be made right, while modern planning departments often have difficulties in this area (*see* DEAN OF GUILD COURT).

Cricket

Although not usually thought of as a Scottish sport, cricket has a strong foothold in the Edinburgh sporting scene. The city is home to the Scottish Cricket Union, and has 13 clubs playing in organised leagues (in 1993). At the time of writing a national league has just been established, while the Scottish county championship does not carry the same significance as the English version, and a national cup competition has yet to gain the stature it deserves.

Edinburgh's clubs in 1993 were as follows:

CLUB	GROUND
Carlton	Grange Loan
Corstorphine	Union Park
Edinburgh Academicals	Raeburn Place
Edinburgh University	
Saff	Peffermill
Grange	Raeburn Place
Heriot's FPs	Goldenacre
Holy Cross Academicals	Arboretum
Leith Franklin/	
Academicals	Leith Links
Mitre	Inch Park
Royal High	East Barnton Avenue
Scottish Widows Fund	Inch Park
Stewart's/Melville	Inverleith
Watsonians	Myreside

The best-equipped grounds in the city are probably Myreside, Inverleith, and Grange (the latter two just off Raeburn Place). All three have been used in recent years by Scottish XIs to play visiting Test sides (the West Indies visited Grange in 1995). Edinburgh's grounds are picturesque (none more so than Carlton's ground at Grange Loan) and, with their comparatively limited playing areas, highly-amenable to century-seeking batsmen.

No Edinburgh cricketers have gone on to achieve outstanding fame and fortune in the English county system, unless one counts Brian Hardie as a capital cricketer. This Edinburgh University graduate (although previously with Stenhousemuir) scored a double century against the MCC when studying in the city in 1973 and went on to a distinguished career with Essex, one of only two English counties at that time never to have won a major trophy. Along with fellow-Scot Mike Denness, Hardie helped to make his adopted county the most successful in England over a 14-year period.

Scottish teams have regularly attracted foreign professionals to play and coach on a temporary basis, Australia's Kim Hughes enjoying a season with Watsonians in the 1980s and West Indian batsman Jimmy Adams starring with Royal High.

History

Probably the most momentous occasion in Edinburgh cricket history occurred in 1882, when Scotland recorded its only victory over a visiting Test side, by defeating Australia in a one-day match at Raeburn Place on 29 July. Scotland's top scorer was Leslie Balfour (later Leslie Balfour-Melville) who found time for cricket when not representing his country at rugby, or defending his lawn tennis and golf championships.

The Grange club in Edinburgh acted as the national association for the sport in Scotland from 1883-1909, when the Scottish Cricket Union went through a hiatus.

Crime

In the year 1993, the number of crimes reported in the three Edinburgh operational divisions (B,C, and D) of Lothian and Borders Police (*see also* POLICE) came to 59,931. Of these, approximately 35 per cent were solved. This is around 143 crimes reported per 1,000 of the city's population per annum; in 1962 the number of crimes and offences totalled 28,625, to a ratio of 60 per 1,000. This may merely indicate an increase in the reporting of crime; it could equally signify a decline in social values. The statistics can be used to support either argument.

The classification of crimes reported in 1993 was as follows:

Serious Assault	480
Robbery (assault with intent)	745
Rape	41
Indecent Assault	183
Indecent Exposure	221
Theft by housebreaking	5,633
Housebreaking (with intent)	3,401
Theft (breaking lockfast)	11,261
Other theft	13,064
Motor vehicle theft	3,544
Pedal cycle theft	1,797
Fireraising	452
Vandalism	6,654
Other crimes	12,455

Murder seems to be something of an Edinburgh speciality. It is no surprise that the Scottish capital has inspired such literary fiction as *Dr Jekyll and Mr Hyde*, and the Sherlock Holmes stories of Arthur Conan Doyle, when the horrific activities of Burke and Hare in the city were only too factual. Two Ulstermen who emigrated to Scotland to work on the Union Canal, William Burke and William Hare were aware of the illicit trade of supplying newly-buried corpses to the university for dissection demonstrations. Deciding to accelerate the supply of cadavers to the anatomy tutors by cutting out the burial part of the process, they murdered no fewer than 16 unfortunates before being brought to account, and even then a conviction could only be secured when one (Hare) turned King's evidence against the other.

Burke was executed in January 1829, but his accomplice lived on in London until about 1860 (*see also* EXECUTIONS). The surgeon who took delivery of the bodies, Robert Knox, escaped accusations of complicity, but his dubious 'no questions asked' role in the matter led to the Anatomy Act of 1832, which regularised the supply of corpses for teaching purposes.

Edinburgh has even produced a child killer (Jessie King), and two foreign-born men convicted of insurance murders (Chantrelle and Dumoulin) in the mid-19th century and 1972 respectively. Of course, these were only the murder cases actually solved. Perhaps the most tragic and perplexing of unsolved murders at the time of writing is the 1977 'World's End' murders of two teenage girls who left the pub of that name in Edinburgh's High Street with two unidentified men and were later found dead in the East Lothian countryside. The men responsible have never been identified.

'In Edinburgh, ***prostitution*** tends to be hidden indoors – in bars, dance halls, and hotels' – so concluded the *Third Statistical Account* in 1966. Its authors would have been interested to learn that in the 1990s the local District Council licensed saunas in the city despite widespread reports that these were fronts for prostitution (which is not strictly speaking a crime, although soliciting is).

Indeed, an English newspaper journalist assigned to investigate Edinburgh's sex industry in 1995, reported that prostitution was undoubtedly taking place in the licensed saunas he visited, and that all the clients he spoke to were from North East England. Whether this suggests that the local Council was right to tacitly believe that it was taking prostitution off the streets, or whether it was unwittingly creating a special market for sex tourists, is a moot point. Suffice it to say, that Edinburgh, the hinterland of a major port, and with three military bases within a few miles, has always been a major centre for the sex industry.

Murder and prostitution are often two of the by-products of *drug-related offences*. But the supply of drugs is quite enough of a crime in itself, and, in Edinburgh, took on an even more sinister aspect when an HIV-infected family moved into the city in 1983. A subsequent crackdown on the supply of injecting equipment brought into existence 'shooting galleries' where needle-sharing took place, and HIV soon escalated to the horrifying extent of infecting 51% of intravenous drug-abusers in the city. From 1987, a needle-exchange scheme has been operated by worried authorities, although both the police and the judiciary had originally argued that this was in itself a criminal activity. To make matters worse, it was found in 1990 that the threat of contracting AIDS was not itself sufficient to deter drug users from needle-sharing.

'Edinburgh had been shown to have the most serious HIV epidemic in Britain; this reservoir of infection among heterosexuals means that the potential for spread was unlimited'. This observation was made by visiting medical author, Dr Louis Appleby (*see* BIBLIOGRAPHY), and November 1995 figures showed that Edinburgh's level of intravenuous drug abuse, with its potential for passing on infection, was more of a problem than homosexual spread, where Edinburgh's rate was well below the national average. HIV has brought the dreaded spectre of AIDS in its wake, and for some time Edinburgh was dubbed 'AIDS capital of Europe', although the number of subsequent fatalities, while providing no grounds for complacency, have not fulfilled the lurid predictions being made in the late 1980s (*see also* SOCIAL WORK).

The 'Good Old Days' were exactly that, if William Creech was to be believed. This one-time Lord Provost of Edinburgh, publisher of Robert Burns's poetry, recorded that:

> during the winter 1790-92 (sic) there was not a robbery, housebreaking, shopbreaking, nor a theft publicly known to the amount of forty shillings within the city of Edinburgh; not one person accused of a capital crime...

Creech wrote this two years after serving on the jury which tried Deacon Brodie, Edinburgh's greatest exponent of **burglary**, and finding him guilty. In contrast to the current annual figure of 9,000 housebreakings (in Lothian and Borders), the total accumulated by Brodie was somewhat more modest, but the fact that he was an Edinburgh councillor and head of the Incorporation of Wrights and Masons, gave his crimes more than a little piquancy.

Brodie even attempted to steal the revenues of Scotland, and his lifestyle of respectable townsman by day, notorious burglar by night, is believed to have inspired Robert Louis Stevenson's creation of Dr Jekyll and Mr Hyde. Unlike today's housebreakers, Brodie paid with his life for his crimes; he was hanged at the Tolbooth on 1 October 1788. An excellent account of Brodie, his Edinburgh surroundings, and his trial, is to be found in *Deacon Brodie; Father to Jekyll and Hyde* by John S. Gibson (Saltire Society, 1993).

Dancing

Edinburgh dances to many different tunes. The Scottish Country Dance scene is healthy, dedicated ballroom dancers practise their craft to almost athletic standards, while the Ross Open Air Theatre in Princes Street Gardens hosts examples of both forms of dancing on most summer evenings.

The Royal Scottish Country Dance Society has its headquarters at Coates Crescent in Edinburgh's West End, along with one local branch, and no fewer than six affiliated dance groups, including one based at South Queensferry. This is the largest total of such groups in any Scottish city.

The capital has a number of popular discos, and the biggest 'raves' in Scotland are held at Ingliston, but the age of the commercially-run ballroom, with its syncopated rhythms and a dance floor thick with foxtrotting couples, is very much consigned to the past. Interestingly, Edinburgh boasted the largest ballroom of them all.

History
As a capital city with a royal court, Edinburgh was no stranger to the formal dance. The Palace of Holyroodhouse had a surprisingly short history as a court, and was probably at its best intermittently in the 60 years from the reign of James IV up to the mid-1560s, when Mary Stewart, who enjoyed dancing, had returned from France, while there was something of a revival when the future James VII took a personal interest in the palace in the next century (*see* ROYAL RESIDENCES).

At all times, dancing was targeted by the religious authorities as a potentially sinful activity, and after the court went south in 1603, precious little dancing seems to have been done in the capital, at least by the aristocracy. The city's taverns were a different matter, with oyster parties usually ending in dancing (*see* PUBS). However, buildings devoted to Terpsichorean activites only appeared in the 18th century, when Assemblies were held in a room in the West Bow from 1710, and then in what is now Old Assembly Close, near St Giles, in 1723.

Polite society found the Assembly (in other words, a ball) a convenient way for the sexes to mingle, albeit in a highly formalised way; Lord Cockburn commented at the time that popes had been elected with 'less jobbing' than had the partnering arrangements at assemblies. Meanwhile, the dancing habit spread to the New Town. The Assembly Rooms opened in 1786, their centre-piece a cavernous ballroom with a floor area of nearly 4,000 square feet and a ceiling 40 feet high, while in Leith, an Assembly Rooms was opened during the Napoleonic wars with only slightly less aplomb. Formal dancing had come to stay in Edinburgh; less formalised dancing carried on as before in taverns and at weddings.

Increased leisure time and the spread of Negro-inspired music and culture from the USA, led to a huge enthusiasm for

Mere men fade into the background in this attractive line-up of competitors in an Open Amateur Championship held at the Eldorado Ballroom in Leith in June 1958. The Eldorado later specialised in the less graceful art of all-in wrestling, and burned down in 1988. (The Scotsman)

dancing in the first half of the 20th century. Dance-halls began to cater for this on a commercial basis from the 1920s, when such names as the Cavendish, Plaza, and Palais de Dance made their appearance on the city scene, while the biggest ballroom of them all, at Marine Gardens near Portobello, was a converted roller-skating rink. Unfortunately, its conversion into a vehicle-assembly plant during the Second World War brought its entertainment role to an end.

The '20s and '30s had seen the development of a popular culture of dancing to celebrity bands and singers whose distinctive sounds could also be heard on the phonograph or wireless at home. Edinburgh embraced its dancing years.

Dean of Guild Court

Until the local government reorganisation of 1975, planning matters in Edinburgh were administered by a court with legal powers, presided over by the Dean of Guild. Situated in the City Chambers, this was the body which decided municipal planning matters ranging from the erection of a shop sign, to the permission necessary for the construction of a new housing scheme.

The Court consisted of 15 members, seven of them members of the former Town Council, and seven qualified laymen. Presiding over this assembly was the Lord Dean of Guild, also an unelected layman, but who became an ex officio member of the Council. His appointment was made by the Council on the recommendation of the Incorporation of the Brethern of the Guildry, and therein lay the main reason for the Court's demise, since the system was obviously archaic in origin, deriving from a time when local government had a very restricted franchise.

While anachronistic, the Dean of Guild Court did have the power to fine those who transgressed planning regulations, while latter-day planning departments in the District Councils often appeared to encounter difficulty in enforcing their decisions.

History

Guilds appear to have become established in Edinburgh in the 14th century, furthering and protecting the interests of those working together in a skilled occupation or commercial cause. Merchants appear to have bonded together in a guild of trade, although their early history is not fully documented. However, it is known that the first Dean of Guild was Symon de Schele, elected as 'Dene of Gilde and Keeper of the Kirk Work' on 3 October 1403. Elections to the position of Dean continued annually from that time, unless interrupted by military matters, such as the arrival of an English army in 1650–1 and the Jacobites in 1745.

Perhaps the most noteworthy of the Deans of Guild was George Mortimer, who in 1865 sacrificed his life trying to save a victim buried under rubble in one of the numerous fires which afflicted the Theatre Royal in Broughton Street.

Districts

ABBEYHILL
Occupying the ridge immediately to the north of Holyrood Abbey, and part of the slope stretching away to the Forth from there, Abbeyhill stands on a fork where incoming road traffic from Portobello or the A1 decides to make for Leith Walk, or to the east end of Princes Street. It is an industrious area, replete with tenements and 'colony' style housing, although a number of local industries have either moved out to Midlothian (printing, glassmaking), or closed down altogether (metalworking at London Road Foundry).

BALERNO
Nowadays very much a dormitory of Edinburgh, Balerno, some five miles west of the city, has a long history as an independent community at the highest point on the Water of Leith where its water could be put to work. Corn mills are recorded here from the 14th century and paper mills from the 18th. The village was connected to Princes Street by rail from 1874 to the 1970s, passenger trains last running in 1943. Balerno was part of Midlothian until 1975, when it was absorbed by Edinburgh.

BARNTON
A popular residential suburb to the south of Cramond, Barnton is essentialy a postwar addition to the cityscape, one transport historian pointing out that major development began in earnest here as soon as the railway link with Princes Street was

closed in 1951! It was as if its inaccessibility for the general public was its greatest perceived attraction for the better-off (although the Queensferry Road is not far away). Golf moved here from the Meadows in 1895 (*see* GOLF).

BLACKFORD

This is a southside residential suburb which is often frequently known as Blackford Hill, for the hill has played a major part in the development of the area, hosting the Royal Observatory since the 1890s (*see* HILLS and OBSERVATORIES), and providing local houses with a superb viewpoint. The road approach to the hill is through the impressive Harrison arch commemorating Sir George Harrison, former Lord Provost and first MP for Edinburgh South (*see* LORD PROVOSTS and PARLIAMENTARY REPRESENT-ATION).

BROUGHTON

Once notorious for its witches and warlocks, Broughton is now an amorphous area to the east and north-east of the New Town, running as far eastwards as Leith Walk. No signs remain in this heavily built-up area of its past supernatural connections, nor of its pastoral nature, where Edinburgh's first zoo was created in 1839 (*see* ZOOS). Broughton school opened in 1909 but has now moved to the Fettes area (*see* SCHOOLS), and a huge industrial hall was built here in the 1920s, hosting exhibitions and boxing matches before becoming the city's largest bus garage.

CANONGATE

Now normally thought of as that part of the Royal Mile below the Netherbow crossroads down to Holyrood, Canongate was in fact a burgh quite separate from Edinburgh, although very much under its domination, until 1856. Technically, Canongate was a royal burgh, having been the product of a royal gift from David I to the Augustinian canons of Holyrood. It was less well defended than the city of Edinburgh (*see* CITY WALLS), but boasted its own Tolbooth (still extant, *see* LOCAL GOVERNMENT and MUSEUMS), while its kirkyard, just off the High Street, rivals Greyfriars in importance (*see* CHURCHES). The Canongate enjoyed its own police, banking, and theatres, often in advance of the city itself (*see* POLICE, BANKS, and THEATRES) but in 1856 an amalgamation took place which was perhaps long overdue.

CANONMILLS

Occupying the Water of Leith valley immediately east of Stockbridge, Canonmills, as the name suggests, was a corn-milling settlement worked by the monks of Holyrood from the 12th century. The playground and small industrial estate just off Eyre Place occupy the site of Canonmills Loch (*see* LOCHS), where the city's first curling club first met around 1750, and was later the venue for St Bernard's football club (*see* FOOTBALL). Edinburgh Academy is located here (*see* SCHOOLS), as well as the Post Office Philatelic Bureau (*see* POSTAL SERVICES), and one of Edinburgh finest examples of 'colony' houses (*see* HOUSING).

COLINTON

Originally a self-contained village community employing the power of the Water of Leith in milling and snuff-making, Colinton is now a western suburb of the city. Redford Barracks were established here in 1915, resulting in the village becoming one of the first localities in Scotland to be bombed from the air, by Zeppelin in the following year. Connected by railway from 1874 – allowing passage to the city's West End in only 14 minutes – Colinton was formally absorbed into Edinburgh in 1920, although it still retains much of its pastoral charm. With passenger trains withdrawn in 1943, journeys into the city by public transport now take longer!

COMELY BANK

An almost wholly tenemental area, Comely Bank is the Marchmont of north Edinburgh, and surely does not deserve a reputation for snobbishness and genteel behaviour often also attributed to Morningside. The area is really a western adjunct of Stockbridge, with Inverleith Park, Fettes, and the Western General Hospital, to the north. The naming of its primary school, for Flora Stevenson, pioneering Edinburgh educationalist, is a pleasant touch (*see* SCHOOLS).

CORSTORPHINE

Like Colinton, Corstorphine is a Midlothian village which has been swallowed up by Edinburgh. Originally situated just to the north of the isthmus between Corstorphine and Gogar Lochs (*see* LOCHS), the village was a one-street community which was a farming centre for its surrounding area. By the 19th century,

market gardening developed to supply the burgeoning city to the east, and the railway arrived nearby in 1842 (although the first Corstorphine station was some distance to the south, at Saughton).

Corstorphine rapidly became an attractive suburb for commuters, particularly with the city's west end only 11 minutes away by train, although the area attracts visitors in its own right, with Edinburgh's Zoo established here during the First World War (*see* ZOOS). The Forestry Commission offices are a newer arrival, and the former village now finds a huge retail and business development growing at South Gyle to the south-west. The branch railway line (opened 1902) closed inexplicably in 1969, sentencing the locals to nearly 15 years of continuing traffic congestion, now slightly eased by long-overdue highway developments to the west and south.

CRAIGLOCKHART

A south-western suburb, one of the most pleasant in the city, lying to the north of the twin peaks of Craiglockhart Hill (*see* HILLS). Mainly commuter country, Craiglockhart holds an unusual place in First World War history, as its military hospital (now Napier University, *see* UNIVERSITIES AND COLLEGES) housed Siegfried Sassoon and the doomed Wilfred Owen during their convalesence from the Western Front (*see* LITERATURE). The site of the former Happy Valley leisure complex is now Scotland's top venue for tennis and badminton (*see* SPORTS and TENNIS).

CRAIGMILLAR

Once a rural area noted for its cream produce, and within the last 50 years the location for one of Britain's biggest brewing centres, Craigmillar is now essentially a residential area. Situated south-east of the city centre and south of Portobello, Craigmillar has a population of between 15,000 and 20,000 people, almost entirely accommodated in council housing. Unemployment is worse here than anywhere else in the city, (see POPULATION), with the social problems and vandalism that often come in its wake, following the closure of two coal-mines in the area, six out of seven breweries, and an ice-cream factory.

In 1964 a group of local residents led by Helen Crummy decided to take positive action to improve their environment and their communal lifestyle. By forming the Craigmillar Festival Society, they set in train a series of local events which stretched beyond the Festival which was the centrepiece of their plan. The Society also has a permanent office and undertakes community activities all the year round, staffed by volunteers and social work trainees.

In 1991 both the District and Regional Councils decided to build on the foundations laid down by the Society to launch the Craigmillar Initiative. This is a community enterprise involving a total of 27 interested local groups and is principally intended to improve the immediate environment by creating the Craigmillar Castle Country Park and promote interest in the wildlife corridors which enter the area from the south. With backing from Scottish Natural Heritage, the Initiative will involve tree-planting, landscape design, and environmental clean-ups, some of them miles from Craigmillar on the Niddrie Burn (Braid Burn) to the south.

CRAMOND
see VILLAGES

CURRIE
Situated between Juniper Green and Balerno, Currie has much in common with both of them – a riverside village with a number of mills based on the Water of Leith, but with a modern suburbanite population enjoying the fresh air of this former Midlothian community.

DALMENY
One of the West Lothian communities which passed into Edinburgh at the 1975 local government reorganisation, Dalmeny is a surprisingly large parish almost enclosing South Queensferry to the north. Dalmeny village itself is centred round a charming village green, with the Norman church nearby, its 1937 tower perfectly blending with the rest of the 12th century building. The village was boosted by the building of the Forth railway bridge (1883–1890), and its principal occupations are the Ministry of Defence depot, and the tank farm which is carefully landscaped. Otherwise, Dalmeny, like its neighbouring community of South Queensferry, is fast becoming an Edinburgh dormitory.

DALRY
South-west of Haymarket is an intensively-populated area, known as Dalry, after the burn which once drained the Burgh Loch to the Water of Leith (see RIVERS AND STREAMS). Nearly all the housing here dates from Victorian times, and is almost invariably tenemental, although there are some 'colony' houses (see HOUSING). Railway depots and yards once provided

much employment here, as well as breweries, although both industries have now almost entirely receded. To the west, the area merges with Gorgie, with which Dalry shares a community council.

DAVIDSON'S MAINS

Like so many parts of Edinburgh, Davidson's Mains thinks of itself as a self-contained community, complete with its east-west village street. Its annual gala reinforces the message that this is no mere suburb, although the spread of bungalows to the north suggests otherwise, and the area now has many daily visitors to its supermarket. This is built on the site of the former railway goods station; ironically, the railway closed as the population swelled. Lauriston Castle is a fascinating feature to the north.

DEAN VILLAGE
see VILLAGES

DUDDINGSTON
see VILLAGES

GILMERTON

While almost qualifying for an entry in the VILLAGES chapter, having its origins as a community back in the 12th century, present-day Gilmerton has been swallowed up in the great swathe of new housing on the southern outskirts of the city. Its past industries were part agricultural – an annual Carters Play was held (*see* FAIRS) – and partly based on coal mining, the local mine closing in 1961 (*see also* INDUSTRY: COALMINING). The most interesting antiquity in the area is Gilmerton Cove, a series of underground chambers believed to

have been hewn in the early 18th century (although probably on the site of an earlier work). It contains living and storage chambers, but its purpose and precise function are unclear.

GORGIE

Like Dalry to the east, this is an industrious area, which accommodated the city's slaughterhouses from 1911, as well as breweries, railway and tram depots, and latterly a huge telephone exchange. Nearly all of this has now vanished, although an electronics factory compensates. Gorgie is the home of Heart of Midlothian FC, at Tynecastle, and the City Farm (*see* FOOTBALL and AGRICULTURE respectively). The area shares a community council with its neighbour, Dalry.

GRANTON
see PORTS

HAYMARKET

Like Tollcross on the south-west corner of the city centre, Haymarket is a nerve-centre; here the main roads from Princes Street and the Old Town, split into westward routes via either Corstorphine or Dalry. Centring on its railway station, once the eastern terminus of the Edinburgh & Glasgow Railway, Haymarket is a contrasting mix of working-class housing in Dalry, including a 'colony' (*see* HOUSING), facing the more measured terraces and crescents of the western New Town to the north. A major road redevelopment here in the early 1970s made Morrison Street, Torphichen Street, and part of West Maitland Street into one-way streets, with considerable success in keeping traffic moving. All this meant the moving of the Hearts memorial (*see* MILITARY HISTORY), but its prominence is undiminished.

JUNIPER GREEN

Like Balerno and Currie, Juniper Green is a riverine community once a village in its own right in the Water of Leith valley. The river powered a number of mills here, with snuff being produced from 1749 until the 1940s, as well as agricultural milling, and some light industry. The coming of the railway in 1874 made Juniper Green popular as a pleasant dormitory for the city, and the area is now very much suburbanised, the railway track a riverside walkway.

KIRKLISTON

To the motorist passing close by on the M9, Kirkliston is a community apparently dominated by one of its major industries, a distillery. It is in fact a pleasant village, formerly in West Lothian, but transferred to Edinburgh District in 1975.

The village has a parish church rivalling Dalmeny and Duddingston's in antiquity, having been dedicated in 1244, and in continuous use ever since. Despite its pleasant surroundings, the village enjoys considerable industry; apart from the distillery, rubber and electronic concerns have made their way to the area from central Edinburgh over the last half century. Pink shale bings are evidence of 19th century enterprise.

LEITH

see LEITH (main heading)

LIBERTON

Historians now dispute whether this placename does in fact denote a 'lepers' town' outside the city, there being records of a community at Liberton some 140 years before the disease was recognised in the city. Modern day Liberton straddles the top of its brae on the A701 south of the city centre, and is predominately residential. Edinburgh University's King's Buildings campus is situated at the foot of the brae, and the Cameron Toll shopping complex is a new development (*see* SHOPS). The area includes the Roman Catholic cemetery at Mount Vernon, and Liberton Hospital (*see* HOSPITALS).

MARCHMONT

An almost wholly tenemental area, Marchmont lies to the south of the Meadows, providing a useful dormitory for those who work at the Royal Infirmary or study at the university. It has its own community council, but otherwise fails to give the impression of a self-contained community, with too few shops and even fewer places of employment or entertainment. The eastern end of Marchmont is known as Sciennes, believed to be named after St Catherine of Sienna, and this is home to the Royal Hospital for Sick Children, and had until 1985 a single factory, Bertram's, producing paper-making equipment.

MERCHISTON

An indeterminate area south of Gorgie and Dalry and north of Morningside, Merchiston's housing represents a complete cross-section, ranging from tenement to villa, with two 'colonies' of artisans' houses.

One of these is situated next to the former Merchiston railway station, closed in 1965, and there is no recognisable main road or 'high street' for this community to configure around. There is, however, an active community council.

MORNINGSIDE

Undeservedly vilified for being snobby and pretentious, Morningsiders occupy an area on the city's southside straddling the A702 road to Dumfries. Modern Morningside has merged to east and west with Marchmont (or Grange) and Craiglockhart respectively as part of the southside commuter belt. The area has always been residential, but local dairies and farms were to be found well into the 20th century, even after tenemental housing was built in the centre of the area. Rail transport from 1884 may have hastened the potential for commuters, and villas fringe the edge of Morningside. Morningside is an excellent shopping centre, and has good bus services in and out of the city, although radial services east and west are less reliable.

Morningsiders have had thrust upon them an unenviable reputation for being hypocritical or puritanical or something of the kind (reputations are not usually very specific), so much so, that a 1994 TV programme, finding real Morningsiders surprisingly normal and good-humoured, used professional actors to represent them as puritanical, snobbish etc!

MUIRHOUSE

Along with Pilton, Muirhouse was the biggest council housing development of the 1950s, creating a huge residential scheme in the north-west of the city from 1953 onwards. Located south-west of Granton and north-east of Davidson's Mains, Muirhouse suffered from the usual thoughtless urban planning which combined high density housing – the city's largest concentration of two-room and three-room houses (*see* HOUSING) – with a serious lack of communal and shopping facilities (the shopping centre was not built until 1971).

A recent TV feature on urban deprivation alighted on Muirhouse in the way the 1930s newspapers might have featured Glasgow's Gorbals. The reduction in the gas industry nearby has worsened employment prospects here, although a local initiative scheme is currently doing its best to improve opportunities for residents in the area.

MURRAYFIELD

A residential area, Murrayfield has grown westwards from the hamlet of Coltbridge (Roseburn), the area north of the Glasgow Road being feued for housing in the mid-19th century as far as the present-day Zoo. The earliest existing dwelling in the vicinity is the 16th century Roseburn House, now dwarfed by Murrayfield Stadium, the finest sports venue in the country (*see* RUGBY). The ice-rink is north-west of here (*see* ICE SPORTS). South of the Water of Leith, sprang up some brewing and railway-orientated industry, but new housing developments are now reinforcing Murrayfield's residential image.

NEWCRAIGHALL
see VILLAGES

NEWHAVEN

'Our port of grace' is a phrase well-applied to Newhaven, a former fishing community which was originally created by James IV as a shipbuilding site to produce his mighty warship *Michael* at the beginning of the 16th century. Situated immediately west of Leith, Newhaven maintained its links with the sea as a fishing port, although the harbour was not built in its present form until the 1860s with a fishmarket also being built on the eastern quay some 30 years later (*see* PORTS). This harbour is now given over to leisure sailing, and there is an interesting heritage museum and restaurant on the quayside. The village itself is now conserved and bypassed by the main Leith–Granton road. It is something of a pantiled gem, well worth visiting.

NIDDRIE

Once an active part of the Midlothian coalfield, its 'Jewel' seam commemorated in the name of a nearby college (*see* UNIVERSITIES AND COLLEGES), Niddrie is now very much a residential area with Portobello and Duddingston to the north and west. Niddrie shares a huge swathe of council housing with Craigmillar next door. A number of large retail units provide local employment for an area of some deprivation.

OXGANGS

A council house development begun by the City Council in 1954, Oxgangs sprawls southwards from the slopes of Craiglockhart Hill towards the Green Belt. Unlike some such schemes, there are community facilities here, but little local employment, making good public transport so much more of a necessity.

PILTON

Pilton is a 1930s slum-clearance solution to the prevalent problem at that time of overcrowded housing in central Edinburgh and Leith. West Pilton, between Granton and Ferry Road, was developed first, in 1937, with two- and three-room housing being built in terraced and high-rise configurations. The lack of shopping and social facilities should have served as a warning when Muirhouse was planned 15 years later. The reduction in the nearby gas and electronics industries has affected local employment prospects badly, and, with Muirhouse and Craigmillar, this represents the most highly deprived area of the city.

PORTOBELLO

Situated about three miles east of Edinburgh city centre, Portobello was a separate burgh until 1896, its industries comprising brick- and bottle-making, salt production, and potteries. The area was originally known as the Figgate Whins, an early resident naming his house here after the Battle of Puerto Bello in Panama in 1739.

'Porty' is probably best known as a seaside resort, although its best days are past. A pier stretched into the Forth here for almost 40 years until its demolition in 1917 (*see* FIRTH OF FORTH). With a funfair standing on the site of its old harbour (*see* PORTS), and with a promenade stretching some two miles along the seafront, Portobello once made a serious attempt to attract trippers, enjoying considerable popularity with Glaswegian visitors at one time. Perhaps they felt at home, with Portobello's tenements coming right down to the sea.

That seems to sum up the town's character – never quite able to turn its back on the sea completely, yet quite prepared to have industrial or housing facilities built within yards of the beach. The 1920s power-station, with its 300 feet (90 metres) high chimney (*see* ELECTRICITY SUPPLY) was demolished in 1983, but more of a loss for a potential holiday resort was the open-air bathing pool (*see* SWIMMING). Bathing was recently prohibited at Portobello altogether because of sewage contamination. With climatologists predicting warmer and drier summers on Scotland's east coast in future, perhaps more investment in Portobello as a holiday resort would not be inappropriate.

RESTALRIG

Another former village in its own right, Restalrig traces its roots back to the Middle Ages, when the local ruling family, the Logans, controlled much of Leith. Local antiquities include the intriguing Craigentinny House and Lochend House (*see* CASTLES AND TOWERS) and St Triduana's well (*see* WATER SUPPLY), and there is still a recognisable village street. Surrounded by council housing to the north and east, and bungalow-land to the south, Restalrig is an interesting relic of times past, and can claim a footnote in aeronautical history as the landing-site of Britain's first balloon flight (*see* BALLOONING).

ROSEBURN
see MURRAYFIELD

SOUTH QUEENSFERRY

Separated from the rest of Edinburgh by the Green Belt, South Queensferry was added to the city's administrative area by the local government reorganisation of 1975. It was perhaps a surprising move, and one not entirely welcome in the town, up to that time, a Royal Burgh. 'This loss of autonomy is still a matter of resentment; Queensferry still thinks of itself as part of West Lothian', advised the *Third Statistical Account* as recently as 1990.

The former burgh is dominated by the two bridges spanning the Forth to the north, although local sources of employment were the distillery (although closed in 1985), the naval depot and minesweeping base at Port Edgar (the former reduced in size, the latter closed), and a new electronics factory. This last-mentioned is a welcome addition to the local economy, and there is also employment to be had at the nearby tank farm and oil-loading utility at Hound Point (both strictly speaking in Dalmeny).

Central South Queensferry is now a conservation area, and architecturally very attractive. Much of the town's hinterland has become ringed with new housing, putting considerable pressure on schools and local facilities, as the town increasingly sees itself becoming an Edinburgh dormitory.

STOCKBRIDGE

Once a village independent of Edinburgh, Stockbridge now enjoys a reputation for being one of the most cosmopolitan and

South Queensferry's Tollbooth Tower dates from the 17th century, although its appearance was considerably altered by the addition of the Jubilee clocktower in 1887. In this 1995 view of the High Street, one of the support arches of the Forth Road Bridge can be seen in the far background.

intriguing areas of the city. Straddling the Water of Leith west of Canonmills, and not a mile from the city's West End, 'Stockaree' offers the visitor a wide range of exotic shops including The Lighting Museum in St Stephen's Street, as well as an array of pubs, restaurants, and shops catering for alternative lifestyles. No longer centred round its market (*see* MARKETS), the area nevertheless has a good library and its own theatre (Theatre Workshop, *see* THEATRES), while Inverleith Park and Pond, and the Royal Botanic Garden are immediately to the north.

SWANSTON
see VILLAGES

TOLLCROSS
A vibrant and cosmopolitan community, despite losing much of its housing and industry, Tollcross has changed considerably in the years since the Second World War. The loss of such industries as the rubber factories, slaughterhouses, co-operative warehousing, and a reduction in brewing, is reflected in the opening up of the centre of Tollcross, with the eastern side of Earl Grey Street demolished in the early 1970s to facilitate traffic flow. This certainly justifies the local history of the area being published under the title *By Three Great Roads* (*see* BIBLIOGRAPHY).

Tollcross still has its Fountain Brewery, but much of its other features are less prominent nowadays – namely its one-time variety of shops and places of entertainments. These include such retailers as Goldberg's, now closed and demolished, but which brought Sunday shopping to the capital, and the Palladium, the Coliseum (later the Palais ballroom), and such cinemas as the King's (Cameo), the Beverley (Blue Halls), and Tollcross, to say nothing of the King's Theatre.

WESTER HAILES

Open country until 1966, Wester Hailes is now one of the principal council house areas in the city, its 11,000 population giving it almost the status of a satellite town. The scheme had few of a town's facilities when first built, unfortunately, apart from an excellent education centre which doubles as a sports and community facility. The housing in the area is now undergoing a regeneration, particularly of its 25 tower blocks, six of which are being reclad and the rest scheduled for demolition. A railway station and public library have opened in recent years, and more attention given to the need to generate community awareness.

Electricity Supply

Edinburgh no longer generates its own electricity, but receives power from the national network via Scottish Power, the now-privatised power supply authority whose headquarters are based in Glasgow.

The power station closest to Edinburgh is Cockenzie in East Lothian, fuelled by coal, as are stations within a 30 miles radius at Longannet and Kincardine-on-Forth both

in Fife. Nuclear-generated power is fed into the grid from Torness, on the other side of Dunbar, and the United Kingdom headquarters of the new British Energy authority, the privatised merger of Nuclear Electric and Scottish Nuclear, are presently being established in Edinburgh.

History

As with gas provision, the earliest use of electricity on a large scale was in street lighting. The first electric light to be publicly operated in Edinburgh was a demonstration light which shone for nearly an hour on Castle Hill on Boxing Day 1854, and was visible for miles around.

Practical lighting for the streets made a short-lived debut on North Bridge as early as 1881; although highly effective, the contractors had trouble with their cable connections from their steam-driven plant in Market Street due to high winds, and it was not until 1895 that permanent electric lighting came to Edinburgh, by which time Edinburgh was dragging behind many other British cities. The first power station in Dewar Place supplied the current to a lighting network in the New Town, and this was extended considerably, even into parts of neighbouring Midlothian, after a second power station had been opened at McDonald Road four years later in 1899.

The capital's first shop to utilise electric lighting was Baildon's, chemists at 73 and 144a Princes Street; the first domestic user being a Miss Murray at 11 Chester Street, both sites being connected to the new supply in May 1895. Growing demand for domestic electricity soon indicated the need for greater generating capacity – one city butcher employing an electric mincing machine had been asked not to operate it during the hours of darkness as it seriously compromised the city's supply!

This increase in demand necessitated the building of a third station, intended to be the largest of them all in the city, and this was opened at Portobello in two stages. The first section began generating after a formal opening by George V on 11 July 1923. At that time the Portobello power station had eight squat chimneys but these were replaced by a 350 feet high 16-sided redbrick monster chimney when the station was brought up to full strength after 12 April 1939, supplying Edinburgh through 400 sub-stations.

Portobello was one of the two principal stations serving Central Scotland in the immediate postwar years, and achieved the highest thermal efficiency figures for any power-generating unit in the United Kingdom in the years 1952-55. At one time the station was consuming 2,400 tons of coal daily, with sea water being taken in through a tunnel system burrowing under the Forth. However, the station was certainly not a good neighbour to the townspeople, regularly waking them with emissions of waste steam at high volume in the early hours of each morning.

The appropriateness of locating this utility on the promenade of a then-popular holiday resort was also highly questionable, although at least some effort was made to harness the waste heat from the station by warming the waters of the outdoor swimming pool opened next door in 1936 (see SWIMMING). Ever-increasing demand for power led to additional power having to be brought in from the National Grid at Gorgie and Telford Road from 1960, and the Portobello station closed on 31 March 1977 when the present trio of coal-fired stations came fully on stream. Ironically, and presumably coincidentally, Portobello has been less popular as a holiday resort since the station's removal.

Edinburgh street lighting was all-electric by April 1965 when the last gas lamp was extinguished (see also GAS SUPPLY and ROADS AND STREETS). Little now remains of the power stations at Dewar Place (closed in 1930, although offices remain) or Portobello, although the shell of the McDonald Road building (actually Shrubhill) is still substantially complete at the time of writing. It had become a sub-station by 1928, and was closed completely on 23 September 1957, when the city supply was converted to AC from DC.

Leith's tramways were electric by 1904, some 18 years before Edinburgh's, and these were powered from the town's small power station off Junction Street (closed in 1923). The city caught up in 1922, with power being supplied to the new amalgamated tramway system from its own power station at Tollcross.

Hydro-electric power is not normally associated with the Scottish lowlands, but in fact Edinburgh was selected as the site of the North of Scotland Hydro-Electric Board when it was set up in 1943. Offices were taken by the new authority in Rothesay Place in the West End, and occupied until the overdue decision was made to move the organisation, newly rechristened Hydro Electric, to Perth in 1994.

Enlightenment

The Scottish Enlightenment was a glorious flowering of talent in science, economics, and the arts, in the 70 years from around 1775. It is important to remember that it was a *national* outburst of creative activity, although Edinburgh's status as capital city and largest community ensured that it comprised the nucleus of the Enlightenment.

It was at Edinburgh's Mercat Cross that an English visitor reported that he could 'in a few minutes, take 50 men of genius and learning by the hand'. Glasgow comedian Billy Connolly, in a 1994 television programme, pertinently asked 'Where did Edinburgh go wrong since then?' The answer is − around 1850, when it became possible for a career scientist, doctor, or writer, to reach London within the course of a single day, by train.

Listing some of these men of genius could hardly be done by subject, since so many of them were polymaths. Further details of the 50 listed below can be found in *The Dictionary of National Biography* or *Collins Encyclopaedia of Scotland*. The names below represent an arbitrary choice from the Enlightment period of 1775–1850, dates on which not all historians agree. Not all of those listed were born in the city, but all have a capital connection:

Adam, Robert (1728–92). Architect of Register House and Charlotte Square.

Adamson, Robert (1821–48). Pioneering photographer.

Black, Joseph (1728–99). Chemist, discoverer of carbon dioxide.

Blane, Gilbert (1749–1834). Antiscorbutic specialist.

Brewster, Sir David (1781–1868). Optical scientist, inventor of the kaleidoscope.

Brougham, Henry, Lord (1778–1868). Judge, anti-slavery campaigner and founder of London University.

Brown, Robert (1773–1858). Botanist, discoverer of cell nucleus, and 'Brownian Movement' in plant fluid systems.

Burnett, James (Lord Monboddo)(1714–99). Judge, formulated pre-Darwinian theory of evolution.

Burns, Robert (1759–96). National Bard.

Carlyle, Thomas (1795–1881). Writer, founder of the London Library.

Chambers, Robert (1802–71). Historian, biographer of Burns, also formulated pre-Darwinian evolutionary theory.

Chambers, William (1800–83). Encyclopedia publisher.

Clerk Maxwell, James (1831–79). Eminent physicist, producer of world's first colour photograph.

Clerk of Eldin, John (1728–1812). Water colourist, naval strategist.

Cockburn, Henry, Lord (1779–1854). Judge and social historian.

Constable, Archibald (1774–1827). Publisher of Scott's works and of *Encyclopaedia Britannica*.

Craig, James (1744–95). Architect of New Town.

Cullen, William (1710–90). Chemist, produced first modern pharmacopoeia.

Darwin, Charles (1809–82). Edinburgh student, later published theory of evolution.

Ferguson, Adam (1723–1816). Philosopher, influenced Schiller and Hegel.

Fergusson, Robert (1750–74). Poet, influenced Burns.

Hall, James (1761–1832). Experimental geologist.

Hill, David Octavius (1801–70). Painter and pioneering photographer.

Hogg, James (1770–1835). Poet, novelist.

Hope, John (1725–86). Botanist, enlarged Royal Botanical Gardens.

Hume, David (1711–76). Philosopher.

Hutton, James (1726–97). 'Founder of modern Geology'.

Jameson, Robert (1774–1854). Wernerian geologist, collector of 70,000 natural history specimens.

Jeffrey, Francis, Lord (1773–1850). Writer and polemicist, drafted Scottish Reform Bill, later M.P.

Lind, James (1716–94). Antiscorbutic discoverer.

Mackenzie, Henry (1745–1832). Novelist, popularised Burns's poetry.

Monro, Alexander (1733–1817). Physician, researched nervous system.

Nasmyth, Alexander (1758–1840). Landscape painter.

Nasmyth, Robert (1808–90). Engineer, machine tool designer.

Playfair, John (1748–1819). Mathematician, championed geological theory of James Hutton.

Playfair, William (1790–1857). Architect of National Gallery and Royal Scottish Academy.

Raeburn, Sir Henry (1756–1823). Portrait painter.

Ramsay, Allan (1684–1758). Poet, editor, and dramatist.

Ramsay, Allan (1713–1884). Portrait painter.

Runciman, Alexander (1736–85). Landscape painter.

Rutherford, Daniel (1749–1819). Chemist, discovered nitrogen.

Scott, Sir Walter (1771–1832). Novelist, poet.

Simpson, Sir James (1811–70). Anaesthetics pioneer.

Smellie, William (1740–95). Edited first edition of *Encyclopaedia Britannica*.

Smiles, Samuel (1812-96). Author of *Self-Help*.

Smith, Adam (1723–90). Economist.

Stevenson, Robert (1772–1850). Lighthouse and bridge engineer.

Stewart, Dugald (1753–1828). Philosopher, biographer of Adam Smith.

Tytler, James (1745–1804). Polemicist, editor of the second (much-enlarged) edition of the *Encyclopaedia Britannica*.

Tytler, Patrick (1791–1849). Historian.

Executions

Edinburgh's history is awash with the blood of those executed in the city. State traitors, common criminals, religious martyrs, and those men and women unfortunate enough to be denounced as witches and warlocks, all met their fate by hanging, beheading, burning, or drowning (or a combination of these ordeals) in various parts of the city, from time immemorial up to 1951, when the last execution took place at Saughton Prison. Indeed, so intensive was the city's purging of its inhabitants, that Edinburgh had its own guillotine-like device two centuries before France.

Executions and other public punishments, such as pillorying, were for many centuries a preventative substitute for proper detective methods and forensic science, resulting in a huge number of Scots meeting their doom in the middle of a crowd of leering Edinburgh spectators. As capital city, Edinburgh was the last view of the world seen by those who had offended against the monarch, or for the monarch, depending on the current circumstances, while the capital had a particularly detestable habit of persecuting the aged or psychiatrically ill who might be castigated as witches.

Those wishing to read in detail on this

macabre subject must do so elsewhere. Suffice to say that executions took place in such city locations as the Grassmarket, Castlehill, Tolbooth, Gallowlee (Leith Walk), at the Mercat Cross, and in the Nor' Loch. So intensive was Edinburgh's despatching of its mortals that a guillotine-like machine known as the 'Maiden' was built in 1565, and used to behead some 120 people, including its designer, the fourth Earl of Morton. It is still to be seen, in the National Museums of Scotland collection.

Some of those unfortunates killed in the name of religious intolerance during Covenanting times have been commemorated on a plaque in the east end of the Grassmarket. Erected by the Scottish Convenanters' Memorials Association and the Scottish Reformation Society in 1988, the memorial lists those executed in or near Edinburgh in the period 1661-88, because of their beliefs.

Edinburgh's last public execution at the scene of the crime, was the despatching of two Irishmen convicted of highway robbery committed at Braid Road, Morningside. On 25 January 1815, the two were hanged at the exact location of their crime, and the scene was marked in 1992 with a commemorative pavement plaque (near the corner of Braid Road and Comiston Terrace).

The last public execution in the city took place at the top of Liberton Wynd, at the north-west corner of Parliament Square in 1864. The site is marked by a plaque and three brass setts. The last woman to be hanged in the city was Jessie King, a child-murderer from Stockbridge, despatched at the Calton Gaol in 1889 (see also CRIME). The last execution of all in Edinburgh took place at Saughton Prison on 15 September 1951, when Robert Dobie Smith was hanged for shooting a police officer (see also PRISONS).

Fairs and Folk Festivals

Edinburgh does not include traditional fairs or festivals prominently in its community life. Such fairs as Allhallows and Trinity are no longer observed as municipal events, and there has been no Riding of the Marches since 1946. The Edinburgh Folk Festival is not considered in this entry (see FESTIVALS).

History

According to historian Florence McNeill, Allhallows Fair was the only one to be held in Edinburgh before 1447, when Trinity Fair was established, before itself falling into disuse. The first site for Allhallows, better known as Hallowe'en, was the Calton Hill, before the Grassmarket was used. The proceedings there were presided over by a Lord of Misrule, and there are records of 'Guisers' calling at Holyrood in 1585 (which is a surprise, as the city was gripped with plague in that winter).

Beltane rites were, and still are, observed on the morning of 1 May, with early morning climbers on Arthur's Seat washing their faces in dew while on their way to the summit for the Sunrise Service – a much more recent custom. First held in 1940 by the Minister of the Canongate, the service appropriately includes a reading from the Sermon on the Mount, but has become merged in most citizens' minds with the face-washing ritual (which strictly speaking should be confined to the female sex).

The Riding of the Marches is very much a part of the calendar for smaller Scottish communities, particularly in the Borders, but has not been observed in the Scottish capital since 1946. On 8 June of that year, after an interregnum of no less than 228 years, the ceremony was revived, although it was considered that the city's boundaries were too far-flung to be circumnavigated in the time available. Instead, a total of 70 riders converged on the city centre from the four principal points of the compass, reporting to the Lord Provost at the Mercat Cross.

One of the companies was led by the Captain of the Orange, whose office is the last reminder of the city's Trained Bands (see MILITARY HISTORY). Formed in 1580 from survivors of Edinburgh's reservists, the 16 Bands followed standards of a particular colour, the Orange being the only one to survive. A purely ceremonial office since the 18th century, this tradition, in this most traditional of cities, has become less well observed than might be expected, since the colour of the remaining standard has become coincidentally associated with one variety of religious bigotry.

South Queensferry and Gilmerton are two areas in Edinburgh District with their own folk-based festivals. South Queensferry is a Royal Burgh dating from 1636, only being absorbed into Edinburgh District in 1975. The town's two rituals, the Ferry Fair and the Procession of the Burry Man are unique to Queensferry (the 'South' is increasingly being dropped) and are not really part of the city's story at all. The reader interested in these festivals is directed to McNeill's classic book *The Silver Bough* (Volume 4).

Gilmerton is now very much a suburb of south Edinburgh, but had its own traditional festival, the Gilmerton Play, until 1935. This took the form of a procession and race (for carthorses!) along a public road, followed by an evening of dining and a barn dance not noted for its sobriety. It appears that the event may have been organised as an annual outing for the local friendly society, and therefore may not strictly qualify as a folk festival, although there was little doubt of its venerable status, dating back almost to the 16th century.

Funfairs (or 'the Shows') were annual visitors to the Waverley Market for 100 years until its closure in 1977. At the time of writing, there is an annual visit by a funfair to the Meadows every May, and to Leith Links in July.

Ferries

Edinburgh no longer counts a ferry terminal among its transport utilities. For many years, a ferry operated from Granton to Burntisland, while the best-known ferries on the Forth – those plying across the Queensferry Narrows – ceased to operate in 1964, 11 years before South Queensferry became part of Edinburgh District.

Although there are proposals currently being mooted for a ferry link from Leith, Rosyth, or East Lothian, to the continent,

Edinburgh's only ferry at the present time is a humble rowboat owned by the Dalmeny Estate, carrying walkers across the River Almond at Cramond village when en route to or from Queensferry.

History

Ferries had been crossing the Queensferry Narrows for 800 years before the opening of the Forth Road Bridge in 1964. In their final years they were carrying 1.25 million passengers each year, and a new ferry boat had to be added to the fleet as recently as 1955. This service, run by the railway companies from 1863, is outside the geographical scope of this book, although Edinburgh had its own railway-operated ferry across the Forth, operating out of Granton.

From around 1849, the often-renamed company (best known as the North British Railway) which built Canal Street station in the city (*see* RAILWAYS), pioneered a roll-on roll-off ferry, the *Leviathan*, for rail vehicles at Granton. The ramp design was by Thomas Bouch, the ill-starred engineer whose life did not long survive the loss of one of his less successful creations, the first Tay Bridge. Bouch's ferry design was little more than a flexible wheeled ramp with rails which could be laid down temporarily on a slipway, thus allowing services to continue irrespective of the state of the tide. Passengers travelling between Granton and Fife could either hire a ferry cabin for one shilling (5p) or make themselves as comfortable as possible among the rail vehicles as the crossing was undertaken, at a sixpenny fare.

This service ran seven days a week, operated at one time by no fewer than four passenger and five freight ferries. These offered the quickest method of travel to and from Fife, Dundee, and Aberdeen, until 1890, when the Forth Bridge opened (*see* BRIDGES). Rail traffic immediately switched to the Bridge route, but the railway company continued the Granton-Burntisland ferry until 1940, when wartime strictures brought it to an end. For the final 58 years, the principal operating vessel was the Kinghorn-built paddle steamer *William Muir* which carried 800,000 passengers on the passage until its retirement in 1939.

In 1950 an attempt was made to restart a ferry passage from Granton to Burntisland, using converted wartime landing-craft. This concern lasted only five years – surprisingly, considering the congestion awaiting the Queensferry crossing passenger. In 1991–93 a motorised catamaran called *Spirit of Fife* was used to try and revive the service, with a free bus connection being offered into central Edinburgh, but this did not thrive, possibly because of the opening of a new east-west dual carriageway in Fife, connecting with the Forth Road Bridge.

Festivals

Now firmly established as one of the most important arts festivals in the world, Edinburgh's International Festival is an integral part of the Scottish tourist industry. It has a host of imitators throughout Scotland, not least in Edinburgh itself, and the table below lists the city's rich feast of events taking place throughout the year. Established in 1947, the EIF is the trail-blazer, along with the Film Festival, with the Fringe taking on its amorphous existence from 1948.

Research published by the Scottish Tourist Board in 1992 (*see* BIBLIOGRAPHY) suggested that the Military Tattoo was far and away the most successful of the city's festivals in encouraging tourist spending, and the Folk Festival the least successful in those terms. Of course, inducing tourists to part with their hard-earned pounds, dollars, or marks, is not the primary purpose of a cultural festival!

EDINBURGH'S INTERNATIONAL FESTIVAL OF MUSIC, DRAMA AND THE ARTS

This takes place every year for three weeks from mid-August. This is *the* Festival, its principal intention being 'to promote and encourage arts of the highest possible standard', while presenting international culture to Scottish audiences and Scottish culture to a wider world.

Performers and artists appear at the Festival by invitation only; their selection is in the hands of the event's Artistic Director, and on his judgement (the appointee has always so far been male) rests the reputation of the Festival. Fortunately, this trust has never been misplaced, and it is believed that many companies and orchestras have tolerated the less-than-satisfactory facilities in Edinburgh in past years out of regard for the city and its Festival Director. Hopefully, with the recent opening of the Festival Theatre (*see* THEATRES) the standard of accommodation offered is improving.

FESTIVAL DIRECTORS	
Sir Rudolf Bing	1947–49
Ian Hunter	1950–55
Robert Ponsonby	1956–60
George Henry Lascelles, 7th Earl of Harewood	1961–65
Peter Diamand	1966–78
John Drummond	1979–83
Frank Dunlop	1984–92
Brian McMaster	1993–

The Artistic Director is responsible to the Festival Society's governing body, its Council. This consists of 21 members, seven currently nominated by Edinburgh District Council, with the Lord Provost as Chairman, seven elected by the Society, one each nominated by the Edinburgh Chambers of Commerce and Edinburgh Trades Council, and two co-opted by the Council itself.

The Festival administration and box offices are presently located in Market Street, just round the corner from the bottom of Cockburn Street. Proposals are currently being considered for a move to the empty Highland Tolbooth church in the Lawnmarket area, and this would present the Festival with a more prominent profile, as well as allowing a social meeting place for Festival-goers, something the accommodation at the present headquarters does not permit.

Income from its own ticket sales comprises 30 per cent of the Festival's budget, but subsidies are received from the Scottish Arts Council and the two local authorities (at the time of writing), Edinburgh District and Lothian Regional Councils, making up 40 per cent. Business sponsorship is a growing, and indispensable, source of revenue (22 per

FESTIVALS	EVENTS	VENUES	AUDIENCE	YEAR
International Festival	205	13	472,000	1992
Festival Fringe	1,996	140	585,600	1992
Military Tattoo	1	1	209,000	1993
Science Festival	400	51	200,000	1994
Jazz Festival	275	20	65,000	1993
Book Festival (Biennial)	184	1	65,000	1993
Children's Festival	80	1	37,000	1993
Film Festival	155	3	25,000	1993
Folk Festival	50	6	8,000	1993
Hogmanay Festival	2	3 (est)	150,000	1994–5

cent), individual performances and exhibitions being supported by commercial companies, as well as through donations to the Edinburgh International Festival Endowment Fund. The remaining eight per cent of income comes from merchandising and broadcasting fees.

The extent to which the Scottish tourist budget is stimulated by the Festival is less easily computed; in 1992 the Scottish Tourist Board estimated that all the city's Festivals generated a total of £72 million for the Scottish economy, and resulted in the creation of 3,034 jobs, although it appears that the latter is a theoretical figure obtained by dividing visitors' estimated expenditure by an average wage quotient. Suffice to say that the Festival has a positive effect on local business and hotel turnover.

Following the recent introduction of computerised ticketing, it has become possible to produce a profile of the geographical location of Festival devotees, the 1992 survey showing, to nobody's great surprise, a predominance of both local people and English-based ticket purchasers. Around ten per cent of ticket purchasers have addresses in London and south-east England, a welcome statistic at a time when the Scottish tourist industry has recently shown an overall fall in the number of English visitors. Analysis of this English sample showed that nearly half of those coming from the London area were new patrons, confirming a high turnover quotient.

The survey also disclosed a dearth of bookings from people in Strathclyde, despite its comparative proximity. One Glasgow-based journalist suggested at the time that this was because Glasgow's own cultural life could stand comparison with Edinburgh's at any time, although one wonders if the same sheer range of cultural choice is available in Glasgow (or anywhere else) in those three weeks in August.

So, when the *Guardian* newspaper declared in 1994 that 'Edinburgh's is everybody's favourite arts festival', this was not totally correct. Perhaps the Glaswegians' attitude is similar to the couple featured in the Monty Python TV sketch; they would love to visit the Edinburgh Festival, provided they don't have to travel to Edinburgh! (In defence of Strathclyde-based Festival visitors, it must be pointed out that their 1995 attendance statistics improved when late-night rail services connecting the two cities continued until well after midnight.)

The first-ever Festival event took place on 24 August 1947 (*see* History *below*). This was very late in the holiday year, and a decision was made in the late 1970s to begin the event, by now a three-week celebration of the arts, in mid-August, with only a few days overspill into September. This followed complaints from performers that the third week held in mid-September was too late in the year to ensure tourist-boosted audiences. The fact that August was chosen as the month to launch the Festival in 1947 is perhaps indicative of the English influences behind its establishment, (after all, July is the holiday period in Scotland's central belt), but this has at least guaranteed continuing interest from visitors from south of the Border.

One very sad coincidence was the choice of an opening date which clashed with the return to school for the city's pupils after the summer holidays. For around 30 years, the message came over loud and clear to successive generations of Edinburgh's youngsters attending state schools – 'Europe's greatest arts festival is about to begin, but it's not for the likes of you'. Even although the city's state schools strove to organise class visits to exhibitions, the timetabling was too tight, at the beginning of the new academic year, for this to happen to any major extent. Bringing the Festival's dates forward at least gave local youngsters a chance to 'festivalise' on their own initiative, if they had not been put off already by the event's image of being intended exclusively for visitors from the south.

In spite of fairly chronic accommodation difficulties, the Edinburgh International Festival is a confirmed success story, as its countless numbers of imitators up and down the land confirms. Its success can, of course, create a difficult standard for the city to follow for the rest of the year. For example, a recent Consumers Association publication, while generally giving Edinburgh a 'good review' commented on the city's 'reputation for spending six months going to bed early to recover from its Festival, and the following five months going to bed early to prepare for the next'.

History

Historians of the Festival appear to agree that its establishment is owed almost entirely to the determination of Rudolf Bing, first general manager of the Glyndebourne Opera House, that the Second World War should not bring down a curtain on Europe's cultural activities. Bing claimed that he had visited a number of towns and cities close to London, such as Oxford and Cambridge, hoping to establish a postwar festival of the arts, but received no encouragement from the local authorities concerned.

Edinburgh, however, was much more responsive. With the local officer of the British Council, Harvey Wood, acting as a catalyst, Lord Provost Sir John Falconer extolled the advantages of Edinburgh as a centre for an arts-orientated event. Bing was impressed and grateful. 1947 was seen as the earliest possible starting time, and Edinbugh Corporation and the Arts Council were two of the principal funding bodies. Interestingly, one of Bing's Glyndebourne associates later recalled that the Festival's first director had considered the Scottish capital as a potential festival site as far back as 1939.

In our own time, with great films, operas, music, and drama available for only a little pressure on the TV remote control switch, it is difficult to imagine just how epoch-making Bing's initiative was. In the mid-1940s, people had forgotten what it was like for a logistical initiative to be put into operation that was not intended to kill the maximum possible number of people in another country, or minimise casualties here. The Festival grew in that infertile soil of disappointed expectations, in a nation still echoing to the sound of marching feet, air raid sirens, and aeroplane engines.

Bing and the Edinburgh city fathers of the time were probably unaware that the capital had already hosted three festivals of music, in 1815, 1819, and 1824. Such venues as Parliament House, the Theatre Royal, and Corri's Rooms (later the second Theatre Royal in Broughton Street, *see* THEATRES) were used. According to an anonymous diarist, whose journal is preserved in the City Libraries, the third of these made a profit of only £500, a considerable reduction on the previous two, and this appeared to seal the fate of Edinburgh's first cultural festivals, which were obviously intended to be money-making ventures.

One of the highlights of the first (1947) International Festival was the reuniting of conductor Bruno Walter with his beloved Vienna Philharmonic, an event whose significance is perhaps not immediately apparent to us nowadays. The following year saw the revolutionary production of the traditional Scottish play *The Thrie Estates* by Sir David Lyndsay, take place in the Church of Scotland's Assembly Hall, a superb example of Theatre in the Round, and a revival of a classic of Scottish literature. Kathleen Ferrier was another immortal name associated with the early years of a cultural event which has become one of the most important in the British calendar.

Edinburgh's International Festival was on its way.

EDINBURGH FILM FESTIVAL (DRAMBUIE INTERNATIONAL FILM FESTIVAL)

Held each August simultaneously with the International Festival, the Film Festival is believed to be the oldest cinema event of its kind in continuous existence. Begun as an eight-day event in 1947, at the initiative of the Edinburgh Film Guild, and under the direction of Forsyth Hardy, the Filmfest rapidly forged itself a reputation for championing documentary films; indeed 'Documentary' was part of this festival's original title, although feature films spiced the programme from the start.

The festival was headed by, among others, Forsyth Hardy and by Murray Grigor, the latter from 1968 to 1973, working from the Edinburgh Film Guild cinema premises in, firstly, Hill Street – where the cinema incongruously had a fireplace on a side wall – and then in Randolph Crescent (until 1982), while hiring commercial cinemas for the showing of the more popular films. Robert Flaherty, Carl Dreyer, Fred Zinnemann, and John Huston (who described Edinburgh's as 'the only film festival that's worth a damn'), were among the early distinguished visitors to an event that was successful, if sometimes regarded as a little dull.

Grigor's appointment made the Filmfest jump a few sprocket holes. It was obvious that TV had virtually killed off the cinema documentary, and Grigor successfully turned Edinburgh's attention to young feature-film makers often working independently, like Roger Corman. Grigor's successor, Lynda Myles, continued this trend after taking over in 1973. Championing the 'bratpack' concept of film director, Myles arranged early showings of the work of Scorsese and De Palma, and continued the presentation of retrospectives. Associated publications issued by the Film Festival at this time teetered dangerously on the precipice of pretentiousness, but at least the festival's continuance was guaranteed, even as costs threatened to overwhelm an event which was badly underfunded.

In 1982 Jim Hickey succeeded as event director, starting with a vintage crop of showings of such films as *Angel* and *The Draughtsman's Contract*, with Hickey working from the (eventually) more commodious base of Filmhouse in Lothian Road. In 1983 a programme called 'Scotch Reels' was held, compiled by Murray and Barbara Grigor and contributing considerably to the study of Scotland's place in cinema fact and myth.

In 1989–91, David Robinson was in charge, introducing a range of competitive prizes, whose previous absence, apart from the Golden Thistle Award, was very much a characteristic of a film festival more dominated by critics and cineastes than by the box office. In 1992, Penny Thomson took over as director, with Mark Cousins succeeding her in 1995. A commercial sponsor was prominent from 1994 onwards.

More information can be had from the Festival's office at Filmhouse, 88 Lothian Road.

In 1992, the Scottish Tourist Board noted with approval that Edinburgh's was one of the few film festivals in the world to offer tickets to ordinary filmgoers, and those resident in the Edinburgh area made up nearly half of the festival's audience. A survey conducted by the STB that year found that the average festival filmgoer was likely to be male, and among the youngest attending any of the Edinburgh festivals.

While it is probably impossible to nominate the best film ever shown by the Film Festival (so many have gone on to achieve acclaim worldwide), regular festival-goers may agree that the film which was *worst* received at Edinburgh was the experimental feature *Tom, Tom, the Piper's son* (1979). Its constant repetition of the same silent images – backwards, upside-down etc – cleared the Cameo in record time.

The history of the Film Festival is told by its first director, the late Forsyth Hardy, in his book *Slightly Mad and Full of Dangers* (*see* BIBLIOGRAPHY). Although highly informative, the book's reviewers felt that it was disappointingly bland, failing to 'spill the beans' on what must have been a Festival organisation riven by conflicting ideologies from time to time, but which nevertheless is older than Cannes and can claim to be Edinburgh's contribution to Life's big picture.

FESTIVAL FRINGE

Since its inception, Edinburgh's International Festival has been accompanied by a 'fringe' event, an unhomogeneous collection of plays, reviews, sketches, and comedy routines not invited to participate in the official Festival (and in many cases, never likely to be!).

The Fringe has now become, in terms of sheer quantity, even bigger than the Festival itself, the 1995 event comprising 13,378 performances of 1,237 events performed by 8,517 individuals in 174 venues. No wonder that Edinburgh's principal annual event has been described as 'the Festival with the Fringe on top'. The Fringe is particularly popular with young visitors from the south-east of England, a Scottish Tourist Board survey which disclosed this fact also discovering that the popularity of the Fringe was largely spread by word of mouth, although generous covering of Fringe events on television, particularly the BBC, can only have been extremely helpful.

The Fringe prides itself on its casual easy-going nature. Far from being invited to take part, Fringe performers, whether individuals or groups, simply turn up and perform. The Festival Fringe Society, based at 170 High Street since 1977, assists in finding both living and performing accommodation, and the latter (the venue) has to be licensed by the local authority, currently the District Council, as suitable and safe for the public. Otherwise, there is no centralisation, no control, and almost no censorship. This has fuelled criticism of the Fringe; its anarchic, 'anyone can be an entertainer' character, can frequently provide a platform for the bombastic, the ill-prepared, and sometimes the downright untalented.

Answering criticisms that 90 per cent of Fringe productions were 'rubbish', a former Fringe organiser acknowledged in 1980 that this was so, but maintained that the good productions were well worth searching for, among the dross. Since that time, an overall improvement in the average standard of performance has been detectable; a number of prestigious awards from such sponsors as The Scotsman and Perrier have attracted an increasing number of professional performers, and audiences themselves are perhaps more discerning. This is rather more than can be said for many of the critics; productions often highly praised in Edinburgh by English reviewers have a tendency to be ill-received if transferred to London, almost as if visiting critics had been in too much of holiday mood!

In recent years, the Fringe has seen a move towards stand-up comedy as opposed to full-scale theatrical drama as the backbone of the event; this has gone very much hand in hand with the setting up of such entertainment complexes as the Assembly (at the Assembly Rooms) or the Pleasance, both of which even go so far as to produce their own listings. The Fringe Programme is in itself a major production in printing logistics, one which the Loanhead firm of MacDonald Lindsay Pindar can be justly proud of over a number of years. Indeed, Fringe performers have praised the organisation of the Festival Fringe, in particular its provision of useful information to would-be actors, directors, and comedians who see Edinburgh as an important step in their careers.

While the Fringe will always have its critics, it can be credited with taking culture a little less seriously than the 'official' Festival, which is often a mite too intellectual for its own good. The Fringe attracts far more media attention – most of it favourable and indulgent – than the 'serious' Festival; no small consideration in attracting visitors. And any institution that brings the work of such writers as Tom Stoppard or such performers as Hinge and Bracket and Rowan Atkinson to the fore, has some claim to a smile from Posterity.

EDINBURGH MILITARY TATTOO

The first Edinburgh Festival, in 1947, featured a closing ceremony on the Castle Esplanade, and those present must have glimpsed the potential for the site to play host to a military tattoo complete with the striking backdrop of Scotland's best-known castle. So it was that in 1950 the first Edinburgh Military Tattoo was held, attracting a nightly audience of 7,000 in makeshift seating.

To call the Tattoo a success is to understate the case; this is the only Edinburgh festival which can sell its tickets to package tour operators, and, according to a 1992 Scottish Tourist Board survey, generates more tourist spending than all the other festivals put together. Audiences regularly total over 200,000 for an event taking place over approximately 20 evenings, two performances per evening, the event beginning one week before the International Festival itself, and terminating one week earlier. The open air seating is a considerable improvement on the improvised galleries of previous years, not least in the speed with which it can be erected and disassembled.

While Tattoo audiences were estimated to spend £44 million out of £72 million generated for the Scottish economy by Edinburgh's festivals (nearly £20 million out of £44 million in the city itself and Lothians), Tattoo visitors have shown a disappointing lack of interest in the other festivals taking place in the capital. Its lack of 'cultural' content has tended to class the Tattoo as an event not wholly wedded to the International Festival, merely another city attraction which happens to take place at around the same time of year. This is an unfortunate mistake for Festival administrators to make; the Military Tattoo is a success story without equal on the Festival scene, and this is surely a case for the old military maxim to be brought into play – 'always reinforce success'. Festival organisers should consider ways of encouraging Tattoo visitors to dip their toes in the cultural pond!

EDINBURGH FESTIVALS CREATED SINCE 1977

TELEVISION FESTIVAL

For a city which lives in a 'TV shadow' (*see* BROADCASTING), Edinburgh is perhaps a surprising location for one of the television industry's principal annual meetings. First convened in 1977, and financed jointly at that time by the BBC and ITV, 200 programme-makers met to discuss issues facing their profession. Since then, the festival, held over the first or second weekend of the main International Festival, has grown hugely, and has had to move from its first venue, the Physicans' Hall in Queen Street, to find more spacious accommodation. The annual keynote lecture has attracted some of the biggest names in the TV world as speakers – from media moguls like Rupert Murdoch to programme executives like Janet Street-Porter.

In 1995 the organisers admitted they were

considering other cities as possible venues, as pressure on hotel accommodation made it impossible for the festival to negotiate discounts for large numbers of delegates – in other words, if TV executives didn't want the rooms at full price, the hotels could rent them easily to tourists. Hopefully, this problem can be budgeted for, as Edinburgh in August is a useful opportunity for television producers to catch new talent on the Fringe, and in turn makes Edinburgh even more attractive to new talent.

FOLK FESTIVAL

First held in April 1979, the Edinburgh Folk Festival has overcome the reservations of its critics to take its place among the periodic attractions of the Festival City. When first proposed by the Scottish Tourist Board in 1978, the suggestion of a folk festival prompted criticism that it would attract only the low-spending 'knapsack brigade' as one city businessman put it, and this criticism had a certain validity, the 1993 event, for example, attracting a total audience of only 8,000, whose spending habits are unrecorded. However, this is to overlook the point that a festival has other purposes than just making money, and Scotland's long tradition of folksong was well worth glorifying through a festival in the capital city.

The first Folk Festival opened with a concert in the Odeon Cinema, and operated on a budget of £13,000, much of it donated by a brewing company.

JAZZ FESTIVAL

Founded in 1979, when 12 bands totalling 100 players were involved, the Edinburgh International Jazz Festival is usually held in the week preceding the full International Festival each August. In 1995, the event included a series of modern jazz concerts, as well as a Mardi Gras in the Grassmarket, a network of Old Town pubs hosting recitals, and an outdoor event. St Giles was imaginatively used as a venue, as well as the more conventional concert halls including the Festival Theatre and Queen's Hall, and an impressive list of sponsors were involved.

The festival is produced by a limited company run by officials and an army of volunteers, reporting to a board of directors on which the Edinburgh District and Lothian Regional Council, two of the principal sponsors, are represented.

BOOK FESTIVAL

Differing from the other Edinburgh festivals in being held only every second year, the Edinburgh Book Festival occupies Charlotte Square Gardens for a fortnight in August. The 1995 event engaged approximately 200 authors to talk about or read their work, with about half the events being provided free of charge once an overall entry fee had been charged. Attendance in 1993 was 65,000, and the organisers were expecting 70,000 in 1995.

Since its inception in 1983 the Festival has earned itself an admirable reputation for being a national book event which is not 'trade-driven'; the organisers are more concerned in attracting public interest than in promoting a trade fair for the publishing and bookselling professions.

EDINBURGH FLING (SPRING FLING)

Unique among the city's festivals in having a political origin, the Edinburgh Fling was begun as the Spring Fling by the District

Council's Labour majority in 1985. From the start, the emphasis has been on public participation through groups, in performing drama, organising music evenings, or talks. In successive recent years (1994 and 1995), the theme of the Fling was 'My town, your town'; in 1996 it was to celebrate the centenary of the cinema (but unfortunately this was cancelled). The Fling appears successful in encouraging young people to become involved in community affairs, and is very much an Edinburgh Peoples' Festival.

EDINBURGH INTERNATIONAL SCIENCE FESTIVAL

Founded in 1989, Edinburgh's Science Festival is a natural product of the city's prowess in science over the centuries. The Festival has the double aim of developing the science and technological base in the capital, while making science and technology more accessible to the public, particularly the young. In 1993 it was the fourth largest of Edinburgh's festivals in terms of audience size and second only to the Fringe in its number of venues.

Operated by a commercial company which is the offshoot of a charity, Edinburgh International Festival of Science and Technology, the Festival is sponsored by the District Council and the Scottish Office. The Festival is usually held in April each year, 1994's attracting an audience of 200,000 (up from 58,000 in its first year) to about 400 events at 51 venues. Eighty-six per cent of the audience are Scottish-based.

A regular feature of the event is the geodesic Science Dome in Princes Street Gardens. This is a centre where visitors are encouraged to adopt a 'hands on' approach to science, and where demonstrations and projects, such as building a bird's nest by hand, can be tackled. Exhibitions and lectures make up what is invariably a fascinating programme. One of the features of the Festival is the award of the Edinburgh Medal, awarded to suitable recipients from any part of the world for their contribution to science.

EDINBURGH CHILDREN'S FESTIVAL

Children have been able to enjoy their own Edinburgh Festival since 1990. This is held annually, in late May and early June, in a tented village in Inverleith Park, and attracts a high proportion of school parties.

EDINBURGH HOGMANAY FESTIVAL

New Year has been seen in by revellers outside the Tron Kirk in Edinburgh for many years. From 1992, the local authorities, Edinburgh District and Lothian Region, decided to turn the occasion into an even greater attraction for residents and tourists alike by organising a programme of events beginning a couple of nights before Hogmanay.

A torchlight procession has become a feature of the new regular event, while on 31 December itself, popular entertainers are booked to play at the Ross Bandstand. Clear weather is hoped for, to ensure that the firework display immediately after midnight is spectacular. The public have taken to this with enthusiasm, no fewer than 150,000 spectators packing Princes Street from end to end in 1994/5 and nearly twice as many at the following Hogmanay. There were some 20 arrests in 1994/5; in contrast, London's celebration had three times as many arrests from a crowd half as big. Television coverage in 1994/5 was sparse, as one has grown to expect in the capital of Scotland.

The 1995/6 holiday event included the creation of a skating rink on the roof of the Waverley Market and a repeat of the highly successful formula of popular music, fireworks, and a torchlight procession. Local authorities, so often criticised for failures in public services, can be congratulated for their positive efforts to take New Year away from its deadly bottle-party image.

Films

Feature films made for the cinema rarely show a particular location to advantage, so Edinburgh's near-exclusion from the Silver Screen is perhaps a blessing. It can hardly be argued that police thrillers set in the barrios of Los Angeles or the housing schemes of Glasgow have made these cities more attractive to visitors, but they are more likely backgrounds for feature films than Edinburgh, with its beautiful views and rich story-telling heritage.

The fact that Edinburgh is not a broadcasting centre further reduces the capital's opportunity to capture the attention of film-makers. It is all very disappointing for a city which has inspired such cinema stalwarts as Sherlock Holmes, Dr Jekyll, Long John Silver, Burke and Hare, and Greyfriars Bobby.

The city has been used as a backdrop for some location shooting for a number of films which might reasonably have been expected to be set entirely in Edinburgh. It is perhaps to be expected that even Hollywood feature films with Scottish themes or backgrounds would use the city's topography only sketchily, given that most films are studio-based. For this reason it is understandable that such films as *The Thirty-Nine Steps* (the Hitchcock and Ralph Thomas versions), *Journey to the Centre of the Earth*, and the aforementioned *Greyfriars Bobby*, contain only token scenes shot in the city. However, this kind of token location-shooting has produced unusual results.

No film has made more eccentric use of Edinburgh locations than the 1959 feature *Battle of the Sexes*, recounting how a female American executive played havoc with the conservative management values of a staid Edinburgh business. The film-makers decided that the Royal Scottish Academy would be ideal as a railway station exterior, while the Queen's Park doubled as the Highlands! (Convincingly too!) *The Prime of Miss Jean Brodie* contained location footage in the city – street scenes were shot in Henderson Row and off the Grassmarket, but the bulk of the film was made in the studio.

Even the increasing use of hand-held cameras and faster filmstock has not greatly increased the city's role as a film backdrop. Independent film-makers will make films wherever finance is available, and Edinburgh has seen likely projects moved to other cities where backing can be more readily obtained. In 1994, the Glasgow Development Fund enjoyed a total budget of £343,000, and was prepared to invest £150,000 in a locally-made feature film such as the independent feature film *Shallow*

Grave, while the Edinburgh Development Fund was able to invest only £40,000 per annum in the development of film projects. Not surprisingly, *Shallow Grave*, although set in Edinburgh, was shot in Glasgow for 28 out of its 30 days location work.

Nevertheless, the makers of *Chariots of Fire* found that using Salisbury Crags as a backdrop, and the Café Royal for interior scenes, provided no obstacle to its Oscar-winning way, and Edinburgh-born actor Ian Charleson (1949–90) won high praise for his sensitive portrayal of athlete Eric Liddell who refused to run in the 1924 Olympics on a Sunday (*see* ATHLETICS).

Other, less well-known films have followed. Orkney film-maker Margaret Tait used stunning images of the city centre for her 1993 film *Blue Black Permanent* (with some financial help from Edinburgh District Council), and Gillies Mackinnon utilised Leith as a setting for an adaptation of the Manfred Karge play *Conquest of the South Pole*. Brian Crumlish's *Tickets for the Zoo* used local acting talent and was partly set at Corstorphine, and in Leith.

A series of films which mercifully omitted to emphasise their Edinburgh origin, was that featuring St Trinian's girls' school, so delightfully presided over by Alastair Sim in drag. The casting of an Edinburgh actor (perhaps Edinburgh's greatest) as headmistress was made doubly apt by the fact that the original for the school was the now-defunct St Trinnean's in Edinburgh (*see* SCHOOLS), an institution whose innocuous history fails to suggest any behavioural basis for spawning such films as *The Belles of St Trinians*! Sim, incidentally, was an elocution expert in Edinburgh who was so absorbed by amateur dramatics that he decided to try his luck professionally, going on to become one of Britain's greatest-ever character actors. His claim to having been Edinburgh's leading cinema eminence has been eclipsed by only one man – Sean Connery.

Born in the city's Fountainbridge area in 1930, Tom (Sean) Connery held a number of miscellaneous jobs in the city, including that of a lifeguard at the Portobello outdoor pool, but his bodybuilding supplied him with the muscle required to successfully pursue an acting career as a leading man. The decision to chose him to play James Bond was entirely suitable, as Ian Fleming's hero fictionally attended Fettes College in the city. Connery later commented that he had visited the school regularly – when delivering milk.

Connery starred as Bond in five films in the 1960s – *Dr No*, *From Russia with Love*, *Goldfinger*, *Thunderball*, and *You Only Live Twice*, and one in the early 1970s – *Diamonds are Forever*. More demanding, but less popular, roles in the 1970s and '80s flagged up Connery's determination to be taken seriously as an actor, although he could not resist returning to the part of 007 in 1983 with *Never Say Never Again*. Connery subsequently won an Oscar for Best Supporting Actor in the film *The Untouchables* in 1988, and his home city honoured him by making him a Freeman in 1991. The public's demand to attend the award ceremony in the Usher Hall exceeded the ticket supply nine times over (*see* FREEDOM OF THE CITY). At the last count, there were six biographies in print about him.

Possibly the only film which has portrayed the reality of working-class life in the city is *My Childhood*, directed by Newcraighall's Bill Douglas (1934–91). This evokes the gritty lifestyle of the coalmining village in 1945 (*see* VILLAGES), and is still regarded as one of Britain's finest postwar films. *My Ain Folk* and *My Way Home* complete an impressive trilogy. When Douglas died in 1991, he was mourned as a talent lost, having completed only four feature films, the fourth and last being *Comrades*, the story of the Tolpuddle Martyrs.

The Edinburgh Film Festival (*see* FESTIVALS) was established in 1947 and featured documentaries from the outset. As it happens, Edinburgh was the location of one of the most historic prewar documentaries, directed by John Grierson in 1934 – *Granton Trawler*. This featured a voyage of the Leith-registered trawler *Isabella Greig*. In 1947 the city of Edinburgh itself was the subject of a whimsical quasi-documentary called *Waverley Steps*, directed by John Eldridge. Featuring a day in the life of a Danish seaman visiting Leith, and a number of Scottish characters, the film lacked a central theme binding the characters together in a strengthened story-line. If nothing more, Eldridge's work is an exciting peepshow of approximately what everyday life was like back in 1947. Much of the city's immediate postwar atmosphere has been recorded in the 16mm films made by a group of teachers at Norton Park School in the early 1950s, particularly *The Singing Street* and *The Grey Metropolis*.

Despite the setting up of the Edinburgh and Lothian Screen Industries Office, intended to encourage the use of the city for film and media events, Edinburgh still awaits a feature film which will sufficiently convey the beauty and drama of its cityscape. In 1952 Forsyth Hardy, the Film Festival's first director, wrote :

> I see no limit to the films which could be made about Edinburgh. Perhaps among them will be one which will look both at the face of Edinburgh and the character behind it, a film which will proclaim Edinburgh to the modern world as a distinctive unit in that world.

Perhaps that is a contradiction in terms – feature films rarely show their locations to advantage anyway. Edinburgh citizens should possibly be grateful to avoid the cameraman's lens.

This was proved yet again when, as this encyclopedia went to press, the film *Trainspotting* was released, adapted from the Irvine Welsh novel (*see* LITERATURE) and featuring the Edinburgh drugs scene. Filmed in Glasgow, its token location shots of Edinburgh have irritated some city cinema-goers, and the film-makers ditched many of the subtleties of the Edinburgh versus Leith rivalry in producing an account of drug abuse which failed to address the question as to why Edinburgh should have such a major drug culture (*see* CRIME and SOCIAL WORK).

Fire Fighting

Edinburgh's fire fighting facility is the Lothian and Borders Fire Brigade, the

Firemaster being answerable to the regional Fire Board. The principal headquarters are in Lauriston Place, with stations in the city at Tollcross, Macdonald Road, Kirkbrae (Liberton), Sighthill and Newcraighall. The strength of the brigade was 1,056 in 1995, spread over the entire Lothians and Borders area. There were 72 fire appliances available.

In 1993, the brigade answered over 17,000 calls (throughout Lothian and Borders), a slight decrease from the previous three years' figures. In the same period, the brigade experienced a 50 per cent reduction in the number of malicious calls, no doubt due to the introduction of new telephone technology; curiously, the Lothian and Borders Brigade had suffered more from this nuisance than any other UK force.

Not surprisingly, the brigade places great emphasis on educating the community in greater safety consciousness and in a more responsible attitude to the emergency services. It maintains the Museum of Fire, including a museum of fire-fighting vehicles, the Braidwood-Rushbrook collection at Lauriston Place, its headquarters and former principal city fire station.

History

Edinburgh's early fire service was synonymous with the name of James Braidwood. In 1824 Braidwood was employed by the police to take charge of the fire brigade; at that time the police and fire brigade worked together and had the same pay structure. But with its closely-packed housing in the Old Town, Edinburgh needed a specialised fire-fighting service instead of being yet another

added responsibility of the Commissioners of Police.

Before 1824, fire fighting had been carried on without a guaranteed water supply, or any means of transporting large amounts of water to a conflagration. On 20 March 1702, the Town Council decreed that 12 prominent citizens had to assume the role of 'Firemasters', and leather hoses and 300 leather buckets were kept in reserve by the Town Guard. What water could be collected from the city supply (see WATER SUPPLY) was administered with the use of 'squirts' (small hand pumps). In 1771 a number of insurance companies formed fire-fighting crews, with limited expertise and an even more limited remit to protect only the property invested with that company, leading to the unhappy sight of 'firemen' standing by as buildings, insured with another concern, burned to the ground (see also INSURANCE).

In the 1820s, six insurance companies saw the logic in contributing to fire fighting on a communal basis, and appropriate vehicles were constructed, with Braidwood appointed as Master of Fire Engines on £50 a year, implying that he probably kept on his police career at first. The force was called the Edinburgh Municipal Fire Brigade.

Braidwood's force was still in the throes of being organised when a conflagration, apparently with two separate seats of fire, took hold in the Tron and Parliament Square, in October 1824. The woeful attempts to put these out were made worse by the huge number of spectators, while civic figures vied with one another in shouting conflicting instructions to the hapless fire-fighters.

This disaster allowed Braidwood to assume total command of his force, which he soon had exercising at four o'clock in the mornings, and even lowering themselves down the 75 feet of the North Bridge to accustom themselves to attempting rescue from Edinburgh's 12-storey tenements. His equipment included mobile fire-pumps, manually operated and propelled, kept at high points of the city (Parliament Square, where the brigade was headquartered, Rose Street, and the West Port), to make man-hauling easier downhill. He even designed a crossbow which would fire a twine over a high building, allowing a rope to be hauled over and secured at the other side to haul a collapsible ladder up to a high window.

Braidwood, meanwhile, had proved too innovative for Edinburgh to hold on to, and he took up the prestigious appointment of Superintendent of the London Fire Brigade establishment in 1833. He died fighting the Tooley Street fire near London Bridge in 1861.

Improvements in fire-fighting techniques were limited by the quantity of the water supply available in Edinburgh, and it was not until 1873 that a horse-drawn fire engine with steam-powered pumps was introduced. In contrast, the independent burgh of Leith, with its own fire brigade from 1837, bought two such machines. There was an unfortunate incident in 1897 when the Edinburgh force tackled a blaze just over the municipal border in Leith,

The Great Fire in autumn 1824 was a disaster for Edinburgh in the short term, but provided the impetus for the setting up of the world's first professional local authority fire brigade. This print was available commercially within two days of the fire, selling for 1/6d (7 ½ pence). (Edinburgh City Libraries)

arriving before the local crew, the latter promptly disconnecting the Edinburgh hose before their own was ready for use!

The service reached something of a nadir under Richard Williams, who had to be replaced as Firemaster in 1876, due to his unprofessional, indeed apparently indifferent, attitude to a fire in the Stockbridge area. Improvements were made under his successors Samuel Wilkins and Arthur Pordage, with the firemen becoming full-time, and horses being permanently used for engine haulage, somewhat belatedly. Soon, the Edinburgh brigade was forging a reputation for efficiency that has never been lost; it was even said that the Edinburgh fire horses would answer the alarm bell by making their own way to their places in front of the engines.

Braidwood's successors were James Paterson (1832–1839), Robert Hardie (1839–1846), John Wood (1846–1849), John Mitchell (1849–1872), Richard Williams (1872–76), Samuel Wilkins (1876–1895), Arthur Pordage (1896–1927), Peter Methven (1927–1941), William Bell Muir (1941–1948), Alexander Craig, (1948–1962), Frank Rushbrook (1962–1970), James Anderson (1970–80), William Kerr (1980–1984), Richard Edmonds (1985–1989), Peter Scott (1989–1994) and Colin Cranston (1994–).

Perhaps the most memorable of Edinburgh's fires broke out at the Empire Theatre (now the Festival Theatre) in Nicolson Street on 9 May 1911. An electrical fuse set fire to highly-combustible props being used by the famous illusionist and magician, Lafayette. While the safety curtain protected the audience, who made an orderly exit, no fewer than 11 people,

one of them Lafayette, perished backstage, and eight were injured, including a fireman. (*see also* THEATRES)

In August 1941 the nation's fire-fighting services were effectively nationalised, with Edinburgh coming under the jurisdiction of the South Eastern Fire Brigade, answerable to the Secretary of State for Scotland, and administered by councillors from Edinburgh and eight other authorities. In 1975, with local government reorganisation, the new regions were given responsibility for fire safety. The reorganisation of 1996 is expected to create a new brigade, but details were unknown at the time of writing.

Firth of Forth

Edinburgh's coastline on the Firth of Forth is approximately 16 miles (25.6 kilometres) in length, stretching from near the southern base of the Forth Road Bridge (*see* BRIDGES) at South Queensferry, to the mouth of the Brunstane Burn (*see* RIVERS AND STREAMS) just west of Musselburgh.

This length has been the northern boundary of the local government area since 1975 (although there are islands in the Forth which come under Edinburgh's jurisdiction, *see* ISLANDS). At various times Edinburgh's shoreline boundary has been aligned more to the east – that is, starting with its western boundary at the River Almond and stretching eastwards to the Levenhall area, immediately east of Musselburgh racecourse. These were the exact parameters laid down by James VI for the city of Edinburgh, although disputed by

Musselburgh, and subsequently modified (*see* LOCAL GOVERNMENT).

Edinburgh's present-day coastline constitutes the southern shore of the Firth of Forth ('firth' is Scots for 'arm of the sea'). This is the River Forth in its final, tidal, form as it becomes part of the North Sea. Having risen near Aberfoyle, the Forth flows for 115 miles (184 kilometres) before losing its identity at an imaginary line drawn between Dunbar in East Lothian and Fife Ness in the 'wee kingdom'. The firth is just over 17 miles (27.2 kilometres) wide at its greatest extent.

The coastline forming most of the city's northern boundary contains three SSSIs (Sites of Special Scientific Interest) in the stretch between Cramond eastwards to Fisherrow. For much of that distance it is intensively commercialised, the 1994 *Scottish Abstract of Statistics* published by the Scottish Office, classifying 10.4 miles (16 kilometres) of the coastline as 'developed', despite the inclusion of the SSSIs.

Ironically, the coast west from Cramond to Dalmeny is probably the most scenic of the whole stretch, and provides considerable wildlife interest. Commercial utilities on the shore include the oil-loading terminal at Hound Point, Dalmeny, where North Sea oil pumped from Grangemouth is loaded into tankers of up to 325,000 tons. Farther east are Leith Docks and the harbours at Granton and Newhaven. Both of the latter two are tidal; Leith has a lock entry which maintains high water in the Water of Leith well into the city (*see* PORTS and RIVERS AND STREAMS).

There are promenades and beaches of varying quality at Cramond/Silverknowes,

1995 was the year of the Tall Ships visit to Leith, an event witnessed by over a million people. In this picture the Polish barquentine Pogoria slips into the tranquil waters of Leith's western harbour a few days before the event. (The Scotsman)

and at Portobello (from Seafield to Joppa). In 1994 the *Good Beaches Guide* opined that the three Edinburgh beaches had 'not a lot to commend them', pointing out that Portobello failed EC mandatory standards. Cramond and Silverknowes achieved one star status (out of a possible four stars), and passed the EC standard, but it was scarcely a ringing endorsement of the capital's seashore.

Piers once existed at Trinity and Portobello. The former was a 500 feet (150 metres) long structure suspended from four wooden towers, lasting from 1821 to 1898 (look for the Old Chain Pier bar between Granton and Newhaven). The 1,250 feet (375 metres) long Portobello pier was constructed in 1870–71 at the foot of Bath Street by Thomas Bouch, designer of the first (short-lived) Tay Bridge. It was dismantled

Eastern Edinburgh and the Firth of Forth, as seen from the northern slope of Arthur's Seat. One of most prominent buildings in view is the new stand for Hibernian's ground, Easter Road.

in 1917 when considered unsafe, but during its working life was a recognised port of call for all the firth's steamers, and the father of this Encyclopedia's author used to recall the pierrots in the Portobello Pier Show. (For details of Forth cruising in yesteryear, see the book by Ian Brodie listed in the BIBLIOGRAPHY under Transport).

Ferries operated to and from Fife from Trinity and Newhaven until Granton harbour was available, and this only ceased to be a ferry port in 1993. Nowadays the only ferry in the area is a rowboat crossing the Almond (*see* FERRIES). Local oyster and mussel fisheries no longer exist in the Forth because of the effects of sea-dumped sewage, and even nowadays information on water quality should be sought before swimming at Portobello. Lifeboats operate from North Berwick and South Queensferry.

Edinburgh citizens can be forgiven for thinking that the 1995 Tall Ships Race represented the finest assembly of shipping seen in the Forth this century, but probably the greatest tonnage of ships ever assembled in the Forth was in 1919 when the defeated German High Seas Fleet sailed into the estuary to report to Admiral Beatty commanding Britain's own Grand Fleet. Beatty ordered the lowering of the German flag, and set in motion the repatriation of the German officers and sailors which might have been handled more sensitively, possibly avoiding the mass scuttling at Scapa Flow later that year (*see* MILITARY HISTORY).

The Forth lost nearly all its military traffic in 1995, when Rosyth naval base closed on 7 November after almost 90 years' service, although the neighbouring dockyard will continue to refit naval vessels.

Football

Edinburgh has two senior association football teams – Heart of Midlothian and Hibernian. A third, Meadowbank Thistle, has just, at the time of writing, moved its base out of the city to Livingston, West Lothian. Three other sides once played senior football in Edinburgh – Edinburgh City, Leith Athletic, and St Bernard's. The last named won the Scottish Cup as recently as 1895, only seven years before Hibernian's 'latest' triumph in that competition.

Hearts are based at Tynecastle Park, on Gorgie Road, although its main entrance is in McLeod Street. Hibernian's ground is Easter Road, about 300 yards east of that thoroughfare, on Albion Road. In 1993/4 both clubs announced that they were abandoning plans to seek permission and financial backing to construct new stadia in the city's Green Belt, at Hermiston (Hearts) and Straiton (Hibs), but would continue to play at their traditional homes.

The performance record of these clubs was second to none in the 15 years after the Second World War, but has been very poor ever since. Indeed, in the 25 seasons since 1970, the city of Edinburgh has seen its teams bring home silverware only twice, out of a possible 75 competitions entered, and on each occasion it was the League Cup, won by Hibernian. Hearts have won nothing in that period, and neither club has won a European trophy. In comparison with other cities, Edinburgh's record is as shown on the bar chart on page 123.

It is difficult to escape the conclusion that, if they cannot offer Edinburgh football fans a greater return for their loyalty, Hearts and Hibs should seriously consider merging. English cities of a similar size to Edinburgh (between one-third and one-half of a million population) provide an interesting comparison. Like Edinburgh, Bristol has two senior teams, neither of which has distinguished itself in postwar football, while Leeds, with one side, has an impressive record, winning a number of League championships, and coming within an ace of lifting the European Cup. A single city team should enable players and supporters to focus on the goal of winning silverware, instead of coming out on top during an occasional 'derby', which is really nothing more than a distraction, and whose result certainly goes un-noticed on the continent.

In the late 1980s an ill-advised share flotation for Hibernian resulted in placing the club's commercial future very much in doubt. An offer by the then Hearts chairman, Mr Wallace Mercer, to purchase a controlling interest in the club, which he was perfectly entitled to do, created a sensation, but despite supporters' outrage, the matter could only be decided commercially, and Hibernian came very close to being acquired by their deadly rivals. It was not the way to create a single Edinburgh club, but the principle is still worth considering, given the two clubs' poor record on the park.

HEART OF MIDLOTHIAN
History
How and when Heart of Midlothian FC came to be formed is not entirely clear, although 1873 seems to be the generally agreed year of origin. It is assumed that the club took its name from a dance-hall in the Cowgate area, not far from where the

former Tolbooth stood until 1817, its fame as the city's prison enhanced by Sir Walter Scott's novel of the same name. Maroon colours appear to have been worn from the start of the club's history, even when its players were taking part in scratch games on the Meadows.

Hearts rapidly established themselves in the Scottish League, becoming champions twice between 1890 and 1914, and Scottish Cup-winners four times. In 1914 the club earned an unusual place in history when the entire first team volunteered for military service, joining the 16th Battalion of the Royal Scots. Seven of them failed to return, their sacrifice commemorated by the war memorial at Haymarket, and at least two of their number resumed their playing careers despite having been gassed when in the trenches.

The inter-war years were particularly difficult for Hearts, who failed to win the

The last Edinburgh team to have won the Scottish Cup was Hearts, and the antiquated bus and tram-lines indicate that this was some time ago. The date was 23 April 1956 and captain Freddie Glidden shows off the silverware as the party progresses westwards along Princes Street. (The Scotsman)

League again until 1957–58, but at least the team avoided relegation – until the end of the 1970s. Hearts, like Hibs, enjoyed halcyon days in the 20 years after the Second World War, winning the championship twice, contesting the European Cup on merit (unlike Hibs who pioneered British involvement in that competition by invitation, *see* below), and collecting the Scottish Cup in 1956, and the League Cup twice.

Much of this was attributable to the 'Terrible Trio' of Alfie Conn, Willie Bauld, and Jimmy Wardhaugh, who lacked only international-standard wingers to make up a complete forward-line on a par with Hibernian's 'Famous Five'. Willie Bauld was probably the most famous, and highly regarded player at Tynecastle, with his film star looks and ability in the air. Curiously, a successor to the centre-forward position, Alex Young, emerged as Bauld approached retirement age, just as Joe Baker matured in time to succeed Lawrie Reilly for the Hibernian number nine jersey. But manager Tommy Walker's most dependable player in postwar years was probably 'Iron Man' John Cumming, a half-back who didn't know when he was beaten and played through the victorious 1956 Cup Final win over Celtic with blood pouring from a head-wound.

In recent years, Hearts have won nothing but the First Division championship (effectively the old Second Division), in 1979–80, and that despite producing a number of outstanding young players from their own resources. Gary Mackay and John Robertson have both proved loyal servants to the club in recent seasons, coincidentally sharing the distinction of having scored a goal on their international debuts.

Both Mackay and Robertson were members of the Hearts side which came within a whisker of establishing a remarkable 'double' of League and Cup wins in season 1985–86. After going 31 games unbeaten, the Tynecastle team were defeated by Dundee seven minutes from time in their last League match to allow Celtic to pip them by the thinnest possible margin – how Hearts must have rued their early away form, when the odd equaliser would have won them the championship later! The side, by now exhausted and demoralised, lost to Aberdeen in the Cup Final a week after losing the League.

Now, with their Tynecastle ground remodelled extensively from 1994, the Gorgie club is looking to a brighter future.

MANAGERS 1948–96	
David McLean	(1948–51)
Tommy Walker	(1951–66)
John Harvey	(1966–69)
Bobby Seith	(1969–74)
John Hagart	(1974–77)
Willie Ormond	(1977–80)
Bobby Moncur	(1980–81)
Tony Ford	(1981–82)
Alec Macdonald	(1982–86)
Alec Macdonald/Sandy Jardine	(1986–88)
Alec Macdonald	(1988–90)
Joe Jordan	(1990–93)
Sandy Clark	(1993–94)
Tommy McLean	(1994–95)
Jim Jefferies	(1995–)

HIBERNIAN

History

Hibernian Football Club was formed from the Young Men's Christian Association in 1875, and from the start enjoyed the backing of the Irish expatriate community in the capital. Like Hearts, Hibs played their first matches on the Meadows, although by the late 1880s, a pitch close to Easter Road, south-west of the present site, was used. The team won the Scottish Cup in 1887 – and was to do so only once again, in 1902 – and the First Division in 1903.

Like Hearts, Hibs fell into the doldrums in the inter-war period. After being forced to move from a pitch at Craigentinny, the club was able to lease the present site of Easter Road stadium in 1924, but no trophies came that way, other than the Second Division championship in 1933, following relegation the previous season.

Hibs' golden age was the ten-year period after the Second World War. Overcoming the disappointment of a Cup Final defeat by Aberdeen in 1947 – after scoring in the first minute – Hibs went on to win three championships in five years, and were denied a fourth by the thinnest of margins. The main reason for this record was the presence of the Famous Five.

It may come as a surprise to younger football fans, but teams used to play with five forwards, and, managed by Willie Macartney (succeeded by Hugh Shaw in 1948), the Easter Road club assembled the best five anywhere. Gordon Smith, Bobby Johnstone, Lawrie Reilly, Eddie Turnbull, and Willie Ormond, were all internationalists, only one of them (Ormond, from Stenhousemuir) being signed from another senior club.

Gordon Smith was an elegant outside-right who scored a record number of goals for a winger, and was a respected captain of both club and country. A fitness fanatic, he had a lengthy playing career which

Only four of the Hibs Famous Five are shown in this 1988 picture, seen holding a framed photograph of all five of them when Messrs Smith, Johnstone, Reilly, Turnbull, and Ormond, were at their best in the 1950s. The remaining four (Willie Ormond was by now deceased) are pictured with two Hibernian directors. (The Scotsman)

exceeded Hibs' expectations and he was allowed to leave for Hearts, whom he helped to a League Championship, and then Dundee, where he repeated the feat. He became the only Scot to win three championship medals with different teams – none of them the Old Firm – and played for three different Scottish clubs in the European Cup.

At inside-right was Bobby Johnstone, who scored too many goals to be considered a midfield player, and who was the only one of the five to be transferred at the peak of his powers. Johnstone moved on to Manchester City in 1955, where he promptly helped his new team to lift the FA Cup. Wearing the number nine jersey was Lawrie Reilly, a centre-forward with an insatiable appetite for the game and able to shoot hard with either foot. Reilly was particularly effective at international level, his injury-time goal against England at Wembley in 1951 earning him the

soubriquet 'Last Minute Reilly', and his goal tally for Scotland came to be bettered only by Law and Dalglish.

Eddie Turnbull was perhaps less highly regarded than the other four forwards, the Scottish selectors deciding in 1952 to field them in a Scottish League representative match but without the Hibernian number ten. Turnbull, a penalty-kick specialist, went on to a distinguished career as a wing-half, performing well in the 1958 World Cup, and subsequently as manager of both Aberdeen and Hibs. The winger outside him, Willie Ormond, was a brave player who overcame three leg-breaks, and who claimed that if he could have played as well with his right foot as his left 'nobody would of heard of Pele'. Ormond went on to manage both Hearts and Hibs, and his tenure of the Scotland management in 1973-77 went largely unappreciated by the Glasgow press, despite his side winning the British Championship and returning from the 1974 World Cup Finals unbeaten.

The Hibs team of the day of course contained 11 players, the remaining six often being outshone by the Famous Five ahead of them. Occupying the yellow jersey was Tommy Younger, an international goalkeeper who was often flown in specially at weekends from national service in Germany. But perhaps the most highly respected member of the team was Bobby Combe, a player whose sheer versatility denied him regular selection in any one position, but who was still good enough to play for Scotland. Nifty footwork had always stood him in good stead – once when complimented on parking his car in a tight space, he replied that it was easy if you had driven a tank during the war!

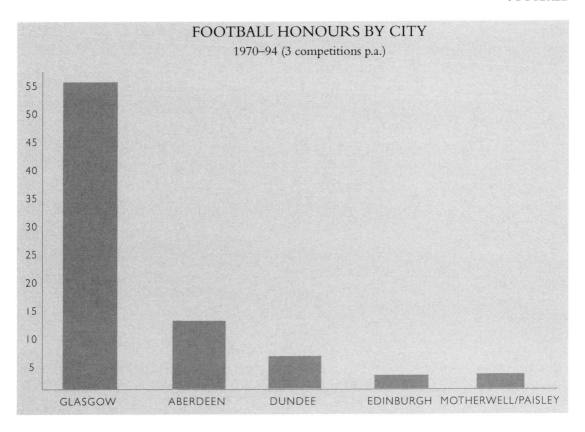

FOOTBALL HONOURS BY CITY
1970–94 (3 competitions p.a.)

Few football teams have inspired poets, but that post-war side played the Muses for James T.R. Ritchie to write in his poem *Easter Road*:

> Frae Arthur's Seat to Restalrig
> the blue's their roof eternally,
> There's no a team as jimp and trig
> as Hybees in their Arcady.

In recent years Hibs have proved less inspirational to poets and football supporters, winning the League Cup in 1972 and 1991, their only feats so far since 1970. Meanwhile the problems caused by the ill-advised share launch seemed likely at one time to make the club the object of asset-stripping. For a three-year period the club lost possession of its ground, an own

goal of massive proportions, and one which means that Easter Road is less well redeveloped than other grounds in Scotland, although improvements are proceeding.

HIBERNIAN MANAGERS 1945–96	
Hugh Shaw	(1948–61)
Walter Galbraith	(1961–64)
Jock Stein	(1964–65)
Bob Shankly	(1965–69)
Willie MacFarlane	(1969–71)
Dave Ewing	(1971)
Eddie Turnbull	(1971–80)
Willie Ormond	(1980)
Bertie Auld	(1980–81)
Pat Stanton	(1981–84)
John Blackley	(1984–86)
Alex Miller	(1986–96)
Jocky Scott	(1996–)

EUROPEAN FOOTBALL IN EDINBURGH

Hibernian can proudly claim to have pioneered playing competitive European football, being the first team in Britain to have entered the prestigious European Cup, in season 1955–56. After defeating Rot Weiss Essen of Germany and Djuurgardens of Sweden, Hibs were knocked out by the Raymond Kopa-inspired Rheims of France, subsequently finalists beaten by the great Real Madrid.

Hearts, however, have played in two European Cup tournaments after becoming Scottish champions (in contrast Hibs competed on invitation). Hearts' participation was short-lived on both occasions, being knocked out by Standard Liège in 1958–59 and by Benfica two years later. The Tynecastle side has probably the better European record in the last 20 years or so, but neither club has ever actually won anything in Europe, in contrast to Glasgow, with wins in 1967 (Celtic) and 1972 (Rangers), while Aberdeen won the European Cup Winners' Cup in 1983, and the city of Dundee saw United reach the UEFA Final in 1987.

Hibs' greatest season in Europe was 1960–61 when, with Joe Baker in brilliant form, the Easter Road side eliminated Barcelona, then the Spanish leaders with a recent victory over Real Madrid. After drawing 4–4 in Spain, Hibs won the return leg 3–2 at Easter Road, with Bobby Kinloch converting a hotly-disputed penalty. The studmarks to be seen on the referee's dressing-room door after the game were testament to Spanish 'disappointment'.

In subsequent years, Hibs' best run in Europe was probably in 1972–73 when they defeated Sporting Lisbon 6–1 and Besa (Albania) 7–1 at home, before under-estimating the wiles of Hajduk Split, although the remarkable victory over Napoli in 1967 takes some beating. Although 1–4 down from the first leg against the Italian leaders, the greens romped home by 5–0 at Easter Road in a result probably bettered only by Dunfermline's even more remarkable comeback against Valencia a few years previously. Nevertheless, despite these feats, Hibernian have never contested a European final. One friendly match against foreign opposition which has never been forgotten by those who saw it was Hibs' 2–0 defeat of Real Madrid at home in 1964. Manager Jock Stein convinced Willie Hamilton and Pat Quinn that their midfield talents were complimentary, and the Puskas-led Spaniards were completely outplayed. What a pity that Stein did not stay longer at Easter Road!

The furthest Hearts have gone in Europe was to reach the last eight in a highly-competitive UEFA Cup in 1987–88, before losing narrowly to Bayern Munich on aggregate. The last ten years have shown Hearts finding a rich vein of form at home in Europe, beating the likes of Bayern, Dukla Prague, Sparta Prague, Dneiperovosk, and Atletico Madrid. Significantly though, away form has tended to let them down, their best away result in Europe probably being a victory in 1987 over an Austria Vienna side which even the great Prohaska could not inspire.

MEADOWBANK THISTLE (NOW LIVINGSTON FC)

Formed in 1974 from the works team Ferranti Thistle, Meadowbank of that ilk joined the Scottish League at a time when the club lacked a ground of its own. Previously playing at City (East Pilton) Park just off Ferry Road, the club were perhaps a little lucky to be admitted to the Second Division, an elevation which was unpopular with Highland League clubs who felt they were comparatively better prepared for the senior grade.

From their first year in League football, Meadowbank played at the District Council stadium of that name, earning notoriety by drawing one of the smallest crowds – 80 – ever attracted to watch a senior game in Britain (against Stenhousemuir in 1979). This chronic lack of support has forced the club administrators to look elsewhere for a permanent home, and Livingston in West Lothian is seen as the answer to the club's problems at the time of writing.

Despite their lack of support, Meadowbank have performed solidly if not sensationally. After climbing to the First Division in 1987, they came very close to promotion to the Premier Division, under the able management of Musselburgh headmaster Terry Christie, who spent 14 years in part-time charge. A curious feature of their football is that, while they have produced such players as Darren Jackson, neither Hearts nor Hibs have looked on their near-neighbour as a reservoir of possible talent, the Easter Road club only signing Jackson after he had served two other senior sides.

DEFUNCT CLUBS

EDINBURGH CITY
Not to be confused with the present club holding the name, (formerly Postal United), the Edinburgh City side which was active from 1928–54 played in the Scottish Second Division from 1931 to 1939 and the Scottish 'C' Division from 1946 to 49. Playing in Edinburgh's colours of white shirts and black shorts, City appeared over the years at Marine Gardens (Portobello), Powderhall, Marine Gardens again, and at East Pilton. The latter is also known as City Park, located not far from Ferry Road.

City appear to have played their last game on 20 April 1955 against Ormiston. It must have been difficult to keep the public interested in the fortunes of such clubs as City when Edinburgh's senior sides were offering such wonderful football at that time. Perhaps City's greatest claim to fame was a certain centre-forward called Willie Bauld, who went on greater things at Tynecastle.

LEITH ATHLETIC
Founded in 1887, Leith Athletic lasted for 80 years, surviving being reconstituted twice, and tolerating the status of being Leith's 'second team', assuming Hibernian as the first. Although the team first sported chocolate and white quarters, they are best remembered in their liquorice and white stripes, enjoying League membership between 1891 and 1915, and again in 1924–26, 1927–40, and 1947–53. Ironically, many of their home games were played outside the Port, including the Powderhall area and (for eight years) at Marine Gardens (Portobello), where they once played Celtic in front of 21,000. Their League career was mainly spent at Old Meadowbank, approximating to where the present stadium's administrative block is now sited.

The Athletic's last game was against Falkirk Reserves in the 'C' Division, a grouping the club protested was less than their right. This last match took place on 27 April 1953, ending in a 2–1 defeat. Although the club entered twice for the Scottish Cup in successive seasons, playing at Fraserburgh in January 1954, the final whistle was about to be blown on a club now totally overshadowed by the Leithers in green a mile to the north. Leith Athletic was dissolved on 2 May 1957.

ST BERNARD'S

Only one of Edinburgh's former clubs has ever won the Scottish Cup, a competition in which the existing city clubs have scarcely distinguished themselves. St Bernard's were formed in 1878, and played for much of the club's existence at the Royal Gymnasium, a former pleasure ground which incorporated a playing field, but since the Second World War has been taken over by commercial properties and King George V Park, just off Eyre Place. Another of the grounds used by the 'Saints' was at Old Logie Green, parallel to Logie Green Road, scene of the 1896 Scottish Cup Final when 16,000 attended. St Bernard's had triumphed in the previous season's final, beating Renton at Ibrox.

Sporting a royal blue strip for most of the club's career up to 1920, and blue and white hoops thereafter, St Bernard's inhabited the First Division from 1893 to 1900 and the Second from 1900 to 1915, where they also spent almost all the inter-war years. Lack of support dogged them during the years up to their demise in 1942, but they were unable to achieve a resurrection in the football-mad years after the Second World War when many of their financial assets were seized by the executors of the estate of a recently demised director.

St Bernard's last match was played at Eyre Place on 16 May 1942, when East Fife won 3–2. For more information on this, and the other defunct city clubs, see the highly-detailed history *Rejected FC of Scotland*, Vol. 1, as listed in the BIBLIOGRAPHY.

Freedom of the City

Now regarded as an accolade awarded only to celebrities, Freedom of the City was at one time a status required by a merchant or craftsman wishing to trade within Edinburgh's boundaries. Such awards were made regularly from the 15th century onwards, the first Honorary award given to a 'celebrity' being made in 1459, when the recipient was Sir Edward de Boncle, Provost of the city's Trinity College at that time.

Since then, not even a local connection is required of a honorary freeman, although the award ceremony itself continues the tradition of the bestowal of a Freedom scroll, a development of the Burgess Ticket, once the licence to carry on trade within the city, but which in return required an offer by the recipient to take part in the city's local government. Until 1812, 'celebrity' freemen were more correctly called Honorary Burgesses of the City and Royal Burgh of Edinburgh.

It is pleasant to record that the latest Freeman at the time of writing is an Edinburgh man, the actor Sean Connery. On the occasion of his award, on 11 June 1991, Freedom of the City was bestowed by

Sean Connery makes a point during his acceptance speech when receiving the Freedom of the City award at the Usher Hall on 11 June 1991. (City of Edinburgh Council)

took the opportunity in his address to suggest that all Scottish schoolchildren should learn more about their legal system. This was met with acclamation by the audience, but he could equally have read the phone book aloud to sustained applause, such was the warmth of the reception accorded to 'Big Tam'.

Some miscellaneous facts about Edinburgh's freemen: including HM The Queen and the Queen Mother, there have been only ten female 'Freemen', the first being the philanthropist Baroness Burdett-Coutts in 1874. A proposal in 1981 to present the award to HRH Prince Charles was defeated in the District Council chamber, something that would have been unheard of even a few years earlier. The only name known to have been expunged from the roll of honour appears to have been that of Charles Parnell, the Irish patriot who was involved in an adulterous scandal. Sean Connery is the only locally-born citizen to be honoured in more than 25 years.

Lord Provost, the Rt. Hon. Eleanor McLaughlin, during an emotional Usher Hall ceremony whose tickets were subscribed nine times over. Glasgow actor Tom Conti gave a handsome tribute and video excerpts from Connery's films were shown. The new Freeman thanked his home city profusely for the honour, and

A noticeable area of activity where eminence has not been deemed a worthy qualification for Freedom status is sport. Such successful sports personalities with strong city connections as Eric Liddell, Gordon Smith, Willie Bauld, Ken Buchanan and Alan Wells, have not been honoured. The list of Freemen is as follows (to 1995):

Sir Edward de Boncle	3 October 1459	Sir John Bellenden (Ballantyne)	29 October 1553
James Adie, merchant in Danzig	8 December 1500	Henri Cleutin, Sieur d'Oysel	10 Janaury 1558
Gavin Douglas		Sir James Balfour of Pittendreich	23 July 1567
(Provost of St Giles)	31 September 1513	Sir William Kirkcaldy of Grange	4 October 1569
Sir Patrick Hamilton (Provost)	4 October 1515	John Craig, religious reformer	6 October 1584
Alexander Guthrie, Town Clerk	10 January 1549	Alexander Guthrie (2), Town Clerk	5 October 1598

Sir Alexander Seton, Provost	7 November 1598	James, Earl of Dalkeith	19 December 1701
George, Earl of Home	16 June 1606	John, Duke of Argyle	28 June 1704
Dr Robert Balcanquell	27 June 1617	Admiral Sir George Byng	19 March 1708
Theodore de Mayerne,		Sir Alexander Erskine of Cambo	27 August 1708
royal physician	27 June 1617	Andrew Fletcher of Saltoun	18 April 1712
Orlando Gibbons	9 July 1617	Duncan Forbes of Culloden	24 February 1714
Ben Johnson, playwright	25 September 1618	John Law, banker	22 July 1719
James, Marquess of Hamilton	6 July 1626	Professor Colin McLaurin	14 September 1726
General Alexander Leslie	22 April 1640	Captain John Porteous	19 June 1728
Alexander Guthrie (3)		Pierre de la Motte,	
Town Clerk	28 October 1640	dancing master	3 December 1735
John Hampden, English patriot	22 October 1641	Sir John Barnard, MP	15 June 1737
John Middleton,		David, Lord Elcho	24 November 1742
Restoration Commissioner	3 July 1646	Captain Augustus Keppel	23 January 1745
James Gordon, minister	5 April 1647	William, Duke of Cumberland	3 January 1747
David Leslie,		William, Earl of Albemarle	3 January 1747
Lieutenant-General	3 September 1647	Commander-in-chief	
Sir Thomas Cunningham	3 September 1647	George Beauclerk	10 December 1756
Peter Jansen	28 February 1649	Matthew Bell,	
General George Monck	26 May 1654	Mayor of Newcastle	14 December 1757
Colonel Robert Lilburne	26 May 1654	Robert Dinwiddie,	
Roger, Lord Broghill	8 August 1656	late Governor of Virginia	2 August 1758
John, Earl of Rothes	12 October 1660	Baron de Grosvelines	15 September 1758
Sir John de Carpenter	31 May 1661	Benjamin Franklin	5 September 1759
Sir George Mackenzie	27 December 1661	William Franklin	
James Sharp, Archbishop	27 June 1662	(Benjamin's son)	5 September 1759
Sir Charles Erskine of Cambo	10 October 1666	Admiral Edward Boscawen	28 November 1759
Sir Alexander Fraser of Dores	18 December 1668	Lieutenant Malcolm Macpherson	23 January 1760
James, Duke of		Tobias Smollett, novelist	30 July 1760
Buccleuch and Monmouth	2 July 1679	Francis Garden, Lord Gardenstone	22 July 1761
James, Duke of Albany		David Graeme of Gorthy	27 January 1762
(later James VII)	26 December 1679	Marquess of Lorne	9 June 1762
Colonel Churchill		Reverend George Whitefield	8 September 1762
(Duke of Marlborough)	26 December 1679	Colonel Isaac Barrhe	6 June 1763
Samuel Pepys	10 May 1682	Robert Keith of Craig	31 August 1763
Sir Robert Grierson of Lag	16 July 1684	John Hume, Conservator, Scottish	
Captain Grenville Collins	4 June 1685	Privileges, Netherlands	6 December 1763
Professor Sir David Sibbald	4 June 1685	James Mounsey, Physician to	
Professor David Gregory	14 September 1687	Russian Empress	22 December 1763
Major-General Mackay	1 November 1689	John Wentworth, New Hampshire	29 August 1764
Edward Lloyd, Oxford	8 December 1699	Count John Baptista Carburi	26 June 1765

Professor John Gregory	12 February 1766
Professor Adam Ferguson	7 May 1766
Robert Drummond,	
Archbishop of York	21 May 1766
Richard Stockton, New Jersey	4 March 1767
James Craig, New Town planner	17 April 1767
Alexander, Lord Colville	17 May 1769
Sir Fletcher Norton	5 July 1769
Francis Forster,	
Mayor of Newcastle	29 November 1769
Adam Smith, economist	6 June 1770
Simon, Earl of Harcourt	22 August 1770
Thomas Pennant, author	20 May 1772
George, Viscount Townshend	13 October 1773
Professor Dugald Stuart	28 June 1775
Douglas, Duke of Hamilton	30 July 1777
Sir Samuel Greig,	
Russian Vice-Admiral	27 August 1777
Rear-Admiral Sir George Rodney	15 March 1780
Andrew Frazer, Chief Engineer	
for Scotland	31 January 1781
Vice-Admiral Hyde Parker	27 June 1781
John Howard, prison reformer	31 July 1782
George, Lord North	30 October 1782
Robert Dundas	3 March 1784
Sir Ilay Campbell	3 March 1784
Vincent Lunardi, balloonist	12 October 1785
John Palmer, Comptroller-General,	
Post Office	22 November 1786
Charles Hope, Lord Advocate	25 May 1801
Earl of Moira, Commander-in-Chief	
Scotland	16 November 1803
Edward Jenner,	
vaccination pioneer	31 October 1804
Professor John Gilchrist	31 October 1804
Professor James Gregory	7 September 1808
Admiral Sir Samuel Hood	23 November 1808
James Neild, philanthropist	28 February 1810
Vice-Admiral William Otway	27 October 1813
General Sir Thomas Graham	22 December 1813
Walter Scott of Abbotsford	22 December 1813

Earl of Dalhousie	22 December 1813
Thomas Coutts, banker	22 December 1813
Francis, Earl of	
Wemyss and March	9 February 1814
Lieutenant-General	
Henry Wynyard	9 February 1814
Gilbert Innes of Stow	9 February 1814
Edmund Antrobus, banker	9 February 1814
David Boyle, Lord Justice Clerk	23 February 1814
Earl of Liverpool	2 March 1814
Viscount Sidmouth	2 March 1814
Viscount Castlereagh	2 March 1814
Nicolas Vansittart,	
Chancellor of Exchequer	2 March 1814
George, Earl of Glasgow	23 March 1814
Rear-Admiral William Hope	23 March 1814
James Clerk of Bonnington	23 March 1814
William Rae, Sheriff Depute	23 March 1814
Henry Jardine,	
Deputy King's Remembrancer	23 March 1814
William Ker, Secretary,	
GPO for Scotland	23 March 1814
Lieutenant-General	
Ranald Fergusson	16 September 1814
Coutts Trotter, banker	16 November 1814
John Smith, MP	7 December 1814
Marquis of Bute	25 January 1815
Lord Niddry	8 February 1815
General Sir James Denham	8 February 1815
John Christison Curwen	8 February 1815
Lord Chief Commissioner Adam	19 July 1815
Charles Forbes MP	19 July 1815
Dr James Gregory	11 October 1815
Archdukes John and Lewis	
of Austria	4 December 1815
Fletcher Norton,	
Baron of the Exchequer	4 September 1816
Grand Duke Nicholas of Russia	18 December 1816
George Arbuthnot,	
Lord Provost's brother	30 April 1817
Professor Thomas Hope	10 September 1817

Lieutenant-General	
Sir Charles Colville	26 November 1817
Grand Duke Michael of Russia	5 August 1818
Archduke Maximillian	
of Austria	11 November 1818
HRH Prince Leopold	18 August 1819
Prince Nicholas Esterhazy	
of Golantha	29 August 1821
Prince Victor of Metternich	29 August 1821
Rear-Admiral Robert Otway	24 October 1821
Major-General	
Sir Thomas Bradford	10 September 1823
Rear-Admiral	
Sir John Beresford	10 September 1823
James Maitland,	
Earl of Lauderdale	1 September 1824
James Wortley MP	1 September 1824
Charles Marjoribanks,	
East India Company	1 September 1824
Henry Brougham MP	30 March 1825
Duke of Brunswick	7 September 1825
Prince Augustus of Brunswick	7 September 1825
Robert, Baron Gifford	5 October 1825
Sir James McGrigor, Director-General,	
Army Medical Department	26 July 1826
Chevalier Masclet,	
French Consul General	29 August 1827
David Wilkie, painter	14 October 1829
James Abercromby MP	24 June 1834
Sir John Campbell,	
Attorney General,	24 June 1834
Charles, Earl Grey	26 August 1834
Sir Thomas	
Makdougall Brisbane	13 September 1834
Dominique Arago, Perpetual Secretary,	
French Academy des Sciences	13 September 1834
Professor Gerrit Moll	13 September 1834
John Dalton of Manchester	13 September 1834
Robert Brown, botanist	13 September 1834
Prince Adam Czartoryski	
of Poland	8 December 1835
Count Ladislas Zamoyski	8 December 1835
Thomas Campbell, poet	2 August 1836
John Charles, Earl Spencer	16 August 1836
Joseph Hume MP	22 August 1837
Sir Astley Cooper, surgeon	5 September 1837
Andrew Rutherford,	
Solicitor General	23 October 1838
Thomas Macaulay MP	4 June 1839
Charles Dickens	29 June 1841
William Gibson Craig MP	29 June 1841
Baboo Dwarkanauth,	
Tagore of Calcutta	30 August 1842
HRH Prince Albert,	
Prince Consort	3 September 1842
Walter, Duke of Buccleuch	6 September 1842
Sir Robert Peel	6 September 1842
George, Earl of Aberdeen	6 September 1842
Richard Cobden MP	19 January 1843
John Talbot, Attorney General	27 September 1843
Professor Justus Liebig	8 October 1844
Sir Henry Pottinger	14 April 1845
Lord John Russell	3 November 1845
Captain Sir Charles Napier	4 December 1845
George Thompson	6 June 1846
Sir Charles Duke,	
Lord Mayor of London	15 August 1849
Lieutenant-General Viscount Gough	5 August 1850
George, Earl of Carlisle	4 April 1853
William Gladstone	27 September 1853
Sir William Molesworth, First Commissioner of	
Works and Public Buildings	30 September 1854
Major Charles Nasmyth	2 March 1855
Dr Merle D'Aubigne of Geneva	7 June 1856
James, Marquis of Dalhousie	1 July 1856
James Moncrieff, Lord Advocate	13 January 1857
David Livingstone	21 September 1857
David Roberts, artist	29 September 1858
Lieutenant-General Sir James Grant	11 July 1861
Viscount Palmerston, Prime Minister	1 April 1863
Guiseppi Garibaldi	11 April 1864
HRH Prince Alfred	17 May 1866

William Lloyd Garrison	18 July 1867
Benjamin Disraeli	30 October 1867
Lord Napier of Magdala	16 September 1868
John Bright MP	3 November 1868
Sir James Young Simpson	26 October 1869
Angela-Georgina,	
Baroness Burdett-Coutts	15 January 1874
William Forster MP	6 November 1875
Earl of Derby	18 December 1875
General Ulysses S. Grant	31 August 1877
Anthony Ashley Cooper,	
Earl of Shaftesbury	13 April 1878
Robert, Marquis of Salisbury	27 November 1882
Archibald, Earl of Rosebery	21 July 1883
John, Earl of Aberdeen	5 August 1885
HRH Albert Victor Prince of Wales	
(Duke of Clarence and Avondale)	6 May 1886
Marquis of Lothian	7 June 1887
Andrew Carnegie	8 July 1887
Henry Morton Stanley	11 June 1890
Sir Daniel Wilson	20 August 1891
HRH George, Duke of York	3 October 1893
General Lord Roberts	18 November 1893
Earl of Elgin	22 December 1893
Earl of Hopetoun	10 July 1895
John Ritchie Findlay	11 December 1896
William McEwan MP	22 October 1897
Field Marshal Viscount Wolseley	15 June 1898
Lord Lister	15 June 1898
Marquis of Dufferin	29 November 1898
Major-General	
Sir Herbert Kitchener	29 November 1898
HRH Albert Edward, Prince of Wales	6 July 1899
Sir Wilfrid Laurier,	
Canadian Prime Minister	26 July 1902
Sir Edmund Barton,	
Australian Prime Minister	26 July 1902
Richard John Seddon,	
New Zealand Prime Minister	26 July 1902
Sir Albert Hime,	
Natal Prime Minister	26 July 1902

Sir Robert Bond,	
Newfoundland Prime Minister	26 July 1902
Lord Balfour of Burleigh	15 April 1903
Lord Strathcona and	
Mount Royal	4 December 1903
Joseph Hodges Choate	21 March 1904
HRH Duke of Connaught	
and Strathearn	6 May 1905
Lord Reay	22 May 1905
Dr George Young	22 May 1905
Flora Clift Stevenson	22 May 1905
Sir George Stuart White	6 July 1905
Arthur James Balfour MP	19 October 1905
Alfred Deakin,	
Australian Prime Minister	10 May 1907
Sir Joseph Ward,	
New Zealand Prime Minister	10 May 1907
Leander Jameson,	
Cape Colony Prime Minister	10 May 1907
Louis Botha,	
Transvaal Prime Minister	10 May 1907
Sir Henry Campbell-Bannerman	30 October 1907
Sir William Turner	10 December 1909
Reverend Alexander Whyte	10 December 1909
Herbert Asquith	20 December 1910
Earl of Minto	28 April 1911
Andrew Fisher,	
Australian Prime Minister	7 July 1911
Sir Edward Morris,	
Newfoundland Prime Minister	7 July 1911
Lord Pentland	18 April 1912
Viscount Haldane	2 November 1912
Lord Dundedin	2 November 1912
William Hughes,	
Australian Prime Minister	26 April 1916
William Massey, New Zealand	
Prime Minister	20 November 1916
Sir Robert Borden,	
Canadian Prime Minister	11 April 1917
Jan Smuts,	
South African Defence Minister	11 April 1917

Sir Ganga Singh Bahadur,	
Maharaja of Bikaner	11 April 1917
Walter Page,	
American Ambassador	2 November 1917
David Lloyd George	24 May 1918
Admiral Sir David Beatty	25 January 1919
Sir Douglas Haig	28 May 1919
Charles Edward Price	24 June 1919
HRH Prince of Wales	
(later Edward VIII)	24 July 1919
Alexander Graham Bell	30 November 1920
Arthur Meighen,	
Canadian Prime Minister	18 July 1921
Sir Robert Horne	12 March 1923
Robert Munro MP	12 March 1923
Viscount Novar	28 September 1923
Sir Robert Cranston	15 October 1923
Reverend Andrew Williamson	15 October 1923
Alexander Grant	15 October 1923
Adolphe Max, Brussels Burgomaster	14 July 1924
James Ramsay Macdonald	28 May 1925
HRH Prince Henry	
(later Duke of Gloucester)	25 July 1925
Stanley Baldwin	7 June 1926
HRH Duke of York	
(later George VI)	9 October 1926
William MacKenzie King,	
Canadian Prime Minister	24 November 1926
Stanley Bruce,	
Australian Prime Minister	24 November 1926
Joseph Coates, New Zealand	
Prime Minister	24 November 1926
Walter Monroe, Newfoundland	
Prime Minister	24 November 1926
Sir Bijay Mahtab, Maharajadhiraja	
of Burdwan	24 November 1926
Alanson Houghton,	
American Ambassador	7 September 1927
Sir Harry Lauder	24 November 1927
Duke of Atholl	21 September 1928
Sir John Gilmour	21 September 1928

Marchioness of Aberdeen	
and Temair	21 September 1928
Sir James Ewing, scientist	18 April 1929
William Adamson MP	29 July 1929
Sir James M. Barrie	29 July 1929
Reverend Alexander Martin	30 September 1929
Reverend John White	30 September 1929
HRH Princess Mary	
(later Princess Royal)	17 September 1930
Richard Bennett MP	19 November 1930
James Scullin MP	19 November 1930
George Forbes MP	19 November 1930
The Nawab of Bhopal	9 January 1931
V.S.S. Sastri	9 January 1931
Earl of Athlone	3 July 1931
Earl of Willingdon,	
Viceroy of India	29 June 1934
Countess of Willingdon	29 June 1934
HRH George, Duke of Kent	20 May 1935
The Maharaja of Patiala	10 June 1935
Joseph Lyons	10 June 1935
John Buchan	10 June 1935
Louise Carnegie	30 September 1935
HRH Duchess of York	
(later the Queen Mother)	1 December 1936
HRH Duchess of Gloucester	28 April 1937
Walter Elliot	19 April 1938
Baron Macmillan of Aberfeldy	19 April 1938
Joseph Kennedy,	
American Ambassador	21 April 1939
John Winant,	
American Ambassador	9 October 1941
Winston Churchill	12 October 1942
Peter Fraser,	
New Zealand Prime Minister	12 May 1944
Thomas Johnston MP	12 May 1944
Sir John Anderson	12 May 1944
Victor, Marquis of Linlithgow	3 October 1944
Admiral Lord Cunningham	15 February 1946
Field-Marshal Alexander	15 February 1946
Air Marshal Sir William Tedder	15 February 1946

Field-Marshal Sir Bernard		Lewis Williams Douglas	21 August 1950
Montgomery	6 March 1946	Earl Mountbatten of Burma	18 January 1954
Dwight D. Eisenhower	3 October 1946	Countess Mountbatten	18 January 1954
HRH Princess Elizabeth		Lord Rowallan	28 February 1957
(later HM the Queen)	16 July 1947	Professor Norman McOmish Dott	6 July 1962
Robert Gordon Menzies	18 November 1948	King Olav V of Norway	17 October 1962
HRH Prince Philip,		Yehudi Menuhin	23 August 1965
Duke of Edinburgh	1 March 1949	Sir Alec Douglas-Home	3 April 1969
Sir Donald Charles Cameron,		Thomas (Sean) Connery	11 June 1991
Mayor of Dunedin	30 August 1949		

Gas Supply

Gas is supplied to Edinburgh householders, as to most other parts of the country, by British Gas Supply, a newly reconstituted part of the now privatised gas industry. This gas is purchased from the long-distance carrier Transco, for onward distribution to consumers. The gas is originally processed from the North Sea and pumped from St Fergus, near Aberdeen.

The city no longer has its own gas-producing capacity, its works at Granton closing as the last producer of substitute natural gas in Britain in 1987. However, the administrative headquarters of Scottish Gas, an area office of British Gas Supply, and including over a million customers in North-East England, are still based at Granton.

History

Gas was first produced and used in the city as an illuminant. In 1816 two shopkeepers in South Bridge set up their own gas-producing equipment in a cellar to illuminate their shops, and within two years this led to the establishment of the Edinburgh Gas Light Company. The High Street enjoyed gaslight in the stretch between the Bridges and Parliament Square by 1820, with a single cockspur light inserted into each oil lamp globe, and Princes Street was illuminated by gas two years later.

Within ten years there were 6,000 street lights in the city and the total was to grow to 15,000 before electricity finally superseded gas in 1965 (see also ROADS AND STREETS). Until the 1930s, gas lights had to be turned on and off manually, leading to the creation of an army of 'leeries' patrolling the streets armed with a dual-purpose pole topped by naked flame for evening duties, and a 'snuffer' device for extinguishing the lights in the mornings.

This gas supply was a by-product of coal and was processed at works at New Street, where the bus garage exists now (its building converted into an indoor market). These works introduced the city's highest chimney into the Edinburgh city skyline. A second site was set up in Leith's Baltic Street.

A rival company was established at Tanfield (Canonmills) in 1824 to extract gas from whale oil, and was distinguished by the presence of Sir Walter Scott on its board; indeed he was either the chairman or president – but he was unsure which! This method of illumination was not, however, a viable option, the supply of the oil being dependent on unpredictable factors, and the company was taken over by its rival in 1828. At least the company left the city with a hall which was to play a hugely important part in the development of Scottish presbyterianism (*see* CHURCHES).

A joint Corporation Gas Commission was established to bring the gas industry of Edinburgh and Leith into local government hands in 1888, including Portobello eight years later, and closing small gasworks there, and in Corstorphine. With the New Street gasworks becoming increasingly cramped, it was decided to move the enterprise to Granton, where 106 acres (43.4 hectares) were acquired from the Duke of Buccleuch in 1898, and where full production began in 1906.

A number of gasholders were built here, none better known to the public than the fixed louvred structure 275 feet (82.5 metres) high, a landmark for Forth sailors since 1933. Fifteen years after construction, the Royal Fine Arts Commission recommended its repainting in shades of blue becoming lighter towards the top to reduce its visual impact on citizens' consciousness. Nevertheless, Granton's gas industry, nationalised in 1948, privatised in 1986, and active until 1987 when it was Britain's last outpost of natural gas production, has proved to be a popular local employer, and redundancies caused by the industry's reorganisation brought about local dismay, although there is still an administrative presence here.

Geology

Edinburgh stands on land sculpted by fire and ice. Although the earliest rocks found in the city area are such sedimentary rocks as sandstones and shales, some laid down as much as 400 million years ago, the most noticeable feature of the city's geomorphology are the hills on which it is largely built.

A number of these are the remains of a huge volcano, active around 354 million years ago (plus or minus seven million years). This was known as Arthur's Seat Volcano, although evidence of its former existence stretches beyond the present Holyrood Park area to include the Castle Rock and Calton Hill. It is believed that the volcano was located under water when it first erupted, although the Firth of Forth did not exist then, the pattern of land and sea at that time being almost unrecognisable. It appears that the site of present-day Edinburgh was submerged in a freshwater or brackish lake extending from the southern part of the present-day city out to West Lothian and Fife.

The cone was quickly projected above sea level, and the vestiges of five volcanic vents still remain – the Lion's Head and Lion's Haunch on Arthur's Seat itself, Pulpit Rock and Crags vents in the Queen's Park, and the Castle Rock (*see also* HILLS and PARKS). Thirteen lava flows can still be identified from four of the vents, while the Calton Hill and Whinny Hill (to the north of Dunsapie Loch) are the remains of the cone itself.

At 822 feet (247 metres), Arthur's Seat is the highest hill within the city centre area. Its profile is often compared to that of a

The igneous sill of Salisbury Crags pictured in an unusual perspective from one of the roads transecting the Queen's Park. Sir Arthur Conan Doyle portrayed his Lost World *of dinosaurs as being isolated on a forgotten plateau remarkably like Edinburgh's Salisbury Crags! .*

crouching lion, and geologists have borrowed the analogy, as mentioned above, identifying two lava flows at the Lion's Head and nine from the Haunch area. These emerged from two cylindrical vents, the Haunch being the larger. One remarkable – and highly visible – product of volcanic activity was that of magma cooling deep inside the volcano being forged into hexagonal dolerite columns which are now visible to the passer-by as 'Samson's Ribs' on the south side of Arthur's Seat.

When the volcano had exhausted itself, its vents were gradually blocked by basaltic rock, by debris and by water, the whole area becoming buried by thousands of feet of sedimentary material. But that was before the ice came. None of the volcanic remains have survived unscathed by the actions of ice. This perhaps arrived around one million years ago, there being a number of ice ages up to 10,000 years ago. The movements came from west to east, stripping away most of the softer sedimentary rocks and physically wearing down the igneous rocks originally produced from under Arthur's Seat.

The grinding of the ice has produced what is known to every Edinburgh schoolchild as 'Crag and Tail Formation', where a protusion standing in the path of the ice has its western face striated by friction and its eastern slope ground down to a gentle slope. Edinburgh has a number of such phenomena – the crag of the Castle Rock gives way eastwards to the High Street stretching to Holyrood, and there are noticeably similar geomorphological features at Blackford and Craiglockhart hills. In each case the walker finds that the stern western crag can be approached easily from the east.

Fossils have been recovered within the city of Edinburgh at a number of quarry sites, including Craigleith and Hailes, before these were filled in (*see* QUARRIES). One of the most striking fossils on public display in Edinburgh is the trunk of *Pitys Withami* found at Craigleith by Henry Witham in 1830, and now displayed outside the glasshouses at the Royal Botanic Garden.

Other fossiliferous sites include Baberton, Colinton, Gilmerton, Granton, Juniper Green, and Straiton, all of whose Carboniferous calciferous sandstone rocks have proved to be of considerable interest to palaeontologists. Most of these fossil remains were non-marine aquatic organisms including crustacea and fish, recovered from deposits left by the fresh or brackish lake occupying the southern half of the city as far south as the Pentlands and stretching to West Lothian and Fife.

For a description of the city's hills as they are today, *see* HILLS. Readers wishing to examine the geology of the area for themselves should take an excursion guidebook with them, or the Edinburgh Natural History Society's publication (*see* BIBLIOGRAPHY under '*Environment*' for details of these titles). The Code of Conduct for geologists should be followed (*see* recommended excursion guide).

The city is one of two major bases for the **British Geological Survey**, whose Scottish headquarters are located at Murchison

Edinburgh's skyline as seen from the Salisbury Crags, where evidence of quarrying can still be seen. The city can boast Britain's first civic society, but 50 years before its formation in 1875, concerned local citizens had successfully brought legal action to prevent further despoliation of the Crags made famous by James Hutton.

House on West Mains Road. Formerly known as the Geological Survey, and later as the Institute of Geological Sciences, this organisation, responsible for the furthering of earth science information and expertise, has had a presence in Edinburgh since 1857. Murchison House is also the location for the **Global Seismology Unit**, responsible for monitoring earth movements around the world.

EDINBURGH AS A CENTRE OF GEOLOGICAL STUDY

'Edinburgh geologists are fortunate in the remarkable variety of rocks and landscape features to be seen in Lothian Region.' So concludes the introduction to the excursion guide to the geology of the Lothian area (*see* BIBLIOGRAPHY). Not only is Edinburgh's geology the product of fire and ice, but it also proved to be an intellectual centre for geological study. In the last quarter of the 18th century, in what became known as the city's Golden Age, Edinburgh was the matrix where conflicting theories about the Earth's formation were formulated, debated, and finally agreed.

James Hutton, born in the city in 1726, concluded from his studies on Salisbury Crags that basaltic rocks had a volcanic origin, and published his findings in *The Theory of the Earth* in 1788. This flouted received beliefs of the time by postulating that the Earth was much older than previously thought, and obviously denied the Biblical theory of creation. But there were scientific objections too. Opposing his theories, and favouring the 'Neptunist' idea that rocks were first formed under water, possibly during Noah's Flood, were the followers of the German professor, Abraham

Gottlieb Werner, and there was no more staunch adherent to these views that Robert Jameson, the long-serving Professor of Natural History at Edinburgh University.

Unlike Jameson, Hutton was not a professional academic, and had no students whom he could infuse with his ideas. However, supported by the fine illustrations made by John Clerk of Eldin, and posthumously championed by John Playfair, who made Hutton's writings more comprehensible by publishing a commentary on them in 1802, Hutton's views eventually prevailed and he became known as the 'Founder of Modern Geology'.

Meanwhile, the energetic Jameson continued to teach his students the Wernerian theory, and Edinburgh produced even more adherents of the German theory, than Werner himself! Leith-born Jameson is best remembered now for presenting his formidable collection of specimens, geological and biological, to what is now the Royal Museum of Scotland, confirming the Museum as one of the most important centres for geological study in Britain.

Golf

Edinburgh has no fewer than 25 golf courses established within the city boundaries since before 1950, and perhaps 90 courses within 20 miles of Princes Street. Six of the city's courses are municipally owned. A recent development to assist the golfer is the driving range, of which there are a number within, or just outside, the city.

The Elf Loch is one of Edinburgh's smallest stretches of freshwater and is located in the middle of the private Mortonhall Golf Course.

The modern expansion of golf within Edinburgh district took place after the foundation of the Scottish tourist industry, in the period between 1890 and 1912, during which 16 courses were opened. A further six courses were opened in the inter-war period between 1920 and 1930.

The idea of golf for the people had been strong at the turn of the century, with the aim of providing public, municipal courses, as an alternative to the sometimes exclusive private courses. The earliest Edinburgh municipal courses were the Braids Number One and Number Two courses set in the Braid Hills to the south of the city, opened in 1893 and 1894. The craggy Braids courses have been described as a combination of hill walking and golf, though the same could be said of other courses built on the volcanic rocks south of the city. The Number One course (5,731 yards/5,238 metres, SSS – Standard Scratch Score – 68) is more challenging than the No. 2 (4,832 yards/4,416 metres, SSS 63). The Carricknowe course (6,299 yards/5757 metres, SSS 70) dates to 1930. The Silverknowes course (6,210 yards/5,675 metres, SSS 70) was opened in 1947. The municipal course of 5418 yards (4,952 metres) which replaced Leith Links was opened just 'over the border' at Craigentinny in Edinburgh in 1907. The nine-hole course at Portobello is now also a municipal course, measuring 4,838 yards (4,421 metres) for two circuits and having a SSS of 64.

The city offers a variety of golfing terrains, but with the notable exception of any true links course, the two types of Edinburgh golfing landscape are parkland and moorland. Several of the city's parkland courses were built in the grounds of large country houses. Baberton (6,140 yards/5,611 metres, SSS of 69, 1893) is an undulating course where the clubhouse building dates from 1622. The Liberton course (5,299 yards/4,843 metres, SSS of 66, 1920) was laid out round the 18th century Kingston Grange, now also the clubhouse. South of Arthur's Seat lies the Prestonfield course (6,216 yards/5,681 metres, SSS of 70, 1920) adjacent to Prestonfield House, which dates from 1687. The Ratho Park course (6,028 yards/5,509 metres, SSS of 69, 1928), designed by James Braid, is laid out in the grounds of a Georgian mansion built in 1824. Braid, from Elie, Fife, was the first golfer to win the Open five times, between 1901 and 1910, and was involved in the design or alteration of ten of Edinburgh's courses. Two of his finest designs are the undulating Dalmahoy East (6,664 yards/6,090 metres, SSS of 72, 1926) and West (5,212 yards/4,763 metres, SSS of 66, 1926) courses.

Notable examples of Edinburgh moorland courses include the municipal Braids mentioned above, Lothianburn (5,750 yards/5,255 metres, SSS of 69, 1893) noted for the mountain golf of its par 4 ninth, Torphin Hill (5,025 yards/4,592 metres, SSS of 66, 1895) whose highest part rises to over 800 feet (240 metres), and Mortonhall (6,557 yards/5,993 metres, SSS of 71, 1892).

The Burgess club became 'royal' in 1929, and has been located at Barnton since 1895, where it plays on a 6,604 yards/6,036 metres course, with SSS of 72. The Bruntsfield Links Golf Club's present home is at Davidson's Mains, adjacent to Royal Burgess, and has a 6,607 yards/6,038 metres course, with SSS of 71. Modern options for Edinburgh golfers include a number of driving ranges, such as the floodlit Port Royal Golf Range, by Edinburgh Airport, which also has a nine-hole pitch and putt course. Ironically, another summertime pitch and putt venue is the part of the original Bruntsfield Links in front of the Golf Tavern, on the western end of the Edinburgh Meadows, which can thus claim to be the oldest course over which golf is still played.

History

St Andrews is universally regarded as the home of golf, and its Royal and Ancient Club as golf's rule-giving authority, other than in the US. However, Edinburgh's claim to originality for both these roles has perhaps the greater historical validity. During Stewart times the links at Leith and St Andrews were the chief golfing centres, but the greatest activity was at Leith, due to its proximity to Edinburgh, the seat of government.

The modern history of golf is reckoned to begin with the formation of the early golf clubs in the eighteenth century, and the presentation of a trophy for competition was the first step in the formation of most golf clubs. The world's oldest golf club is thus the Honourable Company of Edinburgh Golfers, which played its first competition for the trophy of a Silver Club on the Links of Leith, on 7th March 1744. The Honourable Company also devised the first set of rules for its 1744 competition. Although the Royal and Ancient presently has the function of law-giver in golf, the St Andrews club originally simply adopted the

Edinburgh club's rules. It was not until ten years later, in 1754, that the example of the Leith golfers was followed by the men of St Andrews, 22 of whom met to subscribe for a Silver Club.

The original layout at Leith was of five holes measuring 414, 461, 426, 495, and 435 yards, three circuits of the five holes making the recognised round. If such yardages were extrapolated to an 18 hole layout, it would produce a giant course of over 8,000 yards (7,312 metres), and with a probable SSS of 79. The game at Leith was thus primarily a hard-hitting exercise, and it has been observed that if Leith had remained the chief centre of the game, golf might have become a sterner, more monotonous business, than it is today. Leith's five holes were named Thorn-tree, Braehead, Sawmill, North-mid, and South-mid. It was in 1834, while the older Edinburgh club was in a period of eclipse due to the decline of Leith Links owing to overcrowding and related deterioration of the turf itself, that the St Andrews club successfully petitioned King William IV to designate it Royal and Ancient.

Edinburgh also claims the third and fourth oldest golf clubs, these being the Edinburgh Burgess Golfing Society and the Bruntsfield Links Golf Club. The former claims to have existed since 1735, but has records dating back only to 1773. The latter dates to 1761 as a Society, and 1787 as a Club. Both originally played over the five or six holes of the Bruntsfield Links (not true links turf) south of the city, where the present-day Golf Tavern was their clubhouse. Both moved to Musselburgh after the decline of these links, and subsequently to present, adjacent locations at Barnton and Davidson's Mains.

In the mid-19th century the nine-hole Musselburgh course was the focus of Scottish golf, being simultaneously the base for the Honourable Company, the Burgess, the Bruntsfield Links, and the Musselburgh clubs. Musselburgh hosted the Open Championship six times, until in 1891 the Honourable Company moved to Muirfield and took the competition with them. The parchment on which the original 13 rules of golf were drafted is in the Honourable Company's archives, with a copy hanging in the Muirfield clubhouse.

(*George McMurdo*)

Green Belt

Edinburgh's Green Belt was designated by the planning authorities in 1957. It forms a collar round the entire southern perimeter of the city, from South Queensferry in the west to Tranent on the east. Encompassing 40,000 acres (16,400 hectares) of terrain which varies from former industrial land to landscaped estates, the Belt is intended to offer a permanent 'breathing space' free of industrial or housing developments separating the city from other Lothian centres, and preventing the creation of one super-conurbation comprising the city and its satellite communities. Ninety per cent of the Belt consists of private property.

The Belt has three detached areas in Edinburgh itself – Holyrood Park, Cramond, and Corstorphine Hill, while there are two salients into the city from the south, at the Braid and Craiglockhart Hill massifs (*see* HILLS). The Belt is thinnest at

Arthur's Seat dominates the Edinburgh skyline, as seen in this view from another of the city's seven hills, Blackford Hill. Clouds have thrown much of the intervening cityscape into shadow, while a bright patch has illuminated Salisbury Crags and the Lion's Head.

Straiton, a sensitive site where a Local Nature Reserve was no sooner designated at the local pond (*see* WILDLIFE) when development proposals were brought forward, and approved in outline in 1993, for a football stadium, and associated car parking, which would have effectively cut the Belt in two. Thankfully, this proposal has been dropped at the time of writing.

Inevitably, some would-be developers have viewed the Green Belt as a land reservoir to be exploited for commercial and leisure development, with no regard to the environmental issues involved. More public education is perhaps required to explain to many 'captains of industry' that mankind requires a counter-balancing community of plants to produce the oxygen we require, while disposing of our carbon dioxide.

Perhaps to combat this ignorance, but also to further the cause of the Green Belt in general terms, the Edinburgh Green Belt

Trust was formed in 1991. Its board is a mixture of local government, and commercial and environmental interests dedicated to supporting this very necessary city feature. In its short life the Trust has already undertaken conservation work at a number of locations, including Cammo Tower, and has planted some 45,000 trees (to 1995).

Hills

Edinburgh, it has been said, is built on seven hills – the Castle Rock, Calton Hill, Arthur's Seat, Blackford Hill, Corstorphine Hill, Craiglockhart Hill, and the Braid Hills. The truth of that adage seems to depend on what is meant by a hill; Craiglockhart for example can be said to have two hills, giving the city a total of eight. Nevertheless, the capital was not described by Robert Louis Stevenson as 'Precipitous City' for nothing, and one journalist visiting from the West of Scotland was heard to complain that Edinburgh's steepest hill is the Waverley Steps.

Edinburgh's hills are listed below. Their geological formation is discussed under GEOLOGY. Although much of the Pentlands area is outside the city boundary, the borderline runs along the northern-most ridge, and a description of the city's topography would be incomplete without the Pentlands.

ARTHUR'S SEAT

Edinburgh citizens (and geologists) have been known to liken the outline of their highest city hill, Arthur's Seat, to a crouching lion. This may represent some kind of cultural conditioning – a Chinese visitor has remarked on its similarity to the outline of a sleeping elephant. Whichever is more accurate, the 822 feet (247 metres) Arthur's Seat is in fact only one of a number of geomorphological features which make the Queen's Park a unique open space in the middle of the city.

First the origin of the name. There is a school of thought which holds that Arthur's Seat is derived from the Gaelic Ard-na-Said, which translates as 'the height of arrows'. There is no evidence of an Arthurian connection, although southern Scotland has many assocations with the mythical king's wizard, Merlin.

The best way to describe Arthur's Seat is to suggest how to take the quickest route to the summit. (For a description of the hill's surroundings, *see* PARKS). The Queen's Drive (now a one-way street) allows motorists hoping to reach the summit as far as Dunsapie Loch, where there is a carpark, with roughly half the climb to the top accomplished in comfort. From here the summit can be reached in about 20 minutes walking up a path which is steep but manageable for the able-bodied.

The summit is also known as the Lion's Head. With the help of the direction indicator here the successful climber can pick out summits beyond the Ochils, while the Fife and East Lothian coastlines are laid out like a relief map. Since 1940 a sunrise service has been conducted here on 1 May by the Minister of the Canongate, with, appropriately, a reading from the Sermon on the Mount.

Approaching the summit massif from the north is a ridge called the Long Row, running up from St Margaret's Loch (*see* LOCHS) which is watched over by St Anthony's Chapel. It is now a picturesque ruin, believed to have been positioned there to remind sailors leaving Leith to offer their prayers for a safe outward journey, and for thankfulness from those approaching shore.

On the opposite side of Arthur's Seat, is Duddingston Loch (*see* LOCHS), overlooked by prehistoric cultivation terraces on the Lion's Haunch. Further to the west, and lower down, is the impressive geological feature known as Samson's Ribs. These hexagonal dolerite columns bring Fingal's Cave on Staffa to mind. They are best viewed by the pedestrian; there is nowhere here for a car to stop without causing a traffic problem.

The west side of the upland area is dominated by Salisbury Crags, a magnificent mile-long arc of cliff when viewed from the city. Edinburgh's own Sir

Arthur Conan Doyle believed that this cliff was well-known enough to use it as a visual comparison for the impenetrably sheer walls of his dinosaur-populated *Lost World* in the 1912 novel of that name. Technically, it is an igneous sill, whose rocks have inspired and baffled geologists for centuries. Two of its features are named after James Hutton, 'the founder of modern geology', whose studies of Scottish rocks such as these allowed him to correctly define how the Earth was formed. Ironically, modern geologists appear to regard Scotland's rocks as too complex, indeed confusing, to use for teaching purposes, so Hutton's achievement was all the more impressive.

At the base of the Crags runs the Radical Road, from St Leonard's round to Holyrood. Its construction came at the suggestion of Sir Walter Scott in 1820, who was anxious to keep men employed after military service. He feared that otherwise they might have so much time on their hands that they could be swayed by radical orators.

CASTLE ROCK

435 feet (130.5 metres) at its highest point, the Castle Rock is a classic example of a crag and tail formation. The remains of a volcano have been ground down by ice moving eastwards, producing the ridge which now carries the Royal Mile. Textbooks tell us that the junction of basalt crag and grey sedimentary tail is visible at the Portcullis Gate of the castle, but what is more striking is the crag's impregnable appearance.

Although particularly hard, this rock is vertically structured and, where exposed, has become brittle enough to fragment into shards. To prevent dangerous falls of such material, there has been unplanned repair work involving cementing and the removal of loose rock over the decades until 1968. Since that time, a more permanent process of 'rock bolting' has been employed, involving the inserting of 33 feet (9.9 metres) steel bolts through the outer rock into the core and then cementing over the damaged area (*see also* CASTLES).

CALTON HILL

The 328 feet (98.4 metres) high Calton Hill is located due east of Princes Street, giving a splendid panorama of the city. In particular, its view westwards, with Princes Street partly framed by the clocktower of the New Balmoral (formerly North British) Hotel has become world famous. (Or perhaps not. A television quiz competitor recently identified this view as that of central Prague!) Robert Louis Stevenson devoted a chapter to this hill in his 1878 book *Edinburgh: Picturesque Notes*, dryly designating it the best vantage point from which to view the capital:

'since you can see the Castle, which you lose from the Castle, and Arthur's Seat, which you cannot see from Arthur's Seat'.

The Calton is accessible by road almost to its highest point, and the motorist hardly needs to emerge from his or her car to enjoy the view, particularly northwards to the Forth. This is a particularly good vantage point for disabled people wishing to overlook the city. Visitor attractions on the hill include 'Scotland's Disgrace', Nelson Monument (*see* below), City Observatory (*see* OBSERVATORIES), as well as the stupendous 360 degree view. The hill is wooded to south and east, the latter area

The new viewing table on the Braid Hills allows the climber to identify hills in Fife and well into the west of Scotland. On this occasion in 1995, the heatwave has reduced visibility to the extent that the Firth of Forth is hardly visible behind Edinburgh Castle.

comprising private gardens. The hill is not recommended after dark.

The **National Monument** is the correct name for 'Scotland's Disgrace', an unfinished copy of the Parthenon in Athens, designed by Charles Cockerell and William Playfair, and erected between 1826 and 1829 as a tribute to the dead of the Napoleonic Wars. The money ran out after 12 columns had been erected.

Nelson's Monument is over 90 feet (27 metres) in height, built as an inverted telescope in five stages. At its top is a time-ball which is dropped down a mast at precisely one o'clock to give a time signal to Forth shipping. The tower was designed in 1807 as a tribute to the victor of Trafalgar.

BLACKFORD HILL

Geologists have identified this as another volcanic stump, ground eastwards by ice into a crag and tail formation. The western end of the hill shows its basaltic origin with a craggy profile, while the eastern side is a grassy slope. The area to the south of the main summit is known as Corbie's Crag and is particularly striking. Another geological attraction is the Agassiz Rock, located to the south side of the hill, accessible from the footpath running between Liberton and Hermitage of Braid. Originally identified by visiting Swiss scientist Louis Agassiz as evidence of ice action, his interpretation is now subject to reappraisal.

This 539 feet (161.7 metre) high hill can be easily climbed from the east by able-bodied visitors walking from the car park, and their effort will be rewarded with a view as far as the Ochils and Ben Lomond. The hill also plays host to one of Edinburgh's weather stations, as well as a telecommunications mast. On the eastern flank is the Royal Observatory (*see* OBSERVATORIES). To the south-west is the Hermitage of Braid, and immediately to the north, almost invisible from the summit, is Blackford Pond (*see* PARKS).

CRAIGLOCKHART

As indicated previously, Craiglockhart Hill is actually two hills, separated by Glenlockhart Road running between the Craiglockhart and Morningside districts. The higher of the two, Wester Craiglockhart Hill, is 575 feet (172.5 metres) high, the Easter is 519 feet (155.7 metres). As with Blackford, the ascent is easier from the eastern direction and a splendid view is to be had of south-west

Edinburgh. The hills enjoy a wide diversity of botanical life, including such grassland species as Purple Milk Vetch and Maiden Pink, while such plants as Dog's Mercury and Common Dog Violet can be found in the wooded areas (*see* WILDLIFE).

CORSTORPHINE HILL

Probably best known for the Zoo on its southern flank (*see* ZOOS), Corstorphine Hill is a wooded massif running roughly north and south, with its highest point at 531 feet (159.3 metres). Magnificent views of the city, the Forth, and the Pentlands, are available to the climber, whose walk is easiest from the western side. Although pleasantly sylvan in character, the hilltop's paths could benefit from investment in new surfacing. Ironically – considering that the Zoo occupies so much of the hill – naturalists regard Corstorphine Hill as one of the most interesting sites in the city for wildlife (*see* WILDLIFE).

BRAID HILLS

Edinburgh's most southern hill massif entirely within the city boundaries, the Braid Hills have two summits, of 546 feet/163.8 metres (north) and 675 feet/202.5 metres (south). The area accommodates two public golf courses (*see* GOLF), with Mortonhall course immediately to the south. A bridle path encircles almost all of the area, affording the walker or rider refuge from airborne golf-balls, and the southern summit, complete with newly-constructed view indicator (July 1995), is easily accessible from this path. Bird and butterfly populations here reflect the heath-like nature of the Braid Hills, and are noticeably different from other parts of the city (*see* WILDLIFE). The Elf Loch is hidden away in the middle of the (private) Mortonhall golf course (*see* LOCHS).

PENTLAND HILLS

Although the main part of the Pentland massif is located outside Edinburgh, the most northern ridge of the Pentlands represents the city boundary, and is visible from all over south and south-west Edinburgh. Viewed from Morningside, the Pentland ridge comprises Hillend (1,476 feet/442.8 metres), Caerketton (1,540 feet/462 metres), and Allermuir (1,677 feet/503 metres) from east to west.

The ridge hosts one of Britain's first artificial ski-slopes on its north-eastern side, opened in 1965, but many walkers approach the ridge through the picturesque Swanston village, where R.L. Stevenson spent his boyhood summers (*see* VILLAGES). This approach, too difficult for all but the fully fit, involves passing the T wood, so distinctive in the view of the Pentlands from south Edinburgh, although it is in fact planted as a cross. An easier path (although steep) can be taken eastwards to Hillend, before turning westwards along the ridge towards Caerketton summit.

Given favourable weather conditions, the view from the top of these hills is stunning, being so much higher than the other hills within the city. The only drawback is that, on a calm day, the walker is accompanied by the continuous roar of traffic on the by-pass in the valley far below.

Historians

Historians can be placed in one of two categories – contemporary or retrospective. Among contemporary historians chronicling Edinburgh Society as they saw it around them were Lord Cockburn, such English visitors as Edward Topham and Daniel Defoe, and the industrious Church of Scotland ministers recording their three invaluable Statistical Accounts (*see* STATISTICAL ACCOUNTS). Retrospective historians are those using primary sources to glean facts with which to analyse a society which has passed.

CONTEMPORARY HISTORIANS

Henry, Lord Cockburn (1779-1854), holds an important place in the life of Edinburgh even today, for this pioneering conservationist inspired the formation and ideals of the Cockburn Association. As well as being a High Court judge, Cockburn was a prodigious diarist, and two of his published works, *Memorials of his Time* and *Circuit Journeys* have become invaluable source books for later historians to quarry.

Robert Chambers (1802–71), a member of the Peebles family which distinguished itself in Scottish publishing, was an assiduous recorder of current events and mores in the late 18th century. Thankfully, Chambers did not hesitate to record the atmosphere of the drinking 'howffs' just off the High Street, or the details of ladies' contemporary fashions. The latter point is particularly important, given the dearth of contemporary women writers and historians.

An even earlier local recorder of the city scene, was Alexander Carlyle, whose autobiography contains an eye-witness account of his walk among the dead and dying on Prestonpans battlefield, (*see* BIBLIOGRAPHY).

RETROSPECTIVE HISTORIANS

Edinburgh's first historian was William Maitland (1693-1757) who was invited by the Town Council in the early 1740s to undertake a history of the city on the lines of his already successful history of London.

Brechin-born Maitland took nearly 12 years to produce his *History of Edinburgh from its foundation to the present time* and it immediately caused a sensation in 1753 by including attacks on the provost and some magistrates. Apart from this, Maitland had made a highly successful task of creating a broad record of the city's governance and trade, working down into the detail of such matters as the diameter of water-supply pipes, which modern researchers find so fascinating and invaluable. When he cited the height of Arthur's Seat as 650 feet, some 172 feet short, he was careful enough to name a professor of mathematics as his source! Not the least of Maitland's achievements was the inclusion of a useful index. The book appeared in a number of subsequent editions – with new pages inserted softening the attack on the city's bailies!

Edinburgh's second major history appeared in 1779, from the pen of Hugo Arnot and published by William Creech, Burns's publisher and later Lord Provost. Arnot's *History of Edinburgh from its earliest accounts to the present time* is another fount of facts for later historians to relish, with perhaps more of a social slant than Maitland's work, and is particularly well illustrated. Both the above volumes can be examined in the Central Library (Edinburgh Room) or in the National Library of Scotland.

Of 20th century histories of Edinburgh published in a single volume, the works by David Daiches, E.F. Catford, and Charles McKean, are probably best known (*see* BIBLIOGRAPHY). The last-named is a distinguished architectural critic, whose refreshingly iconoclastic attitude to so much of Edinburgh's history makes his work probably the most interesting to read of all the city's historians.

There are many highly competent researchers and writers in our present century who have excelled in the history of one particular area of the city, or one area of its activities. Prominent among these are A.J. Youngson, whose *Making of Classical Edinburgh* (1966) is a classic of its kind. Malcolm Cant has made a major contribution to the history of various communities in the city – Marchmont, Gorgie, the villages – while Charles J. Smith has chronicled the story of communities on the south side, particularly Newington and Morningside.

Leith has been fortunate to have its history written by James Marshall (*The Life and Times of Leith*), and more recently by Sue Mowat (*The Port of Leith*). Portobello and Duddingston were covered in a definitive work by William Baird in his *Annals of Duddingston and Portobello* (1898), with a Mainstream volume by Dennis B. White, *Exploring old Duddingston and Portobello*, bringing the story of that area up to date.

The city's entertainment scene has been well-chronicled by the late George Baird, whose unpublished three volume collection of facts about circuses, theatres and cinemas, is an important source. The Public Library (Edinburgh Room) which holds this, has done well to provide an excellent index. Baird has also written his reminiscences of working-class life in 20th century Edinburgh, and this is another important historical source, also to be found in the Edinburgh Room. David L.G. Hunter is the city's principal transport historian, his definitive *Edinburgh's Transport* recently republished in a new edition, although with a regrettably weak index.

One historical source which should not be ignored by the researcher is the irregular periodical, *The Book of the Old Edinburgh Club*. This contains highly-scholarly articles on detailed aspects of the city's history. It has included the work of such important city historians of bygone years as William Cowan and Charles Boog-Watson, both of whom have donated much invaluable original material to the city's Edinburgh Room at the Central Library.

Hospitals

Edinburgh had 17 public hospitals in 1993. On the day of the Census two years earlier, the population enumerated within Edinburgh care establishments was 5,179, of whom 1,627 were in National Health hospitals, excluding psychiatric hospitals.

The pattern of hospital provision is a fluid one, and the number may have varied by the time of publication of this book, as indeed may the ownership of some of the city's hospitals, with the increase in the number of independent trust-owned establishments. In addition there are a number of private hospitals in the city, and a military hospital.

The basic governing body for the city's hospitals is the Lothian Health Board, although recent years have seen the establishment of six new health care services. In 1992/3 the Board had a budget of £531 million, representing revenue of £708 per head of Lothian population (as opposed to £815 in the Glasgow area, and £671 nationally). The staffing ratio per 1,000 population was superior to that of the national position – 21.5 staff compared to 20.3 nationally, although the number of beds per 1,000 population was identical in Lothian and in Scotland at large, at 9.

The work of the Lothian Health Board and the new NHS Trusts are monitored by the Lothian Health Council, a statutory body comprising 20 members, charged with the tasks of public consultation on health matters, gauging the effectiveness of such services, and advising on such provision when required.

The six health care trusts operating since 1993/4, with the hospitals they run, are as follows:

Edinburgh Healthcare National Health Service (NHS) Trust

Formed 1 April 1994, HQ at the Astley Ainslie Hospital, responsible for the Astley Ainslie, Corstorphine, Gogarburn, Northern General, Royal Edinburgh and Southfield Hospitals, South East of Scotland Breast Screening Service, Family Planning and Well Woman services, Community Dental Services.

Royal Infirmary Edinburgh NHS Trust

Founded on 1 April 1994, responsible for the Royal Infirmary, Chalmers, and City Hospitals, Edinburgh Dental Hospital, Royal Alexandra Eye Pavilion, Princess Margaret Rose Hospital, Simpson Memorial Maternity Pavilion.

Western General NHS Trust

Founded on 1 April 1993, responsible for the Western General, and Royal Victoria Hospitals.

Edinburgh Sick Children's NHS Trust

Founded on 1 April 1994, responsible for the Royal Hospital for Sick Children (Sciennes) and Forteviot House (Hope Terrace).

East and Midlothian NHS Trust

Founded on 1 April 1994 and based at Musselburgh. Responsible for (in Edinburgh) Eastern General, Leith, and Liberton Hospitals.

West Lothian NHS Trust

Founded on 1 April 1993 and based at Howden, Livingston. Responsible (*inter alia*) for a number of specialist units to which Edinburgh patients may be referred, i.e. Burns Unit at St John's Hospital, Howden, Livingston, West Lothian.

At this time of fundamental changes in the Health Service, it must be noted that a number of hospitals have closed in Edinburgh since the Second World War. They are the Longmore, Deaconness, and Bruntsfield hospitals, and perhaps the most famous of them all, the Elsie Inglis (*see* below). At the time of writing there are proposals to close smaller hospitals such as the Chalmers and Southfield, but even some of the larger units, such as the Eastern General and City hospitals, appear to be threatened. The increase of antibiotics prescribable by GPs has been responsible for the decrease in the previous heavy workload of medical cases formerly treated in hospital, while the Care in the Community policy has led to a reduction in the number of elderly and psychiatric patients being 'institutionalised'.

ROYAL INFIRMARY

All this is a far cry from the establishment of Edinburgh's Royal Infirmary, when Provost George Drummond appealed in 1725 for funds to start such a utility. Four years later a house was rented for the purpose at the top of Robertson's Close. The Infirmary's archivist was later to identify this as being on the site of the present James Thin bookshop at the south-west end of Infirmary Street, and a commemorative plaque was unveiled at that spot in 1969. It appears that the first Infirmary had a maximum of five beds, successfully discharging a total of 30 patients in its first year. Their average stay was five weeks, and the annual expenditure on the new facility was almost £98.

The hospital was administered by a Court of Contributors – the Infirmary was dependent on voluntary contributions until 1948 – and George II bestowed a Royal Charter on this rather amorphous body in 1736. Two years later a new building began construction, in Infirmary Street. Not until 1870 was the present site at Lauriston Place acquired through an Act of Parliament which also allowed the Infirmary's administration to

be improved by the establishment of a Board of Management, comprising representatives of the Town Council, University, Royal Colleges of Physicians and Surgeons of Edinburgh, Chamber of Commerce, and other local bodies.

The Infirmary settled down in its new David Bryce-designed baronial-style building in Hailes stone, which in those early days lacked the auxiliary buildings and extensions which have filled the gaps between the ward wings. Doctors and surgeons gave their services free until 1948, apart from some honoraria when teaching was involved, depending for their livelihoods on either academic posts at the university, or a lucrative private practice, or both. In 1948 the financial position was regularised with the coming of the National Health Service, and the Infirmary is now the centrepiece of the Royal Infirmary NHS Trust.

Major adjuncts to the Royal Infirmary are the Queen Alexandra Eye Pavilion, and the Scottish Blood Transfusion Service. In March 1993, the staff complement at the Royal was 2,214. At the time of writing, the Infirmary is planning to break its links with the centre of the city – and not least with the University medical school on the other side of Middle Meadow Walk – and move to a green-field site at Little France.

ASTLEY AINSLIE

Established in 1923 in a picturesque site between Morningside and Grange, the Astley Ainslie hospital originally provided convalescent facilities for the Royal Infirmary, in addition to its existing facility at Corstorphine. The name commemorates the Ainslie family of Midlothian, whose bequest made possible the purchase of a number of large properties in the area which could be run together to form a campus-style environment.

By the 1970s no fewer than 200 beds were available here in the shadow of Blackford Hill (probably not far from Henrysoun's 1580s plague camp!, *see* PUBLIC HEALTH) and the hospital, with its staff of 313 (March 1993), is no longer exclusively linked to the Infirmary. Some specialised therapies are now available for disabled patients, and the site is the headquarters of the Edinburgh Healthcare NHS Trust. From 1995 it has housed the Lothian College of Heath Studies. *Southfield Hospital*, which specialises in geriatric care, is also part of the Edinburgh Trust and had a staff of 66 in March 1993.

Also historically associated with the Royal Infirmary are the *Chalmers Hospital* and Simpson Memorial Maternity Pavilion. The former is almost a cottage hospital off Lauriston Place in the centre of the city, and only a stone's throw from the Infirmary itself. Plumbing must have been a lucrative occupation in the 19th century Canongate for it was George Chalmers of that calling who left funds for the hospital's establishment in 1864. It was originally managed by the Faculty of Advocates by the benefactor's wish, but was 'nationalised' in 1948, and came under the wing of the Royal Infirmary in 1970. In recent years it has served as an overspill for minor surgery for the Infirmary (with a staff of 109 in March 1993), and still has an active out-patients department at the time of writing.

SIMPSON MEMORIAL MATERNITY PAVILION

Expectant mothers, requiring hospital care, had been catered for at the Edinburgh Lying-in Hospital since 1793. Within 50 years this had become the Edinburgh Royal Maternity Hospital, its most famous staff member being Sir James Young Simpson, the pioneer of anaesthesia. After a nomadic existence, occupying seven buildings in 80 years, none of them purpose-built, the hospital's governors settled on a site in Lauriston Place close to the Infirmary, although no new building was immediately forthcoming.

By the 1920s the need for new maternity facilites was becoming unarguable, and it was decided to develop a site close to the Infirmary for both the Simpson – for it was determined that Sir James's services to medicine should be commemorated – and a new nurses' home. Unfortunately the Merchant Company had to be compensated for the loss of a playing field and the foundation stone was not laid for another ten years, the opening not being accomplished until 1939. The Simpson nowadays has an enviable reputation for being the best facility of its kind, and is a member unit of the Royal Infirmary NHS Trust. It was serviced by 432 staff in March 1993.

WESTERN GENERAL HOSPITAL

What is now one of Britain's finest hospitals, and the centrepiece of its own NHS Trust, began as a parish council hospital called Craigleith. Taken over by the Town Council by Act of Parliament in 1929, the Western became one of the leading municipal hospitals, renamed the Western General in February 1932, with

280 beds available. It has accumulated a postwar reputation for the excellence of its surgery, is a noted cancer-treatment centre, and is the centrepiece of its own NHS Trust. Its staff complement of 1,392 in March 1993 was the second highest in Edinburgh at that time.

Coming under the administration of the new Western General NHS Trust, is the Royal Victoria Hospital, a short distance to the south on Craigleith Road. Originally a TB hospital in Craigleith House from 1894, the hospital with its staff of 353 in March 1993, has expanded into a network of single-storey outbuildings situated in pleasant gardens.

NORTHERN GENERAL HOSPITAL

Formerly Leith's fever hospital at East Pilton, the Northern was set up at the same time as the Western General in 1932 as a municipal hospital with 260 beds. By the 1960s the Northern was specialising in the treatment of rheumatism, neurology and respiratory diseases, its capacity greatly increased by a welter of outbuildings. Situated on Ferry Road, it is now managed by the Edinburgh Healthcare NHS Trust, with a hospital staff of 55 in March 1993.

EASTERN GENERAL HOSPITAL

Like the Western General, the Eastern began as a parish council hospital transferred to the Town Council by Act of Parliament in 1929. Originally called Seafield, it was given its present name when reconstituted as a municipal hospital in 1932 with 360 beds – the largest of the three 'northern' hospitals. With some specialisation made into the fields of tropical diseases and thoracic surgery, the

Eastern scarcely deserves its description as 'possibly the bleakest of the municipal institutions' by the *Third Statistical Account*, although the establishment of Edinburgh's main sewage utility a few hundred yards to the north possibly stimulates patients to recover as quickly as possible! There were 540 staff in March 1993. This hospital is now (1995) thought to have been reprieved from proposed closure.

The Eastern is now one of the three East and Midlothian NHS Trust hospitals based in the city itself. The others are **Leith** and **Liberton** Hospitals.

LEITH HOSPITAL

Leith's own hospital has now been reduced to out-patient work as part of the East and Midlothian NHS Trust, with a staff of 19 in March 1993. The hospital was established in 1851, drawing together the work of the local Humane Society branch, the Public Dispensary, and the rudimentary Casualty Hospital.

Leith had previously been served only by the traditional medical care at St Nicholas's church in North Leith, while Trinity House looked after senior seamen. As the docks area built up, it was felt that there should be a proper hospital service in the town to cater for industrial injuries and near-drowning accidents. Leith Hospital thus came into being in 1851 as a voluntary hospital, dependent on gift and bequest until the creation of the National Health Service in 1948.

LIBERTON HOSPITAL

Whether the placename of Liberton is derived from 'Lepers' Town' seems to be a matter of debate among historians (*see*

DISTRICTS). Leper hospitals, the first called the Dyngwall, were established on the present site of the Waverley Station, outside the city walls, until 1591, when a new refuge for them was established at Greenside, near the Calton Hill. Costs for the latter were met by a local merchant, John Robertson, who had vowed to help the afflicted if only the storm his ship was caught by, would abate. It did, and he was as good as his word. The city met the cost of pensioning the lepers themselves. Liberton Hospital is a 20th century establishment, formerly a cottage hospital, situated in Lasswade Road, and now part of the East and Midlothian NHS Trust, with a staff of 223 in March 1993.

CITY HOSPITAL
Founded as Edinburgh's fever hospital in 1903 at Colinton Mains, the City has always specialised in caring for patients with infectious diseases. A virological laboratory is established here, and it was a logical location for the AIDS hospice run by the Milestone Trust to be created in 1990. The ENT (Ear Nose & Throat) patients' department was transferred here from the Royal Infirmary in 1965. There is a major ambulance depot nearby. The City is now administered by the Royal Infirmary NHS Trust, and was run by 744 staff in March 1993. The City is believed to be unlikely to see in its centenary in 2003, with closure a distinct probability before then.

PRINCESS MARGARET ROSE HOSPITAL
Situated in the Fairmilehead area of the city, the 'PMR' was opened in 1932 with 170 beds as the Edinburgh Hospital for Crippled Children. It presently specialises in orthopedics as a member hospital of the Royal Infirmary NHS Trust. It was staffed by 297 in March 1993, and justifiably has a reputation for excellence in dealing with sports injuries.

ROYAL EDINBURGH HOSPITAL
One of the largest psychiatric hospitals in the country, the 'Royal Ed' was opened in 1813 at the instigation of Dr Andrew Duncan who was determined that the mentally ill should be treated more scientifically and sympathetically than was normal at that time. Situated near Morningside Road, the hospital originally included an annexe at Craighouse, also in Morningside, although this is now owned by Napier University. The Royal Edinburgh itself, staffed by 904, is now a leading centre in the treatment of the alcohol dependent, as well as other major categories of the psychiatrically ill.

ROYAL EDINBURGH HOSPITAL FOR SICK CHILDREN
The welfare of slum children in the Old Town led to popular demand for a hospital specialising in the treatment of children. This was financed by public subscription and opened in Lauriston Lane in 1860. A move was made to custom-built facilities on the other side of the Meadows in 1895, when the present building at Sciennes was occupied. The 'Sick Kids' is administered by its own NHS Trust, staffed by 407 in March 1993, and has an psychiatric annexe in Hope Terrace, about a mile to the south-west.

The blind and deaf are cared for by the **Royal Blind School and Asylum**, and by

Donaldson's School, respectively. Visually impaired patients are cared for at the *Royal Blind School* in Newington, and at a new site in Canaan Lane, Morningside.

DONALDSON'S HOSPITAL

This an impressive palace-like edifice on the Glasgow Road just west of Haymarket. Opened for the care of deaf children in 1851, the hospital was designed by William Playfair and built from the bequest of James Donaldson. One contemporary critic complained that the building was far too ornate for children of the poor, deaf or not, and Queen Victoria is believed to have offered to exchange it for Holyrood. Up to 200 children are educated here, both as boarders and day pupils.

EDINBURGH DENTAL HOSPITAL

One of Britain's most famous dental colleges, the Edinburgh hospital has, like so many others, undergone considerable restructuring in recent years. It is, however, still based in Chambers Street, its venue since 1894, with a staff of 116 in March 1993. It was founded in 1880 as the successor to the Edinburgh Dental Dispensary, established 20 years earlier in Drummond Street. The Dental Hospital was scheduled to be completely reconstructed from 4 September 1939, but Hitler had other ideas, and modernisation was not completed until 1953.

HOSPICES

The best-known centre for the terminally ill to die with dignity in Edinburgh is *St Columba's Hospice*, founded in 1975 at Challenger Lodge in the Trinity area. The *Fairmile Hospice* serves a similar function at the Princess Margaret Rose Hospital site,

and AIDS sufferers are catered for at the *Milestone Trust* hospice immediately west of the City Hospital.

CLOSED HOSPITALS

LONGMORE HOSPITAL

Situated in Salisbury Place from its inception in March 1884, the Longmore was originally termed the Edinburgh Hospital for Incurables. Accommodating patients with TB, spina bifida, or forms of paraplegia, the hospital also built up a fine reputation in postwar years for its part in a breast-screening programme. Rationalisation in the late 1980s led to the Longmore being scheduled for closure, with the breast work being transferred to the Western General. The Longmore closed in 1991 and its building has now been acquired by Historic Scotland for its offices.

BRUNTSFIELD HOSPITAL FOR WOMEN AND CHILDREN

Founded in Whitehouse Loan in 1886 by Sophia Jex-Blake, Edinburgh's first woman medical graduate, Bruntsfield offered general medical services for women and children, with 81 beds available by the 1950s. In that decade, the requirement for female practitioners to be given first consideration for posts at Bruntsfield was confirmed in the Court of Session in 1957. Despite its excellent reputation, the Bruntsfield barely achieved its centenary before closing at the end of the 1980s, and its building was unceremoniously demolished in 1995.

ELSIE INGLIS MEMORIAL HOSPITAL

Founded in the Abbeyhill area in 1925, the 'Elsie Inglis' was held in great affection by

One of Edinburgh's best-known landmarks, the Balmoral (formerly the North British) Hotel dominates the east end of Princes Street. This summer 1995 view across the uncharacteristically empty Mound Place, shows the incline of North Bridge to the right.

the capital's citizens, who were taken aback by its closure in 1988, following a reorganisation of maternity services. The hospital's name had commemorated the work in the First World War of Dr Elsie Inglis who founded the Scottish Women's Hospitals. Edinburgh-educated Dr Inglis had led field hospital units, almost entirely staffed by women, into France, Serbia, and Russia, after her offer of service had been rebuffed by Britain's War Office and the Red Cross. She died of cancer in 1917, and was buried in the Dean Cemetery, crowds standing eight deep on Princes Street to see her funeral cortege pass.

At the time of writing (1995) a commercial nursing home has opened in the former hospital, continuing the name but with a logo appearing to portray a Florence Nightingale-like figure. One hopes this is not supposed to represent Dr Inglis, who was very much a 20th century doctor, one who voluntarily carried out her work in appalling and dangerous conditions in the 'war to end all wars'.

Hotels

As befits a major tourist centre, Edinburgh has a considerable array of hotel accommodation. At the 1991 Census, 232 hotels were open in the Edinburgh area, providing 11,721 bedspaces and representing 8 per cent of the total number of Scotland's hotels, while a District Council survey found 162 hotels (11,185 beds) in the city in 1992/3, the lower number possibly explained by a decline in the tourist trade, even in that short time (*see also* TOURISM).

The *Third Statistical Account* observed in 1966 that not one new hotel had been opened in Edinburgh in the previous half-century, and complained that local people did not seem to realise that a visitor's impression of a city was based on the comfort or otherwise of their hotel room. Nevertheless, the last 25 years of the century have seen a new generation of hotel construction, with the opening of the Sheraton, Hilton, and Scandic Crown, all in the city centre, and the Post House, Holiday Inn, and Royal Scot hotels built on the western outskirts.

Probably the two best-known hotels in the capital are the Caledonian in the West End, and the **Balmoral** (formerly the North British) at the junction of Princes Street and North Bridge.

The latter is the older of the two, opened by the North British Railway Company in 1902, with a lift connecting station and hotel. Distinguished by its 175 feet clock-tower (the clock is traditionally maintained two minutes fast) the 'NB' was sold into private hands in 1981 and underwent considerable refurbishment before reopening as the Balmoral in 1991. No doubt the new owners have modernised the wiring in the building, which was designed by the railway company to ensure that no more than one light could be turned on in any room!

The **Caledonian** opened the year after its rival at the other end of Princes Street, but rapidly secured a reputation as one of the nation's finest hotels. Constructed of red Dumfriesshire sandstone by the Caledonian Railway Company, the hotel straddled Princes Street railway terminus until the latter's closure in 1965. The site has since been rationalised, with the former station entrance forming the entry to a new bar. The 'Caley' moved into private ownership in 1981, its Pompadour restaurant still famed for its haute cuisine. At the 1992 European Summit, this hotel accommodated the British government delegation led by Prime Minister John Major.

History
In the 1770s, travel writer Edward Topham observed of Edinburgh's hospitality:

> One can scarcely form in imagination the distress of a miserable stranger on his first entrance into this city, as there is no inn better than an alehouse, nor any accommodation that is decent, cleanly or fit to receive a gentleman.

Travellers in Topham's time would normally stay in coaching inns, and there was scarcely room for those in the congested wynds and alleys of the Old Town. Neighbouring areas could, however, provide convivial hostelries for the traveller – the Sheep Heid at Duddingston, the Old and New Ship Inns in Leith, and from the second half of the 18th century, the Peacock Hotel at Newhaven.

In the city itself, the White Horse Inn flourished in St Mary's Wynd between 1635 and 1868, perhaps undiscovered by Topham, although it reputedly hosted George III, travelling incognito in 1758, and Dr Johnson in 1773. Possibly they transferred to private accommodation as quickly as possible, historian Henry Grey Graham recording that 'hostelries in Edinburgh were meant for putting up horses rather than travellers, who were expected to seek lodgings elsewhere'. In the Grassmarket, the White Hart Inn has an even longer pedigree than the White Horse, surviving nowadays as a public house (*see also* PUBS).

The construction of the New Town spurred the opening of more hotel accommodation for a city which had begun to glory in its attractions for travellers, and there were hotels in St Andrew's Square from the late 1770s. But it was the arrival of the railway which proved the greatest single boost to the hotel business, with Thomas Cook organising trips to the city from the 1850s. The North British Railway opened its hotel, the 'NB' in October 1902, and the rival Caledonian company built its hotel above Princes Street station, opening in December 1903.

Hotels have proved over the decades to be the only commercial undertakings in Princes Street which could compete in turnover with the shops in that famous thoroughfare. The street once had no fewer than four cinemas, at least two of them highly popular, but none could match the earning-power of retail shops in the years before the retail recession started around 1985. Hotels such as the Mount Royal, the Royal British, and the Old Waverley, have managed to resist being sold for yet more Princes Street shops – an indication of the strength of the hotel trade in Scotland's capital.

Housing

Edinburgh's housing, like that of all British cities, is a patchwork of owner-occupier, privately rented, and local authority homes, with housing association stock taking up an increasing share of the pattern.

The number of Edinburgh housing units at the 1991 Census were as follows, with percentage comparisons from the previous Census:

	1991	%	1981%
Owner/Occupier	123,352	66.4	52.7
Edinburgh District Council	35,452	19.1	33.0
Privately rented	15,893	8.6	9.7
Rented from employer	2,110	1.1	1.5
Housing Association (inc. SSHA)	7,359	4.0	3.0
Scottish Homes	1,498	0.8	-

In 1995 Edinburgh District Council announced that its programme of 'right to buy' by former Council tenants, coupled with private house completions, had pushed the number of owner/occupier houses to around 132,000, above two-thirds of all the stock in the city. This is believed to be the highest proportion of owner-occupier houses in any Scottish city, and the market value of the average Edinburgh house continued to be the highest in the central belt.

The number of council houses in the city in 1995 was 37,013 (from 35,452 in 1991, despite 'right to buy' sales). Nearly 40 per cent of these houses are situated in Wester Hailes, Craigmillar/Niddrie and Muirhouse/Pilton. The largest proportion of the houses in Craigmillar (64 per cent) contain three apartments, compared to 45 per cent in the newer Wester Hailes scheme, while the latter area has 25 per cent two-apartments and 24 per cent four-apartments as compared to 18 per cent and 16 per cent respectively in Craigmillar. Unfortunately, half of this publicly-owned stock was identified by the Local House Condition Survey in 1995 as being subject to damp or condensation problems, a higher proportion than estimated (38 per cent) two years earlier. Nearly two-thirds of these houses were in a category where dampness was defined by Scottish Office guidelines as 'inconvenient but tolerable with minimum mould growth'. More severe categories covered some 450 houses.

In 1994 the number of applicants on the waiting list for a council house stood at 28,910, with the number of successful applicants numbering 4,434, a decrease on the 5,500 allocations three years previously. This decrease had no doubt much to do with the reduction in housing available due to government-introduced 'right to buy' schemes, and represents an effective six-year waiting list to rent a council house in a city where the alternative cost of purchasing a house remains high compared with other communities in central Scotland.

Anyone living or working in Edinburgh can apply for a council house, under existing arrangements, and every applicant is automatically awarded 100 points, which increases by one point for every two months spent on the housing list. Additional points are awarded depending on the applicant's present housing situation – from eight points for having to share a kitchen, to 60 points for suffering racial harrassment.

Housing in Leith. Awaiting a decision on its future, the multi-storey Grampian Tower, empty and derelict 30 years after its construction, looms over the traditional tenements of Lindsay Road which are still home to generations of new Leithers. (Frank Reid)

As for the type of housing, 1991 Census figures showed that more than half of all of Edinburgh's homes were apartments, or purpose-built flats (57.7 per cent of the total housing stock), with 15.8 per cent terraced, 11.9 per cent semi-detached, 10.2 per cent detached, 4.2 per cent converted flats, and 0.2 per cent 'other'.

In 1991, a four-room house represented the largest proportion of housing stock across the city (29 per cent), with three rooms as the second most common number. Fewer than one house in five had six rooms or more. Interestingly, Cramond had the highest proportion of six-room houses in the city (no less than 60 per cent), with the Fairmilehead and Baberton wards scoring between 45 per cent and 50 per cent. The New Town ward, historically the result of the 18th century Edinburgh middle classes' need for more space, reported only 28.3 per cent of its housing stock comprising six rooms or more.

In 1995, the city had 65 multi-storey blocks, ten of them scheduled for closure or demolition, and comprising an average of 81 apartments per block. At the time of writing, the Council is planning to improve the amenity of these blocks by introducing a concierge scheme in more than half of its remaining 55 high-rise locations.

One of the particular problems facing housing authorities in Edinburgh is the high proportion of housing with lead piping as part of their water-supply systems, a historical result of having such an early conduited water supply (*see* WATER SUPPLY). Nearly 12,000 council houses in 1995 were identified as retaining lead piping or lead 'tails' connecting with the mains.

History

A characteristic of the Old Town of Edinburgh before the end of the 18th century was the co-existence of citizens of different social classes in the same buildings, with the aristocracy and merchant class living nearer the fresh air and sunlight than their social inferiors who were literally below them. According to historian Henry Grey Graham, a typical tenement would accommodate:

> the sweep and caddie in the cellars, poor mechanics in the garrets, while in the intermediate stories might live a noble, a lord

of session, a doctor, or city minister, a dowager duchess, or writer (to the Signet); higher up, over their heads, lived shopkeepers, dancing masters, or clerks.

Even the building of the New Town in the late 18th century (*see* NEW TOWN) did not entirely split society into geographically-delineated areas, if only because the large houses of the New Town required so many servants who 'lived in', or in nearby mews cottages.

The tenement has been Edinburgh's traditional dwelling-house for working-class people from the mid-19th century up until the First World War. Solidly-built, these flatted buildings can be found from Portobello to Morningside, and comprise almost the entire housing stock in areas like Gorgie and Leith. In spirit they reflect the earliest, wooden, houses which comprised the Old Town of Edinburgh while it still huddled within its city walls, and houseowners had to build ever upwards.

The word 'tenement' means a piece of land; a landowner could then exploit his limited area by building as many storeys as possible for would-be tenants, and 12 storeys were not uncommon in the Old Town, even in the 19th century. Curiously, the levels of such buildings were known as 'lands', possibly because they multiplied the original small area being so intensively developed by the landlord. These Old Town buildings were, as mentioned above, divided by class; the 19th century tenements built to cope with the swelling workforce created by the Industrial Revolution were entirely working-class.

An average tenement in Scotland's central belt comprises three to five storeys with thick external walls, although internal walls can be surprisingly thin. There is usually a pitched roof, and up to 16 chimney pots on each gable – 27 can be seen on one Portobello tenement visible from the Promenade. A central common stairway rises from an indoor well reached by a passageway, or 'close'. There is also an exit to the back green from the central well.

Some distinctions could be discerned. A 'wally' close, for example, is one with a tiled passageway, and many tenements can be pleasant places in which to live, provided neighbours make a conscious effort to live together. The widespread fitting of security systems has made it more difficult to gain access to such buildings unless the visitor is expected. Previously, a dumb-bell shaped key was used to gain entry to the passage; a 'pinkie' would do just as well, although all occupiers in the tenement, or stair, hold keys to the front and back doors.

Lighting in the stair is the responsibility of the District Council, but the occupiers are required to maintain the passage and staircase in a clean condition, taking turns to do so on a weekly basis. Older residents frequently complain that young purchasers fail to take their turn on such a sensible hygienic task; this problem will increase as more young people, not themselves raised in a tenement community, purchase tenement flats as they become available. One might reasonably think that a new houseowner would be anxious to see the stair kept clean, but this often is not the case, and the problem is made worse by flats being sub-let to students who may not recognise any such obligations. Suffice to say, as mentioned above, a degree of co-operation is required to co-exist happily in tenemental housing.

Colony housing by the Water of Leith. First built in the 1880s, these houses remain popular in such city locations as here at Stockbridge/Canonmills, as well as Abbeyhill, Shandon, Merchiston, and Dalry.

Artisans' dwellings are a pleasant exception to the housing segregation which developed in the 18th and 19th centuries, and the best example of these dwellings are 'colony' one-storey terraced houses at such locations as Abbeyhill, Canonmills/ Stockbridge, Dalry, and at Merchiston/ Shandon. Built from 1861 by the Edinburgh Co-operative Building Company, a co-operative established by masons and other craftsmen involved in the building industry, these dwellings were sold for £100, or for £5 deposit and £125 repaid to an investment company over 14 years. Colony houses now accommodate a total of 10,000 people across the city and continue to be much sought-after.

'Segregation began in the 19th century', concludes the *Third Statistical Account*, 'but not until the 1920s did open development allow of the creation of coherent areas not only housing one social stratum of the city's community, but separated by open space.' Nowadays, we accept without thinking –

and more's the pity — that Edinburgh's aristocracy or successful professionals will live in such locations as Moray Place or Heriot Row, business people in villas in pleasant spots like Barnton or Grange, but that working people are more likely to have addresses in Wester Hailes, Craigmillar, or Leith.

In the 1930s, the concept of the mass housing estate came to Edinburgh, or more accurately, to its outskirts. While privately-owned houses rarely exceed 12 to the acre, early municipal housing schemes reached 24 per acre at Niddrie, and 16 elsewhere. Prestonfield received 662 dwellings in the 1930s, Restalrig/Craigentinny 2,643, and Craigmillar/Niddrie 2,593. After the Second World War, thousands more houses were built at Southfield, The Inch, Moredun, Ferniehill, Gracemount and Hyvots Bank, Bingham, Muirhouse and Pilrig. Often these schemes lacked social and shopping facilities to an extent which compromised traditional social values and encouraged juvenile crime.

The *Third Statistical Account* averred in the 1960s that 'skyscrapers and multi-storey flats are nothing new to Edinburgh', giving Gladstone's Land, just off the Lawnmarket, as an early example of high-rise building. Even higher was Robertson's Land, a 17th century tenement towering up to 14 storeys from the Cowgate before being burnt down in 1700. Its 11-storey replacement was destroyed in the 1824 blaze which inspired the establishment of Britain's first municipal fire brigade (*see* FIRE FIGHTING). Two-thirds of the Old Town's housing was swept away in improvements in the 40 years before 1900, and modern successors to Robertson's

Land would quite literally put it in the the shade.

The city's first block of multi-storey flats rose at Gorgie in 1952, soon to be dwarfed by later developments including a 23-storey block at Muirhouse, 21 storeys at Leith Fort, and 16 storeys at Restalrig and Sighthill. As indicated above, these seemingly quick solutions to the dire need to clear slum areas have produced their own share of subsequent problems, currently being tackled by the District Council, with no less than 10 of their 65 multi-storey buildings scheduled to be taken out of use or demolished altogether.

'Prefabs', more than 4,000 in number, proved a temporary phenomenon in the housing field, although they endured longer than expected. Although the city built no more of these factory-built prefabricated buildings after 1949, they were well-equipped for their time and proved popular with the public, if less cost-effective than permanent housing.

Since the Second World War, the largest area of expansion for Council housing has been at Oxgangs, Pilton, and at Wester Hailes, originally outside the city boundary. The last-named has been described as a 'dense 4,800-house township for expatriate Leithers plonked on Pentland foothills in tall white vaguely Scots fortresses', according to architect-historian Charles McKean.

Ice Sports

Edinburgh's principal centre for ice sports is Murrayfield Ice Rink, located between Corstorphine Road and the rugby stadium.

With an ice pad 61.8 yards (60 metres) by 34 yards (33 metres), and seating for over 4,000, this represents one of the biggest facilities of its kind in Scotland, although its changing accommodation is perhaps a little on the spartan side. A curling rink has been built on at right angles, and there is another curling rink at Gogar, on the city's western outskirts. There were a number of now-defunct rinks, both indoor and outdoor, which should be mentioned, and they are described under 'History' below.

Edinburgh has played a large part in the development of *ice skating*. A skating club was formed in the city in 1744, well before London, whose club dates from 1830. The country's oldest existing club, Murrayfield ISC, is based at the rink of the same name, where the Scottish Ice Skating Association is also located. Local skater Stephanie Main has won the British Senior Ladies title twice in the last three years, at the time of writing.

Ice hockey attracts large crowds to Murrayfield on a regular basis, usually on Sunday evenings. Called Murrayfield Racers until 1994, the team has had a troubled history in recent years, but prospects had appeared brighter when the team contested the 1995 British Championship final at Wembley. This was only narrowly lost to the Sheffield Steelers, but a greater defeat which came along that year was a financial crisis which led to the team dropping out of Britain's Premier League. When it is remembered that none of Edinburgh's football, rugby, or cricket, teams compete in any British competitions in this supposedly United Kingdom, the Murrayfield team's self-sought demotion is all the more regrettable. The team is now once again known as the Murrayfield Royals (*see* below).

Curling was first codified by Duddingston Curling Society in 1804, providing the basis for a game which has become popular across the globe. Canonmills Loch claimed to have a curling club before Duddingston's began in 1761, although all of the city's curling activity is now indoors. Nowadays Edinburgh is the location for both the Royal Caledonian Curling Club (RCCC), instituted in 1838 and 'Royal' from 1843, and the World Curling Federation, set up in 1973 (renamed from the International Curling Federation in 1991).

There were 54 curling clubs registered in the RCCC's Area 5 based on the city's two rinks, at Murrayfield and Gogar in 1995. These were as follows (clubs from other areas, such as the Borders, and using Edinburgh facilities, are not included here):

Murrayfield

37 Club, Abbotsford, Bank of Scotland, Boswall (also uses Gogar), Bruce, Bruntsfield, Chartered Surveyors, Clydesdale Bank, Coates, Colinton Ladies, Corstorphine, Corstorphine Ladies, Dalkeith, DAFS, Duddingston, Dundas & Wilson, Edinburgh Academicals, Edinburgh BMA Ladies, Edinburgh Curling Club, Edinburgh Ladies, Edinburgh Medical, Edinburgh Plumbing Employers, Edinburgh Rotary, Ford Ladies, George Heriot's, George Watson's, Holyrood, Lothian Health Board Staff, Lothian Ladies, Lowland Brigade, Merchiston, Midcalder, Musketeers, Musselburgh, National Coal Board, Oxenfoord, Penicuik, Pentland Ladies, Royal Bank of Scotland, SIAE, Scottish Widows, Stewart's Melville FP, Super, Watsonian.

Gogar

Carrington (also uses Murrayfield), Currie & Balerno, Dominies, Dundas, Eglinton, Gogar Park, Gogar Park Young Curlers, Haymarket, Owl.

History of Edinburgh ice sports

Skating and curling were developed as sports on frozen lochs and ponds, indoor rinks only becoming available as freezing technology developed towards the end of the 19th century. Canonmills Loch was drained by the 1840s, Duddingston Loch, long popular with skaters, became a bird sanctuary in the 1920s, and the last outpost for outdoor ice skating in Edinburgh appears to have been at Happy Valley, the sports complex at Craiglockhart. Here the pond was given over to skating, floodlit after dark, when conditions in winter were suitable – 'frost holding', as a 1930s newspaper advert rather ominously put it. (see also LOCHS).

The Edinburgh Skating Club was formed in 1744, and a century later boasted Prince Albert as its patron, with Lord Cockburn as a member of its council. In fact, high office counted for nothing in the Club membership, according to an 1846 publication about the Club:

> 'nobility, judges, and eminent men of the land; all of them however, without distinction of rank, were required to go through regular trials of their qualifications on the ice before they could be admitted as members'.

Two indoor rinks opened in 1912, at Lochrin and Haymarket. The former was incorporated into a car showroom in 1920, and may have closed for skating as early as 1914, but the Haymarket Rink had a longer pedigree.

Described as Britain's largest when opened by Lord Provost William Brown in February 1912, Haymarket Rink (officially Edinburgh Ice Rink) was a popular venue for ice sports, although it lacked spectator accommodation. With the coming of the Second World War, the Admiralty requisitioned the building and buried the freezing pipes under a massive concrete floor. Although it reopened postwar, it was dwarfed by the newer Murrayfield facility to the west, and closed in the 1970s.

Murrayfield Ice Rink was scheduled to open on 15 September 1939, but a less appropriate time for a new sporting initiative could scarcely be imagined, and the huge building became a NAAFI store until 1942, and then a depot for His Majesty's Stationery Office until 1951. On 8 August 1952, Lord Provost James Miller declared the facility open to the public after a 13 year wait, with the first ice hockey match scheduled between the Murrayfield Royals and Falkirk Lions in September of that year.

Industry

At the 1991 Census, 30,978 people were employed in industry in Edinburgh, out of a total workforce of 225,654. This industrial workforce was down from 42,349 in 1981, a reduction of approximately one-third, but perhaps not a matter of surprise for a nation which has gone through such serious recession in the marketplace, and in particular seen the diminution of its manufacturing industries in a national context.

For the record, Edinburgh's workforce in 1981 and 1991 was distributed as follows:

	1981	1991
Electrical/Electronic Engineering	8,225	7,519
Food & Drink	14,819	8,347
Paper/Printing/Publishing	6,302	4,259
Construction	13,003	10,853

The 15 largest companies with their head office in the city, arranged by 1992 turnover (except where indicated) were:

Standard Life (Life Assurance)	£5,480m
Royal Bank of Scotland (1993)	2,968m
Scottish Widows (Life Assurance)	2,598m
Bank of Scotland	2,577m
Scottish & Newcastle	1,514m
Scottish Equitable (Life Assurance)	1,322m
John Menzies (Retailing) (1993)	1,168m
United Distillers	965m
Scottish Provident (Life Assurance)	826m
Scottish Life (Life Assurance)	703m
Christian Salvesen (Distribution)	528m
Dawson International (Textiles)	432m
TSB Scotland (Banking)	376m
Miller Group (Construction)	258m
Kwik-Fit (Vehicle maintenance)	234m

Source: Edinburgh District Council.

In 1994 Edinburgh District Council listed the following companies as the city's largest manufacturers:

GEC Marconi Avionics	Defence-related electronics
Uniroyal Englebert	Tyres
Scottish & Newcastle	Brewing/Leisure
Burton's Biscuits	Food
D.B. Marshall	Food
Scotsman Publications	Publishing
Hewlett-Packard	Electronics
Racal-MESL	Electronics
Ethicon	Pharmaceuticals
William Thyne	Packaging

City tourist guides at one time assured visitors that Edinburgh's principal products were 'beer, brains, and books'. TOURISM itself is now one of the most important industries in the capital and has an entry of its own, as have BANKS and INSURANCE. More specifically, the following can be regarded as Edinburgh's manufacturing industries, past or present, worthy of greater examination :

Biscuit-making, Brewing, Coalmining, Confectionery, Crystal-making, Electronics, Papermaking, Printing and Publishing, Rubber, Shipbuilding.

BISCUIT-MAKING

Edinburgh claims to be the home of the Digestive Biscuit, and certainly deserves to be considered as one of the most important biscuit-manufacturing centres in Britain, even if the industry has changed considerably in the last 50 years. The biggest producer is ***Burton's (United Biscuits)***, their Sighthill factory, founded in 1968, representing the fourth largest manufacturing site in the city, and was the biggest of its kind in Britain when opened.

Smaller-scale production continues at **Simmers**' Mitchelhill factory near Craigmillar, employing around 100 people, while the **Waverley Biscuit Company** in Rodney Street still produces wafer biscuits for the ice-cream industry.

History

Biscuit manufacturers no longer producing their wares in Edinburgh include **McVitie Price**, **Crawfords**, **Mackies**, and **Middlemass**. Robert McVitie began retailing bakery products in the 1830s before deciding to produce his own, first under the arch of George IV Bridge at Merchant Street and then at Robertson Avenue. Despite the latter site being badly affected by fire in 1894, his company became a major trader in the Edinburgh area, complete with retail and restaurant premises in Princes Street and Charlotte Street. In 1965 the firm amalgamated with Alex Ferguson's confectioners, producers of Edinburgh Rock, but soon after became part of the United Biscuits Group.

Crawfords are a well-known name in the city, although they no longer produce biscuits in the capital. Beginning with a shop at Leith's Shore, and then in Elbe Street, Crawfords grew to become a nationwide bakery chain, employing 3,000 people by 1938. Female workers at the Bellevue bakery, McDonald Place, were affectionately known as 'White Mice' from the appearance of their overalls and turbans. In 1965 the firm joined with other major producers, including McVitie and MacFarlane Lang to form United Biscuits.

Mackies were established in Edinburgh in 1825 and became particularly noted for their shortbread. With their headquarters at 108 Princes Street, they advertised themselves in 1960 as 'purveyors of rusks and shortbread to the late King George V'. Robert Middlemass is credited with the invention of the Digestive Biscuit, and was a famous trading name based at Causewayside, the firm being absorbed by United Biscuits in 1971. The biscuit factory site now hosts the futuristic towers of the Science Library (*see* LIBRARIES).

BREWING

At the time of writing, beer is produced in Edinburgh at two major sites, one of them run by one of the biggest 'national' brewers, the other by an independent. The bigger of these is Scottish & Newcastle, the Caledonian Brewery being an independent concern which has been saved from closure. There are also a number of 'brew pubs' which produce their own beer on the premises.

SCOTTISH & NEWCASTLE (S&N)

Best known by its McEwan's and Youngers brand-names, S & N is currently bidding to become the largest brewing company in Britain, and already controls some 3,500 licenced premises. With its Fountain Brewery at West Fountainbridge and its administrative headquarters at the foot of the Royal Mile and Holyrood Road, the company's presence in the city is less than it once was, although a new office building is presently under construction in Dundee Street, and S & N remains the city's third largest manufacturer, whose products are still consumed with relish both in and beyond Scotland (*see also* PUBS).

CALEDONIAN BREWERY

Situated just off Slateford Road, the 'Caley' is a phoenix resurrected on the Scottish brewing scene. Brewing had taken place here – and still does – using direct-fired open coppers from 1869, and from 1919 came under the control of the Vaux company. In 1987 a management buy-out prevented the brewery's closure, and now some 350 free trade outlets are serviced by this enterprising independent with its Edinburgh Real Ale, 60/- and 70/- ales, amongst others.

'Brew Pubs' are something of a throwback to the time when individual pubs brewed their own ales, and these bring welcome variety to the tippler's market choice. Local Edinburgh centres of this kind at the time of writing include the **Physician and Firkin**, opposite the Royal Commonwealth Pool, and the **Rose Street Brewery**. The latter was founded in 1983 by the Alloa Brewery, and supplies six other local pubs.

History

Brewing appears to have first been undertaken in Edinburgh at Holyrood Abbey from its establishment in the 12th century. By the 16th, the production of ale had become secularised, its importance not to be underestimated in a community which was chronically short of water. Indeed, public draw wells in the city had to be locked at night to prevent brewers using them (*see* WATER SUPPLY), despite the fact that there was a well for brewers' use in the Canongate, and water supplies were also found on the fringes of Holyrood, particularly at Craigmillar. At one time

water was being taken from the Burgh Loch (*see* LOCHS) using a windmill-driven pump. The area round the Bristo Port became known as Society, after the association of brewers in the area, 'Bristo' itself being a corruption of the word brewer or brewster.

The year 1710 saw the establishment of Archibald Campbell's brewery in the city, with William Younger opening in Leith some 40 years later. This was to become the biggest of the Edinburgh, indeed Scottish, breweries, the company moving up the road to Edinburgh in 1778 and even going to the trouble of sinking an artesian well in the Grange area and then piping this private water supply to its brewery at Craigmillar (*see* WATER). By 1800 there were 14 brewing concerns in Edinburgh, by far the largest concentration of brewing in Scotland, and by 1825 this had increased to 29, with Glasgow beginning to develop a rivalry with 22.

In 1931 Youngers merged with McEwan, begun in 1856, its patron William McEwan responsible for donating the McEwan Hall to Edinburgh University. Each company maintained a degree of autonomy, but a full merger took place in 1959, forming Scottish Brewers, now Scottish & Newcastle. The company's brewing activities ceased in the Canongate in 1986, but in July 1973 they had opened a new Fountain Brewery on an 11 acre site in Fountainbridge.

Tennents removed themselves from the city brewing scene in the 1980s, their Slateford site becoming the subject of a management buy-out.

By 1937 Edinburgh was the second most important brewing centre in Britain, with no fewer than 23 working breweries. The

Edinburgh is one of the few locations in Britain where deep coalmining still takes place. This May 1993 picture shows men on an early morning shift at Monktonhall entering the cage to take them hundreds of feet below. Monktonhall was bought by the miners themselves when closure loomed, although a commercial company has now become involved. (The Scotsman)

present-day complement of two breweries, plus a number which are basically pubs, hardly stands comparison.

Edinburgh's brewing industry has been responsible for the building of two of the finest halls in the city – the McEwan Hall in Teviot Place, and the Usher Hall. The former is the scene of Edinburgh University's graduation ceremonies, and was built between 1888 and 1897 (*see* UNIVERSITIES AND COLLEGES). The Usher Hall is the city's largest. Built with a £100,000 donation from Andrew Usher, the 2,900 seat auditorium was designed by J.S. Harrison and opened in 1914.

CAR MANUFACTURE

This is not an industry normally associated with Edinburgh, but a number of road vehicles were produced in the city from the opening of the 20th century to around 1930. Unfortunately, the history of the Scottish car industry still remains less well documented than it might be – we know that a steam road vehicle called the Bon Car was produced in Leith around 1905, but details are lacking, and more information about the Madelvic company of Granton would be welcome. This company, owned at one time by a member of the Peck family best known in the city for stationery supply, succeeded in obtaining a licence to carry mail between

Edinburgh and Leith in 1899, although its success appears to have been short-lived.

COALMINING

Coal is still mined within the city boundaries at Monktonhall colliery on the south-east fringe of the city. Here in 1992 117 miners refused to accept the prospect of their pit closing and formed the industry's first collective buy-out by each making an individual investment of £10,000.

So far their enterprise has succeeded in as much as 6,000 tons of high-quality coal is produced weekly, but commercial investors have also come in to attempt to secure the site's long-term future. In November 1995 it was announced that the need to open a new seam would require the scale of investment that only a commercial company could offer, and an overwhelming majority of the miners decided to take the opportunity to sell their shareholdings in exchange for shares in the new owning company.

In recent decades pits existed at Gilmerton, closed in 1961, and Newcraighall, the latter only closing in 1968. Other pits, such as Woolmet, lay just over the pre-1975 city boundary, but had closed by that year.

History

From the Middle Ages, Edinburgh had a powerful appetite for coal, although transport links with the Midlothian coalfield to the south were slow to develop. This trade was the *raison d'etre* of the Edinburgh & Dalkeith Railway in 1831 (*see* RAILWAYS), and the necessity for weighing coals for the practical purposes of transporting it, proved to be a bonus for city customers, as 'railway coal' could be guaranteed to reach its advertised weight.

So important was coal traffic to the North British Railway Company that it constructed the 'Lothian Lines' to facilitate the transport of coal from the Lothian pits to Leith just before the First World War, virtually superimposing a new railway on the existing system. The Union Canal (*see* CANAL TRANSPORT) also imported coal to the city from around 1822, mainly from West Lothian.

Edinburgh and Leith are believed to have been consuming 200,000 tons of coal annually in 1800 – before canal and rail connections were available, so inevitably there were smaller mines and pits existing within carting distance of the city to satisfy this demand, particularly as there appears to have been negligible import of English coal through Leith before 1820. Mining historian Baron Duckham records that, by 1800, pits at Duddingston, Edmonstone, Loanhead, Newton, Sheriffhall, and Woolmet (sites now all within District Council boundaries) were equipped with steam engines for drainage purposes, so there should be no doubt about the economic importance of the Midlothian coalfield, with its ever-demanding market to the north.

Despite the gradual run down of the mining industry in the last 50 years, it was decided in postwar times by the then new National Coal Board that four pits in the east of Scotland merited considerable investment. This virtually amounted to creating new mines from scratch in the case of Bilston Glen and Monktonhall, both then just outside Edinburgh. Work began on both in the 1950s, Bilston not reaching full production until 1964 after a 2,550 foot shaft had been sunk at a cost of £10.4 million. Production targets of one million tons annually were met, but even this failed to guarantee the pit's future, and closure resulted in June 1989.

No such fate has befallen the other new pit in the area, Monktonhall, where a 3,000 foot shaft was sunk at a cost of £9 million, its uncharacteristic colliery towers visible from most vantage points on the east of the city. Coal is still produced here.

CONFECTIONERY

Edinburgh Rock is still produced in segment form (as opposed to stick rock which is more associated with seaside resorts). Local manufacturers include **Cameo Confectionary**, based on the outskirts of Portobello and **James Ross and Co.**, another former Edinburgh company, based in Roseburn Street in the 1960s, now removed out to Loanhead to take advantage of favourable development incentives.

History
In 1960 Edinburgh had five confectionery and chocolate manufacturers. To say that this was a 'high-profile' industry is to state the obvious – its products included Duncan's Hazlenut chocolate, and Edinburgh Rock.

Duncan's began confectionery manufacturing in Edinburgh in 1884, establishing a factory in Beaverhall Road, near Powderhall, 11 years later. Claiming to be 'the Scots word for chocolate', the company produced milk chocolate bars, hazlenut whirls, and Parisian creams which were justifiably popular, and Duncan's became a major source of local employment. Using conveyor-belt technology to its maximum, and with a stratified management structure (uniforms and epaulettes were used to signify a manager's level of seniority) Duncan's were regarded as a strict, but fair, employer. Eventually taken over by Rowntrees, Duncan's produced only the latter company's branded products from 1967, and some 20 years later, closure was announced. Following a management buyout in 1988, a new slimmed-down Duncan's carried on the business by reintroducing their brand name products, but a regrettable decision was soon made to transfer the industry to Lanarkshire.

Alex. Ferguson's was a comparatively small concern with a factory in East Crosscauseway and a shop in Grindlay Street, but their principal product was hugely popular. This was Edinburgh Rock, probably best remembered in its coloured form and boxed with an illustration of Princes Street on its tartan cover. The firm merged with McVitie's in 1965 (*see* INDUSTRY – BISCUIT MAKING).

CRYSTAL

Edinburgh Crystal is no longer produced in Edinburgh, but in Penicuik some eight miles to the south. This is because the premises where this prestige product was created in the city were becoming too cramped, while the financial incentives to move factories out of the city (i.e. regional assistance schemes) made such a move profitable.

History
Glass appears to have been produced in Edinburgh and Leith from the middle of 17th century, taking advantage of plentiful

supplies of sand and kelp, the latter producing potash when burned. Edinburgh's upper classes represented a lucrative market for producers of drinking glasses, while the growing brewing industry required bottles, and plenty of them. Leith was employing 120 glassblowers in 1700, and bottle production later became a major industry at nearby Portobello. From 1760 to 1790 the demand for glass increased more than five times over, and Leith had six separate glassworks by 1792.

The second Jacobite rebellion appears to have produced its own 'heritage industry' in the years after 1745 with the production of Jacobite glasses and goblets, those made after 1746 emblazoned only with symbolic references to the Young Pretender, whose likeness was as proscribed as a graven image in Exodus. It was this trend towards the more decorative end of the market that became a characteristic of Edinburgh glassware, with the evolution of the Edinburgh Crystal Glass Company through a number of name changes and amalgamations with English companies.

The firm worked from two different addresses in Leith Walk before establishing itself at Norton Park, just north of Abbeyhill by the beginning of the 20th century. Here the firm's finest work was produced, much of it to exhibition standard. Apart from interruptions by more utilitarian demands in two world wars – when such essentials as light bulbs and glass envelopes for cathode ray tubes were produced – crystal became the firm's staple product. A move was made to Midlothian when it was realised that a modern plant was required, and this was opened in 1969. A history of the crystal industry can be found in H.W. Woodward's book *The Story of Edinburgh Crystal* (*see* BIBLIOGRAPHY).

Glass bottle production ceased in Portobello in 1968, the Woods company, which operated in the Baileyfield area, being taken over by Distillers Ltd and then by United Glass Bottle Manufacturers.

ELECTRONICS

Three of the city's ten largest manufacturers are involved in electronics – GEC Marconi Avionics, Hewlett-Packard, and Racal-MESL Electronics.

GEC Marconi Avionics, formerly Ferranti, are based at Crewe Toll, just off Ferry Road. As defence contractors this concern has been affected by the 'Peace Dividend' following the end of the Cold War, but is still heavily engaged in aeronautical projects. The factory was founded in the city in 1943, and in the 1960s represented Edinburgh's biggest employer, although it has now slipped to sixth.

Hewlett-Packard is a well-known electronic company employing 1,200 people at South Queensferry, producing personal computers and printers, computer systems, and test and measurement equipment. In 1995 it was estimated that the Queensferry plant was producing 20 per cent of the company's output in the United Kingdom, with an impressive 32 per cent increase being recorded over the previous year.

Racal-MESL Electronics is based at Ratho. This company produces a wide range of microwave and acoustic wave components, representing a major contributor to the local economy.

PAPERMAKING

No longer produced in Edinburgh, paper was an essential commodity in a city involved in the writing and production of books, the daily processes of government, and, from the 18th century, the issuing of banknotes.

Scotland's first mill was established in 1590 by Mungo and Gideon Russell at a location identified by historical records as Dalry, on a tributary of the Water of Leith. By 1700, six of Scotland's first 12 mills had been established, some temporarily, in Edinburgh, and a seventh in Colinton. As well as Dalry (two), there were mill sites at Canonmills (two), Upper Spylaw, Restalrig and Braid. One of the most prominent papermakers in the years before 1700 was Peter Breusch (Bruce) who obtained a patent to produce playing-cards as well as becoming King's Printer, despite suffering religious persecution as a Roman Catholic. He figures more largely in Edinburgh's story in solving the city's water-supply problem (*see* WATER SUPPLY).

So established did papermaking become in the river-valleys to the south of Edinburgh, that it required considerable importing of raw materials through Leith, including wood pulp and esparto grass. Its history is inextricably tied in with that of printing and publishing (*see* below).

An Edinburgh company distinguished for its manufacture of paper-making machinery was Bertrams of Sciennes. As late as 1985, this now-defunct firm was producing its wares on a site it had occupied since 1821, only a stone's throw from the Meadows.

PRINTING AND PUBLISHING

As can be seen from the census figures, the numbers employed in printing and publishing in Edinburgh have decreased by around 50 per cent in the 1981-91 decade. Yet the decline between 1963 and 1981 was even more pronounced, with a drop from around 11,100 to 6,300. This decline probably has a lot to do with the computerisation of the industry, where a typist can typeset a book on a computer costing a few hundred pounds, instead of a specially-trained typesetter having to be employed to operate hot metal equipment, while book production itself has also become more machine-manageable.

In place of such great printing works as Neils at Causewayside, or Morrison & Gibb at Tanfield, a plethora of high street print shops have emerged to take over much of the 'short-run' end of the trade. In addition, the recession has seen considerable rationalisation in the twin worlds of printing and publishing, which share a historical base. Nearly all the names listed in the 1960s *Third Statistical Account*, as representing Edinburgh's contribution to the world of the printed word, no longer do so – Thomas Nelson, Oliver & Boyd (now an imprint of Longmans), Bartholomew (in printing only), W. & A.K. Johnston, and T. & A. Constable.

Nowadays, Edinburgh's most famous publishers include, at the academic end of the market, **Edinburgh University Press** and the former **Chambers** empire, the latter also trading under the French brand name of **Larousse**. Thus, Edinburgh, the birthplace of the *Encyclopaedia Britannica*, and first home to the firm **A. & C. Black** which owns *Who's Who*, continues its production of high-quality reference works. Independent Edinburgh publishers include in their number **Mainstream** and **Canongate**, with many local titles emerging from such firms as **Mercat Press** (owned by booksellers James Thin's) and **John Donald**, and from **Gordon Wright**, an individual with a distinguished record of publishing on Scottish, and particularly, Edinburgh, topics.

Unfortunately, the great **John Bartholomew and Son's** map publishing enterprise was taken over in 1980, later came under the Collins banner, and its editorial division relocated to Glasgow in October 1995 (although the printing is still undertaken in Edinburgh at the time of writing).

History

Scotland's first printing press was established in Edinburgh's Cowgate in 1507 by Walter Chepman and Andro Millar. Granted a patent by James IV, Chepman and Millar were charged with producing the Acts of the Scottish Parliament as well as religious works, using a printing-press they brought from France. Their work was continued by Thomas Davidson in the 1520s, and John Scot and Robert Leekprevik later in the century. The latter produced the first book printed in Gaelic, in 1567, and the first medical treatise, a description of the plague, by Gilbert Skeyne, in the following year.

With royalty taking a strong interest in printed works, it was inevitable that the departure of the Court to London in 1603, would affect the printing industry, but from 1638 to 1711 the royal imprimatur was held by Glasgow printers. During this time, in 1641, Scotland's first newspaper, the *Diurnal Occurrances touching the Dailie Procedings in Parliament*, was printed in Edinburgh but it was a pale copy of a similar publication in London.

Up to the nineteenth century there was little differentiation to be made between printers and publishers, as the latter produced their own books. It was in this way that the *Encyclopaedia Britannica* was created, not by a 'Society of Gentlemen' as indicated on the first title-page when it emerged as a 'piecework' publication in 1768, but as the product of Edinburgh printer Colin McFarquhar and engraver Andrew Bell. They employed William Smellie to edit the first edition, and none of them could have dreamed what they were starting. When the publisher/printers decided they wanted to produce a second edition, one much larger than the first, Smellie declined to undertake the writing and editing of ten volumes, so they employed the impecunious James Tytler. Tytler, who also features in Edinburgh's story as Britain's first balloonist (*see* BALLOONING), wrote the bulk of the seven additional volumes himself in Duddingston village, then part of Holyrood sanctuary, for which he was paid sixteen shillings (80p) a week, between 1777-84.

The *Britannica*, now published in the United States since 1921, is a good means of outlining the spread of Edinburgh publishing, since it has been owned by a number of publishing houses, such as Constable, and A. & C. Black. Adam Black was a highly successful member of the Edinburgh publishing industry, and was both Lord Provost and the city's MP (taking his seat at Westminster when aged 72). After 1851 this firm also acquired the copyright of Scott's novels. Despite these bonds, Black's soon moved to London.

On the distributive side of the publishing business is **John Menzies**, a company which recorded Scotland's most profitable results in 1994. Menzies is now known nationally for its chain of retail shops selling books, newspapers, magazines, and confectionery, as well as stationery and audio-visual products. It is also active in wholesale distribution.

The retail aspect of bookselling is well catered for in the city by the presence of such well-known bookshops as **James Thin** and **Bauermeisters**, two local concerns which have stepped up their opening hours and opened new branches in a largely successful effort to match the efforts of the enterprising **Waterstone** chain, which now has three branches in central Edinburgh.

RUBBER

Rubber product manufacturing occupied no fewer than 4,400 employees in Edinburgh in 1951, with the **North British Rubber Company** the largest single employer in the city at that time, its Castle Mills site encompassing 22 acres. The work undertaken included the production of oilfield hoses, car floormats, golf balls, hot water bottles, as well as tyres, with North British operating only one of three tyre reclamation centres in Britain. 130 tons of scrap rubber were converted into 100 tons of reclaimed products every week in an early example of recycling.

Rubber products had been produced in the capital since 1855, with Scottish industrialists able to take advantage of the chaotic patent system in Britain –

vulcanisation patents registered in England did not apply north of the Border (a similar anomaly arose over cameras, *see* PHOTO-GRAPHY) and by 1856 Goodyear products were appearing from Castle Mills (now demolished) beside the Union Canal, the latter proving to be a useful water conduit. United States capital was invested in this Edinburgh enterprise from the start, the *Third Statistical Account* asserting that this 'may have been the first direct investment of United States capital in British manufacturing history', although control was held by British executives within ten years of establishment.

The rubber industry, which was so innovative in character as an example of inward investment and in its recycling programmes, ceased to be part of the city's industrial scene around 1967, with the move to a Uniroyal plant at Newbridge (now Uniroyal Englebert, and still operating within the District Council area). The **Victoria India Rubber Mills** off Leith Walk, a smaller concern specialising in producing waterproofed apparel for the emergency and military services, closed around the same time.

SHIPBUILDING

LEITH

More than 450 years of Leith shipbuilding came to an end in 1984 with the closure of the Robb Caledon shipyard, fronting on to the Western Harbour. Known as Henry Robb's from 1924 to 1977, this was an industrious concern which absorbed two other well-known shipbuilders in Leith – Cran & Somerville and Ramage & Ferguson.

Originally specialising in dredger and pontoon building, Robbs soon geared up to the construction of merchant and auxiliary shipping of up to 10,000 tons. A number of corvettes and frigates were built in the Second World War, and it was a later naval vessel which was one of the yard's most famous – HMS *Herald*, a survey ship, completed in 1974, which took its place (as a hospital tender) in the South Atlantic Task Force in the Falklands conflict in 1982, as well as the Gulf War in 1991.

The tradition of Leith shipbuilding, which began with the production of the port's first warship, the *Margaret*, ordered by James IV and launched on 3 February 1517, ended with the completion by Robb Caledon in 1984 of the *St Helen*, a Sealink ferry for the Solent launched on 15 September 1983. It was a proud tradition, one which produced the *Sirius* in 1838, built by Robert Menzies, and immortalised as the first steamship to cross the Atlantic.

NEWHAVEN

Shipbuilding at Newhaven was introduced by James IV, who needed deeper water at the launch-site to accommodate larger warships. Historians describe the woods of Fife being destroyed for the best-known ship to be built at Leith, the *Michael*, although a modern historian has argued that it was the shipyard itself which required timber from comparatively nearby, and that the most famous warship constructed there wasted the forests of even farther away.

Seven years under construction, the warship *Michael* was 240 feet (72 metres) long and 36 feet (10.8 metres) wide, with a crew of 300. She was the largest vessel to be built in Scotland at the time, and was not excelled for many years. She appears to have been involved in only one military exercise, in association with the land war which ended disastrously for James IV and Scotland at Flodden. Bought by France in 1514, the *Michael* appears to have been little used in subsequent years.

PORTOBELLO

There was some shipbuilding in the Portobello area on a limited scale in the early 19th century, and amphibious vehicles were produced at an improvised factory in the Marine Gardens during the Second World War.

SHIPPING

Edinburgh's marine activities have always centred almost entirely on Leith, and have traditionally been variations of fishing, and merchant shipping. For centuries, Leith specialised in polar fishing, i.e. whaling and sealing, at both ends of the earth. Leith boats travelled to Greenland at one extreme and to the Antarctic at the other.

The need to establish new whaling grounds in both the northern and southern seas drove sailors from Scotland's principal port to pioneer new paths into the unknown. Unlike the products of London's clubland in the early 20th century, who made the exploration of the earth's extremes a test of manliness, Leith explorers were driven by commercial concerns. Not for nothing is the Weddell Sea named after James Weddell (1787–1834), a Lanarkshire man who accepted a commission to lead a commercial foray from Leith as far south as possible, and it is no surprise to find a Leith Harbour in South Georgia, and an 'Edinburgh' part of the way southwards, in the mid-Atlantic island of Tristan da Cunha (*see* TWINNING).

The shipping (and shipbuilding) industries of Leith have been well documented by Captain John Landels in Sue Mowat's book *The Port of Leith* (*see* BIBLIOGRAPHY). One of the most famous of these companies, the Ben Line, withdrew from the shipping business in 1993, yet it hardly seems very long ago when the progress of the Ben ships from port to port, usually in the Far East, could be followed on a specially-made announcement board in a window of the company's office in St Andrew's Square. Gone are the days when there were regular sailings from Leith to almost 90 destinations, from Aalborg to Windau, as listed in the 1929 Post Office Directory.

Other Leith Industries

Leith's industries have usually been marine-orientated, and chandlers' and chart-sellers are still to be found in the port and surrounding hinterland. One of the most famous industries of them all was the **Roperie**, a rope-producing factory between the Links and the sea, which only went out of business postwar. Ropemaking in Leith goes as far back as 1638, and at one time there were two roperies opposite each other in the area of Bath Street.

LOST INDUSTRIES

Those industrial concerns lost to Edinburgh are unfortunately extensive. Edinburgh has given other British localities such enterprises as Duncan's Chocolates (relocated to Motherwell), Edinburgh Crystal (to Penicuik), the *Encyclopaedia Britannica* (Chicago), *Who's Who* (London), Bartholomew's atlases (to Glasgow), while even the *Daily Mail*, when deciding to re-establish its Scottish operation, plumped for Glasgow instead of its former Edinburgh base. The reduction from 23 Edinburgh breweries in 1937 to three in 1995, suggests that, even allowing for the decline in the industry, much of Edinburgh's former brewing activity is being carried out elsewhere.

Many of these losses may have been politically-fostered. The introduction of selective assistance schemes for manufacturers opening new factories, persistently omitted Edinburgh in postwar years, and it is hardly surprising that such industries as rubber manufacturing and crystal making moved out of the city to subsidised sites outside in the late 1960s. Conspiracy theorists may notice that, at that time, Edinburgh was a Conservative-controlled city in a Labour hinterland. On the other hand, when Duncan's Chocolates moved westwards in the 1990s to take advantage of an 'Enterprise' subsidy offer, devised by a Conservative government, Edinburgh was Labour-controlled!

The apparent lack of discussion about such losses in Edinburgh society suggests that many citizens are simply unaware of the problem. Yet more losses are currently threatening in the biggest industry of them all – tourism, with a local authority in the west of Scotland pushing hard for the establishment of a national art gallery whose only logical location should be the Scottish capital (*see* ART GALLERIES and TOURISM).

Insurance

It is not necessary to consult statistical tables to grasp the fact that insurance is one of Edinburgh's most important industries. Most of the city's newest and most imaginative buildings are in fact insurance offices – the new Standard Life buildings in the West End and beside the Water of Leith at Canonmills, Scottish Widows' HQ with its surrounding moat at Dalkeith Road, and the triangular facade of the Life Association building in Dundas Street, are four very striking examples of how the insurance and life assurance industries are prospering in the Scottish capital. Nor is this architectural distinction a recent development – *The Scotsman* was complimenting the insurance industry on its contribution to the cityscape back in 1932.

Please note that the terms 'insurance' and 'life assurance' are used interchangeably in this chapter. Of the top ten commercial concerns whose headquarters were based in Edinburgh in 1992, five were insurance companies. The following list, arranged by turnover, can be found in full under INDUSTRY.

1st	Standard Life Assurance	£5,480 million
3rd	Scottish Widows	£2,598 million
6th	Scottish Equitable	£1,322 million
9th	Scottish Provident	£826 million
10th	Scottish Life	£703 million

To put this in perspective, it should be added that the second and fourth of the companies ranked in the table were the Royal Bank of Scotland and the Bank of Scotland respectively. The highest earning manufacturing concern with its HQ in Edinburgh was Scottish & Newcastle, occupying fifth place in the list.

STANDARD LIFE ASSURANCE

Formed as a proprietary life concern in 1825, its first office in George Street. Almost exactly a century later it converted to mutual status, effectively transferring its ownership to its policyholders. By 1960 its assets almost equalled those of its two largest rivals in the city, and the table above shows that the company has maintained its supremacy. At the time of writing, its main building is still in George Street, spilling over into Thistle Street behind, while a new building is taking impressive shape at the junction of Lothian Road and the Western Approach Road. The Standard's computer facility is based at Canonmills, described by Charles McKean as 'three top-lit, stone, glass and lead quasi-octogons grouped around the service core and a grand staircase. Lavish roof gardens'.

SCOTTISH WIDOWS FUND AND LIFE ASSURANCE

This is the oldest Scottish life assurance company, founded in St Andrew's Square in 1815. By forging a fine trading record, the company was second only to Standard Life in its assets total by 1960, enlisting Edinburgh's own Basil Spence to design its offices facing eastwards across the Square in 1962, and then more boldly opening a new centre on Dalkeith Road ten years later, again designed by Spence's company. The architecture of the latter building has been widely praised, not least for its landscaping and imaginative moat concept.

SCOTTISH EQUITABLE

Its headquarters presently based on the north side of St Andrew's Square, the Scottish Equitable Life Assurance Company (now Scottish Equitable PLC) was set up in the Square in 1831, and ranked sixth in turnover in 1992 among those companies centred on Edinburgh. It is currently expanding with a new building under construction at South Gyle.

SCOTTISH PROVIDENT

Formed in 1837, the Scottish Provident Institution has its headquarters on the south side of St Andrew's Square in a 1961 modernistic building described by more than one architect as one of the most pleasing designs yet integrated into an existing terrace.

SCOTTISH LIFE

The Scottish Life Assurance Company began trading in St Andrew's Square in 1881, the youngest of the five companies listed in the top ten of those companies whose headquarters are based in Edinburgh. It now boasts a major office development in Henderson Row, occupying the former cable tram depot, and imaginatively displaying the winding wheels once used to power Edinburgh's cable cars round the city.

History

Edinburgh's insurance industry appears to date back at least to 1475, when the United Corporations of St Mary's Chapel was founded to financially assist the widows of deceased members of the Edinburgh Trades Guilds, and continues to do so to this day.

Insurance, particularly against fire, became something of a growth industry in Edinburgh over the centuries – scarcely surprising in a city of such densely-packed housing. In 1720 the Edinburgh Friendly Insurance against Losses by Fire was formed, trading until absorbed by the Sun Life Company in 1847. In 1805 the Caledonian Insurance Company was established, reputedly by a city shopkeeper whose one day delay in paying an insurance premium left him without insurance when he lost £600-worth of property (whether the Edinburgh Friendly was the unsympathetic company or not is unrecorded), but he lost no time in forming his own company, the Caledonian's first office being established in Hunter's Square.

Insurance companies appear to have been particularly active in trying to remedy Edinburgh's chronic inability to fight fires, arranging fire-fighting units on a single-company basis, with the often unfortunate result, commented on under FIRE FIGHTING, that buildings were left to burn to the ground by these commercial 'firemen' if insured with the wrong company or not insured at all, but an inter-company force did come into being in the first quarter of the 19th century. It required an inspiring individual, James Braidwood, to tackle the perennial problem of fire on a more professional local-authority basis.

Life assurance on the other hand, was more of an English speciality until the second quarter of the 19th century, when, as observed above, Edinburgh companies began to concentrate on an aspect of insurance in which they now excel. By 1887, eight of the top 12 life assurance companies based in Scotland had their headquarters in Edinburgh, including the five with the richest assets. Curiously, their history has, in the words of Charles W. Munn (*see* BIBLIOGRAPHY) writing in 1994, 'received very little attention from historians. Public sources of information about the industry are scarce and they are often unreliable'.

Islands

The most northernly parts of the Edinburgh local government area comprise three of the islands in the Firth of Forth. They are, in order of decreasing size, Cramond, Inchmickery, and Cow and Calves. All are uninhabited. In 1603, the Golden Charter granted to the city by James VI stipulated the middle of the Firth of Forth as the city's northern boundary, and this still pertains today.

Inchkeith, so prominently situated opposite Leith, is part of Fife, as are Inchcolm and the Isle of May.

CRAMOND ISLAND
Connected by a causeway with the western end of the Silverknowes promenade, this eight-acre (3.28 hectares) island, with its highest point 19 feet (5.7 metres) above sea level, is the nearest and most-visited of the city's islands, and is of particular interest to birdwatchers. It is accessible, with care, at low tide from Cramond.

INCHMICKERY
Two miles north of Cramond Island is Inchmickery, a rarely visited island 30 acres (12.3 hectares) in area and rendered largely

unattractive by its wartime defensive works. The highest point is 48 feet (14.4 metres) above sea level, with one of the more interesting landmarks being the Mickery Stone, a 14 feet (4.2 metres) high natural pillar on the south side of the island. A reserve maintained by the Royal Society for the Protection of Birds, Inchmickery used to be noted as an important nesting area for the Roseate Tern until about 1990. Pressure from the more common tern species unfortunately has all but driven out this attractive bird.

COW AND CALVES
A rock formation to the north of Inchmickery, and technically the most northern part of the city.

Other offshore rock formations once known to local people, but now lost to land reclamation schemes are the **Mussel Cape Rock**, on which the Martello Tower was built in 1809 (*see* PORTS), now incorporated into the land area to the north of the 1969 entrance lock at Leith. The **Penny Bap** was a solitary rock close to shore at Seafield, but is now enclosed in the area of the new sewage farm.

Keys to the City

Edinburgh presents the Keys to the City to the Monarch on royal visits, or to their representative at the General Assembly of the Church of Scotland, the Lord High Commissioner.

This symbolic gesture involves ceremonially handing over (and hastily retrieving for safe keeping) two silver keys and chains commissioned by the City Treasurer in the 1620s (at a cost of £37.6s.4d.). Their first use was to mark the visit of Charles I in 1633, although previous ceremonies were arranged to commemorate the arrivals of Queen Mary (Queen of Scots) in 1561, and later her son James VI in 1579. On these occasions the real keys to the city's ports (gates) may have been used. Mary entered by the West Port from Holyrood – her obvious route, through the Netherbow, would have taken the Queen through the enemy's gate, the one nearest the English invader.

At the West Port a special 'cloud' made from soft fabric had been positioned above the gate, and from this a child descended to present the keys, as well as a bible and psalter. James VI received the keys, also at the West Port, from a boy emerging from a globe above the gate.

After the defeat at Pinkie in 1547, the city's ports were closed each night at eight o'clock and the keys handed over to the Bailie of the quarter in which the gate was located. The keys were lost after 1649; certainly there appears to have been no formal presentation until 1813, when the Lord High Commissioner received them from the Lord Provost. Nowadays, the keys are held in the posession of the Director of Finance, who before the local government reorganisation of 1975 enjoyed the more imposing title of City Chamberlain.

For information on the city's ports (i.e. gates), *see* CITY WALLS.

Keys to the City, ceremonially presented to monarchs or their representatives. These are believed to have been lost from the mid-17th century to 1813. (City of Edinburgh Council)

Learned Societies

As befits the capital city of a nation noted for its contribution to science and medicine, Edinburgh is home to a number of learned societies. While many of these no longer enjoy the prestige and renown they once knew – greater travel opportunities mean that conferences are a more frequent means for scientists and researchers to disseminate new research discoveries or the latest formulated ideas – societies can still make a major contribution to the intellectual life of the nation through their publications and meetings. The medical colleges are also prestigious examining bodies.

Scotland's national academy of science, founded for 'the advancement of learning and useful knowledge', is the **Royal Society of Edinburgh**, in George Street. This was established in 1783 to formalise much of the scientific and artistic energy of the city during the golden age of the Enlightenment, but, more prosaically, was a means of preventing the controversial Earl of Buchan securing a prominent place in the intellectual hierarchy with his Society of Antiquaries (*see* page 179).

Sir Walter Scott was an early president, but the literary side of the Society's work virtually died with him, science becoming the principal preoccupation for most of the succeeding decades. The Society's *Transactions* first appeared in 1788, containing no less than James Hutton's seminal paper on his 'Theory of the Earth' (*see* GEOLOGY), and *Proceedings* of the meetings began publication in the mid-19th century. In 1909 the RSE surrendered its quarters in the Royal Institution building (henceforth, the Royal Scottish Academy) and moved to its present building in what was then the commercial heart of the New Town.

Following a reorganisation in the late 1970s, the Society's literary side has been revived, and the building refurbished at the expense of disposing, partly through sales, of a very fine library of scientific literature, some of it dating back to beyond the time of the RSE's creation. An offer in 1968 to make the collection available to the Scottish nation was apparently not even acknowledged by the government of the day (*see* LIBRARIES).

Older than the Royal Society of Edinburgh are the three medical societies in the city, all of them holding royal charters. Of these, the ***Royal College of Surgeons of Edinburgh*** is the oldest, and is in fact the oldest surgical incorporation in Britain. Founded in 1505, the College carried out practical instruction in anatomy and surgical techniques until 1948, when the National Health Service came into being, but the College continues its examining function, and Fellowship is an essential prerequisite for a successful surgical career. Surgeon's Hall, designed by William Playfair and opened in 1832, is a city landmark in Nicolson Street, and contains the College's museum, which is open to the public (*see* MUSEUMS).

The oldest medical society in Britain, the ***Royal Medical Society*** dates back to 1737, and is composed of medical students and qualified practioners, enjoying the probably unique distinction of being largely an undergraduate's society with a royal charter. So passionate have its debates been in past years that, in 1780, the Society had to ban duelling among its members, following disagreements on differing medical philosophies. Located at Melbourne Place, just off George IV Bridge, until the 1960s, the Society is now housed in the Students' Centre off Bristo Street.

The ***Royal College of Physicians of Edinburgh*** received a royal charter from Charles II in 1681 and was closely involved in the opening of the city's first Infirmary in 1729. The college has now become one of the most important postgraduate examining bodies in Britain for the education of doctors to the highest level. Its magnificent Queen Street building, fronted by statues of Hippocrates, Aesculapius, and Hygeia, contains an important medical library and conference facilities available for hire.

Still active in Edinburgh is the ***Society of Antiquaries***. Founded by the Earl of Buchan in 1780, the Society has the National Museum of Antiquities as its base, and has a long working association with the museum. Its membership of 2,800 shows that there is still considerable interest in the nation's ancient history, and the Society publishes annual proceedings and irregular monographs.

While the Royal Scottish Geographical Society has now transferred its headquarters to Glasgow, there are still a number of other important learned societies left in the capital. One of the oldest of these is the **Royal Physical Society of Edinburgh**, which dates from 1788, intended to study all aspects of natural sciences. Nowadays, based at Edinburgh University's Department of Genetics, it concentrates on experimental biology and genetics.

The Scottish History Society was founded in 1886 to further the study of Scotland's past, and specialises in reproducing previously unpublished documents of historical interest. With some 800 members, it is based at Edinburgh University.

The **Edinburgh Botanical** and **Edinburgh Geological** societies are active in their subject areas, and are located at the Royal Botanic Garden, and Edinburgh University's Grant Institute of Geology, respectively.

Leith

Although technically no more than the EH6 postal district of Edinburgh nowadays, such a description is never likely to meet with a Leither's approval. In fact, Leith could do very well with an encyclopedia of its own!

To any visitor unsure of the wheareabouts of Leith, the advice can be given to find the most northern mainland part of the city and there you are. Leith's shoreline stretches from a point between Newhaven and Granton on the west to Seafield on the east, (see also FIRTH OF FORTH). Bisecting the area is the Water of Leith (see RIVERS AND STREAMS), and the town developed around the river-mouth before the docks began construction at the beginning of the 19th century. The area to the west of the river is known as North Leith, that to the east as South Leith.

The port's main road connection with Edinburgh has always been Leith Walk, the boundary point between the two former municipalities being sited at Pilrig. (As will become obvious later, Edinburgh and Leith were separate burghs between 1833 and 1920.) The boundary between Edinburgh and Leith is more difficult to discern in other parts of the present-day conurbation.

Leith is entitled to four community councils to deal with local issues, if the public were to demand them, but at the time of writing has only one, the Links Community Council. It seems a pity that Leithers have not taken up this opportunity of creating their own statutorily-funded assemblies.

History

Leith's maritime history is referred to more fully in this volume under PORTS, although it is interesting to examine the reasons for the residual antipathy which may still exist between the inhabitants of Edinburgh and its principal port. According to Leith historian, Sue Mowat (see BIBLIOGRAPHY):

So successful was the port that Edinburgh periodically took vigorous measures to ensure that it was not outshone by its satellite. Leith

A Leith quayside scene in 1995. The Water of Leith here is now maintained to high-water level, and the former swing-bridge carrying Bernard Street across the river has been replaced by a fixed structure, seen here blocked with traffic. In the right upper background can be seen Calton Hill, where Nelson's Monument still drops a time-ball at one o'clock on weekdays for the shipping in the Forth to use as a time-check. This will not include the vessel on the left; now a popular restaurant, it is landlocked by the new road bridge near the Victoria Dock. (Frank Reid)

was subject to a series of restrictions on its trade long after the laws on which they were based had become obsolete in the rest of Europe, causing much resentment . . .

Following the granting of Leith Harbour to Edinburgh's burgesses by Robert the Bruce in 1329, it became impossible for a ship returning to Leith to unload its cargo unless its captain had paid the appropriate dues at the Tolbooth in Edinburgh, some three miles away! Inevitably this led to much evasion of port regulations, as well as creating needless enmity.

Leith's fortified status always made it a threat to Edinburgh, should it fall into the wrong hands. The town's independence became little more than a bargaining counter in the mid–16th century, with the Regent Mary selling burgh status to the inhabitants of South Leith, although no charter appears to have been issued. Mary Stewart allowed the Edinburgh Town Council to acquire Leith in return for a loan, although, in a complicated series of transactions, the Council appear to have had to purchase the charter outright from Lord Thirlestane. Historian Marguerite Wood comments that the whole issue 'bred an ill-feeling between the two places which lasted for centuries, and is still remembered, in spite of subsequent developments'.

Leith was independent of Edinburgh only between 1833 and 1920, when it had its own town council, but the town has enjoyed its own parliamentary representation since the former date, although the constitutency dropped its links with Portobello and Musselburgh in 1950, and ceased to be called the anachronistic 'Leith Burghs'. For a list of MPs, *see* PARLIAMENTARY REPRESENTATION; it is a diverse listing; in 1886 the burgh voted in Prime Minister William Gladstone but he decided to represent Edinburghshire (Midlothian) instead! His successor, Ronald Munro-Ferguson held the constituency for 28 years before going off to become Governor General of Australia.

In 1927 the consistently Liberal town of Leith turned its back on William Wedgwood Benn, father of Tony Benn, who dared to join the Labour Party, while in John Murray, Andrew Rutherford, James Moncrieff, and Ronald King Murray, Leith has had no fewer than four Lord Advocates among its representatives, as well as Alfred Brown, Secretary of State for Scotland and Minister of Health while representing the port. More recently Labour's Ron Brown proved to be a controversial MP, finally defeated after he had been deselected by his party and stood unsuccessfully as an independent at the General Election in 1992.

The first municipal election was held in Leith on 5 November 1833, with the first meeting of the 16 members of the Town Council taking place on the 12th of the month. As the town's Tolbooth (traditionally a municipal building incorporating a meeting place as well as a prison) had been demolished as recently as 1824, a town hall for the new burgh was hurriedly improvised from the then-new Sheriff Court building. This still stands as the police station at the corner of Queen Charlotte Street and Constitution Street. The building still contains the one-time Council chamber, adorned with portraits of former provosts as well as that of Ronald Munro-Ferguson, Leith's longest-serving MP. Pride of place goes to the famous painting by Alexander Carse of George IV's landing at Leith in 1822; the actual site of the landing is commemorated by a free-standing plaque on the Shore.

Owing to a legislative anomaly, fund-raising powers were not granted to the new burgh until 1838; its creation took place against the background of a continuing squabble over the funding of the docks system at Leith (specifically the East and West Old Docks, now filled in). In 1813 it was discovered that the amount owing on the construction came to £240,000 owed to individuals, and £25,000 to government. There were complaints from Leithers that the new docks were not properly fitted out, and there was certainly a high rate of drownings owing to the lack of railings and proper lighting.

In 1825 the docks were effectively nationalised when the Government of the day bought the outstanding debt, but it was to be many years before this matter was laid to rest, with Edinburgh prepared to call itself bankrupt and Leith being liberated to chart its own course as a municipality in its own right, (*see also* LOCAL GOVERNMENT). The Act dividing Leith from Edinburgh did not include reserving powers to the smaller town to raise finance through levying its own petty customs, which had always been paid to Edinburgh. With the city now technically bankrupt, an amending Act had to be sought, and it was not until 1838 that this matter was put right, mainly with help from its MP, John Archibald Murray, who happened to be Lord Advocate from 1835. Leith did not start its independent status auspiciously.

The Provosts appointed during Leith's 'independence' were as follows :

1833	Adam White
1839	James Reoch
1845	Thomas Hutchison
1848	George McLaren
1851	Robert Philip
1855	James Taylor
1860	William Lindsay
1866	James Watt
1875	Dr John Henderson
1881	James Pringle
1886	Dr John Henderson
1887	Thomas Aitken
1893	John Bennet
1899	Richard Mackie
1908	Malcolm Smith
1917	John A. Lindsay

PUBLIC SERVICES
Leith's *water* came originally from Lochend Loch (*see also* LOCHS), conduited by a wooden pipe. Even at the time, 1753, this undertaking was criticised, the contractor being regarded as too inexperienced for the task, and the pipe too narrow. In 1771 the appointment of Police Commissioners, with a wide remit to improve the town's water, sanitation, and public order, arranged for some of Edinburgh's new Crawley supply to be piped to the port, although this Leith extension was the first to be cut off at a time of shortage. Interestingly, a domestic supply appears to have been laid on to some Leith houses – in return for a special water rate – some 30 years before Edinburgh householders enjoyed such a privilege. Again, Lochend water was used, and it was not until the formation of the Edinburgh and District Water Trust in 1869, that the supply of water was regularised, (*see* WATER SUPPLY).

Leith appears to have had its own *police* constables from at least 1610, and a formal force existed up to the Amalgamation with Edinburgh. In 1913, the Leith force was stretched to breaking point because of the Dock Strike that year (*see* POLICE).

Leith had its own *fire* brigade from 1837 until amalgamation. It boasted two steam pump vehicles to Edinburgh's one in 1873, and a building in Junction Place still carries the legend of 'Fire Engine House', (*see also* FIRE FIGHTING).

TRANSPORT
For the best part of 30 years, Leith had its own tram system, one which shamed Edinburgh by being electrically-operated some 20 years before the capital's (*see* TRAMS). For a short time around 1904, the port had no fewer than four railway termini – at Constitution Street (1831-1904), at the Citadel (North Leith station at Commercial Street, 1846-1947), Leith Central (the largest and probably least used, 1903-52), and Leith North at Lindsay Street (1879-1962), (*see* RAILWAYS). The town even had

its own airport at one time! (*see* AIRPORTS).

For information about Leith Hospital, *see* HOSPITALS. For details of such Leith industries as shipping and ropemaking, *see* INDUSTRY. More information on education in Leith can be found under SCHOOLS.

For details of Leith's sporting history, *see* GOLF – for the town outrivalled St Andrews at one time as the true home of the sport – and FOOTBALL. Details of theatre and cinemas in the port can be found respectively under those headings. Scotland's first novel was published in Leith – *see* LITERATURE.

HISTORY OF LEITH LINKS

The Links were originally an uncultivated area of whin and bracken fringing the sea, and incorporating part of the town's race meet (*see* RACING), while it was on the Links in the 15th century that a Scottish king brought his imprimatur to the game of golf (*see* GOLF). In 1560, English artillery units constructed two mounds on the Links on which to base their cannon when attacking Leith Fort, and these earthworks are still visible today. These are the Somerset and Pelham mounds, named after the captains of the gun crews which constructed them, although they are now known locally as Giant's Brae and Lady Fyfe's Brae, respectively.

From the time that the track of the Edinburgh & Dalkeith Railway's Leith branch was laid in 1830 (*see* RAILWAYS and INDUSTRY), the Links were separated from the sea, and later industrial developments – slaughterhouses, the 'Roperie', and the docks – were built to the north of the dunes.

The Links were owned by Edinburgh until the Leith Town Council purchased them in 1856, and the area was levelled in 1880. Leith historian James Scott Marshall records that local councillors betrayed their ignorance of the game of cricket by giving permission for no fewer than 11 clubs to lay out their own pitches(!), but golf was banned in 1907, when the new Craigentinny course was opened. The last tournament had been played on the Links 40 years earlier.

Perhaps Leithers should think themselves lucky they did not lose the ground altogether, but at least a park was laid out, with football and cricket catered for. Long-serving member of parliament, Ronald Munro-Ferguson, (*see* PARLIAMENTARY REPRESENTATION) donated 100 trees from his estate to beautify the new park. A little more imagination in urban planning might have prevented the laying out of Links Gardens which bisects the park (although it dates from Edinburgh's ownership of the

Leith's Western Harbour simmers on a hot July day during the 1995 heatwave, with a North Sea oil supply vessel on the right. In the distance can be seen the control tower for the port's lock gates which maintain high water in the docks and the Water of Leith. (Frank Reid)

Links), preventing the park from fulfilling its full potential role as a sporting area.

AMALGAMATION

It may appear puzzling that such a fiercely independent community as Leith should be forced to accept its reabsorption into Edinburgh less than a century after it had been rendered independent. Certainly, public opinion was not in favour of amalgamation when it was mooted in 1919, an opinion poll conducted by the Leith Town Clerk finding that citizens were divided between 5,357 in favour as opposed to 29,891 against.

In his *Life and Times of Leith*, historian James Scott Marshall emphasises that the public had scarcely been given a balanced analysis of the problems facing the town, which had struggled from 1832 to overcome its fiscal problems, and then took no initiative in securing its hinterland at a time when more *lebensraum* was required for the burgeoning population. In contrast, Edinburgh completed a pincer movement round Leith during this period, by acquiring Granton on one side and Seafield on the other.

With the cost of running municipal functions continually rising, there was a strong case for merging these, which Parliament evidently recognised. Leith and Edinburgh merged in 1920, but for many years a pedestrian in Leith Walk could observe the lamp standards exchange their castles for ships half way up the Walk, and the lounge bar of a particular hostelry (the Boundary Bar) is still ceremonially divided between city and port, although standardised licensing conditions have brought to an end the movement of tipplers from one end of the bar to the other, as the different licensing hours were strictly observed (*see also* PUBS).

Libraries

Besides its own municipal public library, Edinburgh is home to the National Library of Scotland, and the headquarters of these two storehouses of knowledge face one another from opposite sides of George IV Bridge. The city also hosts libraries of three universities and a number of colleges, as well as some institutional libraries not open to the public, making a total of 107 in addition to the public, national and university networks, and 23 school libraries.

NATIONAL LIBRARY OF SCOTLAND (NLS)

It is something of a surprise to learn that such an important body as Scotland's national library was not formed until 1925, although in fact its function was previously exercised by the Faculty of Advocates' Library. With more than five million volumes stored on 270 miles (432 kilometres) of shelves, the NLS benefits from being one of the Deposit libraries in the British Isles, entitling it to receive automatically a free copy of every book published in Scotland, and those published elsewhere in the United Kingdom on request. This has obviously allowed the Library to build up a collection of material unrivalled in Scotland, and bearing comparison with the largest libraries in England and Ireland.

It is presently a multi-site library, with its Map and Science collections located at Causewayside, away from the main building in George IV Bridge, and with an interim bookstore, not open to the public, at Sighthill (and expected to be relocated to Causewayside in 1996). Material held at the last-named site cannot be made immediately available to readers visiting the George IV building, so it is advisable to telephone the Library before calling to see a particular book or periodical. There are some restrictions on student use of the National, but there are times, particularly before Final exams, when it is almost impossible to find a seat in the Reading Room. An evening visit is invariably more comfortable and quieter, although no delivery service to the reader's seat is operated at that time.

The National has excellent micro facilities, particularly useful for searching newspapers, and a Manuscripts department with a vigorous acquisitions policy (*see* ARCHIVES). The Lending Services Division maintains the Scottish Union Catalogue – a record of where individual books, even individual editions, can be found throughout Scotland's libraries – and there is a heavily-used exhibition hall and well-stocked shop.

The Enquiries staff are helpful and friendly to a degree which hardly seems possible, given the queries they have to deal with from overseas visitors anxious to talk interminably with someone, anyone, about their Scottish forebears, and from students whose arrogance would have made Evelyn Waugh blush.

History
The Faculty of Advocates, so inextricably linked with the life of Scotland's capital and the government of the nation, set up a library largely at the instigation of Lord Advocate George Mackenzie of Rosehaugh. As recounted in the section on LITERATURE – for Sir George is credited with having written Scotland's first novel, published in Leith in 1660 – this can scarcely atone for his ruthless persecution of the Covenanters around 1690. The library appears to date from 1679 or 1680, although there is evidence of such a facility some 80 years earlier. In 1700 the new library had to be evacuated because of fire, although many volunteers were able to rescue books from the conflagration.

Deposit privilege was assigned to the Advocates' Library by the Copyright Act of 1710. Its name apparently did not appear in the bill's first draft but at a later committee stage, possibly to demonstrate the benefits of the new Act of Union to those Scots requiring to be convinced. Whatever the provenance of this privilege, it launched the library on a course to make it one of Britain's most important.

The Library's first premises were in a private house off Parliament Close, but the fire rendered urgent the need for a new home, and the Laigh Parliament Hall became the new site for the library for the next 250 years. By the 19th century, the Advocates were finding the upkeep of the library increasingly burdensome, and a lengthy correspondence was entered into with government for state assistance.

This finally came to pass in 1925 when the Faculty generously donated its library, with the exception of the legal collection, to the nation. It was decided to allocate a new site for the National Library on George IV Bridge, replacing the former Sheriff Court, with a generous donation of

£100,000 being made by Sir Alexander Grant to speed the process. Work on the new building began in 1937, but was interrupted by war, and the new facility was not opened by HM The Queen until 1956. The blank, windowless, facade of the NLS, facing its municipal neighbour opposite, is not to everyone's taste, Charles McKean commenting critically that the building's 'lack of presence (is) the outcome of interminable client indecision and timidity'. A library is, of course, a living functioning organism, and aesthetic considerations are perhaps of secondary importance, particularly when the library and its staff are a credit to the nation.

EDINBURGH CITY LIBRARIES

The city's own library network comprises a headquarters, as already mentioned, in George IV Bridge, as well as 22 branches, and a mobile service. At a time of falling library use nationally, it is pleasing to report that in 1994 the Edinburgh service had seen an increase of nearly 20 per cent in membership, and of 11 per cent in book issues. Ninety-two per cent of users interviewed in 1993/4 expressed themselves satisfied with the service.

It is hoped to expand the headquarters area by taking over a redundant bank building nearby, while the Children's and Music departments have already spilled over to the other side of the Cowgate. Particularly gratifying has been the increase in usage of the specialist departments in George IV Bridge – Reference, Home Reading, Fiction, Scottish, Edinburgh Room, and Fine Arts, as well as those mentioned above. Considerable emphasis is placed on new media such as computers,

compact discs etc, and the needs of ethnic minorities are assigned a high priority.

CITY LIBRARIANS	
1887	Hew Morrison
1922	Ernest Savage
1942	Robert Butchart
1953	Charles S. Minto
1970	James Cockburn
1973	Alan Howe
1975	Anthony Shearman
1986	Margaret Sharp

History

For a city with such a 'bookish' reputation, Edinburgh was slow to adopt the provisions of the Public Libraries Acts, being the last Scottish city to do so. Two attempts were made to set up a municipal service, in 1868 and 1881, but were rejected by ratepayers anxious not to be burdened with the expense of running a free library service. This speaks volumes, if that is not an inappropriate phrase, for the unrepresentative nature of local government enfranchisement at that time. (Curiously, a supply of fresh water to the city in the 17th century was held up by a previous display of selfish parsimony, *see* WATER SUPPLY).

Generously funded by Andrew Carnegie, a new attempt was made to open a municipal library at the end of the 1880s, and this resulted in the towering edifice which is still the capital's public library, opened in 1890. Although the public consider George IV Bridge as its address, the building is actually built on the Cowgate on the site of the 17th century house of Sir Thomas Hope.

Although the service's first head, Dr Hew

Morrison, was in charge for no fewer than 35 years, it was Edinburgh's second Chief Librarian, Ernest Savage, who is probably best remembered as an outstanding contributor to the city's cultural scene. Savage liberated the service from its previous 'closed access' regime, where the reader was forced to enquire if a particular book was 'in', and where there was no question of browsing being allowed. On a technical point, it was Savage who adopted the use of the Library of Congress classification scheme for the bookstock, believing that it lent itself best to a departmental organisation, but which means that Edinburgh is very much different from most other public library systems, which employ the Dewey Decimal Classification. The Congress system is probably as good as any; one local reader interested in books on Hollywood films knows to find them under the notation PN1990, the mnemonic unintentionally suggesting 'Pictures, North America, in our own times'!

OTHER LIBRARIES

These exist in Edinburgh at each one of the three universities, the oldest obviously being Edinburgh University, whose main library centre is the Basil Spence-designed building in George Square. The 107 other libraries are listed in the volume *Scottish Library and Information Resources* published by the Scottish Library Association, and 23 of Edinburgh's schools have their own libraries.

Some of the smaller libraries in the city comprise not much more than a cupboard housing boxes of pamphlets and periodicals relevant to the work of the business or institute, but the capital boasts some of the country's finest special libraries ('special' in that they contain specialised stock or cater for a particular readership). Into this category comes the Signet Library, housed in a magnificent building just off the High

BRANCH LIBRARIES	OPENED		
West, (Dundee Street)	1897	Blackhall	1966
Portobello, (Portobello High Street)	1897	Sighthill	1968
North, (Stockbridge)	1900	Muirhouse	1970
East, (McDonald Road)	1904	Colinton	1970
Morningside, (Morningside Road)	1905	Gilmerton	1974
Leith, (Ferry Road)	1932	Craigmillar	1974
Craigmillar School Branch	1934	Balerno, Currie, South	1974
Colinton	1934	Queensferry integrated into	
Balgreen School Branch	1935	new Edinburgh City Libraries	1975
Corstorphine	1936	Newington	1975
Granton School Branch	1936	Moredun	1975
Craigentinny School Branch	1936	Kirkliston	1978
Pilton Temporary Branch	1945	Oxgangs	1990
Blackhall Temporary Branch	1948	Piershill	1995
Mobile services began	1949	Wester Hailes	Planned
Portobello (Roseburn Avenue)	1963	Ratho	Planned

Street at St Giles, while the Royal Botanic Garden's library is the oldest of its kind in Britain (*see* BOTANIC GARDENS).

LOST LIBRARIES

The biggest library to be lost to Edinburgh is that of the Royal Society of Edinburgh, in George Street. In the late 1970s the Society decided to divest itself of its outstanding collection of scientific periodicals dating back to the 17th century and numbering upwards of half a million volumes, but which was making increasing demands on space. A number of monographs and lengthy 'runs' of periodicals were sold commercially, but a substantial part of the foreign-language material was incorporated into the Science Library at Causewayside.

Incredibly, in 1968 the Society had generously offered to donate the entire collection to the Scottish nation, an offer which was not even officially acknowledged! (*see* the Society's submission to Sir Frederick Dainton's enquiry into national libraries, 1967-69.) Ironically, so many commercial organisations have now vacated George Street that the library would have had ample room for expansion had it remained where it was.

COMMERCIAL LIBRARIES

George Street was the home of one of the first libraries in the city to be commercially run – the Edinburgh Subscription Library, established in 1794. This was by no means the first, however, the versatile Allan Ramsay (*see also* THEATRES) having operated a library as part of his bookselling business at the Luckenbooths from 1726. Its volumes were perused by Walter Scott well into the next century, before it was broken up at auction in 1832, its stock swelling a number of circulating libraries in Victorian times.

At least two major subscription libraries survived into the 1970s, including the former collection of Robert Grant and Son which became part of the Edinburgh Bookshop in George Street, while Douglas and Foulis operated a well-known library in Castle Street until around the same time. Boots, rather better known as chemists, operated a subscription library in the city from 1911 to the early 1960s.

The suburbs have always boasted their own, less grandiose, commercial libraries; even today there are shops allowing regular callers to swop paperbacks featuring action stories and romance, especially the latter, for a small outlay, a system video shops have made commonplace in recent years. Portobello citizens were even better off for leisure reading in the 1950s and '60s, their every whim catered for by a unique commercial mobile enterprise known as 'Tom's Travelling Library'. This well-known feature of the seaside community presumably did not survive the extension of the Public Library's housebound scheme.

Literature

Edinburgh's status as a literary centre is not exactly as coruscating as it once was. No present-day writers can begin to match the prestige of such Edinburgh writers of yesteryear as Scott, Stevenson, and Conan Doyle, and with broadcasting focusing so much attention on transmitted media, as opposed to the book, the city has lost much of its importance as a centre of intellectual

Allan Ramsay 1686-1758. A remarkable polymath, Ramsay the elder was a poet, bookseller, playwright, and father of the famous portrait painter of the same name. (Edinburgh City Libraries)

creativity. (*see also* BROADCASTING, and FILMS).

HISTORY OF EDINBURGH LITERATURE

POETRY

Because poetry was as integral to court ceremony as drama and dancing, Scotland's earliest recognised poets, such as Dunbar, Douglas, and Lyndsay, were associated with the royal court at Holyrood, although none of them were born in the city.

William Dunbar (1460–1513), about whom comparatively little is known, was probably dependent on royal patronage to some degree. Indeed he may be considered as Scotland's Poet Laureate of his time, history only losing track of him when his name disappeared from royal accounts following the Flodden disaster. Twentieth century authors such as Christopher Grieve have admired Dunbar's mastery of verse and vocabulary in works ranging from the celebratory *The Thrissill and the Rois*, marking the marriage of James IV and England's Margaret Tudor, to the farcical *The Fenzeit Freir of Tungland*.

Born in East Lothian, Gavin Douglas (1476–1522) was another poet who was closely associated with the royal establishment, and who indeed fell foul of it, enduring imprisonment in Edinburgh Castle, but his contemporary, Sir David Lyndsay (1486–1555), is better remembered nowadays. Lindsay was born in Fife, working both as a writer – his *Ane Satyre of the Thrie Estaitis* is a landmark in Scottish poetic drama, first performed in the city in 1554 and gloriously revived at the 1948 Festival – and as Lord Lyon, King of Arms. Present-day critic Maurice Lindsay believes that, until the career of Robert Burns reached its ascendancy, 'Sir David Lyndsay of the Mount has some claim to be regarded as the national bard.'

It was not until the 18th century that poetry once again became part of the Edinburgh scene, and by that time the Court had long ago moved south. Allan Ramsay (1684–1758), father of the more famous painter, combined the writing of poetry with bookselling and the running of a theatre at Carrubber's Close on the north side of the city (the Old Town), despite an official ban on theatre performances anywhere outside London (*see* THEATRES).

Only a few years after Ramsay, an Edinburgh-born man enjoyed a meteoric career as a poet who is best remembered as one who inspired and influenced Robert Burns. Robert Fergusson was born near the present site of North Bridge in 1750 but failed to graduate at university and returned to work in his birthplace as a clerk. He enjoyed city nightlife to the full, and his poetry was read by Burns in 1782, the latter's debt to Fergusson not being difficult to discern, particularly in such a poem as *The Cottar's Saturday Night*, when compared to Fergusson's *The Farmer's Ingle*. Ironically, the city-bred Fergusson's poem evokes a controlled sentimentality about rural life, while in Burns's, it seems excessive, despite the latter genuinely coming from a farming background.

Fergusson died tragically young in 1774, after confinement in the city's Bedlam, and despite the attempts by Dr Andrew Duncan, a pioneer of proper psychiatric treatment (*see* SOCIAL WORK) to find him a more salubrious refuge. Burns later insisted on paying for a proper headstone for Fergusson in Canongate churchyard.

Burns himself came to Edinburgh in 1786, where he appears to have alternated between the literary and social salons of the New Town and the bibulous nightlife of the Old. Sir Walter Scott's account of meeting Burns, or more exactly, of seeing Burns in a crowded drawing-room, leaves no doubt about the way that the 'Ploughman poet' was lionised by city society. Anxious to consolidate his reputation after the publication of his Kilmarnock edition, Burns was pleased to place his new

collection with William Creech (later Lord Provost 1811–13), although probably to no great remunerative advantage.

During his time in the city he wrote *Address to Edinburgh*, which is not one of his more memorable pieces, and *Address to a Haggis*, which is. His description of the city as 'Edina's, Scotia's darling seat' was seized on as a commercial trade-name for a toilet manufacturer. Nevertheless, his two successive winters spent in the capital consolidated his literary reputation, indeed, projected him firmly into celebrity status, even if his poems written in, or about, the city, are not among his best.

More modern poets with Edinburgh connections include William McGonagall, more usually associated with Dundee, but born in the city in 1830, while Christopher Grieve (Hugh MacDiarmid) taught at Broughton High School before the First World War. That conflict also brought two of Britain's most illustrious modern poets to the city – Siegfried Sassoon and Wilfred Owen. Sassoon was a wounded officer who courageously published a letter in a newspaper in 1917 questioning Britain's conduct of the war for which, in the words of historian Martin Gilbert, he 'was fortunate to be hospitalised rather than court-martialled'. Admitted to the Craiglockhart War Hospital for Neurasthenic Officers (*see also* DISTRICTS), Sassoon met Wilfred Owen there and encouraged him in his work. The result was Owen's poem *Dulce et decorum est*, one of the most noteworthy written during a war remembered at least for the quality of the poetry generated during that dreadful time.

The capital's 20th century own poetic fraternity include Sydney Goodsir Smith, Norman McCaig, and Hamish Henderson, of whom only the last survives. Among Edinburgh publishers, Macdonald's, now based at Loanhead in Midlothian, has an excellent record of poetry publishing.

Scottish Poetry Library

With so many poetic connotations, it was entirely appropriate that Edinburgh should become the home for the Scottish Poetry Library, established in 1984. Focusing its emphasis on 20th century Scottish works, the Library offers its members poetry on casette, video, and in printed form. The SPL is based in Tweeddale Court, 14 High Street.

NOVELS

Leith was the place of publication of the first Scottish novel – *Aretina* by the notorious Sir George Mackenzie of Rosehaugh (1636–1691). Mackenzie was a ruthless persecutor of the Covenanters, and can scarcely be adjudged to have atoned by founding the Advocates' Library, the basis for the later National Library of Scotland (where he is commemorated in an inscribed window on the grand staircase). *Aretina*, subtitled *The Serious Romance*, was supposedly published by Robert Brown in 1660, but the printer is thought to have been Evan Tyler, the Englishman who was the 17th century equivalent of HMSO, and who set up a printing-press in Leith.

The novel is an allegorical work, telling of the efforts of Megistus and Philarites to overcome treachery at the Egyptian court, being rewarded with the love of Aretima and Agopeta respectively. Present-day critic Maurice Lindsay concludes that the work is 'too interlaced with political and philosophical references to be succesful as a romance'.

Edinburgh's earliest novelists were invariably professionals who were involved in uninspiring day-to-day jobs, and Henry Mackenzie (1745–1831) was no exception to this. A senior tax official, he has left behind a substantial archive of correspondence with other writers (and taxpayers) now preserved in the National Library of Scotland, but his literary reputation has proved less durable. His most famous novel *The Man of Feeling*, little read nowadays, made it fashionable for young men to burst into tears in polite company, as one critic sourly remarked.

But it is Sir Walter Scott's novels which tower over Edinburgh literature in the manner that his monument dominates Princes Street. Like the monument, they are a little the worse for wear, or more accurately perhaps, neglect. Scott is not a popular novelist nowadays, and his work no longer commands the admiration, the film-star adulation, it enjoyed in the first half of the 19th century.

> Today, perhaps, we can scarcely realise the almost overwhelming impact of the Waverley novels upon the cultured public of the day... could one imagine a popular novel of the present time giving its name to a great airport; or of airliners, motor-cars, diesel-electric locomotives, or even a great trade-route, all taking the same name?

Transport writer O.S. Nock was writing in 1960 of how Scott's literary creations had come to be eponymously immortalised through the naming of railway routes, stations, and ships in the 19th century. Meanwhile, Scott's narrative legacy was picked up by Edinburgh's Robert Louis Stevenson, and the latter's novels are more fashionable nowadays, endlessly produced in dramatised form on TV, radio, and film. At the time of writing, his tale of Jekyll and Hyde is receiving Hollywood treatment in a film involving two of the USA's highest-paid stars – proof of the enduring appeal of Stevenson's work.

While so much of Glasgow's prose fiction is grittily proletarian in subject and background – novels by Kelman, McIlvanney, Hind, Burgess – Edinburgh's has tended to reflect the city's professional social base. This is puzzling, since Edinburgh has proportionately as much of a working-class element to its demographic make-up as its western neighbour. Perhaps the reading public – or the publishers who supply reading material – simply *expect* novels in Edinburgh to feature teachers, doctors, police officers or lawyers? A newer generation of novelist has however started to buck the trend.

It is surely debateable if Edinburgh can claim to be flattered by Muriel Spark's portrayal of an Edinburgh teacher in *The Prime of Miss Jean Brodie*, first published in 1961, although curiously, it has proved to be probably the best-known individual novel featuring Edinburgh's professions. (No wonder Glasgow author Maurice Lindsay exclaimed in 1977 'How tiresome . . .to find these good middle-class folk cherishing the absurd notion that Edinburgh is still a capital city!' To many outsiders, it seems, Edinburgh population profile is dominated by a swollen middle-class).

Spark herself is no longer resident in the city, but has paid tribute to what she sees as the influence Edinburgh had on her work. To her, the city 'means rationalism, believing in a strong difference between

Robert Louis Stevenson (1850-94), Edinburgh's most famous author, commemorated at the Writers' Museum in Lady Stair's House, just off the Mound. (City of Edinburgh Council)

right and wrong'. Perhaps a little more clearly, she credits Edinburgh with being more of a European city than English-influenced; an opinion of considerable merit coming as it does from the writer whom Ian Rankin has described as 'the most 'European' writer whom Scotland has produced'. Spark claims that Edinburgh has influenced 'her way of thinking', prompting comparisons with another writer born in the city, and who lived far from it in adult life, but whose most famous literary work opens in a mole's burrow.

> For Kenneth Grahame, who was not old enough to understand the city in any conscious way when his parents removed him from it, the sense of powerful landscape more real and dependable than any construct of human beings remained, throughout his life, the most dominating influence.

Thus writes Alison Prince in her biography of Kenneth Grahame, author of *The Wind in the Willows*, born in Edinburgh in 1859. The reader can make up his or her own mind about the validity of the biographer's obervation. What is interesting about the plaque raised on Grahame's birthplace in Castle Street is that it was only recently modified from associating Grahame with *The Golden Age*, the title of a comparatively unknown work nowadays, to crediting him with the immortal *Wind in the Willows*. But an Edinburgh influence? This is difficult to envisage.

Sir Arthur Conan Doyle, coincidentally born in the same year as Grahame, was another Edinburgh writer on whom the city's influence was insufficient to persuade him to stay in Edinburgh, and his greatest literary creation, Sherlock Holmes, is very much a London-based character. This has not prevented the recent erection of a statue to Conan Doyle overlooking the Picardy Place roundabout, his local admirers citing Edinburgh University professor Joseph Bell (1837–1911) as the model for Holmes. But Conan Doyle's possibly most intriguing Edinburgh reference is his comparison of the impenetrably sheer walls of his dinosaur-populated *Lost World* with the city's Salisbury Crags!

Postwar Edinburgh Novels

Although James Allan Ford's best known work is probably *The Brave White Flag*, set in a Japanese POW camp, his two Edinburgh novels feature the professions – *A Statue for a Public Place* (civil service), and *A Judge of Men* (law). Doubtless he would have written more had his professional duties not intervened – among a number of important postings, he was Registrar General for Scotland for 1966–69.

One of the most 'professional' of Edinburgh's current novelists is Colin Douglas, the pseudonym for a prominent geriatrician, who has produced a string of medical novels since 1975, when Canongate published his first novel, the superb *The Houseman's Tale*.

Douglas's formula has provided an irresistible mixture of death, disease, and sex. His hero David Campbell is a newly-qualified doctor – from furth of the city – finding his way among the dragons and warlords of Edinburgh medical society, showing a gift for diagnosis not always to the taste of his contemporaries, while rarely failing to seek out the bedworthy amongst his female colleagues.

The use of a central character from outside Edinburgh provides an ideal platform to examine the capital's medical profession, particularly its 'dynastic' structure comprising successive generations of Edinburgh-educated medical graduates, often of doubtful quality, and perceived as a bar to promotion for those from outside the city. All this was totally lost when televised in the 1980s, the action being crassly transferred to Glasgow. Douglas's hero has also seen service in the Royal Naval Reserve (*Wellies from the Queen*) and on job exchange in the USA (*A Cure for Dying* – one of the best of the series). A recurring theme of Douglas's work is his exploration of the ethical side of medicine – from the seemingly-sadistic vivisection of animals where nothing of medical value is likely to accrue, to the casual experimentation with drug treatments on uninformed patients.

Probably Edinburgh's best-known contemporary novelist is Candia McWilliam, who was born and bred in the city. Daughter of Colin McWilliam, the author/architect responsible for launching the 'Pevsner' series of books about Scotland's buildings, McWilliam is a dextrous wordsmith whose first novel, *A Case of Knives*, was criticised for an over-elaborate dressing up of a weak story line. However, her later works show a sincere attempt to communicate what McWilliam thinks of the human condition – admittedly from a rather middle-class point of view. In that sense she is very much in the traditionally-perceived Edinburgh idiom, although her latest work at the time of writing, *Debateable Land* (1994) has been highly praised, and this author is undoubtedly in the top rank of contemporary imaginative writers.

Two of Scotland's best-known contemporary novelists have Edinburgh connections to a greater or lesser degree. Although a former resident of the city, Allan Massie's novels look furth of Edinburgh for their settings, particularly Italy, either modern or in the days of Ancient Rome. In contrast the much-acclaimed William Boyd was partly educated in Glasgow, which may

explain a geographical error in the Edinburgh sequence of *The New Confessions* which sits strangely in a novel so meticulously researched to impressively reproduce the horrors of the Western Front in the First World War.

Two Edinburgh-born writers with a working-class view of the world should be mentioned. The first is Fred Urquhart (1912–95), a novelist and short-story writer whose critical acclaim outstripped its public renown. Such novels as *Time will knit* reflect his own experiences of growing up in Edinburgh, as do the books of the young present-day writer, Irvine Welsh. In interviews, Welsh insists that he began writing because he was irritated by the determinedly middle-class flavour of British novels, and his own are unlikely to be seen in that light. His first novel *Trainspotting* (1993) may have been displayed in the transport section of the bookshop, but not for long. This was a hard-hitting look at Edinburgh's drug sub-culture which made Trocchi look tame by comparison.

Welsh currently rivals Dorothy Dunnett as Scotland's best-selling author. The latter is a popular novelist with a huge following, her Lymond historical novels guaranteeing her a unique place, indeed, a unique category, in the annals of contemporary Scottish literature. Unlike many of her successful contemporaries, Mrs Dunnett is happily resident in the city.

Comic Edinburgh novels are few and far between, but one which should never have been allowed to go out of print is *The Edinburgh Caper* by American author St Clair McElway, whose 1962 account of a paranoid tourist trying to prevent an imagined assassination of a visiting

City Chambers and the Mercat Cross. This 1912 view shows the intervening High Street free of traffic, something which is rarely the case nowadays. (Edinburgh City Libraries)

American president would have been worthy of a film. There aren't enough good Edinburgh films as it is (*see* FILMS).

Local Government

At the time of writing, Edinburgh's local government is in the hands of two authorities – the City of Edinburgh District Council, and Lothian Regional Council. Their respective functions are listed overleaf. These councils were established in 1975 following the Local Government (Scotland) Act, which implemented the findings of the Royal Commission on Local Government set up by the Wilson government in 1966, and chaired by Lord Wheatley. Following a new reorganisation, to take effect in 1996 after a consultation process but no Royal Commission, it is expected that Edinburgh will revert to the single-tier style of authority which it enjoyed before 1975 (*see* opposite).

The *City of Edinburgh District Council* covered nearly all the territory of the previous city authority, with the addition of Balerno, Currie, Kirkliston, and South Queensferry. Its headquarters were the City Chambers in the High Street, where the 62 elected councillors made up the District Council itself. In 1993 the Council was rated the 13th largest employer in the city, with 4,869 employees, 39 fewer than the previous year. 2,887 of these were salaried, with 1,982 manual workers. In 1994 the Council's budget was made up from the following sources:

Housing Subsidies	24%
Housing Rents	21%
Revenue Support Grant	25%
Fees & Charges	15%
Council Tax	12%
Other	3%

Net expenditure was along the following lines:

Recreation	33%
Environmental Services	24%
Housing	26%
Estates	4%
Planning	3%
Property Services	3%
Others	7%

In 1984 there was a break with political tradition when Labour became the controlling party in Edinburgh, sustaining its position after the 1988 and 1992 local elections, although on the latter occasion only doing so through a deal with the Scottish National Party members which saw the latter party have the honour of appointing the Lord Provost – the Rt. Hon. Norman Irons. Previous District Council and Town Council Lord Provosts are listed separately under LORD PROVOSTS.

The District Council's functions involved: allotments, building control, burial and cremation, caravan sites, cleansing, community centres (along with Region), conservation areas, countryside (with Region), development control, district courts, environmental health, food hygiene, health and safety in workplace, housing, industrial development (with regions), leisure and recreation, libraries, licensing (of alcohol, places of entertainment & gambling, taxis), listed buildings, local planning, markets, museums & art galleries, nature conservation, parks, public conveniences, refuse collection & disposal, shop hours, slaughterhouses, tourism, urban development, war memorials, young people's employment.

Finance is raised by the Council Tax, currently collected by Lothian Region. In 1994 the District reported that the first year's collection of the new tax achieved a highly satisfactory level of collection compared with the previous Community Charge, which was unpopular and difficult to collect.

For thousands of citizens, Edinburgh District Council was their landlord (see HOUSING). In 1991 35,452 households were housed by the local authority in Edinburgh, roughly 20 per cent of the total, and a decrease of 14 per cent since 1981 of the total housed.

The District Council was responsible for overseeing the setting up, and funding, of the city's Community Councils. Such councils are established if required by public demand, and are funded by the District Council, although they are also free to raise funds themselves. Reforming every third year, it is usually the case that the number of council places available exceeds the numbers of potential community councillors, so elections are necessary in only a few parts of the city. These councils currently (1995) number 25, in the following areas: Balerno, Chesser, Corstorphine, Craiglockhart, Currie,

Drum Brae, Drylaw/Telford, Firrhill, Gorgie/Dalry, Kirkliston, Links, Longstone, Marchmont, Merchiston, Morningside, Newhaven, New Town, Northfield/ Willowbrae, Portobello, Queensferry, Ratho, Stenhouse, Stockbridge, Tollcross, West End.

Lothian Regional Council was also set up by the 1973 Act. Its electorate of 596,236 throughout the Lothians, 58 per cent from Edinburgh, elected 49 councillors who met in the Regional headquarters at Parliament Square. The Council had 12 committees covering such areas of activity as: airports, animal disease, careers service, civil defence, coast protection, consumer protection, education, electoral registration, ferries, fire and flood prevention, harbours, highways, industrial development (with districts), industrial promotion, lighting, police, public transport, registration of births/ marriages/deaths, road safety, social work, strategic planning, valuation and rating, water and sewerage, weights and measures.

Of the above, education and social work represented the highest spending functions of the Region. The Region was responsible, as indicated above, in collecting revenue from the citizenry in the form of Council Tax. In 1995 it allowed business rate relief to some 1,600 community and charitable organisations who had their own premises, in addition to supplying them with £18 million in grants (*see* SOCIAL WORK).

At the time of writing, perhaps the most outstandingly successful of the Region's departments has been Water and Sewerage, ensuring that Edinburgh has been spared the major drought problems prevalent south of the border in 1995.

The Region's Conveners since 1974 have been:

1974-78	Peter Wilson
1978-82	John Crichton
1982-86	Brian Meek
1986-90	James Cook
1990-96	Eric Milligan

From 1 April 1996, the *City of Edinburgh Council* came into being. This is a unitary authority combining most of the powers previously held by District and Region, although, controversially, the administration of water and sewerage has been allocated to an autonomous quango. This has raised fears that water services were being isolated to make them suitable for privatisation, as in England and Wales, although supporters of the move argued that only an authority larger than any one region could guarantee the necessary investments for modernisation (*see* WATER and SEWERAGE).

Edinburgh is the home of *COSLA*, the Convention of Scottish Local Authorities. Based at Rosebery House, next to Haymarket station, COSLA has, since 1975, comprised representatives from all elected Scottish authorities, meeting four times annually in plenary session and in its 14 committees, and representing local government to Scottish Office ministers.

History of local government in Edinburgh

In 1618 the magistrates of Edinburgh assured James VI, in a loyal address, that the city of Edinburgh had been in existence for 330 years before the birth of Christ. In the previous century, an English historian opined that the city had been founded no less than 889 years BC. Modern historians tend not to accept either figure!

The earliest years of Edinburgh as a municipality are not fully documented, historians usually regarding Edward I's demand in 1296 for Edinburgh's allegiance, signed by alderman Edward de Dederyk, as evidence that the community was substantial enough to merit such attention.

The city's early history was tied closely to that of the royal court, even before capital status was officially recognised, if only because of the defensive importance of the castle. The town's physical development came to be controlled by 'royalties', described by A.J. Youngson as the 'rights and privileges in connection with markets, customs, and other dues – powers which became, in effect, those of local government'. Local government was closely linked to trading rights for many centuries; almost as if traders' associations nowadays had the right of governing the communities in which they are based.

In 1603, the year when James VI took his court to London, he granted a charter to Edinburgh confirming its rights and privileges. Known as the Golden Charter, this outlined the boundaries of the Royal Burgh, by no means an academic exercise when this municipal status effectively prevented any nearby community from challenging any of the monopolies enshrined in the charter. The boundaries were stipulated as running from Edgebuckling Brae (the east end of Musselburgh links) on the east, to the River Almond on the west, and from the southern limit of the Sheriffdom of Edinburgh to the middle of the Forth. The eastern boundary delineated

by the Charter allowed Edinburgh's Town Council to successfully challenge Mussel-burgh's aspirations to the status of royal burgh, and hardly created amity between Edinburgh and its eastern neighbour.

By the 1820s Lord Cockburn was describing the Town Council as 'omnipotent, corrupt, impenetrable' adding for good measure 'silent, powerful, submissive, mysterious, and irreponsible'. (The submissiveness was probably to the 'uncrowned' government minister Henry Dundas). Cockburn was a Whig (Liberal); the 33 town councillors Tories to a man (32 elected, plus the Dean of Guild), a not insignificant fact at the time of the General Election in 1832, when they were the only parliamentary voters in the city.

It was at this time that Edinburgh entered into the murkiest period of its municipal history; a time of financial incompetence which led to the city being declared bankrupt. Years of irregular book-keeping – it was discovered in 1799 that the City Chamberlain of 30 years standing had no grasp of the capital's financial affairs – brought the city to the brink of insolvency, and the building of Leith Docks pushed it over. A Government loan for their construction carried ruinous penalties, leading to the Exchequer virtually obtaining all the benefits accruing from the new facility. Leith itself had to be given its 'independence' in 1833 in an effort to regularise the fiscal position, whose history has proved difficult to trace over the years because of the chaotic state of the city's financial records.

The number of members of the Town Council since 1800, and later District Council, has been as follows:

199

	NO OF COUNCILLORS	COMMENT
1800	33	
1850	33	
1856	41	Absorbed Canongate, Calton, Portsburgh
1896	50	Absorbed Portobello
1920	71	Absorbed Leith
1966	71	
1994	62	District Council, includes Currie, Balerno, Queensferry etc, but with many former functions transferred to Region
1996	58	New Edinburgh Council

The 19th century saw the gradual, very gradual, democratisation of the Town Council of Edinburgh. In 1833 Leith was set up as a separate burgh by Act of Parliament, entitled to form its own Council, although it did not appear to have been granted fiscal powers, (*see* LEITH). In 1856, an even more momentous event took place with the absorption by the city of the separate burgh of Canongate, and the baronies of Calton and Portsburgh, effectively all the area administered by the Police Commissioners, apart from the territory now part of Leith. All administrative powers in the newly enlarged area were concentrated on the Town Council, in anticipation of national legislation to that effect some 44 years later.

In 1896 Portobello was absorbed, as was Leith in 1920, very much against public opinion. Ten years later, Edinburgh, designated as one of the four city authorities in Scotland, took on responsibilities for education, mental health, and poor law, previously administered by autonomous boards (*see also* PUBLIC HEALTH, SCHOOLS and SOCIAL WORK).

The Town Council moved into the **City Chambers**, then the Royal Exchange, in 1811, but did not have exclusive use of the building until 1893. Previously, it had been used as a government Customs House, as well as containing coffee houses, shops and the Royal Bank of Scotland. It was built in 1754–61 over three closes, Stewart's, Pearson's and Mary King's, the last of which still exists underneath the Chambers as an early example of a street museum.

An unusual, and controversial, element to Edinburgh's local politics from the 1930s to the early 1960s, was the presence in the Chamber of the Protestant Action Party. Led by John Cormack, this openly anti-Catholic group held no fewer than 12 seats in 1937, claiming to be ever-watchful against the alleged Catholic domination of job patronage and slum landowning. By the 1950s Cormack was the last remnant of the PAP, but was a noted speaker at the Mound, where he regularly defied his advancing years by haranguing the crowd for four hours every Sunday.

By 1963 Edinburgh Town Council was the largest employer by far in the Edinburgh area, with 13,800 full-time and 3,400 part-time employees. These included 2,900 teachers and 1,100 police officers – both of these occupations would presently be serving the regional authority.

The local government reorganisation of 1975 was the product of the Royal Commission on Local Government which was set up by the Wilson administration in 1966, and which reported, under its chairman Lord Wheatley (1908–88), in September 1969. This recommended the adoption of a two-tier system of seven regional and 37 district authorities, dividing local government responsiblities among them. In the resulting legislation of 1973, Edinburgh was one of 53 District Councils, and Lothian one of nine regional authorities to be set up.

In contrast, the 1996 reorganisation was conceived by the Scottish Office, and although a consultation exercise took place, no royal commission was established. The removal of a number of functions from directly-elected councils, for example water and sewerage, has been a source of criticism. The first elections for the new councils were held in April 1995, the successful candidates being expected to 'shadow' the existing councils in their final year of existence.

For the history of the local government of Leith, *see* LEITH.

Lochs

Edinburgh has three stretches of freshwater worthy of being described as lochs, all of them in the Queen's Park – Duddingston, Dunsapie, and St Margaret's. A number of smaller lochs and ponds merit consideration, and mention should also be made of four lochs which no longer exist.

DUDDINGSTON LOCH

A noted bird sanctuary, Duddingston Loch (32 acres/13.1 hectares in area, averaging 7 feet/2.1 metres in depth), is the only naturally-formed loch of the three in the Queen's Park, although it has a history of dredging (for marl, an agricultural fertiliser). The loch was gifted to the nation by the Askew family in 1923. Unlike some such sanctuaries, it is extraordinarily beautiful, and can best be viewed in its landscape situation from the Queen's Drive on the slope above.

The reedbeds on the south side of the loch provide ideal cover for waterfowl, and the triangular area to the south, a former cavalry training ground, is run as a nature reserve by the Scottish Wildlife Trust, complete with hide. In 1971 no fewer than 8,000 Pochard wintered here, but these numbers are now greatly reduced, following changes in feeding patterns on the nearby coastline caused by improved sewage disposal methods.

A colony of 200 Greylag geese is a feature at Duddingston, having grown from 13 released here in 1961. The geese at the loch are in fact remarkably tame, much to the indignation of one visiting birdwatcher from south of the Border who did not expect to find feral geese snapping at his wellingtons demanding bread! A recent visit by a bittern produced the unusual sight of cars parked almost all the way along the park road from Duddingston to Samson's Ribs (*see* HILLS), as ornithologists scanned the reedbeds below with binoculars.

Duddingston Loch has appeared on a postage stamp, when Henry Raeburn's portrait of the Reverend Robert Walker graced the nation's envelopes. It was the site of much skating and curling activity before the bird sanctuary was declared (*see* ICE SPORTS).

DUNSAPIE LOCH

An artifical loch, indeed technically a reservoir, just over three acres (1.23

The Lion's Head of Arthur's Seat is evident in this view from Dunsapie Loch, with the leonine haunch to the left. Dunsapie is not a natural loch, but a reservoir constructed by Prince Albert in the 1840s. (Frank Reid)

hectares) in area, and with an average depth of 14 feet (4.2 metres), Dunsapie was created at the initiative of Prince Albert, when the Queen's Drive was under construction in 1844. Waterfowl are plentiful here, although the loch is not particularly attractive, unusual though it is; a crescent-shaped stretch of water in a hanging valley, with Dunsapie Crag towering above. It is supplied with water from Alnwickhill.

ST MARGARET'S LOCH

The lower of the two artificial lochs in the Queen's Park (4 acres/1.64 hectares in area, less than five feet/1.5 metres deep), St Margaret's is situated next to the east-west road in the Park, close to its junction with the Queen's Drive. Although lacking in indigenous food sources, the loch is home to a considerable number of waterfowl fed by visitors and residents from nearby Meadowbank. It was a boating pond until comparatively recently, but now the swans, geese, and tufted duck have it to themselves.

LOCHEND LOCH

Situated just off Lochend Road, and east of the Hibernian FC football ground, Lochend Loch is fed by subterranean springs, prompting its use at one time as a municipal water supply for Leith. A piped supply was arranged in 1753, but this was soon superseded by water from Edinburgh. When new housing developments were built close by in the first half of the 20th century, the loch came to be regarded as dangerous – locally rumoured to be 'bottomless', probably because the bodies of drowning victims were trapped by underwater ledges – and was partially filled in during the late 1960s to reduce its depth. It is currently fenced, for safety reasons.

One of the largest ponds or smallest loch, if that is not too illogical, is **Straiton Pond**, within earshot of the busy City Bypass. Designated as a Local Nature Reserve in 1991, and with wildlife interest in the form of Great Crested Newt, dabchick, and heron (see also WILDLIFE), this site has survived a threatened infilling to form a car park for a proposed football stadium. The pond's considerable depth is the result of its origin as a pit for blue clay extraction.

Small lochs still exist at Craigcrook, near Blackhall, (evidence of quarrying in years gone by, see QUARRIES), at Granton gasworks site (no public access), and on Mortonhall golf course (the Elf Loch, again, on private ground). Attractive ponds can be found at Inverleith, Blackford, and Figgate (Portobello) Parks, and at Craiglockhart (where floodlit skating took place as late as 1938).

FORMER LOCHS

NOR' LOCH

Formed originally by the damming of the burn exuding from near the present site of the Wellhouse Tower, the Nor' or North Loch is not usually thought of as having been artificial. In fact it does not appear to have existed before 1450, a tournament being held on this site for Prince David, son of Robert III, in 1396. Historian David Robertson has argued that it was the absence of a guaranteed water supply which prevented the Romans from settling on an area whose topography had so much else to offer in terms of ease of defence, and where the damning of the burn at this location fulfilled such a need.

Occupying what is now Princes Street gardens, the Nor' Loch had a sluice at its eastern end, from where the water level was controlled, being raised at time of invasion. Eels from the Nor' Loch were a particular gastronomic treat until the effects of pollution – offal from slaughterhouses and human ordure from the undrained city – rendered the loch sterile and its water undrinkable. A ducking stool is reputed to have existed here until 1685 for the torment of those unfortunate enough to be accused of witchcraft, and a particularly deep pool, known as 'The Pot', in the loch's north-east corner was a favourite location for suicides.

Proposals were frequently made to improve the state of the Loch by incorporating it into a moving water-course, perhaps by chanelling the Water of Leith through the valley, as later considered by James Craig. In the event, a decision was taken around 1750 to drain what had already been described in an Act of Parliament as a 'noxious lake'. This took some 60 years, the area at the west still being boggy when Princes Street Gardens were being developed. In 1825 there was a dispute between the civic authorities and the Princes Street Proprietors about the amount of infilling; it appears that infilling was required to an average depth between 16 and

24 feet, using material excavated from construction sites in the New Town. For the history of the area in its new role as a park (first private, then public, *see* PARKS).

In the mid–1840s, a railway line was laid through the Gardens and continues to be an integral part of the British Inter-City system. If it were not so, the reintroduction of a loch in the area would provide a new perspective of the Castle rock, when seen from Princes Street, by doubling its visual mass, as well as reintroducing an historic part of the city's defences. The preservation of the loch is not a new idea; in 1825 the Princes Street Proprietors requested that the loch be left as it was, east of the Mound, its draining 'having the effect of injuring the romantic appearance of the old town as seen from this quarter'.

BURGH LOCH

Less well-known than the Nor' Loch, the Burgh Loch could be described as its southern counterpart, occupying much of what is now the Meadows. This stretch of water was also artificial in origin, having a sluice at the north-western end, at the appropriately-named Lochrin, whence its waters drained to the Water of Leith via the Dalry burn (*see* RIVERS AND STREAMS). The Town Council attempted to improve the loch in 1685 and again ten years later, being finally drained by Thomas Hope of Rankeillor from 1722, a process which was complete by the 1760s.

CORSTORPHINE LOCH

It comes as something of a surprise to learn of a loch, no less than three miles in length, running from Broomhouse to Haymarket. An isthmus separated this stretch of water from the smaller Gogar Loch to the west. Corstorphine's loch was considered such a natural barrier to travellers that a lamp had to be kept alight in the gable end of the parish church to guide those crossing by boat at night.

CANONMILLS LOCH

Situated between what is now Eyre Place and Royal Crescent, Canonmills Loch, also known as Boyton Pond, was believed to be about four feet deep. It boasted a curling club before Duddingston's (*see* ICE SPORTS), but was drained by the 1840s, when a railway station was built on its eastern extent (Scotland Street, *see* RAILWAYS). Its bed later became the site of the popular fairground known as the Royal Gymnasium, and a playing field used by St Bernard's Football Club until the Second World War (*see* FOOTBALL). A small industrial area and a playpark now occupy the site of a loch once famed for its wildfowl and fighting perch.

Lord Provosts

The earliest years of Edinburgh as a municipality are not fully documented, although it appears that the community was important enough in 1296 for the victorious Edward I of England to seek its allegiance. Alderman William de Dederyk signed on Edinburgh's behalf and he is regarded as being the city's first Provost. The title comes from the Latin 'Praepositus', and the first to be so-called was John de Quhitness in 1376. Although usually selected from among the senior bailies or aldermen, the 16th century saw the monarch regard the Provostship as being within their gift, and in 1561 Queen Mary, newly arrived from France, felt able to dismiss the Lord Provost and the bailies on religious grounds.

The post was no sinecure, and it was not unknown for the Provost to die violently. Sir Alexander Lauder was killed at Flodden in 1513; Adam Otterburne, Provost no fewer than four times, was assassinated in office. Archibald Stewart was regarded as so closely identified with the Jacobite cause that he was tried in London for 'neglect of duty' in the autumn of 1746, his subsequent acquittal being greeted with delight.

There has only ever been one female Provost – Eleanor McLaughlin from 1988–92. One man, James Miller, has held the titles of both Lord Provost of Edinburgh and Lord Mayor of London (i.e. City of London) at different times. The longest in office was Lord Provost Andrew Ramsay who served, if that is the correct term for what historian Thomas Whitson describes as a 'career of time-serving and corruption', a total of 14 years, including 11 in one stretch, and was appointed on 12 different occasions. Ramsay was able to appear amenable to both the Royalist and Cromwellian persuasions of the time, and was the first to be formally called Lord Provost. His enemies attempted to have his office limited to two years only, and this

appears to have taken effect after he stepped down, remaining a two-year term for some 150 years. Although believed by many to be using the office to his own advantage, Ramsay at least left his house in Niddrie's Wynd to the Town College.

Until parliamentary reform took place in 1832, the Lord Provost was usually, although not invariably, one of the city's parliamentary commissioners (at the Scottish Parliament to 1707) and member of parliament representing Edinburgh at Westminster during the 1707–1832 period. (*see* PARLIAMENTARY REPRESENTATION).

Edinburgh's Lord Provosts between 1296 and 1996 are listed below as far as is known. (Leith's Provosts between 1833 and 1920 are shown under LEITH). In the early part of the list the date given is that when the appointment was made, and there may have been intervals between these early Provosts, when appointments were unsupported by documentary sources. Where there are doubts about the exact date or succession of appointments of Provosts, the chronology used here is as established by Sir Thomas Whitson (himself Edinburgh's foremost citizen 1929–32) in his book *The Lord Provosts of Edinburgh, 1296–1932*, cross-checked against a list prepared by William Brown in Edinburgh City Libraries.

1296	William de Dederyk	1391	John de Dalrympill
1343	John Wigmer	1392	John de Camera (Chambers)
1347	John Wigmer	1408	John Rede
1359–69	William Guppild	1409	Adam Farnylie
1371	Adam Forrester	1413	George Lawedre (Lauder)
1376	John de Quhitness	1419	Adam Farnylie
1381	John de Camera (Chambers)	1422	John of Levingtoun (Livingstone)
1387	Andrew Yutson	1423	Thomas de Cranstoun

1425	William de Libertoun		1499	Sir Thomas Tod
1426	George Lawedre (Lauder)		1500	Alexander Lauder of Haltoun
1428	John of Levingtoun (Livingstone)		1501	George of Touris
1429	William de Libertoun		1502	Alexander Lauder of Haltoun
1430	George Lawedre (Lauder)		1504	Richard Lawson of High Riggs
1432	William de Libertoun		1505–13	Alexander Lauder of Haltoun (Blyth)
1434	Sir Henry Preston of Craigmillar		1513	George of Touris
1435	John of Levingtoun (Livingstone)		1514	Alexander Home
1437	Alexander Napier		1515	Sir Patrick Hamilton of Kincavill
1438	Thomas de Cranstoun		1515	David Melville
1443	Thomas de Berwick		1517	Earl of Arran
1445	Thomas de Cranstoun		1518	Archibald Douglas of Kilspindie
1445	Stephen Hunter		1520	Robert Logan of Coitfield
1446	Patrick Cockburn		1522	Sir Adam Otterburne
1449–51	Thomas de Cranstoun		1522	Alan Stewart
1453	Sir Alexander Napier		1523	Francis Bothwell
1455	Thomas Oliphant		1524	Robert, Lord Maxwell
1456	Sir Alexander Napier		1526	Archibald Douglas of Kilspindie
1462	Andrew Ker			(Father)
1466	George Bartraham		1528	Robert, Lord Maxwell
1467	Robert Mure of Polkellie		1528	Sir Adam Otterburne
1469–72	Sir Alexander Napier		1532	James Lawson
1477–78	James Creichton of Ruthven		1535	Robert, Lord Maxwell
1481	Walter (William) Bartraham		1538	Simon Preston
1482	Sir John Murray of Tulchad		1543	Sir Adam Otterburne
1483	Patrick Baron of Spittalfield		1544	Simon Preston
1483	John Napier		1545–46	George Henrison
1485	John Murray (Sir John Murray		1547	Sir Adam Otterburne
	of Tolchad?)		1548	Alexander Ker of Dolphinton
1486	Sir Patrick Baron		1549	Sir Andrew Ker of Littledean
1487	John Murray		1550	Francis Tennant
1487	Patrick Hepburne, Lord Hailes		1551	William Craik
1488	Thomas Tod		1553	William Hamilton
1488	James Creichton of Felde		1554	Archibald Douglas of Kilspindie
1490	Alexander Hepburn of Quhitson			(Son)
1491	Sir Thomas Tod		1557	George, Lord Seton
1491	Richard Lawson of High Riggs		1559	Archibald Douglas of Kilspindie
1492	Sir John Murray		1561	Thomas McCalyeane
1494	Walter Bartraham		1562	Archibald Douglas of Kilspindie
1496	Sir Thomas Tod		1566	Sir Simon Preston
1498	Andrew Bartraham		1569	Sir William Kirkcaldy of Grange

1570	James Macgill of Rankeillor	1687	Sir Magnus Prince
1571	Sir Andrew Ker of Fernihurst	1689	Sir John Hall
1572	Patrick, Lord Lindesay	1691	Archibald Muir or Mure
1576	George Douglas of Parkhead	1692	Sir John Hall
1578	Archibald Stewart	1694	Sir Robert Chieslie of Dalry
1579	Alexander Clerk of Balbirnie	1696	Sir Archibald Muir
1584	James Stewart, Earl of Arran	1698	Sir George Home of Kelso
1585	William Little	1700	Sir Patrick Johnson
1587	Sir John Arnot of Birswick	1702	Sir Hew Cunninghame
1591	William Little	1704	Sir Patrick Johnston
1592	Nicol Uddert or Udward	1706	Sir Samuel McClellan
1593	Alexander Home of North Berwick	1708	Sir Patrick Johnson
1597	Henry Nisbet	1710	Adam Brown of Blackford
1598	Alexander Seton, Lord Fyvie	1711	Sir Robert Blackwood of
1608	Sir John Arnot of Birswick		Pitreaves
1616	Sir William Nisbet	1713	Sir George Warrender of Lochend
1619	Sir Alexander Clerk of Stenton	1715	John Campbell
1620	Sir William Nisbet	1717	William Neilson
1621	David Aikinhead	1719	John Campbell
1623	Sir Alexander Clerk	1721	John Wightman of Mauldslie
1625	David Aikinhead	1723	John Campbell
1630	Sir Alexander Clerk	1725	George Drummond
1634	David Aikinhead	1727	Archibald Macaulay
1637	Sir John Hay	1729	Patrick Lindsay
1638	Sir William Dick	1731	John Osburn
1640	Sir Alexander Clerk	1733	Patrick Lindsay
1643	Sir John Smith	1735	Alexander Wilson
1646	Sir Archibald Tod	1737	Archibald Macaulay
1648–50	Sir James Stewart	1738	James Colquhoun
1652	Sir Archibald Tod	1740	George Haliburton
1655	Sir Andrew Ramsay	1742	John Coutts
1658	Sir James Stewart	1744	Archibald Stewart
1660	Sir Robert Murray	1746	George Drummond
1662	Sir Andrew Ramsay	1748	Archibald Macaulay
1673	James Currie	1750	George Drummond
1675	Sir William Binning	1752	William Alexander
1677	Sir Francis Kinlock	1754	George Drummond,
1679	Sir James Dick	1756	Robert Montgomery
1681	Sir James Fleming	1758	George Drummond
1683	Sir George Drummond	1760	George Lind
1685	Sir Thomas Kennedy	1762	George Drummond

1764	James Stuart	1851	Duncan McLaren
1766	Gilbert Laurie	1854	Sir John Melville
1768	James Stuart	1859	Francis Brown Douglas
1770	John Dalrymple	1862	Charles Lawson of Borthwick Hall
1772	Gilbert Laurie	1865	William Chambers of Glenormiston
1774	James Stoddart	1869	William Law
1776	Alexander Kincaid	1872	James Cowan
1777	John Dalrymple	1874	Sir James Falshaw
1778	Walter Hamilton	1877	Sir Thomas Jamieson Boyd
1780	David Steuart	1882	Sir George Harrison
1782	John Grieve	1885	Sir Thomas Clark
1784	Sir James Hunter Blair	1888	Sir John Boyd of Maxpoffle
1786	John Grieve	1891	Sir James Alexander Russell
1788	Thomas Elder of Forneth	1894	Sir Andrew McDonald
1790	Sir James Stirling of Larbert	1897	Sir Mitchell Mitchell-Thomson
1792	Thomas Elder of Forneth	1900	Sir James Steel of Murieston
1794	Sir James Stirling of Larbert	1903	Sir Robert Cranston
1796	Thomas Elder of Forneth	1906	Sir James Puckering Gibson
1798	Sir James Stirling of Larbert	1909	Sir William Slater Brown
1800	Sir William Fettes of Wamphray and	1912	Sir Robert Kirk Inches
	Comely Bank	1916	Sir John Lorne Macleod
1802	Neil McVicar	1919	John William Chesser
1804	Sir William Fettes of Wamphray	1921	Sir Thomas Hutchison
1806	Donald Smith	1923	Sir William Lowrie Sleigh
1808	William Coulter	1926	Sir Alexander Stevenson
1810	William Calder	1929	Sir Thomas Barnby Whitson
1811	William Creech	1932	Sir William Johnston Thompson-
1813	Sir John Marjoribanks of Lees		Thomson
1815	Sir William Arbuthnot	1935	Sir Louis Stewart Gumley
1817	Kincaid Mackenzie	1938	Sir Henry Steele
1819	John Manderston	1941	Sir William Y. Darling
1821	Sir William Arbuthnot	1944	Sir John Ireland Falconer
1823	Alexander Henderson of Press	1947	Sir Andrew Hunter Arbuthnot
1825	William Trotter of Ballindean		Murray
1827	Walter Brown	1951	Sir James Miller
1829	William Allan of Glen	1954	Sir John Garnet Banks
1831	John Learmonth of Dean	1957	Sir Ian Anderson Johnson-Gilbert
1833	Sir James Spittal	1960	Sir John Greig Dunbar
1837	Sir James Forrest of Comiston	1963	Sir Duncan Weatherstone
1843	Adam Black	1966	Sir Herbert Brechin
1848	Sir William Johnston of Kirkhill	1969	Sir James McKay

1972	Jack Kane		1984	Dr John Mackay
1975	John Millar		1988	Eleanor McLaughlin
1977	Kenneth Borthwick		1992	Norman Irons
1980	Tom Morgan		1996	Eric Milligan

Maps

Until 1980, Edinburgh was a major centre for the production of maps. Two firms were active in the capital until recently – Johnston's and Bartholomew's. The latter still prints maps in the capital, but the editorial work is now carried out in Glasgow (see INDUSTRY), while W. & A. K. Johnston, latterly known as Johnston and Bacon, moved to London in the 1970s. Nevertheless, the British Geological Survey, the largest publisher of specialised maps in the United Kingdom, still has an office in Edinburgh which inputs material into the Survey's map production programme.

History

Maps of Edinburgh appear to date back to the 16th century, and are considered below, although the earliest of these were effectively illustrations from an imaginary bird's eye view, and were neither detailed, nor drawn to scale. The earliest of these, dating from 1544, appears to have been an English drawing of the Earl of Hertford's attack on the city. This was drawn from a northern perspective; the original is in the British Library in London.

Perhaps the best of the 16th century drawings-cum-maps, was *Edenburg, Scotia Metropolis* published by Georg Braun and Franz Hogenberg in their survey of the world's nations, *Civitates Orbis Terrarum*. This shows Edinburgh from a south-eastern perspective, but on such a small scale that the Firth of Forth is out of the picture and the Nor' Loch appears almost as a canal. The representation of the streets and gates is very good, however.

The first known attempt at producing a map of Edinburgh was carried out by James Gordon, minister of Rothiemay to a commission of 500 merks from Edinburgh Town Council on 2 April 1647. The resulting map was published in Amsterdam, and became the standard on which many later maps were based. One which was not, was William Edgar's map of the city surveyed in 1742, and published in Maitland's *History of Edinburgh* (see HISTORIANS).

Further details of these and other early maps of the city can be learned from William Cowan's book *The maps of Edinburgh, 1544–1929*, available for consultation in Edinburgh Public Libraries.

Markets

Edinburgh no longer enjoys the tradition of the open air market so common in English towns and cities, and in Glasgow's 'Barras'. Following the opening of the Waverley Market in 1869, those with wares or produce to sell, but without the wherewithal to own a shop, were expected to lease a stand at the Market, and outdoor selling was not encouraged.

Unfortunately, the Waverley Market's central location in a citycentre increasingly attractive to tourists, led inevitably to its site, roofed over from 1877, being made available for exhibitions and touring funfairs to the detriment of lease-holders, while the predominance of established retailers on the city's council over the decades of the 19th century was never likely to allow the stallholders' point of view to prevail. (In 1832, for example, 15 of the 32 councillors were involved in retail trading, although this had dwindled to single figures, out of 65 councillors, by 1960). The Market site is now, significantly, a shopping mall. In recent years, probably the only city location where it was regularly possible to buy fruit and vegetables from a barrow out of doors was at the top of Infirmary Street.

It is no surprise to find that the biggest market in the Lothians is well outside the citycentre, at Ingliston, while Bonnyrigg and other towns on the capital's environs have regular outdoor markets. Following the recent reorganisation of the bus industry, an indoor market, claiming to be Scotland's biggest, has now opened in the former New Street garage of Scottish Omnibuses.

History of Edinburgh's agricultural markets

The fertile Lothians have traditionally looked on Edinburgh as a ready market for their products. In October 1477, the city's markets were important enough to be reorganised by royal decree from James III, with the Grassmarket's west end being allocated, along with King's Stables Road, for cattle sales even although the latter location was marginally outside the burgh boundaries. By 1840, before the railways arrived to change the distributive pattern, there were many different types of produce market in the city, as listed below, with such locations as the Grassmarket being used for the selling of many diverse commodities (*see also* AGRICULTURE):

Grassmarket	meal/corn/grain horses/cattle Straw
High Riggs	sheep/lamb/pigs
West Port	cattle
King's Stables Road	cattle
North Bridge/ Fishmarket Close	meat meat
Market Street (site of)	wholesale & retail fruit & vegetables also, fish
North Bridge/ Fleshmarket Close	poultry
House o'Muir (Pentlands) then to Meadows	ewes

By 1844, it was decided to centralise most of the livestock activity at Lauriston although this proved to be a less than ideal development, being too close to housing, far from the newly-developing rail network, and, from 1900, a serious problem for the market's new neighbour. This was the Lauriston Place fire station (*see* FIRE FIGHTING), whose crews understandably found difficulty in threading their way through herds of arriving or departing livestock.

By 1911 the livestock market moved, along with corn dealing, to the Gorgie area, but another short-sighted development in the mid-19th century was the centralisation of the city's slaughterhouses on the Lochrin area near Tollcross, from 75 previously scattered and largely unsupervised gory sites. This new locale was too close to housing and was the subject of a complaint from the first Medical Health Officer appointed in the 19th century, Dr Littlejohn (*see* PUBLIC HEALTH). In 1911, the slaughterers moved to Gorgie to continue their trade.

Grain dealing was traditionally carried out in the Grassmarket, where a Cornmarket building, described by a contemporary writer as an 'unsightly arcaded edifice, with a central belfry and clock' stood near the West Port site from 1819 to around 1850, succeeding an earlier building situated only a few yards from the Bow Foot Well, which still stands at the east end of the Grassmarket. The western building was then replaced by one on the south side of the Grassmarket, itself demolished in 1965 to make way for the Mountbatten Building built for Heriot-Watt University (the Mountbatten building is now also demolished). In contrast, the Leith Corn Exchange still stands, on the corner of Constitution and Baltic Streets, about a quarter of a mile from the dock gates. Its frieze illustrating the import of grain, in an unlikely classical style, is outstanding.

The position of the fruit and vegetable markets in the area of what is now Market Street, was affected by the arrival of the railway companies in 1846. Considerable rationalisation was necessary because of the building of the Joint (later Waverley) Station, and a slaughterhouse was demolished altogether. The railways finally took over almost all the site after undertaking to create a custom-built market-place for the vendors of fruit and vegetables.

This was the **Waverley Market**, located directly parallel to, and below, Princes Street, and opened in 1869. After the Corporation had roofed it over, some years later, it rapidly became attractive as a site for travelling exhibitions and menageries, while an aquarium was located here around 1877. On these special occasions the market gardeners' leases did not protect them from being pitched out into the street. Court action followed, but although alternative accommodation for stallholders was found in a building east of North Bridge, no real solution was devised until the demand for market shopping and selling waned in postwar years. Meanwhile, the Waverley Market was demolished 115 years after its opening, the site being resurrected as a shopping mall in 1985 (*see* SHOPS).

Enclosed former market sites can still be found in the city – e.g. Stockbridge Market (now an attractive housing area connecting Hamilton Place with St Stephen's Street, where a handsome gateway remains; the market closed for trading by 1906), and even more visibly, Broughton Market (off Dublin Street). The former dates from around 1826, the latter from the 1840s, and their remains are more obvious than two other markets, at Nicolson Street and at Fountainbridge. In his excellent history of Edinburgh markets, written for the *Third Statistical Account*, E.F. Catford speculates that these markets were opened in defiance of the Town Council monopoly of trade, and this source is well worth consulting for further details of the history of the city's markets.

Although nominally connected with the city's market history, the **Mercat Cross** appears to have lost any direct connection with the city's markets when livestock and foodstuff selling was concentrated in the Grassmarket in the late 15th century. The present cross, situated in the High Street opposite the City Chambers, is not the original structure, but a 19th century replica incorporating a 1970 copy of the original shaft from the 14th century. Royal proclamations are still made here, although another of the Cross's functions – as a place of execution – is no longer continued.

Military History

Nowadays, with no compulsory national service in Britain, the city's military profile is greatly reduced. In 1991, the Census discovered 93 people living in Edinburgh who were employed in the armed forces, 91 of them men. The Army's headquarters are no longer sited at Edinburgh Castle, but have removed to Craigiehall near South Queensferry. The Castle remains the HQ for 52 Lowland Brigade, although the Castle's garrison has been based at Redford Barracks, in the south-west of the city, since 1915. Barracks formerly existed at Piershill, just east of Jock's Lodge, from 1793 and the layout of the housing scheme there somehow preserves an image of the parade-ground, as indeed it might, stone from the barracks, demolished in 1934, having been used in the houses' construction. There are Territorial centres at various locations in the city.

A number of Scottish infantry regiments have Edinburgh connections. The Royal Scots, as discussed below, regard the Lothians as their principal recruiting territory, while the King's Own Scottish Borderers, raised in the Borders and based at Berwick-on-Tweed, is the only regiment permitted to march through Edinburgh with fixed bayonets without seeking prior permission.

With Edinburgh Castle providing a romantic backdrop to the Edinburgh Military Tattoo, the sight of massed pipes and drums is a familiar one to citizen and visitor alike. One historic massing of Scottish troops which met with meteorological defeat was the 'Wet Review' of 25 August 1881, when 40,000 volunteers were drenched awaiting inspection by Queen Victoria on what is now the playing fields area east of the Palace of Holyroodhouse.

In the air, No 603 Squadron of the Royal Air Force was regarded as the city's own, and had a distinguished career in Fighter Command in the Second World War. (The city's military airfields are discussed under AIRPORTS).

At sea the Type 42 destroyer HMS *Edinburgh* is the city's adopted ship. The first British warship of the name appears to have been the pre-1707 Scottish warship *Royal William*, renamed for Edinburgh after the passing of the Act of Union. The present ship's immediate predecessor holding the name was a 10,000-ton cruiser sunk in the Barent's Sea on 2 May 1942 after being torpedoed by a U-boat while conveying Soviet gold to London. The value of the cargo was considered to be a constant lure for bounty hunters when peace returned, so a controlled salvage of the gold was carried out by government contractors in 1981. This was not accomplished without controversy, the ship being a war grave for the men who died on her.

Edinburgh's history has inevitably been one of bloodshed and strife, but the last occasion when Edinburgh citizens had to prepare to fight for their city was during the Second Jacobite Rebellion, in 1745.

In that momentous year, volunteers were sought to augment regular forces defending the city at the Coltbridge (Roseburn). The Reverend Alexander Carlyle, in his *Autobiography*, recalled marching down the West Bow to the Grassmarket with other nervously-bantering volunteers, only to be marched back to High School Yards, where Lord Provost George Drummond informed them that he was unable to bring himself to send such men to a probable early death. A particular twist of the volunteers' predicament was the possibility of being charged with treason for opposing *either* side. This civilian would-be army was to be the last of its kind until 1940, and the birth of the Home Guard. After 1745, when the last Jacobite headed northwards, a distinction could be made between civil and military lifestyles.

An earlier Edinburgh citizens' army (conspicuously missing from accounts of the '45) was represented by the Trained Bands. These were heavily-armed if apparently lightly-trained irregular volunteers who were responsible for the safety of the city, but who may have assisted the Town Guard and Constables from time to time (*see also* POLICE). First mentioned in city histories in 1580, it was not until 1626 that a systematic attempt was being made to drill, on a weekly basis, volunteers grouped into eight companies of two hundred men each. In 1645 the force was reorganised into 16 Bands of 100 men each.

For no obvious reason, the first of these companies was drawn from the householders on the north side of the Grassmarket, between the West Bow and the West Port, its Standard being orange in colour. This is the only one to survive, and should not be confused with the insignia of the Orange Order, with which it has no connection. A map showing the bounds of each company, and a list of their colours, can be found in the Russell Fox typescript on the subject in the City Library Edinburgh Room.

In 1753 the Bands' armoury comprised 1,350 sets of arms, each set consisting of a musket, bayonet, cartridge-box, sword and belt, paid for by the admission fees of the Band members. By this time the Trained Bands were probably no more than decorative; indeed the minutes of the society of Bands' captains, formed in 1663, make no mention of such events as the First and Second Jacobite Rebellions which might reasonably be categorised as events of pressing interest to a military unit, part-time or otherwise.

The Trained Bands in fact became nothing more than a drinking and dining club for their officers, Fortune's Tavern (at the top opening of present-day Cockburn Street opposite the Guardhouse) their favourite venue. In the second half of the 18th century 'celebrity' members were admitted, including Adam Smith and city MP Sir Laurence Dundas. The minutes show an elaborate array of fines for the sloppy wearing of uniforms or swearing. The Captain of the Orange Colours featured in an honoured position in the 1946 Riding of the Marches; the eclipse of this historic figure in an otherwise tradition-conscious city is perhaps because of the erroneous assumption that the colour has some connection with extreme protestantism.

COMPULSORY MILITARY RECRUITMENT

After the Young Pretender's rebellion had been crushed at Culloden in 1746, successive London governments could not face the prospect of supplying arms to potentially rebellious Scots in anything other than regular army conditions. As a result, the raising of militias in Scotland to act as manpower reservoirs for the regular army during the 1790s wars with France, broke with military tradition and met considerable resistance from Scots unaccustomed to being called upon to defend their country.

There were riots throughout most of Scotland against the balloting of able-bodied men for service, and 12 people, not all of them protestors, and including women and a child, were killed when cavalry ran amok at Tranent, some ten miles from the city. While the recruitment terms appear fairly innocuous nowadays – drafting was done by ballot only, and anyone whose name came out of the hat had the right to pay for a replacement to go instead – there is no doubt that the authorities' promise of 'no service overseas' was not kept.

Archival papers at the Scottish Record Office show that government officials and military commanders were worried that the deaths at Tranent might presage a violent reaction from the working population of Edinburgh, then Scotland's largest city, when recruits were sought in the capital. In fact this did not happen, possibly thanks to

a higher proportion of newspaper readers in Edinburgh, who could be fully appraised of the recruitment conditions by military and civil officials.

Enforced enlistment did continue, however, through the 18th and early 19th centuries in the form of 'impressment', particularly for the Royal Navy. Press-gangs frequently combed the Leith and Canongate areas, with local constables giving varying degrees of co-operation in rounding up likely victims. In 1756 a Canongate constable was himself dragged off to sea by a gang, the remaining constables promptly resigning their commissions, enraged by the feeble attempts by the authorities to deal with the Admiralty. In later years, Edinburgh Town Council declined naval requests to search the public houses for likely recruits, unless a search for named individuals, such as deserters, was being undertaken – and no deserter worth his salt was likely to remain within a few miles of the sea!

THE FIRST WORLD WAR

No further compulsory recruitment took place in Edinburgh in modern times until 1916, when the First World War was raging. Edinburgh had already responded gallantly to Lord Kitchener's message of 'Your country needs you', but the terrible campaign of attrition which began on the Western Front soon drained the supply of volunteers. The war diary of the 1st City of Edinburgh Battalion of the Royal Scots records 628 casualties in the first week of the Battle of the Somme in 1916, leaving virtually no Edinburgh men left in that unit.

This particular regiment, the first of the line in the army hierarchy after the Guards battalions, incurred a horrendous loss in the most unexpected way in May 1915. In that month a train of recruits, mainly from Musselburgh and Leith, was involved in Britain's worst rail disaster at Quintinshill, Gretna Green, when on their way to the Front. No fewer than 214 of the total 227 death-toll were Royal Scots. Their remains were buried at Rosebank Cemetery, Pilrig, with full military honours, and their graves are marked by a pink sandstone cross of Celtic design. Visible from Broughton Road, (although the date of the disaster is given wrongly on the notice at the cemetery gates in Pilrig Street) this is a war memorial to soldiers who volunteered but who never had a chance to fight for their country.

Perhaps they would have perished anyway. For the major part of the First World War, Edinburgh-born Sir Douglas Haig was the principal British commander on the Western Front. An officer with cavalry training, Haig seemed more well-equipped to fight a 19th-century war, believing that the lance was the weapon which would defeat Germany in 1914–18. At that time, the horrendous death-toll on the Western Front was apparently accepted by the public as unavoidable, and at the conclusion of the war, Haig was honoured by Edinburgh with the 'Freedom of the City' on 28 May 1919,

in recognition of his distinguished career as a soldier . . . and in testimony of the honour and esteem in which he is held by the whole community.

This was not a case of a favourite son being honoured more by his home town

One of the city's most poignant monuments in Edinburgh is this Celtic cross and list of names over the mass-graves of the Royal Scots killed in the 1915 railway disaster at Quintinshill (Gretna), while on their way to the front. Possibly because of its location at Rosebank Cemetery, Pilrig, well away from the city centre, it is comparatively unknown.

than elsewhere; similar awards were granted by Glasgow and Aberdeen in 1919, and Haig was gifted the Bemersyde Estate near Melrose by 'a grateful nation', as Britain was described at the time.

One of his biographers has pointed out, in the face of subsequent criticism, that Haig *won* the war, although it could equally be argued that Germany simply lost, her last push in the spring of 1918 exhausting a nation that had no prospect of seeing the kind of reinforcements that the Western Allies could expect when the USA came fully into the conflict. From about 1928, the often horrific reminiscences of such articulate former soldiers as Siegfried Sassoon and Robert Graves destroyed Haig's reputation, and the play *Oh What a Lovely War!* by Joan Littlewood, and Richard Attenborough's film based on it, communicated this destruction to a new generation 40 years later.

Earl Haig's equestrian statue on the Castle Esplanade seems somewhat the worse for wear in this autumn 1995 picture, rather like Haig's reputation. Nowadays he is not regarded as one of Edinburgh's more illustrious sons. History does not record if the model for the horse was the one owned by Haig which threw George V in 1915, seriously injuring the monarch.

No community nowadays would wish to boast about being Earl Haig's birthplace – which Edinburgh is – and it was noticeable that a recent Edinburgh District Council souvenir pamphlet, to commemorate Sean Connery's Freedom of the City award, omitted Haig from its list of previous recipients. An article in *The Guardian* newspaper in 1994 named Haig as one of the most notorious men of the 20th century, along with the likes of Hitler and Stalin. No letters to the editor appear to have resulted.

All this may appear a trifle harsh – Haig's main failing seemed to have been a blimpish lack of tactical imagination, and he appeared to enjoy the confidence of his French allies and King George V and his ministers. For those who wish to see it,

Haig's birthplace is at 24 Charlotte Square, and he is commemorated by an equestrian bronze statue on the Castle Esplanade by G.E. Wade.

Also honoured by the city of Edinburgh at the end of the First World War (*see* FREEDOM OF THE CITY), and voted University Rector, was Admiral David Beatty. A contemporary of Haig's, the two could hardly have been more dissimilar. Beatty cut a flamboyant figure, sporting his cap at what became known as a 'Beatty angle', but there was more to him than met the eye.

Commanding a squadron of battleships and battlecruisers from its base at Rosyth, Beatty deployed his ships as a scouting group to tempt the enemy into battle when British reinforcements were waiting just over the horizon, or perhaps just to tempt them into battle, whether reinforced or not. His force was heavily involved in the 1916 Battle of Jutland, where two of his largest warships, the *Indefatigable* and the *Queen Mary*, were blown up. 'Something wrong with our bloody ships today' was his laconic comment at the time, but, unlike Haig, Beatty was in the thick of the battle himself.

Beatty was often to be seen in Edinburgh during the war; to maintain morale he reportedly banned his officers from visiting a fortune-teller in the city who discovered ominously that all the army officers whose palms she examined had shortened life-lines.

One relevant detail of Beatty's later command in the First World War, as Jellicoe's successor as Admiral of the Fleet, was his refusal to accept the ridiculous findings of a board of inquiry into an incident known as the 'Battle of the Isle of

May'. On this occasion in January 1918, two British submarines, and 105 lives, had been lost in a naval manoeuvre which had gone horribly wrong in the Firth of Forth barely 20 miles from Edinburgh. An attempt to blame a hapless, and undoubtedly innocent, signals officer, was crushed by Beatty, who had already seen at first hand that the truth of Matthew Arnold's poetic line about ignorant armies clashing by night, could be extended to fleets too.

Many historians believe that if Beatty had commanded the whole British fleet at Jutland, instead of what was basically a well-armed scouting group, the attack on the numerically-inferior German High Seas Fleet in that action would have been prosecuted with greater determination, possibly shortening Haig's war on land, with its seemingly endless death-toll.

But the First World War was not just an officers' war, (although in the army at least, junior officers were statistically at even greater risk than their men). A young Edinburgh lad named George Baird went cheerfully to war in 1914, excited by the prospect of fighting for his country. He had plenty of time to write his memoirs in later life, crippled from his injuries for the next 48 years. His unpublished manuscripts are to be found in the care of Edinburgh City Libraries, and his fate must have been fairly typical of that of many youngsters who had no idea of how the world was to become a darker place around them.

After training at an extemporised depot at the Marine Gardens, Baird's battalion was marched to entrain in public at Portobello station where, Baird records touchingly, he was able to glimpse his mother in the crowd. Gallipoli was his first destination, and although he was wounded, Baird's account was more concerned with what happened to his company commander whom he saw shot dead a few feet in front of him. As if this was not enough war for anyone, Baird and his comrades were then transferred to the Western Front. Here he was wounded very badly and was invalided out of the war in 1916. Yet his is not one of the names to be seen on the war memorials recording those whom we regard as the victims of war. They *were* victims of course, but so was George Baird.

George Baird used his years of invalidity to hone his skills as an amateur historian, and it is largely thanks to him that we have such excellent records of Edinburgh's places of entertainments – the cinema in particular fascinated him.

Two little-known monuments in the city commemorate aspects of the First World War that, otherwise, are nowadays little remembered. Above warehouse doors in Pitt Street, Leith, can be seen a low-relief sculpture illustrating women and children being killed and wounded by German soldiers, the inscription being *The Valour of German Culture 1914*. Sarcasm is not usually found in plaque inscriptions, and this relief does not figure in any 'must see' list issued for tourists.

The second plaque commemorates the fact that the First World War was the first of the modern 'total' wars, and Edinburgh became one of the earliest cities in Britain to experience bombing from the air.

On the night of 2 April 1916 Zeppelins L14 and L22 flew over Leith and Edinburgh, the former dropping 27 high explosive, and 17 incendiary bombs which killed 13 and injured 24. L22 succeeded only in breaking glass in Colinton and Liberton, but her sister ship, commanded by *Kapitanleutnant* Alois Böcker, exacted this civilian death-toll, two dying in Leith and 11 in the Grassmarket. There is some evidence that Böcker attempted to hit only strategic or military targets – in bombing Leith, whose docks he had visited as a merchant officer in prewar days, he succeeded in also causing £44,000 of damage to a whisky bonded warehouse, which was uninsured against attack from the air.

The raid is commemorated by a little-known plaque on the western side of the Castle Rock above the footpath between King's Stables Road and Johnston Terrace. Positioned high above the path, the plaque cannot be read by a passer-by, and merely records that a bomb fell 'on this spot', presumably aimed at the Castle. It appears that Donaldson's Hospital was also targeted, presumably because of its resemblance to a barracks building and parade grounds. Some commemoration of the raid would have been better placed in Leith or the Grassmarket, where the casualties occurred.

EDINBURGH IN THE SECOND WORLD WAR

Edinburgh faced the war in 1939 with the same elaborate precautions as elsewhere. Air-raid shelters were dug in East Princes Street Gardens, and in five public parks from Barnton to Portobello. 13,538 Anderson shelters were inserted into suburban flowerbeds (some are still there), and it was calculated that by October 1939, around 140,000 people had access to shelter in the event of bombing.

Children were evacuated from city stations in the first weekend of war, although in smaller numbers than anticipated, probably around 26,000. They went mostly to the Borders, camps being built at Broomlee (West Linton) and Middleton (near Gorebridge) – both became 'camp schools' after the war, familiar to successive generations of the city's children. One of the evacuation trains was halted near Peebles when gunfire was heard – it turned out to be thunder in the hills. Not all such alarms proved to be false, however, as the Forth estuary rapidly became the cockpit of early aircraft raids by the Luftwaffe.

Bombs fell near the Forth Bridge on 16 October 1939 in the first air attack of the war on the British Isles, and the first Luftwaffe plane to be downed in Britain was accounted for near Humbie, East Lothian, less than a fortnight later. 602 and 603 vied with one another, as one would expect the air squadrons of Glasgow and Edinburgh to do, in shooting down enemy aircraft, but civilian casualties were soon incurred from shrapnel and badly fused ammunition falling at various locations throughout the Forth valley.

Edinburgh had no fewer than 7,000 Air Raid Wardens at the beginning of the war, 85 per cent of them volunteers, although even the early air-raids failed to raise their status in the eyes of the public, who must have found them officious with their cry of 'Put that light out!'. In his history of Edinburgh at war, Andrew Jeffrey (*see* BIBLIOGRAPHY) records that the most persistent offenders in breaching blackout precautions were the Royal Artillery in St George's Church Hall and a resident in

Succoth Place who turned out to be a Warden himself! No sustained blitz materialised in the first year of war, and when a warehouse in Lothian Road accidentally went on fire in November 1939, no enemy aircraft were around to use the beacon of flame and smoke for bomb-aiming purposes.

The summer that followed was one of perfect weather. As Britain found itself having to face the prospect of standing alone against Germany, a 'fifth column' panic sprang up, with the widespread belief that German spies and disguised troops were everywhere. An innocent walker in the Pentlands was questioned by police on suspicion of attempting to poison the city's reservoirs. More seriously, a nervous spy was arrested at the Waverley Station that autumn, later to be executed in Wandsworth prison.

The Home Guard took up their duties in 1940. While our perception nowadays of this organisation is coloured by the TV comedy series *Dad's Army*, there was no denying that their formation took place against a background of defeat on the continent, and in the shadow of imminent invasion. Whether an Edinburgh Home Guard battalion armed with peeled potatoes was ever going to prove a match for a Panzer unit is something that only the imagination can supply an answer to. The Guard was 'stood down' in December 1944.

Manufacturing industry in the capital geared up to war production without apparent effort. Robb's, the Leith shipbuilders, built 42 naval vessels, most of them corvettes and frigates, and 14 merchant ships. This was despite a strike at the yard in April 1940 when 300 men came

out over the conduct of a foreman. The rubber and electrical industries in the city produced important war equipment, but many a building changed its function within days. Where there had been skating at the Edinburgh (Haymarket) Rink, aero engines were assembled, where couples had danced at the Marine Gardens, amphibious vehicles were prepared for launching across the deserted promenade.

One industrial concern in the middle of the city – the SMT garage at Fountainbridge (now demolished) – underwent an almost overnight conversion to a munitions factory late in 1939. Grotesquely, the top floor was utilised for the production of the heaviest guns. The ground floor was laid out as a canteen for the workers, many of them from the Irish Republic, and, later, the West Indies, and a young domestic science graduate found herself drafted in to run it. On her first day she arrived to find contractors removing all kitchen equipment because of a contractual dispute, while hundreds of workers expressed a strong interest in knowing the provenance of their next meal! By enlisting her former tutors from Atholl Crescent college (now Queen Margaret College) she was able to feed her hungry workers, going on to run 11 such canteens throughout northern Britain.

In 1946 Edinburgh's Chief Constable reported that, in the six years of war, the city had experienced 105 air attack alerts, 15 of which proved to be genuine, bringing about the deaths of 20 citizens, with injuries to a further 210. Two land-mines, 47 high explosive bombs, and more than 600 incendiaries had rained down. One of the saddest features of this report is the realisation that Edinburgh had been very lucky compared to so many other European cities.

WAR MEMORIALS

Edinburgh's – and Scotland's – greatest war memorial is the **Scottish National War Memorial** at Edinburgh Castle. Designed in 1924 by Sir Robert Lorimer, the Memorial takes the form of a shrine opened within the shell of the north barracks, and with an imposing facade. Opened by the then Prince of Wales (later Edward VIII) in July 1927, the memorial features stained-glass windows by Douglas Strachan recalling the paraphernalia of war, and the Rolls of Honour displayed allow for the additional names from later conflicts, including those after the Second World War.

The city's **Cenotaph** is situated in the arcade outside the City Chambers in the High Street. Unlike the Whitehall monolith in London, this is a horizontal stone commemorating dead servicemen and women in many conflicts.

The **Heart of Midlothian War Memorial** commemorates the act of volunteering in 1914 of the entire Hearts first team. In addition to those who did not return from military service, two of the players who resumed their playing careers suffered from gas effects. The monument takes the form of a stone pylon with two clock-faces, designed by Henry Snell Gamley, and erected in 1922. It was moved a short distance westwards 50 years later, but still dominates the crossroads outside Haymarket station.

The **Scottish-American War Memorial** is situated on the long terrace in West Princes Street Gardens opposite the Castle. Its centrepiece is a bronze statue of a kilted soldier who has just received 'The Call'. This was the theme pursued by the sculptor, R. Tait Mackenzie (1867–1938); the work was commissioned by American expatriates and unveiled in 1927.

Britain's first regiment of the line, the Royal Scots, have their own memorial in West Princes Street Gardens, unveiled in 1952 (*see also* MUSEUMS). The Royal Scots Greys are commemorated by an equestrian statue of 1906 opposite the south end of Frederick Street. Viewed from there with the Castle in the background, it presents a particularly impressive sight. The Black Watch's involvement in the Boer War is unlikely to be forgotten, their commemorative statue having stood on the Mound at its corner with Market Street since 1908. This was the work of W. Birnie Rhind, as was the Royal Scots Greys' memorial, and he was also responsible for the memorial to the King's Own Scottish Borderers, located on North Bridge in 1906. More technical detail about these statues can be found in the *Buildings of Edinburgh* volume (*see* BIBLIOGRAPHY).

Museums

Edinburgh is fortunate in hosting two tiers of museums – the national storehouses of the nation's cultural artefacts, and the city's own museum network. Mention 'the museum' to most capital citizens and they will immediately assume you are referring to the Victorian palace in Chambers Street with its breathtaking arcaded hall complete with goldfish ponds. But it is museums such as Huntly House and the People's Story (at Canongate Tolbooth) which more closely reflect the life of the city. Both national and municipal systems are described below, as well as academic and private museums.

While Edinburgh is fortunate to have a municipal museum service which appears determined to strike a popular note by hosting travelling exhibitions with wide appeal, it is surely not inappropriate to wonder if and when the community of Leith is likely to have a museum of its own. Also, a transport museum currently proposed for a gap site off Dundee Street is long overdue for a city which is a traditional route centre, home to the nation's first railway companies, and which once operated one of the world's largest cable-car systems. A museum of computing might also be appropriate for a city which was the home of John Napier, inventor of logarithms, and constructor of one of the world's first mechanical calculating machines.

NATIONAL

ROYAL MUSEUM OF SCOTLAND

Centrepiece of the National Museums of Scotland, the Royal Museum (until recently known as the Royal Scottish Museum) is the prominent feature of the landscape of Chambers Street. Visitors to this fine Victorian edifice enter almost immediately into a lofty galleried atrium, known as the Crystal Palace Main Hall when opened in 1875.

The collection continues to be a happy balance between nature and technology. While the natural history specimens are perhaps less useful to the student or illustrator than they were in pre-television days, the working models in the Power Hall can still fascinate the younger generation. The original intended function of an industrial museum was left behind with the addition of a formidable collection of Oriental Art, and there are specialist satellite museums featuring costume (at New Abbey, near Dumfries), aeronautics (at East Fortune), and gas-making (at Biggar). Curiously, admissions fees are charged at two of these three sites, which are less conveniently placed for the tourist (particularly New Abbey) than in the Scotland's capital city; a similar policy is operated by the Royal Botanic Garden in relation to its outstations (*see* BOTANIC GARDENS).

Public attendance figures were close to half a million in 1994, although the Museum is perhaps a little less crowded than it used to be on a Sunday, when, as the *Third Statistical Account* reported, young people were attracted there 'not by the exhibits alone, but by shelter, warmth, and company'. Newer generations of teenagers seem to have transferred their Sunday quest for 'company' to the city's shopping malls, probably to their own ultimate intellectual deprivation! Chambers Street will be doubly attractive to the museum visitor when the new **Museum of Scotland** is completed next door.

History

The Museum itself dates back further than the opening of its grand hall in 1875, being the product of a Government initiative to construct an Industrial Museum of Scotland while the memory of the Great Exhibition of 1851 was still fresh in collective memory.

Edinburgh Town Council added to it the University's Natural History Museum, which was within their gift (much of it based on the late Robert Jameson's collection, *see* GEOLOGY), and the building's foundation stone was laid in October 1861 by Prince Albert, in one of his last public appearances. Close links with the University remained until 1901 when funding for the Museum passed to the Scottish Education Department.

NATIONAL MUSEUM OF ANTIQUITIES

Currently sharing its Queen Street building with the Scottish National Portrait Gallery, the Antiquities' museum collection will form a major part of the Museum of Scotland currently under construction in Chambers Street. Meanwhile, here can be seen Scottish artefacts dating back to prehistoric times, with the emphasis being very much on man-made exhibits. Roman artefacts are particularly prominent; a reminder to those from south of Hadrian's Wall of the Antonine Wall even farther to the north, straddling the Forth-Clyde isthmus. Perhaps the most memorable single item is the 'Maiden', Scotland's own 16th century precedent of the Guillotine (*see also* EXECUTIONS). The Museum enjoyed an increase in visitors of no less than 30 per cent over 1993-4, to 228,984.

History

This is the second oldest museum in Edinburgh, dating back to 1780, when the 11th Earl of Buchan was the driving force behind the Society of Antiquaries at that time. In many ways, this resembles an older, traditional, concept of a museum, with its glass cases and lifeless artefacts, and the shortage of exhibition space at the Queen Street site has always been only too apparent. This building was first used from 1891, the collection previously having been somewhat nomadic. The Museum has held the right of Treasure Trove since 1859, giving it first refusal of valuable artefacts discovered by chance. Unfortunately, this frequently leads to a conflict with local museums which might badly need all the attractions they can lay hands on to boost their area's tourist trade. However, the Antiquities' conservation capabilities and the need for a national centre for Scottish artefacts are powerful arguments in favour of centralisation in Edinburgh.

SCOTTISH UNITED SERVICES MUSEUM

Covering all aspects of Scotland's warlike past, this museum, a branch of the National Museums, is situated in Edinburgh Castle, and is well worth visiting. Its extensive displays remind the visitor that not all Scots have gone to war decked in tartan, marching to the skirl of the pipes – naval and airborne services are recorded too.

For the ***Royal Observatory Visitor Centre***, *see* OBSERVATORIES, and for ***Scottish Agricultural Museum***, *see* AGRICULTURE.

MUNICIPAL

HUNTLY HOUSE MUSEUM

Although dwarfed by the Royal Scottish Museum almost a mile to the west in Chambers Street, Huntly House in the Canongate is in fact Edinburgh's own museum. Here, housed in a fine 16th century mansion opposite the Canongate Tolbooth (itself housing 'The People's Story', see below) is a collection of artefacts and restored rooms providing a palpable record of Edinburgh's history as a community.

The museum houses collections of Edinburgh and Canongate silver, and glassware from the city and from Leith. Among the more controversial items are memorabilia and personal effects belonging to Earl Haig, not now regarded, perhaps, as Edinburgh's favourite son (*see also* MILITARY HISTORY).

THE PEOPLE'S STORY

Edinburgh's museum's service was determined that popular culture should not go unrepresented in a city which many outsiders often perceive as just a little too upper class for its own good. This museum, founded in 1989 in the Canongate Tolbooth is the result, and records everday life as it was lived by ordinary citizens from the 18th century to the present time. Here are representations of a prison cell, cooper's workshop, 1940s kitchen, and even a pub.

MUSEUM OF CHILDHOOD

Advertised by the District Council at one time as 'the noisiest museum in the world' – a claim since made by other Scottish museums – Edinburgh's Museum of Childhood is one of the most fascinating and enjoyable for visitors of all ages. In 1992 the Museum attracted nearly a quarter of a million children and former children to view its outstanding collection of toys, games, costumes, and all the paraphernalia of the childhood of yesteryear. It is well worth a visit at its High Street site between South Bridge and St Mary's Street, nearly opposite John Knox's House.

The Museum owes its existence to former councillor Partick Murray who saw a need to record the history of childhood through its artefacts. By personally assembling a collection of toys, dolls, comics, etc, he made possible the opening of the Museum at Lady Stair's House in 1955, with the new museum moving to its present base in Hyndford's Close in 1966. A major reorganisation took place in 1986, utilising five galleries.

LAURISTON CASTLE

Situated near Davidson's Mains, Lauriston Castle has been a city museum since 1926, and provides a unique view of how an upper-class Edwardian house would have appeared in the early 1900s, when it was owned by a wealthy cabinetmaker named William Reid. For more information, *see* CASTLES.

NEWHAVEN HERITAGE MUSEUM

Housed in what was once the quayside fishmarket, the community of Newhaven has its own museum, opened in 1993. The formerly vital fishing industry is well illustrated in the collection,which is geared to engage the attention of younger visitors. Your encyclopedia editor was surprised to find on display a photograph of his great-grandmother, a Newhaven fishwife, pictured in a group bound for Windsor Castle to meet Queen Victoria!

QUEENSFERRY MUSEUM

Housed in the former Burgh Council chambers, this small museum, run by Edinburgh District Council, commem-orates community life in the town situated between the bridges, and which has been part of Edinburgh District since 1975 (*see also* DISTRICTS and FAIRS).

Newhaven's Heritage Museum occupies part of the former fishmarket shed on the harbour quayside, and is well worth visiting. (City of Edinburgh Council)

MUSEUM OF FIRE

Maintained by the Lothian and Borders Fire Brigade, the Museum of Fire records the history of Britain's oldest fire-fighting service in continuous existence. It includes the Braidwood-Rushbrook collection of historic fire-fighting vehicles at Lauriston Place, its headquarters and former principal city fire station (*see* FIRE FIGHTING).

WRITERS' MUSEUM

With such famed Scottish authors as Scott, Stevenson, and Burns having so many Edinburgh associations (*see* LITERATURE), it is only appropriate that there should be a city museum commemorating their work. This is to be found in Lady Stair's House, between the Lawnmarket and the section of the upper Mound running east and west. Here are portraits, manuscripts, and memorabilia, of Scotland's most illustrious writers.

Lady Stair's House was built in 1622 by Sir William Gray of Pittendrum, but is now named for a later inhabitant, the 18th century Dowager Countess of Stair. It was presented to the city by the Earl of Rosebery in 1907 and opened as the city's own museum six years later. The major part of the collection was moved out to Huntly House in 1932, and the building also housed the Museum of Childhood from 1955-63, but is now exclusively devoted to wielders of the pen, including less well-known authors through temporary exhibitions.

ACADEMIC

COCKBURN MUSEUM
Housed in Edinburgh University's geology department at King's Buildings, this collection of 150,000 geological specimens, instituted in 1873, is principally intended for teaching purposes, but is open to the public on weekdays.

EDINBURGH UNIVERSITY COLLECTION OF HISTORIC MUSICAL INSTRUMENTS
Located in the Reid School of Music, just off Bristo Square, this collection of some 2,000 instruments was begun in 1855. It includes woodwind, plucked stringed, brass, and percussion instruments, and, needless to say, bagpipes. It is complemented by the Russell collection.

RUSSELL COLLECTION OF EARLY KEYBOARD INSTRUMENTS
Britain's most important collection of early keyboard instruments is housed in St Cecilia's Hall in the Cowgate. It includes such instruments as harpsichords, virginals, clavichords, fortepianos, and organs, some dating back to 1585. The collection is administered by Edinburgh University, and the visitor is prompted to wonder if a more central site could not be found for the collection, perhaps more closely allied with the main University collection of historic instruments. Unlike the main collection, an entry fee is charged.

MUSEUM OF THE ROYAL COLLEGE OF SURGEONS
If a museum of museums is ever established, it should surely include this one, set up by the Royal College of Surgeons in Edinburgh as early as 1505. The collection comprises pathological specimens removed from Edinburgh surgical patients over the centuries, as well as instruments used by this august body of practitioners.

The museum was not governed by an officially-recognised curator for the small matter of its first three centuries, one of its earliest custodians, being Robert Knox, the anatomist who 'bought the beef' from Burke and Hare (*see* CRIME). The collection is open free of charge to the public on weekday afternoons.

OTHER MUSEUMS

ROYAL SCOTS REGIMENTAL MUSEUM
Accorded honourable accommodation in Edinburgh Castle, this Museum commemorates the history of 'Pontius Pilate's Bodyguard', the first and oldest regiment of the line, the Royal Scots. Founded in 1951, this museum attracted no fewer than half a million visitors in 1994. More about the City of Edinburgh Battalion in this regiment in the First World War can be found under MILITARY HISTORY.

THE GEORGIAN HOUSE
Established in 1973, this is a fascinating museum created by the National Trust for Scotland at 7 Charlotte Square, a property the Trust acquired from the Bute family seven years earlier. The ground floor, first floor, and basement have been restored to their appearance as it was in 1796 at the height of Edinburgh's Golden Age. Furnishings, and even such 'fixtures' as

chimneypieces, have been brought to Charlotte Square from all over Scotland to complete the illusion of an upper class domicile of the period.

GLADSTONE'S LAND

Another National Trust for Scotland property which stands as a museum of a certain historical period, is the tenemental property known as Gladstone's Land on the north side of the Lawnmarket. The house was in danger of demolition in 1934 when saved by a private purchaser and handed over to the Trust, which opened it in 1980 as a 17th century merchant's house.

TRANSPORT MUSEUM

At the time of writing, Edinburgh has no such museum, which as already observed, is highly regrettable for a city which is a traditional route centre, the site of the first flight in Great Britain (*see* BALLOONING) and where there were two separate municipal tramcar networks. One of the latter comprised the fifth largest cable-car system in the world (*see* TRAMS). While it is believed that a collection of trams and buses are stored at Shrub Hill, Leith Walk, neither Lothian Region nor the Scottish Museums Council have been able to confirm this information. Let us hope that a proper transport museum is not too far in the future; there is currently a proposal that such a museum should be established on a gap site off Dundee Street.

Newspapers and Periodicals

Edinburgh has long been a centre for publishing and printing, (*see* INDUSTRIES) but is much less of a media centre than it was even 50 years ago. In contrast to Glasgow's ten daily and Sunday newspapers (at the last count), Edinburgh has three, while in comparison to Dundee's production of magazines and comics, Edinburgh is out of the frame. It was not always thus.

PRESENT-DAY NEWSPAPERS

Edinburgh's oldest surviving periodical publication is the *Edinburgh Gazette*, which is not a newspaper, but a twice-weekly listing of official announcements, published by HMSO. It originally appeared in 1671, printed by James Watson for James Donaldson (of the publishing dynasty which donated Donaldson's Hospital). Although Donaldson enjoyed official sanction for his paper from the Scots Privy Council, he nevertheless found himself incarcerated in the Tolbooth on one occasion for displeasing his masters. The *Gazette*'s news function has now vanished.

THE SCOTSMAN

This is Edinburgh's oldest and most prestigious newspaper (if the *Edinburgh Gazette* is excepted). Since its first edition appeared on Burns's Day 1817, *The Scotsman* has endeavoured to maintain a liberal middle-of-the-road stance on political matters, in comparison to nearly all

British broadsheets. The paper has been daily since 1855 and caused consternation in 1957 by replacing the advertisements on its front page with news instead.

Published by Thomson Regional Newspapers Limited until 1995, the paper, along with its sister publications, the *Evening News* and *Scotland on Sunday* (*see* overleaf), was bought by European Press Holdings, run by the brothers David and Frederick Barclay.

Surpassed by Glasgow's *Herald* and the *Aberdeen Press and Journal* in terms of circulation, *The Scotsman* nevertheless has a vigorous advertising department guaranteeing its continuing prosperity. After undergoing two design 'makeovers' in the last few years, the paper nowadays presents an attractive appearance in two sections, with enhanced features, more sport, very good Scottish coverage, but with columnists who are perhaps not to everyone's taste. The paper's policy of trying to improve its market share in the West of Scotland effectively means that Edinburgh has no morning daily of its own, as *The Scotsman* sees itself as a national daily. There is a Weekend section, published in tabloid format. The paper's picture library is the finest in the East of Scotland and some of its products can be enjoyed in the pages of this book.

History

The Scotsman's founding editors were Charles Maclaren (who fought a duel in 1829 with a rival editor after an exchange of insulting remarks got a little out of hand) and William Ritchie. They were weary of the tame newspapers of the time, the longer established of which simply printed whatever the government of the day asked them to. Looking back, 1817 seems a bad time to have started a newspaper, with a repressive government anxious to limit the freedom of the press by various measures, including a tax on advertising. Suprisingly, this helped the new weekly by killing off many of the dailies, and *The Scotsman* began to prosper, eventually moving into prestigious premises on North Bridge (in 1905). The editors have been as follows:

1817	Charles Maclaren/William Ritchie
1831	Charles Maclaren
1845	Alexander Russel
1876	Robert Wallace
1880	Charles Cooper
1906	John P. Croal
1924	Sir George Waters
1944	James Murray Watson
1956	Alistair Dunnett
1973	Eric Mackay
1985	Christopher Baur
1987	Magnus Linklater
1994	Andrew Jaspan
1995	James Seaton

The postwar history of the paper was marked by its becoming the British launchpad for Canadian Roy Thomson to become a major media mogul. In 1955, Edinburgh, then still a very conservative city in every sense of the word, was horrified to find that this myopic colonial wished to purchase Scotland's leading newspaper! Strings were attached to the deal which ensured that the paper could not be sold on by Thomson for a quick profit, but the wily Canadian, although hurt by the snubs he received from Edinburgh high society, used Scotland as a power base to buy into the new Independent Television network, becoming the first proprietor of Scottish Television. His comment about its lucrative nature – 'a licence to print money' – hardly needs repeating, and enabled him to purchase the Kemsley range of papers in 1959, led by the *Sunday Times*. This had serious repercussions for the Edinburgh evening papers (*see* below).

EDINBURGH EVENING NEWS

A stable-mate of *The Scotsman*, the *News* is a tabloid evening daily with a sturdy circulation, and a pink sports section on Saturday. First appearing in 1873, the *News* was publishing no fewer than four daily editions by the beginning of the 1960s, covering the central belt as far west as Clackmannan. It stole a march on its rival, the *Edinburgh Evening Dispatch* (*see* opposite), by attracting a larger volume of small ads, and was soon outselling its older rival by three to one. In 1963 the *News* was acquired from Provincial Newspapers Ltd by the Thomson organisation, who disposed of two Sheffield newspapers in exchange, and which immediately guaranteed the success of the *News* by closing its rival *Dispatch*. This resulted in a number of staff redundancies and caused considerable bitterness.

Today's tabloid *News* offers good local reporting, with a strong campaigning spirit – railing against the construction of a second Forth Road Bridge for example. The paper has also taken on the organisation of the highly-popular cavalcade to open each year's Festival, something which the Festival itself appeared to find too logistically challenging. Sports coverage is excellent, but local interest features appear to have been reduced in recent years in favour of a more glamorous

'News from Hollywood' type of approach. The paper is noted for employing one of the most outspoken and entertaining local columnists in the country, John Gibson. Advertising is still the paper's strongpoint and seems unaffected by its freesheet competitors.

SCOTLAND ON SUNDAY

First published in 1987, this is Scotland's only broadsheet Sunday newspaper, succeeding where Glasgow's *Sunday Standard* failed a few years previously, after appearing from 1981–3. Produced in Edinburgh by Scotsman Publications, *SOS* is a two-part production, with heavy emphasis on features and sport.

HERALD AND POST

Edinburgh's 'freebie' newspaper, first published in 1979, and distributed house to house on a weekly basis. Its copious advertisements are supplemented by community information about sales of work, exhibitions, along with the occasional human interest story. Now published by Scotsman Publications.

FORMER EDINBURGH NEWSPAPERS

Edinburgh's – and Scotland's – first newspaper is generally agreed to have been the *Diurnal Occurrences touching the Dailie Proceedings in Parliament*. First published at the end of 1641, probably by Evan Tyler (*see* LITERATURE), this featured English news reprinted and proved to be very short-lived, lasting barely into 1642. Only slightly less ephemeral was *Mercurius Scoticus*, of which 21 issues were published in Leith in 1651. It was entirely English in content, catering for the interests of those English soldiers occupying the port at that time.

Its successor, *Mercurius Caledonius*, emerged during the comparative freedom of the Restoration, not surprisingly being pro-royalist, edited by Thomas Sydserf. Although dismissed by historian Robert Chambers as 'frivolous and foolish to a degree', it was much more firmly Scottish-based than its two predecessors, comprising a dozen issues early in 1661.

Three Edinburgh newspapers which, although they proved remarkably durable, failed to last into our own times were the *Edinburgh Evening Courant* (1718–1886), the *Caledonian Mercury* (1720–1867), and the *Edinburgh Advertiser* (1764–1859), all of them published three times weekly. All three carried more advertisements than news, most of the latter being reproduced from the London press. Government versions of events usually found space in publications of the day without difficulty, since publishing took place effectively only by government consent. An example of the punitive conditions under which the city's press laboured is best illustrated by the short life of the *Scots Chronicle*.

In the autumn of 1797 this Edinburgh newspaper published an almost entirely accurate description of the Tranent massacre, which had taken place only ten miles from the city. The authorities attempted in vain to pin the blame on a number of innocent bystanders at Tranent, and when an Edinburgh jury failed to convict, the paper's proprietor and printer were then sued for defamation in the Court of Session by one of those involved – and by no means blameless – at Tranent. The paper

was heavily fined, but appealed successfully to the House of Lords. By the time that it had effectively won its case – and without it, modern historians would know considerably less than we do about an appalling incident – the *Chronicle* was ruined (*see also* MILITARY HISTORY).

EVENING DISPATCH

No longer are tourists in Princes Street baffled by the newsvendors' cries of 'Spatch n' News!', the former of these two worthy publications having ceased in 1963.

First published in 1886 as a sister paper to *The Scotsman*, the *Dispatch* was seen by many as the most Conservative of the city's newspapers, although the *Third Statistical Account* comments curiously that 'its old ultra-Conservatism ended in its having no real political attachments at all'. An early switch to tabloid format in postwar years, and a green sports edition every bit as good as the *Pink News*, did not delay its end.

In 1956 new owner Roy (later Lord) Thomson sacked the *Dispatch*'s highly-respected editor Albert Mackie soon after taking over, and finally closed it in 1963 to allow the *News*, with its already higher circulation figures, an unrivalled market share. A number of redundancies resulted, one of those failing to make the transition to the *News* being Jimmy Wardhaugh, the former Hearts player who was surely one of the finest sports journalists ever to tap a typewriter.

DAILY MAIL

While the *Daily Express* settled on Glasgow for its Scottish edition, its rival the *Mail* based itself at Tanfield in the capital for a Scottish edition produced from 1946 to the early

1970s. It gradually suffered with the move away from Conservatism among its readership, while its sports section was not above criticism, but modern technology has allowed the restarting of a Scottish edition with fewer overheads than formerly. In 1995 the *Mail* is once again publishing in Scotland, but now in Glasgow.

PERIODICALS

Gone are the days when Edinburgh published two of the most influential and stimulating magazines in the English-speaking world – the liberal *Edinburgh Review* and its Tory rival, *Blackwood's Magazine*. So successful was the former when first published in 1802, that a Conservative reply was deemed imperative. This first of all took the form of the *Quarterly*, but longer-lasting was *Blackwood's*. First appearing in 1817, the same year as *The Scotsman*, *Blackwood's* outlasted the *Edinburgh Review* by more than half a century, although it had turned almost exclusively to fiction and short features by the time of its closure in 1980.

Literary magazines produced in the city nowadays include *Chapman and Cencrastus*, while the world of science is well represented in the Edinburgh periodical press. The Royal Society of Edinburgh has been publishing its *Transactions* since 1788, the first volume including James Hutton's seminal 'Theory of the Earth' (*see* GEOLOGY), to be joined in the 19th century by the Society's *Proceedings* in both physical and biological branches of science. A number of highly-regarded periodicals are also produced commercially in Edinburgh, examples being *Recent Advances in Surgery* (Churchill Livingstone) and the *Scottish Journal of Geology* (Scottish Academic Press).

For a city which produced so many political, indeed almost revolutionary, periodicals, the scene is a little dull nowadays in comparison with, for example, 20 years ago. Possibly the most interesting anti-establishment publication in postwar years was *Scottish International*, a monthly which succeeded in being both intensely Scottish and outward looking at the same time. It went out of business in the 1970s after publishing inaccurate remarks about an oil company, but not before the magazine had commissioned one of the most enjoyable, and influential plays seen on any Scottish stage – *The Cheviot, the Stag, and the Black Black Oil*, by John McGrath.

New Town

Edinburgh's New Town lies to the north of the Princes Street Gardens valley, comprising around four square miles of Georgian buildings which make up the largest example in Britain of 18th and 19th century town planning.

With its parade of ubiquitous shopfronts, the southern frontier of the New Town – Princes Street – displays a brash facade to the visitor looking down from the Castle, but the area deserves and repays much closer study. Its avenues and circuses stretch as far north as the Water of Leith, and it sends its fingers almost as far west as Haymarket and eastwards to the edge of Abbeyhill. Just as it was the result of systematic and imaginative planning, so is its preservation, its 11,000

Atholl Crescent is part of the western New Town, arcing away from the main A8 just west of Princes Street, but is still very much part of the city's commercial and business centre. (City of Edinburgh Council)

listed properties watched over from 1970 by the New Town Conservation Committee.

History

The New Town was the product of Edinburgh's determination to break out from the confines of the Old Town, once the need for a garrisoned city had died with the defeat of the Second Jacobite Rebellion. As early as 1752 a municipal pamphlet called *Proposals for carrying on certain Public Works in the City of Edinburgh* was published, written by Sir Gilbert Elliott, but believed to have been heavily influenced by George Drummond, six-times Lord Provost of Edinburgh and founder of the Royal Infirmary.

The pamphlet called for a systematic approach to developing the area north of the Nor' Loch on the ridge known as the Lang Dykes and then down its north-facing slope towards the Water of Leith. The pamphlet cited Turin and Berlin as role models for Edinburgh – 'in these cities , what is called the *new town* consists of spacious streets and large buildings'. As A.J. Youngson, the New Town's principal historian, has pointed out 'What is astounding about the *Proposals* of 1752 is that they outlined a scheme which, in the course of the following 80 years, was actually carried out'.

The need to cosmeticise the Nor' Loch, or remove it altogether was regarded as an essential prerequisite. Described some 30 years earlier as a 'noxious lake' in an Act of Parliament, the loch and the bog area immediately to the west of it would either be removed or turned into an ornamental canal fringed by terraces. There were even proposals at around that time to divert the Water of Leith through the valley (*see also* LOCHS). Drainage of the area started around 1759 and took 60 years, enabling gardens to be established by the Princes Street Proprietors after 1820, although the ornamental canal never materialised.

The area 'zoned' for the New Town could now be connected with the Old by the construction of the North Bridge. This is not the present-day three arch structure (1894-5) but an earlier bridge opened in 1772 after a structural collapse had caused loss of life. To design the now opened up New Town area, a competition was advertised in March 1766. There were six entries, the winner being James Craig.

Craig's plan for the first New Town represented a grid-iron design with a central street joining two squares, and with two major streets running east-west parallel to the central one, the area stretching from just west of the Calton Hill to the present city's West End. Some changes in the naming of the streets and squares appears to have been undertaken by Craig at the request of George III, and without the Town Council's agreement, so the idea of St Andrew's and St George's as balancing squares did not survive this redrafting. The latter is of course now Charlotte Square, the main central thoroughfare being George Street, with Queen Street and Prince's Street (as named on the original plan) single-sided and looking to north and south respectively.

Some historians believe Craig to have been heavily influenced by developments in Richelieu (near Tours, France) and Bath, while others have detected the influence of John Adam, with a 1747 plan for Inveraray. The street and pavement widths were even specified, although actual buildings were not. It was felt that individual proprietors would not be amenable to a uniform design, but building controls were enshrined in a number of Acts of Parliament in the 1780s.

Craig's plan shows intelligent use of the site, and cleverly exploited the vistas from Queen and Princes Streets. Its survival more or less *in toto* has been attributed to the fact that its east and west ends are effectively sealed by its own buildings, emphasising to visitors and citizens alike that this is a planned, self-contained living area. Craig's reward for his design was a gold medal bearing the city's insignia, as well as the 'freedom of the city in a silver box', presented on 17 April 1767.

The first houses built in the New Town date from 1767, and represent a tentative entry into the newly-designated area, as they are artisans' houses in the vernacular tradition, and not typical of what we now associate with New Town architecture. Thistle Court (originally Rose Court) is just off the eastern end of Thistle Street, and comprises two rubble-built semi-detached houses. The foundation stone was laid by Craig himself on 26 October 1767, and the houses still stand, one of their gardens serving as a car park.

What is known as the Second (or Northern) New Town dates from the 1800s, developed by Robert Reid and William Sibbald in an area between Queen

Street and the Water of Leith where Lord Cockburn was later to record hearing 'ceaseless rural corncrakes'. Bigger in area than Craig's scheme for the New Town, Reid and Sibbald designed Great King Street as their principal east-west axis, the scheme echoing Craig's by having Drummond Place at one end and Royal Circus at the other. The latter was designed by William Playfair by 1822, incorporating the main road from the first New Town to the village of Stockbridge.

Not long afterwards, the Moray Estate was planned and almost completed by 1836. This is basically a series of two and a half interconnected Places, each smaller than the one before when proceeding westwards (Moray Place, Ainslie Place, and Randolph Crescent), to the design of James Gillespie Graham. The buildings on the north side tower over the Water of Leith, and the main throroughfare of the Estate opens up to the Western New Town .

This is basically a triangular area, with the Water of Leith to the north, the main Glasgow road to the south, and Queensferry Road making up the third side, as far north as the Dean Bridge. The main east-west axis can be defined as Melville Street, flanked by Shandwick Place/Maitland Street to the south and Chester Street to the north, and with three streets crossing to provide a chessboard pattern. West of Palmerston Place are two doubled crescents, totalling four different place-names. The planner responsible was again James Gillespie Graham, but progress here was slow; by 1860 Manor Place was still the western frontier of residential Edinburgh.

North and east is an area of planned development regarded as the Calton section of the New Town, but the overall plan by W. H. Playfair was never completed. Had it been, the *Buildings of Scotland* guide believes this 'would have been by far the most magnificent in the New Town'. London Road is the major thoroughfare, flanked by Hillside Crescent to the north, with three streets radiating from it, and with its classical arc of period buildings ruined by a 1960s addition. The hill to the south of the road is undeveloped up to Royal Terrace, so the lower eastern scarp of Calton Hill bears two residential terraces meeting at a point overlooking Abbeyhill.

Recent press reports (1994) have mooted the possibility of 'completing' the New Town, which as presently constituted, loses itself in unplanned developments to the north, west, and east.

Observatories

Edinburgh turns its eyes to the heavens from two prominent city locations – Calton Hill and Blackford Hill. The former observatory is the older, operated by the Astronomical Society of Edinburgh, while the Royal Observatory on Blackford Hill is one of the most important astronomical research centres in Europe, specialising in interpretation and engineering support for telescope facilities on the other side of the world.

History
Astronomy has been studied in Edinburgh since the Tounis College (Edinburgh University) was founded in 1583, although it was not until 1785 that the first Chair of

City Observatory on Calton Hill was Edinburgh's eye on the heavens from its opening in 1824 until replaced by the present Royal Observatory on Blackford Hill in 1896. The Calton Hill building still serves its original function to a reduced extent, not least because modern street- and flood-lighting reduces night sky visibility. (Edinburgh City Libraries)

Practical Astronomy was established. Its first incumbent, medical graduate Robert Blair, refused to lecture on astronomy, on the not unreasonable grounds that he had neither an observatory nor equipment. An observatory did exist on the Calton Hill by 1792, but its construction (by the Town Council) appears to have left no funds available for the purchase of necessary instruments. The building was leased by a newly-formed learned society called the Astronomical Institution, but they soon brought forward plans for a new observatory designed by William Henry Playfair on classical lines. Completed in 1824, the building still tops Calton Hill a little to the east of the earlier building (which survives).

Named the Royal Observatory of Edinburgh from the 1820s, the new facility became more closely associated with Edinburgh University, its Director now holding three titles – Director, Regius Professor of Astronomy, and Astronomer Royal for Scotland. (In 1995 this last appointment was awarded to a Glasgow astronomer for the first time). The first appointee was Thomas Henderson, who produced important research findings based on earlier work in the southern hemisphere, but who failed to lecture on astronomy. His successor was the colourful Charles Piazzi Smyth, who suggested establishing a mountaintop observatory away from the centre of Auld Reekie. After Smyth's tenure in the years 1864-88, the Royal Observatory was underfunded and Smyth's reputation tarnished by his fascination with the allegedly prophetic measurements of the Great Pyramid.

Out of this crisis, Edinburgh's history as an astronomical research centre took a new turn. In 1888 the 26th Earl of Crawford offered his private collection of instruments and his astronomical library to the nation if the government would build a new Royal Observatory, and when the Town Council made Blackford Hill summit available, the present Observatory was opened for research by April 1896. Its principal instruments were two telescopes, a 15 inch refractor and 24 inch reflector housed in two domes (although drums would be a more accurate physical description), of 33 feet and 22 feet diameter respectively. These still dominate the hill to this day, although neither dome now houses an active telescope.

Nowadays much of the Observatory's deep space research work is accomplished far from Edinburgh, at Mauna Kea in Hawaii, and at Siding Springs in Australia, where atmospheric conditions are more reliable – much as Piazzi Smyth had predicted. However as early as 1959 the Edinburgh centre had adopted an interpretative role, using computers to examine faint photographic images. Considerable expertise has been assembled in infra-red astronomy and in the operation of sub-millimetre radio wavelengths, while the Observatory's workshops provide engineering support for its now far-flung telescopes.

The Earl of Crawford's 15,000 books and manuscripts still grace the Observatory's excellent library, and a prize-winning visitors' centre has been opened to increase public appreciation of one of the finest scientific research centres of its kind in the world, one which is a direct result of Edinburgh's intellectual prowess in the 18th and 19th centuries. The Royal Observatory Edinburgh was administered by the Science Research Council from 1965 to 1994, now coming under the aegis, along with the Royal Greenwich Observatory (Cambridge) of the Particle Physics and Astronomy Research Council, although there is still a strong teaching link with Edinburgh University.

The Calton Hill still casts an eye on the night sky, although the increase in the floodlighting of the city's buildings since 1959 has reduced the observatory's effectiveness. When originally leased to the University, the Town Council had insisted on maintaining an interest in the building, and it is now used by the Astronomical Society of Edinburgh. An amateur learned society, it makes visitors welcome, and evening classes are held. The Observatory's phone number can be found in the directory under 'City Observatory'.

Parks

Edinburgh is fortunate in possessing no less than 3,500 acres (1,435 hectares) of public parks owned by its local authority, (presently the City Council), but also has the Queen's Park, a royal possession, in its midst, as well as a number of private parks in the New Town. While these last-named are open to the public only on special occasions, their existence contributes to the amenity of the city.

The city's local authority parks are nowadays run by a privatised in-house concern under the control of the

Man's reconstruction of the Edinburgh landscape is well summed up in this photograph from Arthur's Seat, which shows Holyrood Palace just beyond the reverse slope of Salisbury Crags, with Nelson's Monument prominent on Calton Hill to the left of the picture. In the middle foreground is Hunter's Bog, and above it an area formerly quarried.

Recreation Department. A modern feature of the city parks is the Mobile Patrol, which, since 1975 has replaced the local 'parkie' with a fleet of 11 cars and one van (in 1995) transporting staff round the city's green places. The largest parks are visited two or three times daily, while the smaller ones receive one visit daily if staff are available. Whether this is an improvement on the days when more than 40 park staff patrolled their own area on foot, is debateable, and it is noticeable that the 'torching' of park buildings in even supposedly genteel neighbourhoods in the suburbs has led to a policy of not replacing buildings in locations attractive to vandals.

LOCAL AUTHORITY PARKS IN EDINBURGH

	AREA ACRES	HA.	YEAR OPENED BY CITY		AREA ACRES	HA.	YEAR OPENED BY CITY
Abercorn (Portobello)	2	0.81	1897	Dovecot Park (Kingsknowe)	14	5.67	1960
Allison (Kirkliston)	13	5.2	1984	Drum Brae	10.8	4.34	1961
Atholl Crescent/Coates Cresc.	1.1	0.44	1948/9	Dunbar's Close Garden	0.75	0.30	1978
Bingham (Lismore)	3.3	1.36	1975	Dundas (South Queensferry)	4.84	1.96	1962/75
Blackford/	157.3	63.7	1884/	East Pilton	7	2.83	1931
Hermitage of Braid			1938	Fairmilehead (Camus)	7.8	3.15	1964
Bloomiehall (Juniper Green)	6.2	2.5	1911	Figgate Burn (Portobello)	27.83	11.27	1933
Braid Hills	231.5	93.75	1890	Gardner's Crescent	0.35	0.14	1886
Braidburn Valley	27.5	11.13	1933	Gayfield Square	0.93	0.38	1886
Brighton (Portobello)	2.1	0.85	1900	Gilmerton	5	2.02	1964
Bruntsfield Links	36.2	14.6	★	Gyle	52.8	21.3	1953
Burdiehouse Burn	14.5	5.87	1955	Hailes Quarry	30	12.15	1967
Cairntows	4.4	1.78	1992	Harrison	17.5	7.08	1886
Calton Hill	22.2	8.9	★	Haugh (Barnton)	1	0.41	1890
Cammo Estate	100	40.5	1975	Hermitage of Braid	see Blackford		
Campbell (Colinton)	8.1	3.28	1936	Hillside Crescent	1.45	0.58	
Clermiston	14	5.67	1956	Hunter's Hall	70	28.3	1955
Coates Crescent	see Atholl Crescent			Hyvot's Bank Valley	12	4.8	1955
Colinton Dell	45	18.2	1975	Inch	61.1	24.74	1975
Colinton Mains	20.8	8.4	1939	Inverleith	54	21.87	1889
Corstorphine Hill	112	45.36	1924	Iona Street	see Dalmeny Street		
Craiglockhart Dell	6.7	2.8	1975	Jewel (Niddrie)	6	2.43	1959
Craiglockhart Hills	87.7	35.5		Joppa Quarry	5.85	2.36	1933
Craiglockhart Wood	8.96	3.62		Keddie (Leith)	1.35	0.55	1920
Cramond Foreshore	150	60.7		King George V (Currie)	7	2.83	1936
Dalmeny St./Iona St.	2	0.81	1922	King George V Memorial (Eyre P.)	2.4	0.97	1948
Davidson's Mains	31.5	12.7	1922	King George V (S. Queensferry)	1.75	0.70	1936

Name	acres	hectares	Year	Name	acres	hectares	Year
Lauriston Castle	30	12.15	1926	Ravelston	3.9	1.57	1994
Leith Links	48	19.44	★	Ravelston Woods	20.75	8.4	1994
Liberton	11	4.4	1975	Redbraes	2.8	1.13	1905
Lochend	21.2	8.5	1907	Redhall (Slateford)	8.34	3.37	
London Road Gardens	10.8	4.37	1893	Regent Road	3.4	1.37	1890
Malleny Park (Balerno)	5	2.02	1975	River Almond Walkway	90	36.4	
Meadows	58.4	22.03	★	Rocheid (Canonmills)	3.8	1.53	
Meadowfield	58	22.02	1952	Roseburn	18.1	7.33	1898/1906
Morningside	3	1.2	1913				
Muirhouse	14	5.67	1947	Rosefield (Portobello)	3.27	1.32	1920
Muirwood Road (Currie)	1	0.4	1975	St Margaret's (Corstorphine)	9	3.64	1923
Murieston	1.3	0.53	1932	St Mark's (Warriston)	10.6	4.29	1905
Newbattle Terrace (Morningside)	1.7	0.71		Saughton	42.5	17.21	1900
				Sighthill	43	17.41	
Newcraighall	9	3.64	1922	Silverknowes	12	4.86	
Orchard Brae	6	2.43	1801/1935	Spylaw (Colinton)	8	3.24	1911
				Starbank (Newhaven)	2.6	1.05	1920
Parkside (Newbridge)	1	0.4		Station Road (S. Queensferry)	6	2.43	1975
Paties Road (near Colinton)	10.9	4.41		Taylor Gardens	0.9	0.28	1920
Pilrig	17.3	7	1920	Union (Corstorphine)	10	4.05	1924
Portobello Golf Course/Park	55.24	22.37	1898	Victoria (Leith)	18.1	7.33	1920
Prestonfield	3.4	1.37	1926	West Pilton	15.6	6.31	
Princes Street Gardens	37	14.98	1876	Whinhill (Calder Road)	11.7	4.73	1934
Quarryhole	7	2.83	1975	White (Gorgie)	0.75	0.3	
Ratho Station	1.22	0.49	1962				
Ratho	2.74	1.1	1975				★Traditionally open land

CITY PARKS

PRINCES STREET GARDENS

The most famous of Edinburgh's parks is Princes Street Gardens. The plural form is used advisedly as there is no physical connection between East and West Princes Street Gardens, effectively divided by the Mound. The West garden is the larger, approximating to 29 acres (12 hectares), the East garden covers nine acres.

Here the Nor' Loch reflected the north face of the Castle Rock, beautifully recalled in such paintings as Naysmith's, although the water was almost certainly polluted and undrinkable by the time the loch, and the bog immediately to the west, were drained between 1759 and 1825, (see also LOCHS). An Act of Parliament passed in 1816 imaginatively preserved the view southwards from Princes Street by banning the construction of all buildings except a 'chapel' – which metamorphised as St John's Church at the West End – and garden buildings such as greenhouses.

After the Mound was completed around 1820, the Princes Street Proprietors invested £7,000 in landscaping the West garden for their exclusive use, although after one year only 100 trees survived, and progress slowed down in the creation of an exclusive refuge for well-to-do city residents.

This private ownership of such a prominent area became a source of contention over the years, particularly with the employment of a constable to patrol the garden and eject intruders. Public demand for access became so widespread that the Governor of Edinburgh Castle refused to allow military bands to perform there unless the public was admitted. In 1876, the city Council took over the Garden compulsorily, although the public were still not admitted to the garden completely until 1882.

The nine acres of East Princes Street Gardens includes an area at street level, where the Scott Monument points to the heavens, as well as the lawns lower down on each side of the railway tracks.

Both East and West Gardens contain a number of intriguing statues and other features. Prominent among these is the **Scott Monument**. 200 feet (60 metres) high, with foundations going down 50 feet (15 metres) underground, this is a Gothic rocket-ship poised for take-off. Its passengers are Sir Walter, sculpted along with his deerhound Maida in Carrara marble by Sir John Steell.

Completed in 1846, the monument was the product of a design competition conducted ten years earlier by admirers of Sir Walter, won by an unknown architect called John Morvo. This was eventually proved to be George Meikle Kemp, a Peeblesshire carpenter. His work was undoubtedly very much of its time, no matter how over-fussy it may appear to modern eyes. It successfully incorporates

three Scottish monarchs, 16 poets, and 64 of Scott's characters into its design, with a 287-step staircase leading to the top. Kemp did not live to see it completed, tragically drowning in the Union Canal in 1844.

Other **monuments** in Princes Street are listed below, in approximate east-to-west order.

David Livingstone. Blantyre-born African explorer (1813–73), made freeman of the city in 1857. Statue by Amelia Robertson Paton.

John Wilson (1785–1854). The English visitor who exclaimed that he 'had never heard of half these people' commemorated by Princes Street statues may have had a point in relation to John Wilson, commemorated near the Mound square. He was a Tory advocate, journalist, and wit, sometimes better known, if at all, as 'Christopher North'.

International Brigade Memorial. A rough-hewn abstract memorial to those from the Lothians and Fife who died in the Spanish Civil War between 1936 and 1939.

Adam Black. A leading member of the city's business community in the 19th century, Black (1784–1874) is commemorated by a statue close to the Scott Monument. Black first represented Edinburgh in parliament at the age of 72 (*see* PARLIAMENTARY REPRESENTATION, LORD PROVOSTS, and INDUSTRY).

Allan Ramsay. Although born in Leadhills, Ramsay (1686-1758) was a very active member of the capital's arts scene in the 18th century, not only proving a poet of note, but opening a theatre in the Canongate in the face of official opposition (*see* THEATRES and LITERATURE).

Scottish–American War Memorial (*see* MILITARY HISTORY).

Falklands Memorial. A comparatively

recent addition to the Gardens, this commemorates the British servicemen who died in the Falklands Conflict of 1982.

Ross Fountain. A massive cast iron fountain created by an unknown sculptor for the International Exhibition of 1862 and gifted to the city by Daniel Ross, gunsmith, although it was not to the taste of Dean Ramsay (*see* below).

Robert Louis Stevenson Memorial. An unusual tribute to 'RLS' is this grove of birch trees laid out to the design of Ian Hamilton Finlay.

Norwegian Memorial. This eight-ton boulder commemorates the links between Scotland and Norway in two world wars.

Royal Scots Memorial (*see* MILITARY HISTORY)

Royal Scots Grey Memorial (*see* MILITARY HISTORY)

Standing Figures. Presented to the city in 1871, this statuesque mother-figure with a child on either side of her, either symbolises motherhood or 'the genius of architecture crowning the theory and practice of Art'.

Dr Thomas Guthrie. An Edinburgh cleric (1803–73) who was noted for his work on behalf of deprived children, through the setting up of his 'ragged school' in Blackfriars Street. His statue was not unveiled until 1901.

Sir James Young Simpson (1811–70). Pioneer in anaesthesia, commemorated with a statue dating from 1876. The Simpson Maternity Hospital also commemorates his vital work in making operations safer, and in gynaecology (*see* HOSPITALS).

Dean Edward Ramsay (1793–1872) is commemorated by a Celtic-style cross opposite South Charlotte Street. An outstanding Episcopalian, he described the Ross Fountain, situated 200 yards away, as 'indecent and disgusting'. Strictly speaking, Ramsay's memorial stands in the grounds of St John's Church, but may at first glance be taken for a Princes Street monument.

Floral Clock. This magnet for tourists has been situated at the south west corner of the Mound's corner with Princes Street since 1903, when it was installed with an hour hand only, the minute hand being added the following year. Comprising 27,000 plants in an average display, the clock measures 36 feet in circumference, and has been driven by electricity since 1973.

MEADOWS

One of Britain's largest and oldest public parks, the Meadows are a relic of the Burgh Muir which flanked the Old Town to the south, at one time stretching as far south as Blackford Hill. The Scots army is reputed to have mustered here on six occasions before invading England, although a good part of the area was under water until the late 17th century (*see* LOCHS), and the south-western end was extensively pitted by quarrying for building materials (*see* QUARRIES).

Nowadays, the Meadows form a valuable 'lung' near the centre of the city, with Middle Meadow Walk permitting walkers and cyclists to travel from Forrest Road on the very edge of the Old Town as far south as Greenhill at Whitehouse Loan, or into Marchmont. With its walks pleasantly fringed by trees, the Meadows offers facilities for cricket, tennis, and (unofficially) for football, as well as a regular funfair and Meadows Festival, but no longer for band concerts, its bandstand being finally dismantled in the 1970s.

Citizens can be congratulated for protecting the Meadows from the ravages of thoughtless planning; in 1873 landscape gardener Edward Kemp successfully campaigned against Middle Meadow Walk being turned into a carriage-drive, which, he calculated, would save the better-off residents of Newington a mere 60 seconds in travelling to and from the city centre. For this, all the trees on one side of the Walk would have been sacrificed. Fortunately, his campaign was successful!

In postwar years, the Abercrombie Report of 1949 recommended sending a freight railway in a tunnel under the area, while the 1965 proposal to bulldoze a six-lane highway through, was even more sacrligeous (*see* ROADS AND STREETS). Nothing worse than a miniature railway, temporarily running through the trees alongside Melville Drive, has ever materialised, and proved to be highly popular with local children in 1952.

LEITH LINKS

Now much reduced in size and significance, Leith's Links, lying to the east of the port, no longer enjoy the fame they once did. The area still represents a welcome 'lung' for local people in an area heavily built up, with housing (including a 'colony', *see* HOUSING), on the south side, and industrial undertakings and more housing to the north, with the former Leith Academy building to the west. The walks are pleasantly tree-lined, but, despite the survival of two 16th century artillery mounds, the Links lack a focal point. For the area's history before it became a park, *see* LEITH.

INVERLEITH PARK

Laid out by Edinburgh Corporation in 1890, this is another of Scotland's largest urban parks. It is quartered by two paths, and is partly given over to playing fields in its northern half, as well as providing a model boating pond. This is overlooked by a south-facing grassy slope formerly used as a bleaching green. The pond itself was partially infilled to a depth of no more than four feet in 1959 for safety reasons, and is popular with model boat enthusiasts from all over the country.

HERMITAGE OF BRAID AND BLACKFORD PARK

One of the most beautiful parks in any British city, this originally consisted of two parks, the first comprising Blackford Hill (*see* HILLS) and the boating pond on its north flank. The 30-acre (12.3 hectare) Hermitage was only added in June 1938 by the gift of John MacDougal. The whole area is now designated as a Local Nature Reserve, and the Blackford Pond is now given over exclusively to wildlife.

The Hermitage of Braid is a valley stretching two miles from Braid Road eastwards to Liberton, following the course of the Braid Burn (*see* RIVERS AND STREAMS). At the centre of the Hermitage is a two-storey villa built in 1785 for the Gordon family, later used as a scout hostel, and nowadays centre for the District Council's Nature Warden department. East of this is the most beautiful part of the valley, where the burn runs through a ravine, planted with trees two centuries ago. To the walker on the valley floor in summer, there is the unforgettable experience of looking up at the towering ceiling of Nature's own cathedral.

The Hermitage of Braid is one of Britain's most beautiful parks, the house of that name dating back to 1785. This eastwards view shows the picnic area in the foreground; the house is now the headquarters for the city's nature wardens. (City of Edinburgh Council)

Like all Edinburgh parks, however, the Hermitage could benefit from more investment in paths and in the provision of interpretation notices. If a connection could be made under Braid and Comiston Roads, it would be possible to connect with Braidburn Valley Park (*see* RIVERS AND STREAMS, also THEATRES as there is an open-air amphitheatre there). This would provide a walkway for some miles through south and south-west Edinburgh. At the time of writing, no details were available of an arboretum proposed by local government for Braidburn Valley.

CAMMO

This open area on the western edge of the city is managed jointly by the District Council and the National Trust for Scotland. Until the site was opened to the public, the once imposing house here was home to a recluse known as 'the Black Widow of Cammo' (Mrs Maitland Tennant), and the dilapidated building was demolished 13 years after the death of her son in 1975. Its 100-acre (41 hectare) estate is now considered a wildlife site, the canal (designed by Sir John Clerk) bringing a formal touch to the landscape, and providing a haven for the most impressive dragonflies the nature-watcher is ever likely to see in the city. Just to the south is a circular water-tower, which despite its archaic appearance, is of surprisingly modern origin, and has recently been restored by the Edinburgh Green Belt Trust (*see* GREEN BELT).

SAUGHTON WINTER GARDEN

A popular park with a glasshouse as its nucleus, located between the Water of Leith and Saughton sports pitches. It contains an impressively large rose-garden with highly distinctive sundial.

Other local authority parks include Figgate Park and Lochend Park (*see* LOCHS for more details).

ROYAL PARKS

Edinburgh's royal park is the Queen's Park, situated immediately to the east of the Palace of Holyroodhouse, and encompassing no less than 640 acres (259 hectares). A Japanese visitor recently expressed astonishment at the size of such a large city-centre area remaining undeveloped, so local citizens should be in no doubt as to the uniqueness of this park. It is presently administered by Historic Scotland, and is an SSSI (Site of Special Scientific Interest, *see* WILDLIFE).

There are four road entrances into the park – from the junction of Holyrood Road and Horse Wynd, from Holyrood Park Road at St Leonard's, from Meadowbank Terrace, and from Duddingston village. It is possible to drive through the park from any one point of entry to another, although these roads are not rights of way, and the St Leonard's and Duddingston entries are closed on Sunday; all are closed when ceremonial occasions require.

Arthur's Seat and Salisbury Crags are described elsewhere in this book (*see* HILLS). They provided the venue for the 1995 World Mountain Running Trophy – there can surely be few capital cities that could host such an event! Hunter's Bog, the hidden valley running approximately north-east/south-west below the peak of Arthur's

The Edinburgh skyline as seen from a corner of the Queen's Park above the St Leonard's road access. The former school of that name can be seen in the left background.

Seat, provides what is surely the greatest 360-degree vista of unspoiled scenery to be seen in any British city. From one of the paths crossing the Bog, formerly a shooting range, no man-made construction can be seen apart from one of the floodlight towers at Meadowbank.

The park's three lochs are dealt with under the appropriate heading. Of these three, Duddingston is the only natural loch; Dunsapie was designed as a reservoir, and St Margaret's was a boating pond until comparatively recently.

Parliamentary Representation

Edinburgh has six parliamentary seats at Westminster at the time of writing. They are, in clockwise order, Edinburgh Leith, Edinburgh East, Edinburgh South, Edinburgh Pentlands, Edinburgh West, with Edinburgh Central in the middle of the imaginary dial. In 1995 four of these seats were Labour-held; Conservative members hold Edinburgh West and Pentlands. Part of the Linlithgow constituency cuts into the Edinburgh district at Kirkliston and South Queensferry, but this is not historically regarded as an Edinburgh seat.

The electorates for each city seat were, at the 1992 General Election:

Edinburgh Central	56,527	(59,529 in 1987)
Leith	56,520	(60,359)
East	45,687	(48,895)
South	61,355	(63,830)
Pentlands	55,567	(58,125)
West	58,998	(62,214)

The longest-serving contemporary MP at the time of writing is Dr Gavin Strang, first elected for Edinburgh East in 1970. He is currently the second-longest serving MP in the city's history, the record of 28 years being held by Ronald Munro-Ferguson (later Viscount Novar) who represented Leith (strictly speaking not then a city constituency) from 1886 to 1914, when he was appointed Governor General of Australia.

HISTORY OF REPRESENTATION

EDINBURGH PARLIAMENT

Scotland's own Parliament ceased to exist in January 1707 when it created a special niche for itself in gubernatorial history by voting itself out of existence, by 100 votes to 67, in accepting the Act of Union with England. In return, Scotland received 45 seats in the House of Commons and 16 in the House of Lords.

This unusual case of political suicide was carried out by what Robert Burns characterised as 'a parcel o' rogues'. It was an unpopular decision; even ordinary Edinburgh citizens, who were not represented in Parliament whether it was in their own city or 400 miles away, took to the streets to protest, and many a Commissioner (MP) feared for his safety. There was to be no welcome for the Scottish representatives at Westminster either; historian Gerrit Judd records that Scottish MPs dreaded having to speak in the Chamber because of the merciless ridicule their accents evoked from the English majority.

The Scottish Parliament comprised the 'Three Estates' – the nobility, clergy, and burgesses – and, until the end of the 16th century, was peripatetic, being called at any one of a number of Royal Burghs or sites convenient to the monarch at the time. From around 1600 it was based permanently in Edinburgh, 'except', as historian Robert Rait puts it dryly, 'during periods of disturbance'. In 1632 Charles I demanded that Edinburgh should provide a proper Parliament House at its own expense, to replace the malodorous Tolbooth (*see* PRISONS), and this was built just north-west of St Giles and was ready by 1639. It now houses the Supreme Law Courts, and its fine hammer-beam ceiling now looks down on bewigged advocates walking with their clients in Parliament Hall.

In 1584 an Act of the Scots Parliament confirmed that Edinburgh would have two seats in the assembly, as appears to have been the case in practice already, although such double representation was not unique to Edinburgh at that time. However, in the last 86 years of the Parliament's life to 1707, Edinburgh was unique in being represented by two MPs, there being 50 commissioners for 49 Scottish burghs.

Edinburgh was represented by a total of 113 commissioners over the years from 1293 to 1707, although some meetings took place when a sederunt does not appear to have been taken, or the records have been subsequently lost. A record of these representatives, nominated by the Town Council, and not of course selected by any democratic process as known today,

can be found in Margaret Young's book *The Parliaments of Scotland*. For a detailed study of Parliament itself, right down to the details of apparel required to be worn when attending – and the fines imposed if not – Professor Rait's book should be consulted, despite its 1924 publication date (*see* BIBLIOGRAPHY for details of both books).

EDINBURGH'S MPS AT WESTMINSTER 1707–1832

The year shown below dates the beginning of the life of the particular parliament at Westminster, sessions being of irregular duration. The first Scottish MPs joined in the middle of the 1705-8 session. The city's MP was usually, although not invariably, the Lord Provost, but towards the end of the unreformed parliametary period, the position was very much in the pocket of the powerful Dundas family.

(This data is extracted from *Parliamentary Papers*, LXII, 1885, cross-checked against the supplementary addenda compiled by W.W. Bean.)

1707	Sir Patrick Johnson
1708	Sir Samuel McClellan
	Sir Patrick Johnson
	(from 25 November 1709)
1710	Sir Patrick Johnson
1713	Sir James Stewart
1714	Sir George Warrender
	John Campbell (from 18 March 1721)
1722	John Campbell
1727	John Campbell
1734	Patrick Lindsay
1741	Archibald Stewart
1747	James Ker
1754	William Alexander

1761	George Lind
	James Coutts (from 27 February 1762)
1768	Sir Laurence Dundas
1774	Sir Laurence Dundas
1780	Sir Laurence Dundas
	James Hunter Blair (from 29 October 1781)
1784	James Hunter Blair
	Sir Adam Fergusson (from 31 August 1784)
1790	Henry Dundas
1796	Henry Dundas
1802	Henry Dundas
	Charles Hope (from 4 January 1803)
	George Abercromby (from 28 January 1805)
1806	Sir Patrick Murray
1807	Sir Patrick Murray
	William Dundas (from 26 March 1812)
1812	William Dundas
1818	William Dundas
1820	William Dundas
1826	William Dundas
1830	William Dundas
1831	Robert Adam Douglas (to end of session in 1833).

Since the Reform Act of 1832 began the modernisation and democratisation of politics, Edinburgh – no longer itself the seat of Scotland's parliament – has been represented as shown in the tables.

From 1832 to 1885 the city had two MPs, representing the city overall. Each voter enjoyed two votes, provided they registered for a sum of one half-crown, and assuming that they were not objected to by either of the principal political parties. It appears that the Tories were in the habit of objecting much more than the Liberals or Whigs, during the early years of the wider franchise. In 1835, 7,748 voters were registered and 3,813 votes cast, rather more than the 32 voters who comprised Edinburgh Town Council and who had obediently voted Tory.

In the first 20 years after the Reform Act, so popular were the Whig/Liberal factions in Edinburgh that the Tories only put up candidates twice between 1835 and 1852. Interestingly, all the city's MPs in the first 77 years after the Reform Act of 1832 were Whig or Liberal (there was a subtle distinction between these), and it was not unknown for Liberals of different persuasions on such subjects as Irish Home Rule to challenge one another for election. As Jeffrey Williams pointed out in his study of those early years of democratic Edinburgh politics (*see* BIBLIOGRAPHY), 'Edinburgh was a Liberal city'.

The city's first Conservative representative was not elected under democratic conditions until 1909. Leith turned to the Conservative cause from 1914 until 1918 – its only flirtation with the blue ribbon (and, interestingly, its only Tory MP, George Welsh Currie, later converted to socialism). Labour also had to wait until 1918 before taking its first capital seat – Edinburgh Central.

After 1885 there were four MPs, sitting for four separate seats in the city, but from 1918 until 1950, there were five seats – Edinburgh Central, North, East, South, and West, with Pentlands and Leith being added in the latter year. The North constituency dropped out in 1983, merged with parts of Leith and Central, bringing the total down from seven to six.

1832–1885 – Two seats; held throughout this period by Liberals (Whigs). By-elections are included below (these were called if an MP had accepted public office):

1832	Francis Jeffrey and James Abercromby
1834	James Abercromby and Sir John Campbell
1834(2)	James Abercromby and Sir John Campbell
1835	James Abercromby and Sir John Campbell
1835(2)	James Abercromby and Sir John Campbell
1837	James Abercromby and Sir John Campbell
1839	Sir John Campbell and Thomas B. Macaulay
1840	Sir John Campbell and Thomas B. Macaulay
1841	Thomas B. Macaulay and William Gibson Craig
1846	Thomas B. Macaulay and William Gibson Craig
1846(2)	Thomas B. Macaulay and William Gibson Craig
1847	William Gibson Craig and Charles Cowan
1847(2)	William Gibson Craig and Charles Cowan
1852	Charles Cowan and Thomas B. Macaulay
1856	Charles Cowan and Adam Black
1857	Charles Cowan and Adam Black
1859	Adam Black and James Moncrieff
1859(2)	Adam Black and James Moncrieff
1865	James Moncrieff and Duncan MacLaren
1868	Duncan McLaren and John Miller
1874	Duncan McLaren and James Cowan
1880	Duncan McLaren and James Cowan
1881	James Cowan and John McLaren
1881(2)	James Cowan and Thomas Ryburn Buchanan
1882	Thomas Ryburn Buchanan and Samuel Danks Waddy

LEITH MPS 1832-85
(All Liberal)

1832	John Archibald Murray
1839	Andrew Rutherford
1851	James Moncrieff
1859	William Miller
1868	Robert Andrew Macfie
1874	Donald Robert McGregor
1878	Andrew Grant

EDINBURGH'S MPS 1885-1994

Leith Burghs included Portobello and Musselburgh until 1918, and was a separate constituency until 1950, when merged into Edinburgh for electoral purposes. It is listed overleaf with the Edinburgh constituencies for ease of reference. The chronology includes by-elections.

Edinburgh is represented in the European Parliament at Strasbourg as part of the Lothians constituency, currently held by Labour.

ELECTION YEAR	CENTRAL	NORTH	EAST	SOUTH	WEST	PENTLANDS	LEITH
1885	J.Wilson Lib		G.J. Goschen Lib	Sir. G Harrison Lib	T.R. Buchanan	Lib U	W. Jacks Lib
1886	W McEwan Lib		R Wallace Lib	HCE Childers Lib			WE Gladstone Lib
1886 (2)							RC Munro– Ferguson Lib
1892				HW Paul Lib	Viscount Wolmer Lib U		
1895				R Cox Lib	L McIver Lib U		
1899			G McCrae Lib	A Dewar Lib			
1900	GM Brown Lib			Sir AN Agnew Lib			
1906	CE Price Lib			A Dewar Lib			
1909			JP Gibson Lib		JA Clyde C		
1910				CH Lyell Lib			
1912			JM Hogge Lib				
1914							GW Currie C
1917				Sir JE Parrott Lib			
1918	W Graham L	JA Clyde C		CD Murray C	JG Jameson C		WW Benn Lib
1920		PJ Ford C					
1922				S Chapman C	HV Phillipps Lib		
1923		PW Raffan Lib					
1924	PJ Ford C	TD Shiels L			I MacIntyre C		

ELECTION YEAR	CENTRAL	NORTH	EAST	SOUTH	WEST	PENTLANDS	LEITH
1927							AE Brown Lib
1929					G Mathers L		
1931	JCM Guy C		DM Mason Lib		WG Normand C		
1935		A Erskine-Hill C	FW Pethick-Lawrence L		TM Cooper C		
1941	FC Watt C				GIC Hutchison C		
1945	A Gilzean L	EG Willis L	GR Thomson L	Sir WY Darling C			JH Hoy L
1947			JT Wheatley L				
1950		JL Clyde C				Lord John Hope C	
1951	T Oswald L						
1954			EG Willis L				
1955		WR Milligan C					
1957				AMC Hutchison C			
1959					JA Stodart C		
1960		Earl of Dalkeith C					
1964						NR Wylie C	
1970			GS Strang L				RK Murray L
1973		A Fletcher C					
1974 Feb	RF Cook L					M Rifkind C	
1974 Oct					Lord J Douglas-Hamilton C		
1979				M Ancram C			R Brown L
1983	A Fletcher C	(Seat Merged)					
1987	A Darling L			N Griffiths L			
1992							M Chisholm L

251

Photographic History

Edinburgh holds a distinguished place in the history of photography, and rightfully is the venue for the Scottish Photographic Archive, although there is currently speculation that this may be moved to Glasgow.

In the 1840s, Edinburgh supplied the setting and much of the inspiration for Hill and Adamson, regarded as the first to turn photography into an art form. One of Europe's leading camera-makers, Thomas Davidson, was based in the capital, finding an eager clientele of amateur scientists working in the new medium, and sharing their experiences at meetings of various learned societies in the city. Edinburgh was also the birthplace of the inventor of colour photography, James Clerk Maxwell, and in the Edinburgh Photographic Society the city has fostered one of the world's oldest societies of its kind. Appropriately, the Scottish Photographic Archive is located in the Scottish National Portrait Gallery, and is a first-rate research and study centre for this most Scottish of art forms.

It is surprising that the Scots did not invent photography in the first place. With such scientists as David Brewster active in the field of optics in the first quarter of the 19th century, and with the chemical technology already available, it only required an imaginative inventor to marry the technology of the camera obscura with the science of chemical image retention. Exactly this was done by Frenchman Joseph Niepce in 1827, his work being developed by the opportunistic Louis Daguerre, who gave his name to the Daguerrotype. While undoubtedly epoch-making in itself, the Daguerrotype could only produce a solitary image, and it is usually Englishman William Fox-Talbot who is credited with perfecting the negative-positive process which we understand today, and which he described as the Calotype process.

Both Daguerre and Fox-Talbot hastened to patent their inventions in England, which they may have assumed meant Britain, and thereby produced a new field of endeavour which the Scots were free to exploit. Until 1852, the patents system was chaotic, with English patents having no validity in Scotland and vice-versa. Scottish scientists freely ordered Calotype cameras, and a new art form was born. (It should be added that such inventors as David Brewster, inventor of the kaleidoscope, suffered financially by the expense of having to patent their work in England as well as their native land, or risk having their inventions pirated).

David Octavius Hill was a landscape artist and Secretary to the Royal Scottish Academy. When asked to paint a composite picture of the dissenting ministers who figured in the great schism in the Church of Scotland in 1843, he realised that Robert Adamson's prowess with the Calotype camera could help him by allowing him to photograph the sitters before painting them (the painting in fact was not finished until 23 years later).

Thus was launched a partnership which produced some of the finest pictorial images ever to come out of Scotland. Photographic historian Helmut Gernsheim believed that their output – the fisherfolk of Newhaven and soldiers at the Castle as well as dissenting ministers – has 'universally awarded Hill and Adamson first place in the annals of photography'. Before the latter's death in

1848, 1,800 pictures had been produced.

Less well-known photographers of that period in Edinburgh were Thomas Keith and Thomas Begbie, both of whom specialised in local views, while Edinburgh-based Charles Piazzi Smyth used a miniature camera and magnesium flash to photograph inside the Pyramids which fascinated him so much, and also took some of the earliest views of St Petersburg. Many of the earliest cameras were made by Thomas Davidson, a Northumbrian working in Edinburgh. His cameras came to be compared to Voigttlander's, and provided the technical basis for Hill and Adamson's fame.

An Edinburgh banker, Mungo Ponton, carried out seminal research on finding a cheaper substitute for silver as an agent reactive to light, and the city was the birthplace of James Clerk Maxwell, among whose many achievements was the production of the first colour photograph in 1861.

Among the commercial photographers who became famous in the city over the last 150 years, probably Yerbury's is the best-known, and the company is still very active at the present time.

Police

Since 1975 the policing of Edinburgh has been in the hands of the Lothian and Borders Police, with its headquarters at Fettes Avenue. The Chief Constable of the force, currently Sir William Sutherland QPM, has statutory obligations to the Lothian and Borders Police Board,

composed of elected councillors from these two regions, and to the Secretary of State for Scotland.

The force's common purpose is 'to uphold the law fairly and firmly, to pursue and identify those who break the law, to take a leading role in the prevention of crime, to keep the peace, and to protect and reassure the community'.

In 1993 the largest part of the force's income (48 per cent, £51 million) was from the Central Government Police Grant, the Region contributing 42 per cent (£44.5 million), with 6 per cent coming from Borders Region and 4 per cent from chargeable income. 65 per cent of the expenditure in 1993 went on police personnel salaries, the next largest single item being 9 per cent for civilian staffing. Total staff, uniformed and civilian, was 3,600 in 1993. In 1991 the percentage of women staff stood at 13 per cent, approximately half as much again as the national average. There were 157 traffic wardens. The number of motor vehicles was 396 (in 1995), 15 per cent of them used exclusively for traffic duties. There were six horses on the force, and 36 dogs, four trained in drug detection, and two in explosives detection.

For administrative purposes the city of Edinburgh is divided into four divisions – A, B, C, and D. The first of these is based at Fettes Avenue headquarters, and is a support division, comprising Community Involvement, Licensing, Lost Property, Nationality, Recruitment, and Traffic Wardens. B Division is basically the south and south-east of the city, with sub-divisional headquarters at St Leonard's, Gayfield Square, and at Howdenhall. C

Division comprises the south-west of the city, from Morningside out to Wester Hailes, with sub-divisional centres at Torphichen Place near Haymarket and at Wester Hailes, and additional stations at Corstorphine, Oxgangs, and at Edinburgh Airport. The north and north-east of the city are covered by D Division, its Divisional HQ at Queen Charlotte Street in Leith, and with stations at Portobello, Drylaw, and Craigmillar.

As well as maintaining public order and tackling crime in the manner of any police force anywhere – and with commendable results (83 per cent of urgent calls responded to within target time in 1993) – Lothians and Borders Police have experience unique in Scotland in dealing with international events, royal visits etc. Such recent occasions as the European Summit in December 1992 and State Visit of the Norwegian Royal Family in 1994 passed off without a hitch, enhancing Edinburgh's reputation as an exemplary host city.

History of policing in Edinburgh

From 1805 until 1975, the city's policing was officially in the hands of the Edinburgh City Police (City of Edinburgh Police from 1920). This force was the successor to no fewer than three organisations designed to keep the peace in the city – the Constables, the Town Guard, and the Trained Bands.

The **Constables** were set up by the Town Council around 1611 at the express command of James VI, who was impressed with the policing system south of Border, such as it was. By the mid 17th century the Constables, unpaid and recruited from the merchant class, appeared to have been the Council's only 'employees'. They were pressed with the task of keeping the peace, but many of their duties appear to have been taken over eventually by the more down-to-earth Town Guard, which was professional.

It is perhaps significant that when the Police Act came into force in 1805, the Constables had to petition the Town Council to ascertain their role in relation to the new professional force, suggesting a fairly marginal status for the Constables in the first place. Five years later they formed themselves into the Society of High Constables of Edinburgh, to avoid confusion with the new police officers, and they appear to have had an uneasy relationship with the Council in the following decades, being completely reconstituted in 1857. Nevertheless, the High Constables were still called out. Beside patrolling during royal visits or at Hogmanay, this fine body of the better-off members of society were ordered in 1823 to put a stop to snowball-fighting between university students and schoolboys!

A force of constables also existed in the separate burgh of Canongate from the time of James VI's proclamation in 1610, and its history is less well-documented, following the loss of the force's records before 1810. In that year there were ten constables; by the time of the winding-up of the force with the amalgamation with Edinburgh in 1856, there were 20. One of the duties of these volunteers, who were also from the merchant class, was to assist pressgangs in the forcible enlistment of recruits for the armed forces, particularly the navy, which did little to make the constables popular. It was a devil too dangerous to sup with anyway, and at least one constable from the

Canongate was himself pressganged to sea in the 1750s!

The **Town Guard** had its origins in the nightwatch arrangements introduced after the defeat at Flodden in 1513, when every fourth man in the city was required to take a turn on watch, but whose subsequent activity appears to have been keeping the peace. In contrast to the constables, in 1700 the Town Guard members were paid sixpence a day for a sentinel or private, one shilling for a corporal. At one period in the 17th century the Guard was reconstituted, but this proved to be a temporary arrangement, a new reorganisation in 1689 bringing the Guard up to a complement of 120.

The Guard had a kenspeckle history, being ill-disciplined and unpopular, poet Robert Fergusson calling them the 'black banditti'. In his time (the 1760s) they appear to have been figures of fun, but this was not invariably the case. In later years the Guard had a reputation for violence; as late as 1814 a running-battle between Guards and numerically-superior soldiers from the Castle ended with the latter being overcome and made prisoner.

The Guard, Trained Bands, and Constables appear to have continued side by side, not even the creation of the Police Force in 1805 terminating the Guards' existence. Its headquarters was a single-storey guardhouse which the Guard shared with chimney-sweeps, and which was unhelpfully built full in the middle of the High Street around 1609, and situated near the present Cockburn Street opening. It was demolished in 1785.

The Guard's single most eventful incident was the lynching of one of its captains, John Porteous. In September 1736, an Edinburgh mob had become convinced that Porteous, under sentence of death for having caused civilian deaths in a recent disturbance, was to be pardoned. The public took the law into its own hands, and the unfortunate Porteous was hanged from a barber's pole in front of Hunter's Close. The London government of the day attempted to bring strong retribution to bear on the Scottish capital, including a fine, the demolition of the Netherbow, and the forced resignation of the Lord Provost. In the event, the Netherbow survived for a further 28 years, and the fine was paid directly to Porteous's widow.

For a list of officers heading the Edinburgh Town Guard from the 17th century to 1817 see *A History of the Lothian and Borders Police* by T.W. Archibald (1990). The Trained Bands remained voluntary, retained a formidable armoury, and are more relevantly dealt with under MILITARY HISTORY.

In 1805 a Police Commission was set up in Edinburgh, dividing the city (but not including Canongate) into six wards, (later 30), governed by commissioners elected by local ratepayers, whose assessments paid for the new service. Fire safety also came under their remit, along with 'cleaning, lighting, and watching'. The Force divested itself of fire fighting responsibilities in 1824 (*see* FIRE FIGHTING) and of cleansing (*see* CLEANSING) in 1856. In the latter year the Commission was absorbed into the Town Council, and in 1896 and 1920 respectively the Portobello and Leith forces were absorbed into the City Police (*see* below), which became the City of Edinburgh Police in the latter year.

Police boxes first made their appearance on the city streets in 1904, a later generation of them, designed by Ebenezer Macrae, being likened by one visitor to miniature Greek temples. A radio-controlled network of 141 boxes and pillars was established in 1933, radio communication with police cars being introduced in the following year, with Blackford Hill being used as the site for a transmitter. A dogs unit was set up as late as 1954.

The city police force has been headed by the following. The post of Chief Constable appears to have originated with William Henderson:

1805–1812 John Tait (Superintendent)
1812–1822 James Brown
1822–1828 Captain Robertson
1828–1842 Captain James Stewart
1842–1848 William Haining
1848–1851 Richard John Moxey
1851–1878 Thomas Linton
1878–1900 William Henderson (Chief Constable)
1900–1935 Roderick Ross
1935–1955 William Morren
1955–1975 John Ritchie Inch

Lothian and Borders Chief Constables:

1975–1983   John Henry Orr
1983–   William Sutherland

Leith Police Commissioners operated independently from Edinburgh during the time of the town's independence (1833–1920) although as early as 1610 ten constables were appointed in the port, each serving six months, and being responsible for the arrest of religious dissenters and the cleaning of the streets. Unfortunately, the records for the Constables' force appear to be missing before 1810, which applied to South Leith only (that is, the area east of the Water of Leith). North Leith appears to have been linked with Canongate for policing purposes. In the 1840s, the Commissioners were still removing horse manure to the Leith foreshore, some of it to be sold for fertiliser, the remainder to be washed away by high tides.

The formation of the new burgh in 1833 brought South and North Leith, as well as Newhaven, under one police jurisdiction, which lasted until 1920. The 1913 Dock strike posed the greatest test for Leith's police, and is worth recounting in some detail. Unrest in previous years, particularly 1911, had led to the construction of a forbidding boundary wall round the eastern side of the docks in order to keep strikers from interfering with strikebreaking labour.

When, in June 1913, 3,000 dockers struck for the same increased pay they saw being awarded at the other Forth ports, the effects were considerable. Dozens of ships were unable to unload or sail, and within days thousands of miners were laid off in the Lothian coalfield. The shipping companies began recruiting 'blackleg' labour from elsewhere, and the strike became violent. A train carrying new labourers had every window broken at the Citadel station by stone-throwing, and part of the hated boundary wall was blown up. A police officer fell into the resulting crater; he was one of 300 who was having to police the strike. Six gunboats were sent to patrol off the port, and all leave was cancelled at the barracks at the Castle, Piershill, and the Fort. A car accident to a leading union leader had delayed a negotiated settlement, but this was eventually achieved, after a seven week strike which had caused considerable bitterness and had stretched Leith's policing to its limits.

British Transport Police operate within the city of Edinburgh, its HQ being centred on the Waverley Station. The BTP presence has greatly reduced over the years as the capital's rail network has shrunk.

The **Military Police** retain a presence in the Edinburgh area, as can be expected of a militarised city. One curiosity about the Military Police road vehicles is their use of EIIR numerals, not seen on other police or postal insignia in Scottish streets.

The **Royal Parks** in the city – the Queen's Park and the Royal Botanic Garden – have their own uniformed constabularies.

Population

The population of Edinburgh at the time of the 1991 Census was 418,914. With a Census area of 26,080 hectares (64,443 acres, approximately 100 square miles), Edinburgh is Scotland's largest city, although the city's developed area (as defined by the Scottish Office in its 1994 *Scottish Abstract of Statistics*) is only 52.1 square miles, as opposed to Glasgow's 67.8 square miles. This speaks volumes for Edinburgh's open space capacity, compared to more intensively built-up conurbations, although the area figures were also distorted in 1975 with the addition of the Dalmeny/Queensferry corridor to the north-west of the city.

The comparative area and population density statistics for Scotland's four cities are as follows:

CITY	AREA(HA)	POPULATION PER HA.
Edinburgh	26,080	16.1
Dundee	23,504	7.1
Glasgow	19,790	33.5
Aberdeen	18,447	11.1

Edinburgh's 196,894 male citizens were outnumbered by 222,020 females; this differential is probably accounted for by the city's high proportion of citizens above retirement age, where there is a noticeably higher ratio of women to men.

There was a loss of around 25,000 Edinburgh residents from the 1981 Census. Most British cities appear to be losing population at the present time, there being a perceptible move to rural areas for city workers with cars; Edinburgh's decline is considerably less in real and percentage terms than other cities'. Of Edinburgh's 'lost' citizens, 0.7 per cent of the figures were accounted by variation in the birth and death rates, but 5.1 per cent by migration. Glasgow's figures in comparison (a loss of 15.5 per cent overall), were 1.3 per cent natural loss and no less than 14.2 per cent by migration.

Population figures are calculated every ten years (when the year ends in the digit 1) from data supplied from the Census, organised by the Registrar General for Scotland at New Register House at the east end of Princes Street.

AGE OF POPULATION
As will be seen from the table, opposite the largest age-group in the city in 1991 were more than 65 years old. Interestingly, at the

257

1981 Census, the largest grouping was the one immediately prior to retirement age. Edinburgh's population is older than Lothian's in every age sub-group from retirement age onwards. In 1991 approximately one-third of Edinburgh's households (60,569 out of 185,664) contained at least one pensioner (of these, 37.4 per cent had no central heating).

The area of Edinburgh with the oldest population is the Stenhouse ward, where no less than 37.7 per cent of the citizenry is retired; South East Corstorphine is second with 30.7 per cent. (Information extracted from District Council Planning Statistics, *see* BIBLIOGRAPHY).

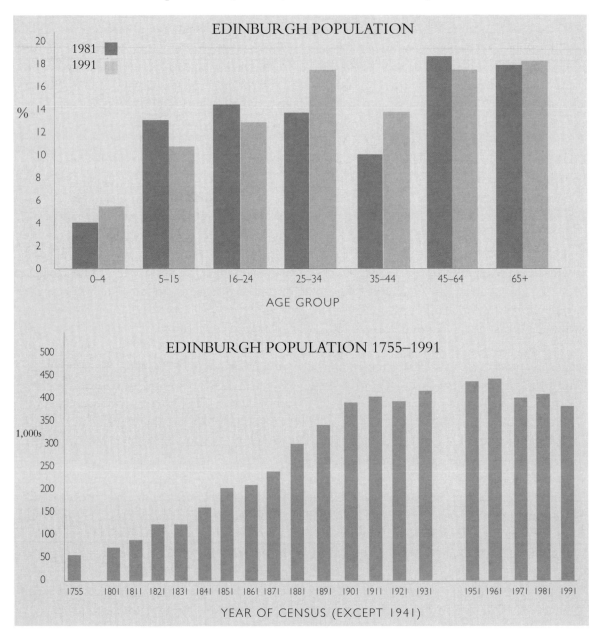

EMPLOYMENT

In 1853 visitor George Measom wrote of Edinburgh:

Edinburgh cannot be called a place of much trade or manufacture, being chiefly supported by persons in the law and medical professions, especially the latter.

Current census figures show that 18,711 people were employed in the medical and health professions in 1991, approximately 8 per cent of the labour force. Legal employees did not appear to be computed separately, but health workers were outnumbered by those in the categories of education, retail distribution, business support, government and local government, in that order. 39 per cent of male workers considered themselves to be professional or managerial in status (as against 35 per cent of employed women).

Perhaps the most surprising information to be gleaned from the bar-chart is the percentage of workers involved with the hotel and catering trades – only 12,403 (5.5 per cent). Of course, it can be argued that a staff member of a car hire agency, or an information assistant on an airline desk is also involved in tourism, so perhaps a classification more closely geared to the tourist industry is required. In 1993 Edinburgh District Council estimated that there were 20,000 employed in its definition of 'tourist industry' in Edinburgh in that year.

The largest employer in the city in 1993 was Lothian Regional Council, which was unfortunate, given its impending demise under local government reorganisation in 1996. The next ten in order of number of employees were – Post Office, Heriot-Watt University, Lothian Health Board, British Telecom, Ethicon, Scottish Office, British Gas, Uniroyal Englebert, University of Edinburgh, and Lothian Region Transport.

Employment History

Recently published research by Helen Dingwall (*see* BIBLIOGRAPHY under History) shows that, according to her painstaking analysis of 1690s poll-tax records, the largest-group of employees in eleven 17th century Edinburgh and Leith parishes were female servants (32 per cent), with male servants comprising around 11 per cent. There were 33 medical doctors registered, compared to one doctor of divinity (a strangely low return), while the files are even specific enough to include two Senators of the College of Justice, and one Master of the Revels, the last-named being a resident of the Tron parish.

The returns anticipate the statement by George Measom in 1853 about Edinburgh's low profile as a manufacturing base. Dingwall concludes that around 16 per cent of taxed individuals were involved in manufacturing – half the proportion of 'living-in' female servants – and a large proportion of manufacturers were producing clothing and clothes accessories, probably mainly for local use. There were 372 merchants, 228 Writers to the Signet (solictors), and 48 masons.

By 1931, Census returns showed that 61 per cent of Edinburgh's population was involved in the service sector, ten per cent more than the proportion of Glasgow's workforce, so there is a strong historical tradition of Edinburgh's working population being largely involved in the non-manufacturing area of commerce.

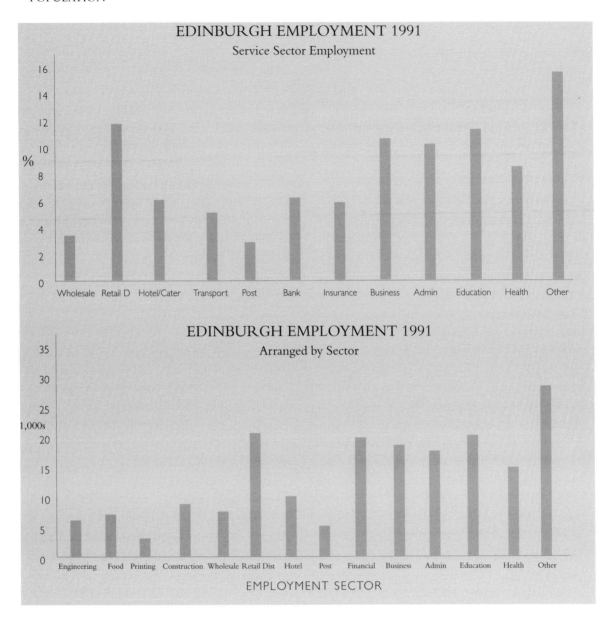

EDINBURGH EMPLOYMENT 1991
Service Sector Employment

(%) Wholesale, Retail D, Hotel/Cater, Transport, Post, Bank, Insurance, Business, Admin, Education, Health, Other

EDINBURGH EMPLOYMENT 1991
Arranged by Sector

(1,000s) Engineering, Food, Printing, Construction, Wholesale, Retail Dist, Hotel, Post, Financial, Business, Admin, Education, Health, Other

EMPLOYMENT SECTOR

UNEMPLOYMENT

In 1991 the proportion of Edinburgh people registered as unemployed was 8.6 per cent (Census figures). This was higher than the national (UK) rate in May 1991 of 7.8 per cent. Edinburgh's worst unemployment blackspot was Craigmillar with no less than one citizen in three drawing unemployment benefit (Edinburgh Topic Sheets 9), and 28.3 per cent of Muirhouse residents were 'on the dole'. One wonders what the editors of the *Third Statistical Account* would have made of this when they drew up their meticulous description of Edinburgh and its people, at a time (1962) when unemployment in the city was a mere 1.7 per cent! This was very close to the national (UK) figure at that time of 1.8 per cent, so

Edinburgh has suffered a marginally worse increase in unemployment than the nation overall in the last 30 years.

ETHNIC MINORITIES

The 1991 Census was the first to contain a question about ethnic origins, and although its results filled something of a gap in knowledge of the city's demographic pattern, its data could be regarded as personally intrusive. 97.6 per cent of Edinburgh's residents considered themselves to be 'white', the largest single grouping of non-white citizens being of Pakistani origin (0.6 per cent of population), approximately half of whom were born in the UK. Interestingly, the *Third Statistical Account* of Edinburgh, published as recently as 1966, relegated the Indian and Pakistani communities to the bottom (in numerical terms) of its list of what it called 'overseas communities', citing treble-figure numbers as a likely population.

Second to the Pakistani community in 1991, was the Chinese (0.5 per cent), followed by the Indian community (0.3 per cent), 'other Asian' (0.2 per cent), with Black African, Black 'other', and Bangladeshis all on 0.1 per cent. Other communities of unspecified origin weighed in at a total of 0.4 per cent.

The proportion of ethnic groups in Edinburgh averaged out at 2.4 per cent across the city. The most cosmopolitan area is Tollcross, where 8.1 per cent of the population is categorised as 'non-white' in District Council statistics. The St Giles ward has the second highest level of mixed population, with Marchmont and Mayfield also showing higher than average percentages. Muirhouse had the lowest ethnic population, followed by Firrhill and Gilmerton. It may be concluded from this demographic breakdown that most coloured citizens work or study in the centre of the city, many of them involved in the restaurant trade or living centrally for easy access to university or college.

No less than 84.2 per cent of the city's population was Scots born. (Only 0.8 per cent of the overall Edinburgh total, Scots or not, could speak Gaelic). The number of Edinburgh citizens born in England was 43,951 in 1991 – approximately 11 per cent, and twice the proportion for the whole of Scotland. The New Town and Sciennes wards are the two areas where English-born citizens exceed 17.5 per cent of the population, more than three times the Scottish average. It is undoubtedly true that Edinburgh has always appeared an attractive place to live for people in England; we can congratulate them on their taste!

HISTORY OF SCOTTISH POPULATION SCIENCE

Edinburgh has always been in the forefront of calculating Scotland's population. Not only is the Registrar General's Office based in Edinburgh, with detailed administration being carried out on census organisation from Ladywell House in the west of the city, but it was an Edinburgh minister who produced what is probably Scotland's first systematic attempt at a population survey.

In 1755 Dr Alexander Webster published *An Account of the Number of People in Scotland*, the product of research he had accumulated through correspondence with other Church of Scotland ministers in as many parishes as possible.

Despite differentiating Catholics from Protestants, Webster nevertheless provided invaluable data for historians. His figures for Edinburgh do not include Canongate, St Cuthbert's, Leith North and South, (South Leith was the more populous), nor 'Libberton', which rivalled Leith in size in that survey. Webster's total for Edinburgh, with these areas added, was 57,195 souls.

Webster's data is of particular interest, representing as it does, contemporary testimony. Writing in the *Third Statistical Account* (1966), Dr Norman Hunter and Dr A.B. Taylor argue that those parishes on the city's outskirts should also be added in, to give a figure of 64,479 for 1755. Earlier figures quoted by Hunter and Taylor, including those taken from the first *Statistical Account* show the following progression in Edinburgh's population growth, again adjusted to include parishes later to be absorbed by the city:

1678	35,000
1722	40,420
1753	48,000
1755	64,479

The sudden increase shown for the two years 1753-55 illustrates how difficult it is to estimate population figures from centuries gone by. The figure for 1753, calculated from the first *Statistical Account*, which was published on a parish-by-parish basis as the information was received (*see* STATISTICAL ACCOUNTS), is almost certainly too low.

Official cenuses began in 1801, but were not conducted on a single day, in the modern manner, until 1841. The registration of births, marriages, and deaths was not mandatory in Scotland in 1855, making all computations of population prior to that year something of an educated guess.

(All population data is reproduced here through the courtesy of the Registrar General for Scotland; all interpretation and comment is the author's alone).

Ports

Edinburgh's working maritime ports are Leith and Granton, both administered by the now-privatised Forth Ports Authority. There are also harbours at Newhaven and South Queensferry, now dedicated to recreational sailing. Former ports on this stretch of coastline and within city boundaries, include Cramond and Portobello. Fisherrow, less than a mile from the city boundary, is of course in Musselburgh, and is not considered in this volume. (For 'Ports', i.e. gates, such as Bristo Port, *see* CITY WALLS).

LEITH

With a cargo turnover of 2.75 million tons in 1992, Leith is once again one of Britain's busiest ports, and nowadays presents a much more bustling appearance than it did in the 1950s and 1960s. Protected by a 1969 lock entrance over 800 feet (240 metres) long by 95 feet (28.5 metres) wide, and 40 feet (12metres) deep at high-water, the harbour installations comprise the Albert (opened 1869), Edinburgh (1881), and Imperial (1904) Docks, as well as the Western Harbour, giving a total of 216 acres (87.5 hectares) of sheltered water area. There are bulk loading and unloading facilities for

This 1995 view of the Leith waterfront sums up the changes in the town's maritime history. In the drydock on the left of the picture is HM minehunter Berkeley, *undergoing repair, although this was before the closure of Rosyth naval base in November 1995 made such visits to Leith less likely in future. Beyond the ship's superstructure can be seen the new Scottish Office nearing completion at Victoria Quay.*

coal, grain, and cement, while North Sea Oil support vessels are regular visitors.

The Western Harbour has recently been modified to take all but the biggest cruise ships, while there are three dry docks for repairs to vessels of up to 500 feet in length. New Spanish-built tugs, the *Dalmeny* and *Cramond*, were delivered to the FPA in 1994, generating enough bollard pull to handle ships of up to 300,000 tons deadweight, and, if unfortunately necessary, recover spilt oil at a rate of 100,000 litres per hour.

Shipbuilding has not been carried on here since 1984 (*see* INDUSTRY: SHIP-BUILDING), while the Victoria Dock (opened 1852) is currently under redevelopment, the new Scottish Office building now occupying its southern quay. The East and West Old Docks have been filled in. In November 1994 the Docks provided an incongruous backdrop to David Mach's municipally-sponsored modern sculpture *The Temple at Tyre*, comprising a Grecian-style temple made of tyres and supported by freight containers. In the following July, 83 entrants in the Cutty Sark Tall Ships Race berthed in the port, being visited by an estimated one million people.

History

Leith's mercantile operations were traditionally centred on the mouth of the Water of Leith, with tidal conditions allowing vessels as far up the river as the present-day area of Junction Street. It was at Leith that Mary (Queen of Scots) arrived to claim her kingdom in 1561. The ill-fated Darien Expedition sailed from the mouth of the river in 1698, and dry docks were built near here in the 1770s, (and not 1720 as sometimes reported). For a detailed history of the port, the reader is recommended to peruse Sue Mowat's excellent book *The Port of Leith* (*see* BIBLIOGRAPHY).

One of the port's most famous landmarks is the 30 feet high Martello Tower built originally on the Mussel Cape Rock in 1809. This fortification against Napoleonic attack was therefore isolated at high water, but is now part of the eastern breakwater, and can be visited by arrangement with the Forth Ports Authority.

The present dock system was reclaimed from the sea during a period of gradual expansion from the 1800s onwards, an exercise initially so expensive that Edinburgh was relieved to see Leith set up as a town in its own right in 1833. The proximity of the Lothian coalfield was a major factor in the expansion of Leith's port facilities, and the Edinburgh & Dalkeith Railway, although nothing more than a horse-drawn tramway to begin with, brought coal to the port from about 1831. Thereafter, rivalry between the North British and Caledonian railway systems assured the dock area of an extensive rail network. Historian Sue Mowat has characterised the 19th century as 'The Coal Age' for Leith Docks. The 20th century she viewed as the 'Grain Age', with the first grain storage elevator being constructed as the century opened, and the port's skyline changed as a result.

In 1929 the Air Ministry designated Leith and Harwich the official east coast ports for passenger flying-boat operations, but potential legal and insurance complications prevented the Leith Dock Commission from proceeding with necessary investment to make Leith into an airport at that time. A second attempt was made in the 1950s (*see* AIRPORTS). Nowadays a helipad suffices, opposite, and east of, the lock entrance. The Commission had been established by Act of Parliament in 1838, being succeeded by the Forth Ports Authority in 1968. The latter is now privatised.

Trinity House is still one of the most important institutions in the port. It was constituted in 1555, originally as a rest home for retired seamen, its name being a gradual corruption from Fraternity House. Financed from 'Prime Gilt', a form of harbour dues, Trinity House became drawn into the administration of the port, and the organisation began providing pilots from 1649, as well as arbitrating in maritime disputes and examining prospective skippers and pilots.

The Custom House in Leith stands in Commercial Street, close to the Water of Leith. It was opened in 1812, the successor to the Customs building in Tolbooth Wynd. The present building is apparently used an as overspill depot for National Museums exhibits – surely something of a wasted opportunity, particularly when Leith has no museum of its own.

NEWHAVEN

Now very much overshadowed by commercial operations fringed around Leith's Western Harbour, Newhaven harbour has settled down to enjoy a recreational role in the life of the waterfront. The Harbour's quays date from the 1860s and '70s, with a lighthouse at the end of the eastern quay. Appropriately, the eastern quay is also occupied by an arcaded timber fish-house now housing Harry Ramsden's restaurant, which has provided space for an excellent community museum to be created by the quayside (*see* MUSEUMS). Among the activites commemorated is the building of the great *Michael* in 1511 (*see* INDUSTRY: SHIPBUILDING), and the fishing industry which was once very active at Newhaven.

With so many houses nearby, a tradition sprang up of fresh fish and oysters being sold round the doors by creel-bearing fishwives, shouting 'caller (fresh) herrin" and 'caller oo' (oysters). So distinctively costumed were they, that pioneer photographers Hill and Adamson (*see* PHOTOGRAPHY) featured them prominently in their work, but these ladies also were so aromatically distinguished that the local railway station staff at Trinity insisted they use a different ticket-window from the rest of the public!

GRANTON

Granton Harbour, like Leith's, is administered by the Forth Ports Authority. Its outline consists of two breakwaters, and so remains tidal, the port entry being over 300 feet (90 metres) wide. The port specialises in handling heavy unit cargoes requiring a roll-on/roll off facility, such as power-station plant, 3000 tons of such commodities being handled in 1992. For many years Granton was a supply base for the Northern Lighthouses support vessels, and the Royal Forth Yacht Club makes its home here.

Granton's harbour was built by the then Duke of Buccleuch between 1834–44, involving the famous Stevenson family as engineers at an early stage. From about 1846 the world's first train ferry (the *Leviathan*) operated from here to Burntisland, not made obsolete until the opening of the Forth Bridge in 1890, after which a passenger ferry continued until the Second World War, and intermittently after that, its last working being undertaken in 1991–3 by a powered catamaran (*see* FERRIES). The harbour is overlooked by the towers of Granton Gasworks, the last installation in Britain to produce domestic gas by traditional methods, as opposed to processing North Sea gas. An unusual industry which tried to establish itself in Granton in the 1900s was an automobile works, owned by the Peck family, a name more usually known in the city as a stationery supplier.

CRAMOND

The present-day picturesque village of Cramond occupies the eastern side of the mouth of the Almond, and this was probably the site of a Roman port around the middle of the first century AD, although structural evidence is lacking. The east bank of the river is quayed with rubble and there is a small wharf at the site of Cockle Mill at the extent of high tide. Cramond's iron mills appear to have provided the spur for the construction of this wharf. Oyster fishing was once carried on from Cramond, and the village is almost

South Queensferry harbour, dating from the 16th century, as glimpsed down a lane from the town's High Street. The middle tower of the Forth Rail Bridge is a ghostly presence in the background.

too picturesque to ever be considered industrial.

The river's mouth is crossed by a rowboat ferry operated by the Dalmeny estate. With the closure of the Granton-Burntisland crossing, this is Edinburgh's only ferry service. (*see* FERRIES).

SOUTH QUEENSFERRY

Although better known as a crossing point for traffic negotiating the Queensferry Narrows, the village also has a small harbour, now used for recreational sailing, at its west end (and not to be confused with Port Edgar, a former minesweeping base just west of the Road Bridge, and now designated as a marina). South Queensferry's was an active fishing harbour for centuries, being extensively rebuilt by John Rennie and Robert Stevenson between 1809 and 1818.

PORTOBELLO

Little now remains of this bottle-mouth harbour constructed at the mouth of the Figgate (or Braid) Burn at around the end of the 1780s. Previously, small craft had traded by beaching here, at a landfall used by the English fleet when attacking Leith in 1560. The construction of a harbour appears to have resulted from the industriousness of pottery owner William Jameson, and stones from nearby Joppa Quarry were utilised, but the harbour was silted up by mid-19th century and was built over by 1860. Two brigs are reputed to have been built at Portobello at a yard immediately east of the burn's mouth, before the harbour was constructed. The harbour's site is now occupied by a funfair area, but exceptionally low tides can occasionally reveal the foundations of the curved eastern sea-wall, last seen in 1981.

For information about Port Hopetoun and Port Hamilton, *see* CANAL TRANSPORT.

Postal Services

Edinburgh is no longer the centre of the Scottish postal network to the extent it was in the days when even Glasgow received its mail from London via the Scottish capital. Nowadays, while Royal Mail operations for both Scotland and Northern Ireland are directed from the West Port building in Edinburgh, Parcel Force and Post Office Counters headquarters are both located in Glasgow. However, the capital is well-known to philatelists as the home of the Philatelic Bureau, whence special edition stamps are issued, and enthusiasts' orders processed.

The principal office of the Royal Mail in Edinburgh was located at 2–4 Waterloo Place from 1861 until 9 November 1995. On the latter date, the counter work undertaken at the GPO was transferred to a rather anonymous service point in the nearby St James Centre, leaving the older, more distinctive, building empty, as the administrative work had already been moved to West Port and sorting to Brunswick Street and Sighthill (*see* below). Along with the new sorting centre, there are ten postal delivery depots in the city, and 17 postcode areas (1995 figures). The 1,466 employees in the Edinburgh postal area deal with 1.2 million letters posted daily, delivering to 371,600 addresses, using 411 vehicles where necessary. There are 1,161 post boxes in local streets.

There is a major sorting depot at Brunswick Street, between Leith Walk and Easter Road, but in September 1995 a new Automated Processing Centre for Edinburgh was opened by Royal Mail on a 13 acre (5.33 hectare) location at Sighthill. This was the second of its kind in Scotland, intended to guarantee high performance standards in an industry where the volume of mail increased by no less than 50 per cent in the years 1985–1995. But even the most sophisticated automation seems unlikely to restore the standard of service which permitted a working man to send a postcard to his wife at lunchtime telling her he might be a little late for his evening meal. With a system of afternoon deliveries, this was perfectly possible in the years after the Second World War!

History

Postal services in Scotland appear to have been established when the Scottish King James VI and his court moved to London in 1603, necessitating some means of communication between Edinburgh and London. The courier system introduced at that time was not open to all, but in 1660 the passing of the General Letter Act offered a limited service for those requiring to send written communications. By 1682 postage between Edinburgh and Glasgow was twopence, and 11 years later the postmark was used in Scotland for the first time.

At the opening of the 18th century, the Edinburgh postmaster was paid £200 annually, assisted by an accountant and two clerks. Their first post office was situated in a High Street shop opposite the Tollbooth until around 1714, when it was relocated in Little's or Barron's Close, which, not surprisingly, later became known as Old Posthouse Close. There were to be no fewer than five later locations for the Post Office in Edinburgh until the opening of the GPO building in the 1860s.

Despatches within Scotland were carried in the earliest years of the service by foot-runners − who never ran, according to historian Henry Graham − being replaced by post-boys, who were men, not boys. Until 1717 a runner set off for Glasgow twice-weekly on Tuesday and Thursday at midnight, arriving the following evening, but after that year a horse-post was introduced, giving a transmission time of ten hours. Post-boys were invariably horse-mounted, but were not supported by 'stages', or relays, of post-horses allowing continuous travel, until about 1750.

At that time postage charges increased with distance, but the entrustment of the mails to the new-fangled railway service from the late 1830s onwards, enforced the need for a more uniform system, one more commensurate with a mechanical form of transport. Charge by distance was replaced by charge by weight, and this principle applies today. The new General Post Office set up in 1840 regularised the mail service, and within 21 years Edinburgh began construction of its new GPO − on the site of the highly successful Theatre Royal (see THEATRES).

This was built on the corner of Waterloo Place and North Bridge, at the east end of Princes Street. Opened in 1861, the building was connected to the railway below by conveyor belt, although vehicular access (from Calton Road) was always less than fully convenient. The building was sold to a commercial developer in 1992 and leased back, but the Royal Mail declined to repurchase and was even prepared to pay a penalty (rumoured to be £2 million) rather than continue in the building. All this came as something of a shock to the city population who rightly regarded 'the GPO' as one of the cornerstones of the capital.

PHILATELY

The Scottish Philatelic Society was founded in the capital on 4 November 1893 as the Edinburgh and Leith Stamp Collectors Club, following the display of a number of privately-owned collections at the International Exhibition in Edinburgh three years earlier. The club was initially so dominated by German denizens of the city that its earliest records were written in German, and the Kaiser was toasted on social occasions!

The club became the Scottish Philatelic Society in 1897, and successfully organised the 5th Philatelic Congress of Great Britain in the city in 1913. A separate Edinburgh Philatelic Society was formed in 1927.

Prisons

Her Majesty's Prison in Edinburgh is situated at Saughton, on the west of the city. Saughton was opened in 1925 to replace the Calton Gaol (see below), and consists of five separate three-storey cell blocks, each arranged around a central atrium. Accommodation comprises 429 cells, plus six for segregation purposes, a dormitory for housing 40, a hospital ward, and a 20-place hostel providing training for freedom. More than 600 prisoners were incarcerated in 1995.

A mesh fence surrounds the 36-acre site, replacing the more conventional wall. The architecture is incongruously described by the Penguin Guide to the *Buildings of Scotland* as 'harled with red sandstone dressings . . . shaped gables and crenellations give a false jollity'. The last execution at Saughton took place on 15 September 1951 (*see* EXECUTIONS).

History

Edinburgh's traditional prison was the Tolbooth, which stood near St Giles until being demolished in 1817. (This should not be confused with the Canongate Tolbooth, built in 1591, and still surviving as a museum, having closed as a prison in 1840. Leith also had a Tolbooth from 1565 until 1824).

Known popularly as 'The Heart of Midlothian', the city's Tolbooth began its municipal service as town hall and customs office, as well as a prison. A two-storey extension at the building's western end was used for public executions. For much of the 16th century, this was the meeting-place for the Scottish Parliament, until Charles I insisted that his northern capital pay for the construction of the present Parliament House (*see* PARLIAMENTARY REPRESENT-ATION).

For a building housing Scotland's parliament, the Tolbooth had a less than effective sewage-disposal system. A visitor

Canongate Tolbooth was built in 1591 and was used as a prison until 1840. It now houses the People's Story Museum, run by the City Council. The site of Edinburgh's city tolbooth is further up the Royal Mile, marked by the Heart of Midlothian emblem. (City of Edinburgh Council)

to the building in the late 18th century had to beat a hasty retreat after finding:

> no ventilation, water nor privy : filth was thrown into a hole at the foot of the stair leading to a drain so completely choked as to serve no other purpose but filling the gaol with a disagreeable stench. (Arnot).

The better-off prisoners therein were able to pay for some semblance of freedom within the building, but debtors and children had to endure dreadful conditions. As late as 1813 an Act of Parliament proposed the construction of a replacement prison, as the Tolbooth, described as 'much decayed, insecure and incommodiously situated', was being used to house those appearing on trial at the High Court.

The aforementioned Act specified that a new prison should be built in the High Street area to the east of Parliament Square, but within a year this was amended to allow a larger site to be selected elsewhere. Two locations considered were East Princes Street Gardens – which resulted in public protest – and the Calton Hill, next to the existing Bridewell. In those days, access to the hill involved climbing, there being no road access from east or west, and an amended Act of 1814 allowed for a new bridge over Leith Wynd from Waterloo Place (see BRIDGES). The foundation stone for the gaol was laid in September 1815, but strangely, by the following year, yet another Act allowed for the building of a small gaol back at Parliament Square, and this was ready by 1817, when the Tolbooth was demolished.

Scotland's largest gaol then took shape on the Calton Hill, adjoining the Robert Adam-designed Bridewell, on the site now occupied by St Andrew's House. Lord Cockburn deplored the choice of site commenting 'it was a piece of undoubted bad taste to give so glorious an eminence to a prison'. This was despite the existence there already of the Bridewell, a 'house of correction' moved from unsuitable accommodation near the Bristo Port. Built in 1791-6, the building housed 52 working cells, 129 sleeping cells, and 13 workrooms in its four storeys. It placed emphasis on 'correction' – what passed then for rehabilitation through forced labour, rather than punishment.

Designed by Archibald Elliot, the new Calton gaol was designed to house prisoners from all over Scotland, the Town Council being required to pay no more than £8,000 towards its £27,500 building costs. The gaol comprised a turreted block facing Regent Road, and castellated watchtowers to west and east, (Robert Louis Stevenson described the gaol as 'castellated to the extent of folly'), all wrapped around by a curtain wall rising sheer from the cliff on the south side. This wall has survived the prison's closure, giving passengers arriving at the Waverley station below, the understandable impression that they are seeing Edinburgh Castle for the first time. To the west of the site, hard against the truncated Burial Ground, is the castellated Governor's House, presently empty.

Probably the most famous prisoners the Calton contained were a number of 'Red Clydesiders' convicted during the First World War for publicly opposing conscription and the drafting of labour. Their written accounts of incarceration on the Calton Hill do not tally, as prison historian Joy Cameron points out, (see

BIBLIOGRAPHY), James Maxton finding the prison officers congenial, and willing to join the Independent Labour Party, while David Kirkwood described the Gaol as 'a terrible place calculated to depress the spirit of the strongest'. Its successor building, St Andrew's House, can be fairly depressing too.

Public Health

Responsibility for the health of Edinburgh's citizens presently lies with the Lothian Health Board, established in 1974. This took over the running of the National Health hospitals in the city, although the recent establishment of N.H.S. Trusts has changed the network of Edinburgh health care (see HOSPITALS). The Board has also taken over some of the functions of the former City Health Department, superseded in 1974, while the Environmental Health Department (of Edinburgh District Council) undertook the city's other former responsibilities to do with physical factors affecting health until April 1996. Since that time, these functions have been taken over by the new City Council.

This covers such areas as food hygiene, control of infectious diseases, sea and airport health, noise control, clean air, pest control and various public health nuisances. It administers the city's mortuaries, skin clinic, the Mortonhall Crematorium, city cemeteries, and the Disinfector Station. Animal welfare is also this department's responsibility, including the conduct of slaughtering, and running of kennels and catteries.

Edinburgh is very fortunate in having a highly-efficient Environmental Health team, one which is a suitable heir to a long tradition of municipal concern about living conditions in the city. It seems that public awareness of the department's work is not as high as it should be, as, for example, many more 'neighbour noise nuisance' problems could be resolved if the city authorities were notified more frequently about this growing social problem.

History

Edinburgh appears to have pioneered the appointment of a city official responsible for health when, in July 1584, surgeon James Henrysoun (c1560–1629) was asked to advise the Town Council on how to combat the Plague. Ten per cent of the population had been lost to an epidemic ten years previously, and when a new outbreak was reported at Wemyss in Fife, Henrysoun was charged with the daunting task of personally confirming this information, and then preparing the city to withstand the spread of the dreaded contagion.

The city's response to the confirmation of the outbreak in Fife comprised the usual measures ranging from the punitive to the compassionate. While threatening its citizens with summary execution for not disclosing news of any outbreak in the city – hanging for men, drowning for women – Edinburgh immediately sent alms for the relief of the Fife victims' families.

Unfortunately, Henrysoun could do little to protect Edinburgh after the first case had been discovered in a house in Fleshmarket Close in April 1585. The house concerned was closed and its remaining inhabitants isolated. Diarist James Melville recorded that in November that year he had walked from the Netherbow to the West Port westwards through the city 'in whilk way we saw not three persons'.

The epidemic was to last five years, during which Henrysoun lost his wife to the illness. Nevertheless, the city appeared well pleased with his work, including the establishment of a camp for sufferers at Purvis Acre, a little to the north of Blackford Hill. The camp was divided into clean and foul areas, the former for those suspected of carrying the illness, the latter for victims who had definitely contracted it. Henrysoun was soon appointed Principal Medical Officer to the city on a salary of £20 annually, while being permitted to carry on private practice. The grateful city also exempted him from the future payment of rates and taxes.

Henrysoun continues to appear in the annals of Edinburgh's medical history, advising on the replacement of the Dyngwall leper's hospital (on the present site of the Waverley Station, outside the city walls). Following his advice, a new hospital was opened at Greenside, to the north-west of the Calton Hill in 1591. Two of the five lepers admitted were allowed to take their wives, who were charged with carrying out all domestic chores. Each patient was pensioned.

In 1618 Henrysoun appears to have accompanied the Lord Provost and councillors on what we would now call a 'fact finding' visit to Comiston Springs to view the possible conduiting of a gravitational water supply into Edinburgh. Undoubtedly, Henrysoun must have realised the value of such a facility; the fact that it was not constructed for another 60 years was due to fund-raising problems (*see* WATER SUPPLY).

That Henrysoun's appointment as City Medical Officer did not survive him is evidenced by the fact that the appointment of a Medical Officer of Health for Edinburgh in 1862 is generally regarded as the city's, and Scotland's, first. It was prompted by the discovery that a collapsed tenement in the city had accommodated 100 people, 35 of whom died in the accident. This tragedy is commemorated at the top of Paisley's Close, 101 High Street, by a relief sculpture dedicated to one of the victims, a young man who, from the debris, urged on his rescuers with the words 'Heave awa' lads, I'm no' deid yet', although he subsequently succumbed to his injuries.

The appointee was Dr Henry Littlejohn (1826–1914), who in 1865 produced *A Report on the Sanitary Condition of the City of Edinburgh*, now regarded as a classic of its kind, and which speedily enabled the necessary reforms in hygiene and housing to be tackled. Littlejohn is credited with the introduction of measures which made certain infectious diseases compulsorily notifiable. This system was adopted nationally, despite the opposition originally put up against it by many members of the medical profession.

Littlejohn held the post until the ripe old age of 82, among his many achievements being the establishment of a fever hospital at Colinton Mains, now the City Hospital. Markets and slaughterhouses were moved out of the Lauriston area, and a start was made on eradicating the city's chronic inability to dispose of its effluent properly (*see also* WATER SUPPLY and SEWERAGE), something the city cannot claim to have dealt with properly until the 1970s.

Littlejohn's successors were:

Dr Maxwell Williamson (1908–23) who was principally concerned with TB, maternity and child welfare problems and the spread of venereal disease.

Dr William Robertson (1923–30), previously Medical Officer for Leith, and a pioneer in the immunisation of schoolchildren against illness. He also introduced a voluntary code of notification of food poisoning, and encouraged public co-operation in health matters.

Dr John Guy (1930–38), Dr William Clark (1938–53), Dr Henry Edmund Seiler (1953-63), and Dr James Leith Gilloran (1964–74), have held the position subsequently.

Pubs

Edinburgh has 662 public houses (1995) licensed by Edinburgh District Council. Taking the city's population as 420,000, this produces a ratio of one pub per 634 inhabitants. Ninety years previously, the ratio was 1:305, in 1920 1:514, and in 1962 1:535, indicating growing control of the licensing trade in Edinburgh.

At the time of writing, only a small number of Edinburgh pubs brew their own beer (*see* INDUSTRY: BREWING), in contrast to the traditional pattern of public houses in centuries gone by invariably selling their own products.

The opening hours of the capital's pubs are among the most liberal in the country, as might be expected of a major tourist centre. Unfortunately this has not always been the case, Scottish licensing laws dating from May 1904 required 'time please, ladies and gentlemen' to be called at ten p.m. each evening (except Sunday, when pubs did not open at all) until the laws were relaxed in December 1976. (At the time of writing, a late-night 'curfew' has been brought into operation because of alcohol-fuelled misbehaviour after midnight, but the licensing times are still more liberal than anyone thought possible up to 1976.)

The Scottish capital played a crucial part in the movement to change the law in the first half of the 1970s, an enterprising licencee in the Polwarth area discovering that the International Festival could be categorised as a special event, like a traditional market or fair, worthy of requesting extended licensing hours from the local authority. Legislation resulting from the recommendations of the Clayson Committee on Licensing has brought about the present, more tolerant, licensing laws.

A full description of the city's pubs would require a sustained campaign of careful research and site visits by the author, and this could only interfere with the speedy production of this book. Instead, a brief mention will be given of the more historic of the city's hostelries (*see also* HOTELS).

Edinburgh's oldest pub is probably the Sheep Heid in Duddingston village, this hostelry claiming to have been serving since the 14th century. The present building, within strolling distance of the bird sanctuary, is comparatively modern. As late as 1952, author Marie Stuart reminisced about seeing cavalry horses from Piershill barracks (*see* MILITARY HISTORY) drawn up in a semi-circle outside the Sheep Heid as

Edinburgh has more than 660 pubs, considerably fewer than in years gone by, with more generous opening hours. This shot shows the interior of the Abbotsford in Rose Street, forever associated with the city's poetic fraternity. (City of Edinburgh Council)

their riders had tankards of beer handed out to them. However, rivalling it for the claim to be the capital's oldest hostelries are the Golf Tavern and the White Hart Inn.

The former looks out over Bruntsfield Links, the date 1456 emblazoned above the door, although the present building appears to date from 1717. The Royal Burgess Golfing Society (*see* GOLF) used to regard this as their '19th hole' throughout most of the 19th century, before moving furth of the city centre, but the pub still prospers. The White Hart Inn, established in the Grassmarket in the 18th century,

claims to be the oldest public house in unbroken existence in the city. Unusually for Edinburgh, it was a genuine coaching-inn, with as many as 96 coach services arriving and departing each week in 1810. Robert Burns and the Wordsworths stayed here, and the pub's window seats were in much demand when public executions took place in the Grassmarket a few yards away.

History

As already noted, Edinburgh's history of licensed premises is slightly unusual in that the city's hostelries, before the 19th century, did not cater for the coaching trade, this business being largely serviced by inns on the city's periphery, as at Duddingston, Leith, and Newhaven. What was characteristic about Edinburgh pubs, or 'howffs', in the years before licensed control of alcohol, was the tradition, in the Old Town at least, of catering for customers arriving direct from their work, whether the drinker be an advocate or water caddie, and for whom an immediate return home to the wife and children seemed not to present a pressing priority.

In many pubs, dining or drinking clubs formed, some of them commemorated by writers and poets, such as Robert Fergusson and Robert Burns, who valued their companionship highly. Burns, for example, relished his membership of the Crochallan Fencibles at Douglas's Tavern in Anchor Close, next to the present City Chambers. One night, one of their number – and the club's military name was entirely facetious – drunkenly made his way to the Castle and demanded its immediate surrender. Since the duty officer had only recently left the same tavern himself, the victorious 'Fencible' was allowed to enter the stronghold where he promptly fell asleep in the officer's quarters. Needless to say, his triumph made him the subject of much ribbing when he made his way groggily back to the city the next day.

This is only one of the many stories which have emanated from the city's hostelries, historian Robert Chambers recording that a High Court judge like Lord Newton did not consider himself at his best until after consuming six bottles of claret, while another encountered no besmirchment of his judicial reputation when found sleeping off his libations among chimney-sweeping equipment in the guardhouse in the High Street.

The casual consumption of alcohol by all classes in Edinburgh before the construction of the New Town may not be unconnected with the city's chronic shortage of water. The largest city in Scotland had, before 1680, a mere handful of draw-wells in addition to hand-drawing water from the Nor' and Burgh lochs, and when the needs of livestock are taken into account, the problem takes on major proportions (see WATER SUPPLY). Small wonder that drinking large amounts of alcohol was regarded as socially acceptable for both sexes – indeed it may have been healthier than drinking the water supply of the time!

Oysters fresh from Newhaven or Cramond, and – until the city's pollution decided otherwise – eels from the Nor' Loch were favourite foodstuffs for the Edinburgh pub tippler. 'Oyster cellars' were popular in the 18th century, English visitor Edward Topham noting with surprise that a large mixed group enjoyed oysters and porter in a 'howff' below street level. Brandy and dancing followed before the ladies of the party departed. They were no doubt anxious to return home before the ten o'clock drum announced Edinburgh's 'slopping out' procedure which was a perpetual menace to city drinkers returning home without a caddie to guide them and shout 'haud your hand' to the unseen residents living above the narrow stinking streets (see SEWERAGE).

A different hazard was encountered by a

group of ladies who were making their merry way down the High Street one moonlit night after what we would nowadays call a 'hen night', only to mistake the shadow of the Tron Kirk for a dark-flowing river. One hopes there were spectators around at the time to enjoy the sight of the female party removing their shoes and stockings before kilting up their skirts and wading to the far 'shore'.

As might be expected, Edinburgh's brewing industry has found plenty of willing customers for its products in its home city, and any modern beer drinker will tell you that the locally-produced beers 'don't travel well' and can only be enjoyed in the city's pubs. This has certainly not slowed the growing popularity in Edinburgh of foreign-produced beers, nor the national trend towards lager consumption, much of which is Scottish-produced. All this is a far cry from the Edinburgh Ale served in the famous Dowie's Tavern, between St Giles and the Cowgate, a libation which historian Robert Chambers recorded was 'a potent fluid which almost glued the lips of the drinker together'.

Quarries

Edinburgh's quarries are used for refuse disposal nowadays rather than for stone production. Yet there is a long tradition of quarrying in the Edinburgh area, including a surprising amount once carried on within the city boundaries. It does not require a geologist's eye to detect quarrying evidence in the artificially pitted topography of Bruntsfield Links, and Salisbury Crags are permanently scarred by excavatory work.

A list of former quarries in Edinburgh appears below. Further information can be obtained from the authoritative book *Building Stones of Edinburgh* (*see* BIBLIOGRAPHY). This also identifies the stone used in the construction of many Edinburgh buildings, and more information on that subject can also be found in the Edinburgh edition of the Penguin *Buildings of Scotland* guide.

FORMER EDINBURGH QUARRIES

ABBEYHILL
Sandstone was quarried in the Abbeyhill area, east of the Quarry Holes complex (*see* overleaf), in the late 17th century. Little else is known of this quarry, including the exact location.

BABERTON
A sandstone quarry opened here in the 1890s was abandoned shortly afterwards 'since the stone was so full of fossils as to be useless' as the book *Building Stones of Edinburgh* records. Palaeontologists should be pleased!

BARNBOUGLE
A coastal quarry is believed to have been worked here in the 1530s, west of the Almond river-mouth, to supply stone by water transport to Leith for Holyrood.

BARNTON PARK
A comparatively recent site for sandstone extraction, Barnton stone seems to have been quarried here in the second half of the

19th century when Craighall stone was proving difficult to extract. The quarry, derelict since 1914, is now flooded and poses as a hazard for golfers on the Bruntsfield course near Davidson's Mains.

BEARFORD'S PARKS

This was the name given to what is now Princes Street, before the construction of the New Town. Sandstone was quarried at various points along the south face of this ridge, the builders of the Scott Monument discovering a 40 feet (12 metre) deep pit which had to be infilled before the monument's foundations were laid.

BLACKFORD

Now completely filled in since 1993, this deep quarry was originally gouged into the south side of Blackford Hill, just east of the Agassiz Rock. It has been used subsequently as a storage site for the local highways authority, although an older and much smaller quarry site survives a few yards to the west, popular with the rock-climbing fraternity.

BLACKHALL

see Maidencraig

BRUNTSFIELD (CITY QUARRY)

The area south of the Burgh Loch (see also LOCHS) was extensively quarried at one time, although to no great depth, from present-day Bruntsfield, through Marchmont to the area beneath Salisbury Crags. The area produced mainly rubble, some of which can still be seen in the remains of the city walls, particularly in the Lauriston area (see CITY WALLS), but sandstone was also worked in the 16th century.

CITY QUARRY

see Bruntsfield

CORSTORPHINE

see Ravelston

CRAIGLEITH

Edinburgh's deepest and most impressive quarry at one time, Craigleith produced pale orange stone from the Lower Carboniferous period. Much of the material found its way into the building of Edinburgh Castle and the National Monument ('Scotland's Disgrace') on the Calton Hill. First worked in 1616, it produced stone only intermittently in the 20th century, and now, filled in, is the site of a retail development. Yet 1860s photographs show an artificially-hewn cliff-face more than 200 feet (60 metres) deep!

CRAIGMILLAR

Rocks of Upper Old Red Sandstone were used to supply the Palace of Holyroodhouse with stone from here in the 16th century, but from the 19th, working had been reduced in a complex of quarries. One of these is now used for waste disposal, west of Craigmillar Castle, which used Craigmillar sandstone in its construction.

CRAMOND

There is evidence that a coastal quarry existed at Cramond around 1535, but like Barnbougle to the west, may have been opened specially for construction materials for Holyrood. Little else is known.

GRANTON

Quarrying appears to have been undertaken at Granton in three phases – in the 1530s when construction at Holyrood placed so much demand on the nation's quarrymen, in the 1550s, when a bulwark was being constructed at Leith, and for about 70 years from the 1830s. The construction of Granton harbour by the Buccleuch family in early Victorian times caused the excavation of Granton Sea Quarry which reached 80 feet in depth and eight acres in area. It was flooded by the sea in 1856 and thereafter serviced the cause of Science by becoming the base for the Scottish Marine Biological station until it moved to Scotland's west coast.

HAILES

Probably second only to Craigleith as Edinburgh's greatest quarry, Hailes seems to have produced mudstone and three types of sandstone for around 350 years. It was recorded as being 90 feet (27 metres) deep in 1845 and no fewer than 139 men worked here 50 years later. At one time quarrying on site was taking place north and south of the Union Canal, with a tunnel connecting the workings. Abandoned after the Second World War, Hailes quarry is now infilled as Hailes Park (1967) and part of Kingsknowe golf course.

JOPPA

Joppa's Quarry Park has playing fields at two different levels, but only the name indicates the existence here of a former quarry, although older residents can still recall the exodus of rats from the site when in-filling reached an advanced stage, some time before the site opened as a park in 1933. Two earlier quarries existed on the shoreline.

LONDON ROAD
see Quarry Holes

MAIDENCRAIG

Immediately west of Craigleith quarry was Maidencraig or Blackhall quarry, first recorded as supplying stone for Edinburgh Castle in 1628. Materials for the original North Bridge, and steps for the Theatre Royal, were produced in the 1770s, but otherwise less is known about this quarry than its larger neighbour to the east. It appears to have been flooded by the middle of the 19th century, and is now filled in and redeveloped.

NIDDRIE

Stone particularly suitable for use in the construction of chimneys was quarried in a site at the west end of Newcraighall Road from the 16th century intermittently up to the 19th.

QUARRY HOLES (LONDON ROAD)

Quarrying for sandstone seems to have been carried on intermittently north of the Calton Hill up to the end of the 17th century.

RAVELSTON

Limestone quarrying was undertaken in the area to the north-east of Corstorphine Hill from the 1530s, continuing intermittently until the Second World War. Monumental stone was a principal product of these workings, all of which are now sealed with the exception of Craigcrook Loch. The south slope of the hill itself, now famously the location of Edinburgh Zoo, has a number of abandoned quarries imaginatively adapted as animal enclosures by Patrick Geddes and Frank Mears (*see* ZOOS).

REDHALL

Sandstone appears to have been worked in this quarry in the Slateford area for around 150 years. Its stone had the useful virtue of been soft enough to work when newly dug, hardening on exposure to the air. The proximity of the canal allowed easy access to central Edinburgh from 1822, but work seems to have ceased by 1895.

SALISBURY

From 1529 to 1821, dolerite on Salisbury Crags, in the Queen's Park, was quarried, the height of the quarries' location making its transport to such building projects as 16th century Holyrood comparatively easy. James Hutton (the 'founder of modern geology') is forever associated with geological investigations at this location, but it required court action, in the increasingly environment-conscious city that was 19th century Edinburgh, to stop the commercial destruction of this great cliff.

SOCIETY

The area round the Bristo Port (near Greyfriars) was sometimes known as Society, after the Society of Brewers whose name became corrupted into 'Bristo'. This particular quarry was situated at the west end of what is now Chambers Street and provided rubble for Parliament House. It is believed to have been sealed in 1654 after around 120 years working, during which time, in 1632, no fewer than 20 labourers were engaged there.

WARDIE

Opened to supply stone for Leith Citadel at the orders of General Monk in 1657, little else is known about this quarry immediately south-east of Granton.

Other Edinburgh quarrying sites have been identified at Broughton (near present-day Picardy Place), in the West End, at Marchmont, and at an unidentified site in Leith.

Racing

Edinburgh's racecourse is outside the city itself, situated some five miles eastwards, at Musselburgh, and officially called Musselburgh from 10 January 1996. The location of the course alongside the shore of the Firth of Forth helps to protect it from the worst of Scotland's weather.

The course is categorised as class D for both Flat and National Hunt racing, being ten furlongs in length, with a four furlongs run-in. The average gate is around 2,000, while the average prize money for owners is £20,000 for a day's racing. Horses winning Flat races in the period 1990–94 comprised 43 per cent of favourites, with 46 per cent of National Hunt favourites winning over the 1989–94 period.

Racing publications suggest that, for flat racing over five furlongs at Musselburgh, horses allocated low numbers have an advantage when the stalls are located on the stand side of the course; when the stalls are on the far rail, the reverse is the case. Over seven furlongs (1,400 metres), high numbers appear best placed. For National

Hunt racing, the hurdles appear to favour front-runners.

While certainly not a Royal Ascot class course, Musselburgh enjoyed a royal visit in July 1995 when HM The Queen opened the new stand there. In comparison with Ascot and other festivals, the cheap entrance fee allows ordinary mortals the opportunity to partake in this sport of kings without having to travel west or, more importantly, south. At the present time, East Lothian District Council subsidises racing at Musselburgh to a certain extent, although there are strong historical reasons for including this sport facility as being within Edinburgh's orbit.

History

Although recognised throughout the British racing fraternity as Edinburgh racecourse, the exact location of this track is in the town of Musselburgh, and that is how it is known in Scotland. But the racecourse here owes its origins to neither of these communities, but to another place on the sea shore west of Musselburgh – the port of Leith.

Leith Links once merged as one with Leith Sands, the area being an extremely popular place with local people, before the construction of the docks in the 19th century deprived them of the seaward site of this local amenity. There was a slight incline from the Links to the Sands which meant that, at low tide, a significant amount of racing area was uncovered. Horse racing had a long history on the Sands, and in 1665, two silver cups were given by Charles II and by the City of Edinburgh as prizes. Thus began the annual formal racing bonanza that divided Leithers as to its worth.

Although annual, races were held at differing times of the year without conforming to any regular date. Eventually, by the middle of the 18th century, agreement had been made to establish this particular meeting during the summer. Also, what had originally been scheduled for one day, expanded to fill two, and then to a racing festival lasting a week, with more prizes on offer. Leith Races attracted entries from all over the country, particularly from the north of England.

The original layout of the course stretched from what is now the foot of Constitution Street to Seafield, amounting to a distance of two miles there and back. Apparently, the rules were such that most races were run as the best of three heats, meaning that 12 miles would be run before a prize was won as each heat consisted of two circuits.

The King's Cup was the most sought-after prize, until it was replaced by a Gold Plate in 1720, and throughout the 18th century, the evolution from Cups to Plates, to Purses and Subscription Races, became the norm. However, Leith Races weren't loved by everyone, and the drunken behaviour by some punters attending the festival was frowned upon by many. Wet boggy conditions were hardly congenial to horse racing anyway, and plans were soon discussed to move the Festival up to the Meadows. This move fell through, and in 1816 the dry flats of Musselburgh won out.

Some 20 years later, Leith Races were revitalised and brought back to life to complement the racing at Musselburgh.

However, church groups objected, and the racing tradition in Leith eventually came to an end, although Leithers continued to use their Sands until further dock developments – the Albert Dock (1869), Edinburgh (1881), and Imperial (1904) – deprived them of this amenity, and permanently exiled racing from the city itself.

(Frank Reid)

Railways

With only 4 per cent of local journeys in Lothian Region being undertaken by rail, it is fair to assume that the railway network in and around Edinburgh is less important than it once was. In particular, where the city once had a total of more than 50 passenger stations within the city boundary, now (1995) it has only seven (Waverley, Haymarket, South Gyle, Dalmeny, Slateford, Kingsknowe and Wester Hailes). A recent study showed that the number of stations served within 15 route-miles from Edinburgh's Waverley Station fell from 65 to 15 between 1910 and 1985 (*see* BIBLIOGRAPHY under Transport).

Edinburgh's railways are nowadays owned by Railtrack and, at the time of writing, operated by a number of sectors of what until recently constituted the national railway system, British Rail. The basic network in Edinburgh is centred on the Waverley station, situated between Princes Street and the Old Town, with services currently supplied by Inter-City Cross-Country, East Coast, West Coast

and by ScotRail. In 1995 Railtrack was about to embark on a £1.5 million initiative to improve the Waverley's overall roof.

Waverley is a major stopping-point on the East Coast main-line between London (King's Cross) and Aberdeen. Indeed, with the line between London and Edinburgh electrified (25kV), and the 133 miles northwards to Aberdeen still operated by diesel traction, a break of journey in Edinburgh is often essential. Interestingly, it is possible to reach London by electric train from Edinburgh in either direction – by the East Coast main-line eastwards via Newcastle, or westwards through Haymarket and Slateford to join the West Coast main-line at Carstairs. Night trains, at the time of writing, use the latter route.

History

Edinburgh's first railway was an unambitious concern called the Edinburgh & Dalkeith Railway, constructed in the 1820s and 30s to a gauge of 4ft 6 in (1.37 metres), to bring coal to the capital at the same time as the Union Canal. The city's first rail terminal was at St Leonards, reached by trains from Niddrie up a 1 in 30 gradient through a 572 yard (522 metre) tunnel from the Duddingston Loch area, with a stationary steam engine supplying assistance by way of a rope. (The tunnel and trackbed are preserved as a walkway, freight services having ceased in the late 1960s, a century after the last regular passengers trains.)

The Edinburgh & Dalkeith used Niddrie as the crucial point of its operations, with 'arms' of its x-shaped system radiating to St

STATION	LOCATION	YEAR OPENED	YEAR CLOSED
Abbeyhill	London Rd (A1)	1869	1964
Balerno	Station Loan	1874	1943
Balgreen Halt	Balgreen Road	1934	1967
Barnton	Whitehouse Rd	1894	1951
Blackford Hill	Blackford Ave	1884	1962
Bonnington Rd	Newhaven Rd	1847	1947
Canal St	Waverley Bridge	1847	1868
Colinton	Bridge Road	1874	1943
Corstorphine	Station Rd	1902	1967
Craigleith	Queensferry Rd	1879	1962
Craiglockhart	Colinton Rd	1887	1962
Currie	Station Rd	1874	1943
Dalry Road	Dalry Rd	1900	1962
Davidson's Mains	Barnton Ave	1894	1951
Duddingston & Craigmillar	Duddingston Rd West	1884	1962
East Pilton	Crewe Rd North	1934	1962
Easter Road	Easter Road	1895	1947
Easter Rd Park	Hawkhill Ave	1950	1967
Gilmerton	A7	1874	1933
Gorgie East	Slateford Rd	1884	1962
Granton	Granton Square	1846	1925
Granton Rd	Granton Rd	1879	1962
Hailes	Lanark Rd	1927	1943
Haymarket	Haymarket Terr.	1842	
House o' Hill Halt	Corbiehill Ave	1937	1951
Jock's Lodge	Restalrig Rd S	1846	1848
Joppa (1)	Milton Rd (A1)	1847	1859
Joppa (2)	Brunstane Rd	1859	1964
Junction Rd	Gt. Junction St	1869	1947
Juniper Green	Station Rd	1874	1943
Kingsknowe	Kingsknowe Rd	1850s	
Leith Central	Leith Walk/Easter Rd	1903	1952
Leith North	Lindsay Rd	1879	1962
Leith Walk	Leith Walk	1868	1930
Lothian Rd	Lothian Rd	1847	1870
Meadowbank	London Rd (A1)	1848	1900
Meadowbank Stadium	Marionville Rd	1986	1988
Merchiston	Bonaly Place	1882	1965
Morningside Rd	Morningside Rd	1884	1962
Murrayfield	West Coates Terr	1879	1962
Newhaven	Craighall Rd	1884	1962
Newington	Mayfield Gardens	1884	1962
Niddrie	Newcraighall	1848	1869
North Leith	Commercial St	1846	1947
Piershill	Clockmill Lane	1891	1964
Pinkhill	Traquair Park East	1902	1967

STATION	LOCATION	YEAR OPENED	YEAR CLOSED
Portobello	Brighton Place	1846	1964
Powderhall	Broughton Road	1895	1917
Princes Street	Rutland St	1870	1965
St Leonard's	St Leonard's Street	1831	1860
Saughton	Saughton Rd N	1842	1921
Scotland Street	Scotland Street	1842	1868
Slateford	Slateford Rd	1848	
South Gyle	South Gyle Rd	1985	
South Leith	Constitution St	1831	1905
Trinity	Trinity Crescent	1842	1925
Waverley	Waverley Bridge	1846	
Wester Hailes	Wester Hailes Drive	1987	

Leonards, to Leith, to Fisherrow (Musselburgh), with the fourth arm penetrating south to the Lothian coalfield, whence came Edinburgh's fuel. The Leith branch was an important limb of the system, running through Portobello (where an embankment can still be seen alongside Baileyfield Road) and Seafield to reach a terminus just off Constitution Street. Passenger services were introduced from 1831 with horses providing motive power. The E & D, while slow to realise the commercial potential of passengers, had enough gumption to introduce a 'bathers' special'. The line was very well-managed, once its 'conductor guards', issuing tickets on the trains themselves, overcame the public's reluctance to tell 'a spierin' loon' where they wished to go, before a ticket could be issued! The line's soubriquet, the 'Innocent Railway', was an apt description of its character, although it is not correct that it was so-called because of its safety record, there having been a number of accidents.

Main-line railways arrived in Edinburgh in the following decade, with the Edinburgh & Glasgow reaching Haymarket from the west in 1842, a line from Granton and Leith climbing to Canal Street, at the north-east end of Waverley Bridge, and the North British Railway opening from Waverley station to Berwick in 1846. A joint station sprang up on the site known as Waverley (named after the abbey of the same name in Surrey, adopted as a character's name by Sir Walter Scott).

Before going on to examine the history of the Waverley Station, it may be interesting to mention Canal Street station, where travellers to Aberdeen in the 1840s and 1850s began their journeys in a train descending to Scotland Street through a 1,000 yard (914 metre) tunnel by cable traction. From Scotland Street, steam power would take the train forward to Granton, where the world's first train ferry, the *Leviathan*, carried the rail vehicles across to Burntisland. There were also services to Leith (Citadel) station from Canal Street, the tunnel with its horrendous 1 in 27 gradient, closing to passenger traffic in 1861 when a new line was constructed through Abbeyhill, Easter Road, Leith Walk (at Shrubhill), and Powderhall, to rejoin the existing line in the Trinity area, and also provide a new route to Leith. The site of the tunnel mouth under Princes Street is still visible from Waverley's platform 19.

Waverley was originally three stations in one, plus three separate freight depots. With only two through passenger platforms, it goes without saying that the Waverley was at one time a nightmare for passengers and staff. It was claimed that the main platform was so narrow that a tall man could straddle its width, and *The Times* devoted a furious editorial to the station's limitations. Not until 1892 was the North British Railway able to rationalise its occupancy of the site, constructing two termini back-to-back, with four through platforms, each capable of dealing with two trains simultaneously. There were 21 platforms (now reduced to 13), and its overall area of 23 acres (9.3 hectares) made it the biggest station in Britain at the time. Its signalling was modernised with colour-lights in 1935-37, replaced in 1976 by a new signalling network centred on a power box immediately to the south of the station controlling over 220 route miles (352 kilometres).

With its modern food court and improved facilities generally, the Waverley Station has made a conscious effort to brighten its image. It could do even more if

Edinburgh suburban trains looked like this in the early 1950s. Here, an Outer Circle train approaches Morningside Road station from the east, with a V1 locomotive hauling a set of articulated non-corridor coaches. The loco was designed by Edinburgh's Sir Nigel Gresley, responsible for the world's fastest steam engine Mallard, *which reached a speed of 126 mph in 1938. Gresley's birthplace in Dublin Street is not marked with a plaque at the time of writing.* (W.S. Sellar)

escalators were installed to improve pedestrian access and egress. In 1925 a newspaper editorial condemned the railway company for having no plans to instal escalators, and predicted that such an omission would make Waverley so unattractive to commuters that Edinburgh's suburban stations would close. It was almost entirely correct.

One closed Edinburgh railway being considered for possible reopening to passengers is the South Suburban railway. Opened in 1884, the line runs from Haymarket Central Junction on the west, the line formerly including stations at Gorgie East, Craiglockhart, Morningside Road, Blackford Hill, Newington, Craigmillar and Duddingston, before joining the East Coast main-line from London just east of Portobello. This last-named station was also considered as part of the circular route, as were those at Piershill and Abbeyhill. Contrary to often-repeated opinion, the line was surveyed and planned by George Trimble of Trimble and Peddie Ltd, and not by Sir Thomas Bouch, builder of the doomed Tay Bridge.

Proposals to reopen the 'Sub', as the line is called, were not helped by a price-tag of £100 million being placed on such a development in the 1980s, regarded by many local groups as excessive (and since scaled down to around £20 million), particularly when the line continues to carry freight, using connections with Millerhill at the eastern end and to Slateford and Haymarket on the west. Perhaps one day passengers will be able to travel the line regularly again as they did before closure in 1962.

Princes Street Gardens were bisected by the Edinburgh and Glasgow Railway arriving at the General Station (Waverley) from the west in 1846, in spite of the fury of pioneer conservationist Lord Cockburn whose pamphlet *The Best Ways of Ruining the Beauties of Edinburgh* was a masterpiece of its kind, although published just a little too late (1849). The lines through the Gardens, and the Haymarket and Mound tunnels, were doubled in the 1890s, when the opening of the Forth Bridge had caused the kind of traffic congestion now confined to the city's roads. But it was at Lothian Road that the first trains arrived from London – via the West Coast route opened throughout in 1848.

The Caledonian Railway (which always fancied that the emphasis should be on *The*) built a terminus at Lothian Road which proved to be less temporary than intended, not being replaced by a properly proportioned Princes Street station until the 1890s. The 'Caley' was quick to build to Granton and then Leith, and in the 1890s faced public uproar by proposing a line under the length of Princes Street and by tunnel through the Calton Hill to complete a northside circle. The rival North British managed to head this off by building a short branch to Leith Central, to the relief of both Edinburgh and Leith Town Councils.

In 1923 Edinburgh's railways were grouped into two super-companies, the London and North Eastern taking over the former North British lines, and the London Midland and Scottish absorbing the Caledonian. A campaign of service withdrawals and closures began almost immediately. On pages 283 and 284 are listed those stations past and present within the city's 1974 boundaries.

Locomotive depots existed in the days of steam power at St Margaret's (now the site of Meadowbank House), Haymarket (actually at Roseburn and still open for diesel maintenance), and at Dalry Road (vanished under the Western Approach Road). There were numerous goods yards throughout the city – in 1900 Leith Town Council complained it already had six freight depots and didn't want any more – and a modern marshalling yard was built outside the city at Millerhill in the late 1950s. Its planners totally failed to anticipate the move to bulk freight traffic which required no remarshalling en route, and half the wide expanse of rails is now closed.

Princes Street station, closed in 1965, was located at the junction of Lothian Road and Rutland Street and was some 50 yards from the thoroughfare whose name it adopted. A terminus with only seven platforms, the 'Caley' station was opened in 1894, before the present hotel was built above it. Lacking awkward pedestrian approaches like Waverley's, this was a popular terminus with the travelling public – and also the Royal Family when visiting Holyrood.

Leith Central station, located at the 'Foot of the Walk' at the Duke Street corner, had a curious history. Archival records show that the North British, convinced that their new Leith station would not pay, did everything they could to avoid building it in return for a free hand from the civic authorities in doubling their western approach to Waverley. This does not explain why it was so big – the largest station built from scratch in Britain in the 20th century. Opened without ceremony in 1903, it provided Leithers with an unprecedented journey time to Waverley of only seven minutes, at a penny (½ pence) single fare. However, the unification of the Edinburgh and Leith tram systems in 1923 (see TRAMS), along with Waverley's steps, made the rail journey less attractive. The station closed to passengers in 1952, being utilised as a maintenance depot for 20 years. Demolition was surprisingly slow in following – 1989, and the site is now occupied by a supermarket and Leith Waterworld.

Rivers and Streams

WATER OF LEITH

Some 22 miles (35.2 kilometres) in length, the Water of Leith flows north-eastwards from the Pentland Hills to the Firth of Forth, falling approximately 900 feet (270 metres). It drains an area of 60 square miles (155 square kilometres), where the rainfall is around 44 inches per year (112 centimetres), and the river receives compensation water as required from Harperrig reservoir (see also WATER SUPPLY).

This is the middle of three north-flowing rivers in the Lothians, with the Almond to the west and the Esk to the east. The Water of Leith's principal tributaries are the Malleny and Murray Burns, the latter being culverted for much of its course through the residential areas south of Calder Road. The river itself used to be tidal as far from the sea as Bowling Green Street Bridge, but the new lock arrangements at the entrance to Leith Docks have maintained water at a permanently high level since 1969.

The Water of Leith has been maintained at its former high-water level since 1969. The bridge over the river here at Junction Street is crowned by the 1930s art-deco building which was formerly the State cinema, now used for bingo, while the area on the left of the picture was once Junction Road railway station. (Frank Reid)

From 1843 the Water of Leith supplemented Edinburgh's water supply, although it also supported a surprising number of water-based industries – flour, paper, and snuff mills, both in the Colinton area, and near the river's mouth at Leith, there being some 36 mills along the river's course in the 19th century alone. Regrettably, the river was also used to remove crude sewage from the city, even as late as the second half of the 19th century, its accumulation at Leith being so bad as to require dredging of the main harbour channel (*see* SEWERAGE). Commissioners of the Water of Leith were appointed in 1889 to eradicate this problem.

The Water of Leith is prone to flooding during heavy rain, particularly in the Murrayfield/Roseburn vicinity. However, the worst flooding in living memory took place in August 1948 on the Warriston to Powderhall stretch of the river. Residents in Warriston Crescent found their cellars and gardens inundated, and a large number of greyhounds at Powderhall stadium were unfortunately drowned in their cages. It was one of the few occasions when a rowing boat was the only means of transport in Edinburgh streets.

The improvement in the present-day amenity of Edinburgh's river is attested by the occasional flash of halcyon blue as the

Kingfishers go about their business, even as deep in the city as Murrayfield (*see* WILDLIFE concerning the fauna and flora of this river, and the streams listed below). The river's course is followed by a number of walkways, not as yet continuous from source to mouth, but including most of the picturesque stretches in the Balerno to Colinton corridor, and from Saughton to Warriston.

The **Braid Burn** is the product of the Bonaly and Howden burns which unite in the Colinton area to form the stream which is now augmented by the famous Comiston springs (*see* WATER SUPPLY) before entering the Braidburn Valley Park. The geological excursion guidebook (*see* BIBLIOGRAPHY) for the area describes the Braid Burn as 'a misfit in such a large valley', the Hermitage of Braid gorge having been gouged by displaced floodwater from melting ice in the Water of Leith at Colinton during prehistoric times. After flowing through the Hermitage – surely Britain's most beautiful urban park (*see* PARKS), and the site of a water mill which once produced paper for banknotes – the present-day burn reaches Liberton and Niddrie, forming a confluence with the Pow (or Jordan) Burn at Peffermill.

It then transects Duddingston House policies and heads seawards under yet another name. As the Figgate burn, the waters from the Pentlands thread through Figgate Burn Park and under Portobello Promenade to meet the Forth between the sites of the former harbour and open air swimming pool, the latter demolished in 1987.

A bearer of even more different identities is the **Niddrie Burn**. This rises in the Pentlands near Swanston and carries the names Swanston Burn, Lothian Burn, Burdiehouse Burn, Niddrie Burn, and Brunstane Burn, before discharging into the sea at the city's eastern boundary at Eastfield.

The **River Almond** formed the city boundary on the western side for three miles inland from Cramond, where it meets the sea. This boundary was confirmed in James VI's charter to the city in 1603, before the line was redrawn farther west with the reorganisation of local government in 1975. A small site on the Almond was designated in 1994 for Hindu funeral ceremonies (*see* CEMETERIES AND CREMATORIA). The Almond's main tributary is the Gogar Burn, unusual in that its course is south-westwards for much of its length.

The **Dalry Burn** is no more; this drained the Burgh Loch from Lochrin, near Tollcross, to the Water of Leith. Edinburgh's first paper mill was established here in 1590 (*see* INDUSTRY), but the loch was dry by the 1760s (*see* LOCHS).

For information about the Firth of Forth, see under that heading.

Roads and Streets

Edinburgh's road system became the responsibility of Edinburgh City Council in April 1996, succeeding Lothian Regional Council. In 1993 the city contained 7.5 miles (12 kilometres) of trunk roads, 124 miles (198 kms) of 'A' roads, 102 miles (163 kms) of 'B' and 'C' roads, and 681 miles (1,089 kms) of unclassified roads, making a total of 914 miles (1,462 kms), the equivalent of the distance between Edinburgh and Exeter and back again.

Local government reorganisation has terminated the division of responsibilities which made the Regional authority in Edinburgh undertake street lighting and road maintenance (the latter carried on by a department called Inroads), while the naming of city streets was a District function. Street cleansing, once also a District responsibility, is now carried out by the City Council (*see* CLEANSING).

Unlike most British cities, the Scottish capital has been left unsullied by inner-city motorways, and while road congestion is an everyday fact of life in the centre of Edinburgh, the city has not sacrificed countless historic buildings for road construction, as has happened elsewhere, while such construction would not have guaranteed any elimination of traffic congestion anyway.

One, perhaps the only, disadvantage of the lack of inner-city motorways, is the resulting absence of motorway connections with other parts of Britain, surely a major drawback for a tourist centre. There seems an apparent indifference to this fact by Edinburgh people, probably glad not to have spaghetti-like flyovers in the Leith Street or

Lothianburn Road junction on the city's southern extremity. The diversity of the road signs on the A702 indicate how the City Bypass, the A720, which the vehicles on the left are about to join, has made an enormous contribution to the transport system in the city.

Tollcross areas, as were once proposed, but the seriousness of the lack of a motorway connection to, for example, England, seems not to be a continuing matter of protest. A car or coach journey to London by the A68, A7, A701, or A702, will involve single-lane driving, with all the possible dangers caused by overtaking, within five miles of leaving Edinburgh, or ten miles in the case of supposedly-prestigious A1, which currently has a reputation as a particularly dangerous road. (In contrast, a Glaswegian driver enjoys two- and three-lane carriageway driving from the heart of his or her own city all the way to London).

Even a road journey to or from Glasgow has, until recently, involved congestion in the Corstorphine area, and even after the opening of the City By-pass, a heavily congested four-lane highway (two lanes each way) has had to carry traffic to and from the M8, M9, and Edinburgh Airport, between the Gogar and Newbridge roundabouts. The fact that Edinburgh continues to be Scotland's most important tourist centre in such circumstances is something of a compliment to its attractions for the much-harrassed traveller.

Edinburgh's City By-pass was completed in 1989. Designated the A720, this runs eastwards from the Gogar roundabout on the A8 round to Sherrifhall roundabout just north of Dalkeith, there connecting with the A68 and A7, as well as a spur leading to the A1. Motorists using it can be forgiven for not regarding it as an all-weather highway, with high crosswinds a frequent occurrence, and winter weather a major problem. More investment in windbreaks and landscaping might not go amiss on what has become a vital part of the region's road infrastructure, now made even busier by the arrival of the M8 from the west.

At the time of writing, there is a proposal to extend the By-pass northwards to the Forth Bridge, thus lightening the pressure on the Barnton roundabout and Queensferry Road by offering citybound motorists the options of entering Edinburgh from Corstorphine, Wester Hailes, Kingsknowe, Redford, Morningside, Burdiehouse, or even by Portobello, if that is near the required destination.

CITY CONGESTION

To the ordinary observer, this seems to be increasing in every part of the city. Statistics suggests however, that road congestion is more random. Regional figures show that traffic in the west of the city increased by one-third in the period 1985-90, while there was no measurable increase in the city-centre. Indeed, traffic in Hanover Street over the same period declined by 2.34 per cent while according to this official source, in the Cowgate the decline was no less than ten per cent.

To tackle the problem of commuter access to the city, Lothian Region formulated its 'Greenways' policy. This is effectively an extension of the already successful 'bus lane' policy from the city centre out to five major routes in the suburbs. The routes selected are the A8, A70, A71, A702, and A900, the last-named as far as the bottom of Leith Walk.

The object is to speed up public transport at the expense of private vehicles, making the former more attractive to commuters. There would be improved facilities for pedestrians and cyclists. 'Traffic calming' measures designed to slow vehicle speeds would also be brought into effect on through

Driver's eye view of the High Street while waiting at the traffic lights at the Lawnmarket and George IV Bridge. The buildings to the left and right are the former Sheriff Court and Lothian Regional headquarters respectively, while the sea is visible in the far background.

side streets currently used as 'rat runs', many of these being residential in character.

The scheme's intention is laudable, although it can be argued that not all suburban main roads are as wide, and suitable for this scheme's implementation as, for example, Earl Grey Street at Tollcross (northbound) and Clerk/Nicolson Street, where bus lanes operate quite well already. There is also the question of allowing enough unloading spaces for local businesses as well as short-term parking spaces for shoppers, and the scheme has already been modified to meet these requirements, as it originally appeared that such restrictions

would last up to eight hours daily. This seems an unresolved problem – it is not uncommon in the mornings to see vehicles being unloaded on the pavement in bus lane throughfares, while a traffic warden tickets the windscreen.

At the time of writing, the Scottish Office has just indicated general approval of the Greenways traffic control scheme, but it has yet to be implemented. In particular, the reopening of the South Suburban Railway might be a useful initiative to mesh with the Greenways scheme, thus further reducing reliance on private means of transport. (*see also* RAILWAYS).

CAR PARKING

In 1994 Edinburgh had nearly 18,000 car parking spaces, including off-street in a number of car parks, three of them purpose-built multi-storey utilities. 57 per cent of these spaces cater for non-residential motorists, an important consideration for a tourist centre, and comparing to 45 per cent in Glasgow, 43 per cent in Bristol, and 41 per cent in Leeds, although these two English cities, approximately the same population as Edinburgh, have created a higher proportion of off-street capacity. The national average is 42 per cent.

Edinburgh has the smallest ratio of spaces per 1,000 local people, perhaps not an unreasonable proportion – although 58 per cent of Lothian households owned a car in 1991, the figure has always been lower in the city of Edinburgh itself (53.5 per cent in 1991). Census statistics show that people in Cramond enjoyed the highest level of car ownership per household – 1.37 cars, with 4 per cent of Cramond motorists owning three or more cars, the highest figures for any Edinburgh area, and approached only by Colinton (1.28 cars per household, with no fewer than 5.1 per cent of motorists living there owning three or more cars). In contrast, Craigmillar households owned 0.18 vehicle per household, with only one local motorist in 100 owning more than two cars.

On-street residential parking in Edinburgh stood at just over 2,000 in 1991. An unforeseen consequence of a comparative lack of designated parking for local motorists has been the tendency for many home-owners to convert their front gardens into car run-ins, with resulting loss of amenity.

ROAD ACCIDENTS IN EDINBURGH

In 1993 no fewer than 2,300 people were killed or injured in 'vehicular accidents' in the city, some 206 less than in 1992. The total for the whole of the Lothians and Borders Police area in 1993 was 4,206. 2,816 of this last statistic comprised car users. Figures for pedestrians killed or injured in Edinburgh were not supplied from this source (Chief Constable's Report, 1993), but national sources of information suggest that it was probably in the region of 24 per cent. In fact it could be proportionately even higher, given the daily problems of pedestrians in such thoroughfares as Princes Street, and bearing in mind the numbers of foreign tourists who unfortunately tend to look left before crossing a Scottish road.

STREETS/ROADS

The Post Office Building (traditionally known as the GPO) at the end-on junction of Princes Street and Waterloo Place is the fount of Edinburgh's road system. Here Britain's most important 'A' road, the A1 or Great North Road, wends its way along Waterloo Place and Regent Road to London. Britain's longest road at 407 miles/651 kms (including the A1M), the A1 is hardly likely to be a popular choice nowadays with most long-distance motorists setting off south from Edinburgh.

The lack of investment in the road north of Berwick-on-Tweed means that many drivers heading for London will take the A701 or A702 instead, aiming to reach the A74/M6 as soon as possible. This has proved to be something of a vicious circle – the A74 has received a large slice of investment on the grounds of traffic figures justifying it, but these statistics include Edinburgh traffic seeking a dual carriageway southwards in preference to the A1, which needs all the investment it can attract.

Westwards from the GPO runs the A8. This, the main Glasgow road, is better known to resident and visitor alike as Princes Street for its first mile. There can be few roads in Britain which carry a regulation by Act of Parliament prohibiting construction on one side to preserve the view from the other! Buildings between the Mound and the West End were banned by law in 1816; the development of the stretch now occupied by the Balmoral Hotel and Waverley Market area was the subject of fierce litigation in the 1770s, a kind of draw being declared which permitted some building provided the chimneytops were below street level. (*see* NEW TOWN)

The A8 continues westwards along Shandwick Place, through Haymarket and outwards via the much-congested St John's Road in Corstorphine. Much of its traffic now takes the Western Approach Road from Lothian Road westwards to Westfield Road, whence the Glasgow Road can be rejoined at Roseburn, east of Murrayfield Stadium or, after Stevenson Road at Balgreen Road, west of it. This new artery also serves the A70 and A71 roads.

Southwards from the Post Office runs the A7 Carlisle road. To Edinburgh people, this throughfare is known as The Bridges, as it crosses North Bridge, immediately, and then South Bridge, across the Cowgate. Nicolson Street and Clerk Street are then followed southwards, with the A68 leaving for Darlington at East Preston Street.

North from the Post Office is the A900 to Leith, via Leith Street and Leith Walk. The latter thoroughfare has, confusingly, other names as well, different on each side.

The three remaining 'A' roads regarded as congested enough to warrant the traffic controls of the Greenways scheme are the A70, A71, and A702. The A71 Kilmarnock road leaves the A8 at Haymarket, heading along Dalry and Gorgie Roads on its way west. Branching from it at Ardmillan Terrace (at the end-on junction of Dalry and Gorgie Roads), the A70 leads to Ayr via Lanark Road. The A702 is one of two roads to Dumfries, in this case running off the A700 Lothian Road at Tollcross and heading southwards through Morningside.

History

Some historians argue that Edinburgh has some of the earliest road 'flyovers' in the world. Such constructions as South Bridge (1788), Regent Bridge (Waterloo Place, 1819), George IV Bridge and Johnston Terrace (over King's Stables Road, 1836), are the result of a policy of directing highways over, and out of the way of, populous areas (*see also* BRIDGES).

Edinburgh earns a footnote in the history of road transport for being only the second authority in Britain to introduce *traffic lights*, at the crossroads of Picardy Place/York Place with Broughton Street. Installed on 21 March 1928, these lights were only advisory at first, but are evidence that Edinburgh's traffic problems have been chronic since long before the Second World War.

STREET LIGHTING
In 1498 Edinburgh Town Council ordered its citizens to carry a lantern after dark in

order to prove their honesty, but wiser residents probably simply stayed at home. Fixed lighting was ordered to be maintained by local shopkeepers from 1554, a requirement extended to ordinary residents ten years later. In practice, little was done until Cromwell condemned the city's failure to light its public places in the mid 17th century, and the records show that the Town Council hastened to burn 45 pounds of candles nightly to rectify the matter.

The building of the New Town generated new interest in the question of street lighting and an Act of Parliament was secured in 1785 to illuminate the New Town. This was probably done with oil lamps, but in 1822 53 gas lamps replaced 79 oil lamps in Princes Street, and gas lighting came to feature in the capital's streets for nearly a century and a half. Until the 1930s, these had to be manually lit and extinguished by a lamplighter (a 'leerie'), and these technicians, immortalised by Robert Louis Stevenson, were still a feature of the cityscape, carrying out repairs on the system, long after the Second World War (*see also* GAS SUPPLY).

Electric lighting made a short-lived debut in the citycentre in 1881; although highly effective, the contractors had trouble with their cable connections from their steam-driven plant in Market Street, and it was not

Wires under the Mound. To improve adhesion in winter conditions, an 'electric blanket' was laid under the Mound road-surface in September 1959, using 47 miles of wire. The facility is still there at the time of writing, but is no longer operational. (The Scotsman)

until 1895 that permanent electric lighting came to Edinburgh (*see also* ELECTRICITY SUPPLY). A power station in Dewar Place initially supplied the current to a lighting network in the New Town, and Edinburgh was all-electric by April 1965 when the last of 15,000 gas lamps was extinguished (in Ramsay Garden, next to the castle). The now-familiar sodium street lighting replaced the previous tungsten bulbs on main streets in the city from 26 May 1959, but with more powerful illumination gradually replacing it subsequently.

An unusual application of electricity to a city highway was the provision of an 'electric blanket' under the Mound, completed on 23 October 1959. Utilising 47 miles of wire, this thermal provision alleviated the adhesion problems caused to tyred traffic by the slope for many winters. Although still in place at the present time, it has proved unreliable in recent years, road salt being applied liberally instead.

For details of **street cleansing**, *see* CLEANSING.

POSTWAR INNER-CITY ROAD PROPOSALS

Abercrombie Report

Published in 1949, the *Civic Survey and Plan for the City and Royal Burgh of Edinburgh*, was prepared by Patrick Abercrombie and Derek Plumstead. Its intention was to formalise the city's approach to both physical and social planning, opening with the announcement 'it is better to guide future development by means of a development plan showing all that can be anticipated, than hope for the best by leaving it to follow an unguided course'.

As far as road planning was concerned, Abercrombie and Plumstead correctly anticipated the need for a City By-pass – their suggestion ran round the city in a course similar to what was opened 40 years later. Less practically, the planners suggested that the Milton Road (A1) enter central Edinburgh through the southern stretch of Holyrood Park, south of Samson's Ribs, something the Royal Parks administration could hardly have been happy about, never mind the feathered inhabitants of Duddingston Loch bird sanctuary.

The report postulated a development for the St James's Square area which would have been infinitely preferable to what was subsequently built, but its suggestion of a freight railway tunnelling east-west under the Meadows seems strange to the modern eye, and Portobello citizens must have been surprised at their being described as on the north-west of the city.

Quinquennial Review

Of all the unpopular ideas postulated for Edinburgh, the idea of an Inner Ring Road was possibly the most notorious. All road plans for the city had included this contentious idea since 1954, but by 1965 the matter had come to a head.

It seems incredible nowadays, but the city Council and planners appeared convinced that a six-lane highway would have to be locked round the centre of Edinburgh, including a path east-west through the Meadows. On the north side, the architectural delight of Warriston Crescent would be demolished, and motorway-type viaducts and flyovers would intrude into the Calton/Greenside area. The matter went to a public enquiry, amid a clamour that the public had been insufficiently informed of the plan. One councillor on the Planning Committee claimed that he had been unaware of the planned course in the Meadows, so the public's position was hardly likely to be much better. The Secretary of State was finally brought into the fight, approving the desecration of the Meadows by the construction of a highway, subject to a consultant's report. Fortunately, this was to be the last of the idea, and the scheme fizzled out, the local authority unprepared to take the matter further.

Perhaps the exercise had been worthwhile in that it had demonstrated that public reverence for the environment was now a weighty consideration indeed – a century previously, even Lord Cockburn had been unable to stop railway lines being driven through Princes Street Gardens. By 1966 the time of the conservationist had come at last in the city which has been home to such men as Cockburn and Geddes.

Buchanan Report

Commissioned in 1970, the planning consultants Freeman, Fox, produced a report the following year which became to be known after Professor Colin Buchanan, one of the principal contributors. While still giving a high level of priority to the private car, this report was less potentially damaging in environmental terms, believing that public transport must be improved. It did however suggest making Queen Street into a heavy traffic-carrier between east and west, while the Morningside and Newington areas would receive new roads only at the expense of existing buildings.

None of these major road-building schemes came to fruition (although Queen Street is now being upgraded to carry more traffic), earning Edinburgh unexpected praise. While such cities as Glasgow and Leeds had 'succeeded' in overcoming objections to inner-city road building, the results were of questionable value. Glasgow, for example, is a city very easy to drive *through*, which is hardly a boost to local tourism, and certainly could never be said of Edinburgh. The City Bypass does of course now offer such a function, but at least keeps any through traffic's exhausts and noise well away from the city itself.

Royal Residences

Edinburgh's principal royal residence is the Palace of Holyroodhouse, situated at the foot of the Royal Mile (High Street). Set at the north-western edge of the 640 acres (259 hectares) of the Queen's Park (*see* PARKS), it commands an uninterrupted view of Arthur's Seat and Salisbury Crags. Edinburgh Castle also contained royal apartments for centuries (*see* CASTLES).

The royal family make Holyrood their base for their annual Scottish week-long visit in June or July, but only rarely at other times. It is not thought to be the Queen's favourite palace, and earlier sovereigns have been similarly disenchanted with it. For a week every May the palace is home to the Lord High Commissioner (the monarch's representative) to the General Assembly of the Church of Scotland. For the rest of the year, the tourists hold it in

297

The Palace of Holyroodhouse is one of the city's major tourist attractions, but is still very much a working building, and site of the 1992 European 'summit'. (City of Edinburgh Council)

thrall, 316,679 of them visiting it in 1992.

In December 1992 Holyroodhouse was the setting for the European Commission 'summit', when the United Kingdom was host country. It was reported at the time that the Foreign Office had previously rejected Edinburgh as a possible venue for such a meeting owing to its lack of a proper conference centre. While the palace undoubtedly supplied a dignified and picturesque backdrop for the meeting of Europe's presidents and prime ministers, no fewer than 600 additional power points had hastily to be fitted.

History

The Palace of Holyroodhouse is a development of the Abbey which was founded on this site in 1128 after David I's apocryphal encounter with a stag with a holy rood (cross) in its antlers. He interpreted this to mean that he must build an abbey for the Augustinian order on this site. Unfortunately it was outside the Canongate, as well as the walls of the city, and it was frequently sacked and damaged, never more so than in the 16th century.

By that time Scotland's monarchs had other plans for the Holyrood site. With Edinburgh Castle regarded as cold and windy, it was natural that Holyrood, outside the filth and noise of the city, would appeal as a royal residence, and James IV was particularly taken with it. It was he who reduced the religious accommodation there and ordered the construction of palace gallery and entrance wing. After the pillaging by the English invader in 1544 and 1547, no major rebuilding was attempted, and only 21 canons remained by 1560.

Strangely, it was to be another 50 years before the palace was completely secularised, while its sanctuary status, which stretched as far as Duddingston village, lasted well into Victorian times, until 1880 when imprisonment for civil debt ceased (*see also* ABBEYS).

Ironically, it was for an English princess, Margaret Tudor, that James IV had built up the palatial element of Holyrood, creating a quadrangle to the west of the abbey, for it was English forces led by the Earl of Hertford, and then by Somerset, who virtually destroyed the abbey. Its remains are still to be seen, as stark and roofless as Melrose or Dryburgh.

The north-west tower of the palace was completed by James V by 1532, and state rooms were created on the western side of the palace by the same monarch. It was this period of the palace's history which will forever be associated with Mary Stewart, Queen of Scots, whose court blossomed against the dark night of Knox-driven Calvinism, but where the brutal murder of her favourite, David Rizzio, took place in front of her in 1566.

Standing alone from this historical period is Queen Mary's Bath house, now isolated beside the main road from Abbeyhill by the laying of the 19th century carriage-drive through the site of the Privy Garden. This curious two-storey building is thought more likely to have been a garden pavilion than having an ablutionary function.

After the departure of James VI's court to London, the palace's development slowed, apart from the preparations for Charles I's Scottish coronation in 1633. After the Stewart dynasty had lost the throne to the Commonwealth, royal interest in Holyrood appears to have waned, even after the Restoration. Cromwell used the Palace as barracks and stables; a Frenchman visiting in 1661 admired Holyrood's wonderful symmetry, but noted considerable fire damage.

This was made good by Charles II's Scottish Commissioner, the Duke of Lauderdale, who ordered the building rebuilt in 'exact ashlar, smooth as paper, loose-joined' to the design of Sir William Bruce. In 1679 the Duke of York, later to be James VII, took up residence at Holyrood and brought a truly royal air to the location. Historian Charles McKean has remarked that the six years which followed saw 'possibly the only time in history that the Palace of Holyrood, as rebuilt by Lauderdale, came close to being used as it had been intended'.

The Young Pretender stayed here in 1745, as did his kinsmens' persecutor, the Duke of Cumberland, the following year. When George IV visited Scotland in 1822, the Palace was really not fit for a king, although it had aristocratic tenants from time to time, the Dukes of Hamilton being curators.

Queen Victoria showed more enthusiasm for all things Scottish than most of her predecessors, or her successors, and with the guidance of Prince Albert, ensured that there was considerable investment in the Palace and park. A new gated approach was created on the Abbeyhill side, the forecourt improved with an octagonal fountain by Robert Matheson, and stables and guardroom rebuilt. Dunsapie and St Margaret's lochs were created at the same time (*see* LOCHS).

Nevertheless, many of the tapestries and fittings in the Palace are part of a royal 'pool', and have no historic connection with Holyrood. The more eye-catching furnishings, such as the four-poster bed in the King's Chamber is 17th century, and never slept in by the monarch it was intended for, Charles II, while many of the tapestries have been brought here from Buckingham Palace.

Tourists insist on seeing those rooms most associated with the tragic Queen Mary. These are situated in the tower built for himself by James V in 1529, and they include the room where Mary's favourite, David Rizzio, was murdered. The proportions of these chambers have been remodelled and the walls hung with tapestries from a later era, although the timber ceilings pre-date Mary.

A tour of Holyrood Palace can be something of a disappointment for the historically-minded tourist. This is essentially a working building, and much of its interest lies in the quality of its objets d'art, and less in the Palace's significance as the nucleus of so much of Scotland's history.

Rugby

Edinburgh can claim to hold an integral place in the world of rugby. While not as popular throughout the social spectrum as in the Borders, the game has a strong grip on the city's sporting community at both club and national level. As well as being home to some of Scotland's most important clubs, the city can boast that Murrayfield Stadium is the largest sports arena in Scotland, one of the four largest in Britain, and one of the finest anywhere.

At the time of writing (1995) Scottish rugby (15-a-side rugby union, mainly played by amateurs) has been newly reorganised into four Premier and seven National leagues by the national association, the Scottish Rugby Union (based at Murrayfield). There were four city teams in Premier Division 1 (Boroughmuir, Edinburgh Academicals, Heriots, and Watsonians), and four more (Corstorphine, Currie, Edinburgh Wanderers, and Stewart's-Melville) in the other premiership divisions. Most of these are FPs, that is, former pupils of the city's schools, although nearly all clubs now operate a policy of 'open' recruitment.

At the end of the 1995–96 Premiership, Academicals were relegated to Division 2, to be replaced by Currie, while Corstorphine and Edinburgh Wanderers were relegated from Divisions 3 and 4 respectively. At the end of that competition, (with Currie the city's only divisional champions), the new Regional leagues came into being for the remainder of the season, to provide competitive rugby at a time when many of the larger clubs were weakened by representative calls at district and international levels. The eight capital clubs listed above were divided between East Leagues 1 and 2.

In the national leagues, ten Edinburgh teams are involved. In addition, in season 1995–96, the Edinburgh & District League included such teams as Edinburgh Royal Infirmary, Ferranti, Heriot-Watt University, Liberton FP, Moray House, Queensferry, and Royal (Dick) Vet College, plus one from outside the city area.

Surprisingly – considering the high proportion of Edinburgh-based players selected to play for the national team – the

EDINBURGH RUGBY TEAMS

TEAM	GROUND	COLOURS
Boroughmuir	Meggetland	Green/blue quarters
Broughton FP	Wardie	Navy blue, red/gold hoops
Corstorphine	Union Park	Navy blue/scarlet quarters
Currie	Malleny Park	Amber/black, black shorts
Edinburgh Academicals	Raeburn Place	Sky blue/white hoops
Edinburgh Borderers	McKane Park (Dunfermline)	Red/white/navy hoops
Edinburgh Northern	Inverleith	Navy/old gold hoops
Edinburgh University	Peffermill	Navy/red & white hoops
Edinburgh Wanderers	Murrayfield	Red/black hoops
Forrester FP	Broomhouse Rd	Green shirt, black shorts
George Heriot's School FP	Goldenacre	Black/white hoops, black shorts
Holy Cross	Ferry Road	Green/yellow quarters
Leith Academicals	Hawkhill	Royal blue/white hoops
Lismore	Inch Park	White with red/blue V neck
Murrayfield	Murrayfield	Navy blue, white shorts
Portobello High FP	Calvary Park	Navy with gold V, navy shorts
Royal High	East Barnton	Black & white hoops
Royal Infirmary of Edinburgh	Kingsinch (Gilmerton Rd)	Red & black quarters
Stewarts-Melville FP	Inverleith	Scarlet, black/gold bands
Trinity Academicals	Bangholm	Black, gold band, black shorts
Watsonians	Myreside	Maroon/white hoops

Championship has been won only twice by Edinburgh sides, by Heriot's in 1978–79 and by Boroughmuir in 1990–91, although the latter won the last unofficial championship, in 1973, before the league structure was begun.

Since 1953, Edinburgh has won the District Championship eight times, and shared it ten times. In the Inter-City competition held annually with Glasgow since 1872, the capital leads with 59 wins to 38, with 19 drawn.

Individual Edinburgh players have made a massive contribution to Scottish rugby at both club and international level; in postwar times Heriot's have provided outstanding Scottish fullbacks in Ken Scotland and Andy Irvine, as well as having the Milne brothers starring in the pack, Boroughmuir have contributed Bruce Hay and adopted-Scot Sean Lineen, Watsonians boast the flying Hastings brothers, while Edinburgh Academicals provided Scotland with arguably its most inspiring captain – David Sole, architect of the Grand Slam 'shoot out' with England at Murrayfield in 1990.

The decision in 1995 to allow professionalism to enter the world of rugby union has completely 'moved the goalposts', as it were, in a game that has always prized its Corinthian traditions, and it remains to be seen how this move will affect the city's clubs. It may well be that the career prospects available to amateur players in Scotland's capital city in the financial and brewing sectors – where traditionally many leading Edinburgh players are employed – will nullify the attractions of moving south to undertake a full-time playing career which could be cut short by injury at any time.

Women's rugby is rapidly becoming more popular in Scotland, and Edinburgh teams are forging a fine reputation for themselves. In recent years, Edinburgh Academicals have been the side for all the others to beat, with Edinburgh Wanderers and Edinburgh University challenging for dominance in the league competition, currently known as the Keyline League.

History

Although there had long been a tradition of handball street games in such Border towns as Hawick and Jedburgh, Edinburgh clubs played a crucial role in the codification of what we now know as rugby. It was an Edinburgh private school, Merchiston Castle, that is usually credited with bringing rugby to Scotland, and in 1858, what is generally accepted as Scotland's first senior rugby match was played in the city between Edinburgh Academicals (Britain's oldest surviving club) and a team from the university. This involved 50 players, and lasted four days! The first rugby international was played between Scotland and England at Raeburn Place on 27 March 1871, resulting in a home win in a 20-a-side encounter.

Until the last quarter of the 19th century the history of rugby and association football (soccer) were so intertwined that it was not uncommon for two teams to arrange a fixture and then discover that each played 'football' in an entirely different way. The establishment of the Scottish Football Union in Edinburgh and the Scottish Football Association in Glasgow – within ten days of one another in 1873 – helped to resolve this confusion and laid the basis for both sports to develop.

The Scottish Football Union became the Scottish Rugby Union in 1924, the year before the opening of Murrayfield which replaced the former international venue at Inverleith. Murrayfield stadium really came into its own in the 1970s, when Scottish nationalism led to unprecedented attendances – for example, 104,000 for the game against Wales in 1975 – and the SRU has since invested heavily in an all-covered venue with cantilevered roofs guaranteeing an uninterrupted view for seated crowds of up to 67,000. The pitch had undersoil heating installed in late 1959, being switched on for the first time on 7 January 1960 for a game scheduled two days later.

With football (soccer) declining in quality and support, particularly at international level, the Scottish rugby team is now the nation's favourite sports team, and the winning of the Grand Slam in 1984 and 1990 represents a record of postwar sporting achievement that the Scottish football team has so far failed to equal.

Schools

Edinburgh has always been noted for its educational establishments, and with good reason. When Queen Victoria decided to send the heir to her throne, the Prince of Wales, to an ordinary school, it was to

Edinburgh's Royal High, and a local authority establishment at that. (Admittedly, he was treated as a private pupil of the headmaster).

Edinburgh has 30,227 primary and 18,858 secondary school pupils attending 102 primary and 23 secondary schools administered by the local authority (Lothian Regional Council at the time of writing). 74 of the primaries provide nursery education, in addition to 18 nursery schools. There were 550 pupils attending 15 special schools also controlled by the authority. The city has 19 private schools, including such nationally-known institutions as Fettes, Heriot's, and Watson's. There are also a number of private special schools for children with particular handicaps. There are no fewer than three universities, and a number of colleges of further education (*see* UNIVERSITIES AND COLLEGES).

In 1996, Edinburgh City Council succeeded Lothian Region as the educational authority for the city, expenditure on education representing the largest single item of the outgoing Lothian annual budget. Of the 68,000 school age pupils throughout the city, one-quarter of these (i.e. approximately 17,000) are educated at private schools, not all of them necessarily in Edinburgh. These figures were published by LRC Education Department in October 1995. The capacity of the city's private schools is around 12,000 according to figures supplied by the Scottish Education Department in 1995, but this includes about 1,700 places for boarders, who are likely to be children from addresses outside Edinburgh.

If the LRC figures are taken as correct, this statistic represents the highest proportion of non-state educated children in any one place in Scotland; indeed, it constitutes around 50 per cent of the nation's entire population of children educated at non-local authority establishments. The Scottish average is just over four per cent (34,000 out of 841,300 educated in Scotland according to the 1994 *Scottish Abstract of Statistics*); in 1961/2 it was also four per cent (according to the *Third Statistical Account*). At that time Edinburgh had 65,750 pupils, approximately 20 per cent of whom attended fee-paying schools. Obviously the present 25 per cent of parents believing that a private education is necessary for their children has grown by a quarter in Edinburgh in the last 30 years, but hardly at all outside the city.

There are strong historical reasons why Edinburgh's private schools play such a large part in the life of the capital, and these will be examined below.

Roman Catholics earned the right for their children to attend separate schools within the state educational framework from 1918 onwards. Prominent among such schools were **Holy Cross Academy**, on the north side of the city (but now closed), and **St Thomas's of Aquin's** in Lauriston, while **St Augustine's** and **Holy Rood** were opened postwar, and there are a large number of Catholic primaries. Whether it is appropriate in this supposedly ecumenical age to segregate Christian children in this way is a moot point, particularly when those from ethnic communities have to accept accommodation in the (nominally) Protestant schools.

Edinburgh's largest state school is Portobello High which in September 1994

Royal High School when newly opened on Regent Road, on the south slope of Calton Hill. This 1829 engraving also shows the National Monument behind, incomplete (as it still is) and cloaked in scaffolding. (Edinburgh City Libraries)

had 1,367 pupils on its roll, well above the roll averages for Lothian and for Scotland, although just outside the top 20 most populous schools in Scotland. The second largest in Edinburgh was Craigmount High with a roll of 1,236 pupils.

The doyen of Edinburgh's schools, the **Royal High School** claims origins going back to Holyrood Abbey in the 12th century, although it appears to have been formally established as the 'Tounis Scule' around 1520, for the education of 'gentilmenis bairnis'.

The school is now situated at Barnton, where it transferred from the impressive Hamilton-designed building on the western edge of Calton Hill in 1968. (This building has been refurbished as a possible site for a future Scottish Assembly, and is currently used as a conference centre). Other important changes just after that time included the ban on local authority schools charging fees for education, and the loss of the Royal High's right to select pupils. Even more epoch-making was the admission in 1973 of girls.

Now regrettably moved from the city centre, the Royal High continues its traditions laid down by such famous former pupils as Sir Walter Scott, Alexander Graham Bell, and innumerable Lord Provosts of Edinburgh and Moderators of the General Assembly of the Church of Scotland.

History of local authority schools

Edinburgh's first schools were probably part of the Abbey establishment at Holyrood from the 12th century, and at St Anthony's preceptory in Leith. The Royal High, as already noted, traces its history back to the establishment of the Abbey.

Although education was more easily available in Scotland than south of the Border from the end of the 17th century (*see also* SOCIAL WORK), it was by no means universally available, and it was not until 1872 that Scottish children were required by law to receive a proper education.

In that year hundreds of elected School Boards were set up in Scotland 'to amend and extend the law of Scotland on the subject of education'. They varied in size from cities like Edinburgh to hamlets like Duddingston, all of them reporting to the new Scotch (sic) Education Department in London. Boards in the Edinburgh area in 1872–1919 were as follows:

NAME OF BOARD	AREA ALSO COVERED	REMARKS
Colinton		
Corstorphine		
Cramond	Davidson's Mains, Granton, Blackhall	1
Duddingston	Easter Duddingston (Joppa)	2
Edinburgh		
Leith		
Liberton	Burdiehouse, Gilmerton, Niddrie, Craigmillar	1
Portobello		2
St Cuthbert's	Gorgie, Coltbridge, South Morningside & Dean	3

Remarks:

1. To Midlothian Education Authority 1919; Edinburgh 1921.

2. To Edinburgh School Board (ESB), May 1902.

3. Gorgie and South Morningside Schools to ESB, May 1895.

One of the most pleasing aspects of the history of School Boards is that, straight

Flora Stevenson Primary School in Stockbridge, as seen in the traffic-free days of the 1950s. The name commemorates the female head of the Edinburgh School Board from a time when women were not allowed to vote, but were allowed a say in their children's education. (Edinburgh City Libraries)

from their inception, women were allowed to stand as, and vote for, board members provided they independently owned property; indeed, Edinburgh's women voters appear to have numbered 25 per cent of the local electorate. At the first election, no fewer than 17 women members were elected to the Board, one of them being Flora Stevenson, who went on to become Chairman from 1900 until her death five years later – this at a time when women were firmly excluded from voting in political elections, whether local or national. Flora Stevenson's name is immortalised in the name of the primary school in Comely Bank.

In 1885, Edinburgh School Board anticipated national legislation by some ten years in opening a gymnasium in every school, and there were inter-school swimming competitions by the 1900s, using pools at Abbeyhill, Broughton, Bruntsfield and Sciennes schools. In 1886 the Board took over three free schools previously run by the Heriot's Trust, and proceeded in the following decades to open such new secondary schools as Broughton (1909), Boroughmuir (1914), and had

EDINBURGH LOCAL AUTHORITY SCHOOLS FROM 1872

SCHOOL	PRESENT ADDRESS	DESIGNATION	OPENED BY: (IF BEFORE ECED IN 1929)
Abbeyhill	Abbey Street	P	ESB (1881)
Ainslie	–	S	
Albion Road	–	P	ESB (1905)
All Saint's	–	P	EPS (1919)
Balerno High	Bridge Road	S	
Balfour Place	–	P	LSB (1921)
Balgreen	Balgreen Road	P	
Bellevue	–	S	EAE
Blackhall	Craigcrook Road	P	
Bonaly	Bonaly Grove	P	
Bonnington	Bonnington Road	P	LSB (1921)
Bonnington Acad (Ferry Rd)	–	S	LSB (1921)
Boroughmuir	Viewforth	S	ESB (1914)
Bristo	–	P	ESB (1877)
Broomhouse	Saughton Road	P	
Broughton	Broughton Road	P	ESB (1896)
	Carrington Road	S	ESB (1904)
Brunstane	Magdalene Drive	P	
Bruntsfield	Montpelier	P	ESB (1895)
Buckstone	Buckstone Loan East	P	
Burdiehouse	Burdiehouse Crescent	P	
Canonmills	Rodney Street	P (now Special)	ESB (1880)
Carrick Knowe	Lampacre Road	P	
Carrickvale	–	S	
Castle Hill	–	P	ESB (1888)
Castlebrae High	Greendykes Road	S	
Causewayside	–	P	ESB (1876)
Clarebank (Special)	–	P	LSB (1921)
Clermiston	Parkgrove Place	P	
Clovenstone	Clovenstone Park	P	
Colinton	Redford Place	P	COSB (1921)
Comiston	Oxgangs Green	P	
Corstorphine	C. High Street	P	CTSB (1921)
Couper Street	–	P	LSB (1921)
Craigentinny	Loganlea Drive	P	
Craiglockhart	Ashley Terrace	P	ESB (1903)

Craigmillar	Harewood Road	P	
Craigmount High	Craigs Road	S	
Craigmuir	West Pilton Park	P	
Craigroyston High	Pennywell Road	S	
Cramond	Cramond Crescent	P	CSB (1921)
Currie	Dolphin Avenue	S	
Curriehill	Lanark Road West	P	
Dalmeny	Carlowrie Crescent	P	WLC (1975)
Dalry	Dalry Road	P	ESB (1878)
Darroch (*see* Gilmore Place)			
David Kilpatrick's	–	S	
Davidson's Mains	Corbiehill Road	P	
Davie Street	–	–	FPF (1886)
Dean	–	P	STCB (1875)
Dean Park	Balerno	P	
Dr. Bell's	–	P	LSB (1921)
Drumbrae	Ardshiel Avenue	P	
Drummond High	Cochran Terrace	S	
Drummond Street	–	P	ESB (1906)
Drylaw	Easter Drylaw Drive	P	
Duddingston (a)	–	P/S	DSB (1902)
Duddingston (b)	Duddingston Road	P	ECED
Dumbryden	Dumbryden Gardens	P	
East Craigs	Craigmount Brae	P	
Echline	South Queensferry	P	WLC (1975)
Fernieside	Moredun Park Road	P	
Ferryhill	Groathill Road N	P	
Firrhill High	Firhill	S	
Flora Stevenson	Comely Bank	P	ESB (1901)
Forrester High	Broomhouse Road	S	
Fort (North Fort)	North Fort Street	P	LSB (1921)
Fountainbridge	–	P	(closed 1918)
Fox Covert	Clerwood Terrace	P	
Fox Covert (RC)	Clerwood Terrace	P	
Gilmerton	Moredun Dykes Road	P	
Gilmore Place	–	P	ESB (1907)
Glenvarloch	Ivanhoe Crescent	P	
	–	P	STCB (1895)
Gracemount	Lasswade Road	P	
Gracemount	Lasswade Road	S	
Granton (a)	–	P	CSB (1902)

Granton (b)	Boswall Parkway	P	
Greendykes	Greendykes Road	P	
Groathill	Groathill Road	P	
Gylemuir	Wester Broom Place	P	
Hailesland	Hailesland Place	P	
Hermitage Park	Leith	P	LSB (1921)
Hillwood	Ratho Station	P	WLC (1975)
Holy Cross (RC)	Craighall Road	P	
Holy Cross Academy	–	S	
Holy Rood RC High	Duddingston Rd West	S	
Hunter's Tryst	Oxgangs Green	P	
Hyvot's Bank	Gilmerton Dykes Drive	P	
The Inch	–	P/S	
Inchview	West Pilton Avenue	P	
James Clark's	–		ESB (1918)
James Gillespie's	–	P/S	FPF (1908)
	Whitehouse Loan	P	
	Lauderdale Street	S	
Juniper Green	Baberton Mains Wynd	P	
Kirkliston	Carmel Road	P	WLC (1975)
Lauriston (Special)	–	P	
Leith	St Andrew's Place, Leith	P	
Leith Academy	Academy Park	S	LSB (1921)
Leith Walk	Brunswick Road	P	ESB (1876)
Liberton	Gilmerton Road	P	EAE
Liberton High	Gilmerton Road	S	
Links Place	–	P	LSB (1921)
Lismore	Bingham Avenue	P	
Lochend Road	–	P	LSB (1921)
Lochrin Nursery	Tollcross		
London Street	–	P	ESB (1889)
Longstone	Redhall Grove	P	
Lorne	Lorne Street	P	LSB (1921)
Lothian Road	–	P	(closed 1912)
Milton House	–	P	ESB (1888)
Moredun	Moredunvale Place	P	
Muirhouse	Muirhouse Place West	P	
Murrayburn	Sighthill Loan	P	
Nether Currie	Thomson Crescent	P	
Newcraighall	Whitehill Street	P	
Niddrie	Niddrie Mains Road	P	

Niddrie Marischal	–	S	EAE
Normal Practising	–	P	EPS (1919)
North Canongate	–	P	ESB (1879)
North Merchiston	–	P	ESB (1883)
North Fort (see Fort)			
Norton Park	–	S	
Orwell	Orwell Place	P	
Oxgangs	Colinton Mains Drive	P	
Parson's Green	Meadowfield Drive	P	ESB (1901)
Peffermill	Craigmillar Castle Ave	P	
Pennywell	Ferry Road Avenue	P	
Pentlands	–	S	
Pirniehall	West Pilton Crescent	P	
Portobello High	–	P/S	PSB (1902)
	Duddingston Road	S	ESB (1897)
Prestonfield	Peffermill Road	P	
Preston Street	Dalkeith Road	P	
Queensferry	Burgess Road	P	WLC (1975)
Queensferry High	Ashburnam Road	S	WLC (1975)
Ratho	School Wynd	P	MCC (1975)
Riccarton	Curriehill Road	P	
Regent Road	–	P	FPF (1886)
Roseburn	Roseburn Street	P	STCB (1894)
Royal High	Northfield Broadway	P	
	East Barnton Ave	S	
Royal Mile	Canongate	P	
Royston	Boswall Parkway	P	
St Ann's RC	–	P	RCS (1920)
St Anthony's RC	–	S	EAE
St Augustine's RC	High Broomhouse Road	S	
St Bernard's	–	P	FPF (1886)
St Catherine's RC	Gracemount Drive	P	
St Columba's RC	–	P	RCS (1920)
St Cuthbert's RC	(Newington)	P	RCS (1920)
	Hutchison Crossway	P	
St David's RC	West Pilton Place	P	
St Francis's RC	Niddrie Mains Road	P	
St Ignatius RC	–	P	RCS (1920)
St James's	–	P	EPS (1919)
St John's RC	Hamilton Terrace	P/S (now P)	RCS (1920)
St John's Vianney RC	Ivanhoe Crescent	P	

St Joseph's RC	Broomhouse Crescent	P	
St Leonard's	–	P	ESB (1880)
St Margaret's RC	South Queensferry	P	WLC (1975)
St Mark's RC	Firhill Crescent	P	
St Mary's RC	York Lane	P	RCS (1920)
	East London Street	P	
St Mary's (Easter Rd).	–	P	EPS (1919)
St Mary's RC	Links Gardens, Leith	P	
St Matthew's	–	P	EPS (1919)
St Ninian's RC	Restalrig Road South	P	RCS (1920)
St Patrick's RC	–	P	RCS (1920)
St Peter's RC	Falcon Gardens	P	RCS (1920)
St Thomas's (Leith)	–	P	(closed 1915)
St Thomas's of Aquin's	Chalmers Street	P/S (now S)	RCS (1920)
Sciennes	Sciennes Road	P	ESB (1892)
Sighthill	Calder Park	P	
Silverknowes	Muirhouse Gardens	P	
South Bridge	–	S	ESB (1886)
South Morningside	Comiston Road	P	STCB (1895)
Stenhouse	Stevenson Drive	P	
Stockbridge	Hamilton Place	P	ESB (1877)
Tollcross	Fountainbridge	P	ESB (1913)
Torphichen Street	–	P	ESB (1888)
Towerbank	Figgate Bank	P	PSB (1902)
Trinity	Newhaven Road	P	LSB (1921)
Trinity Academy	Craighall Avenue	S	LSB (1921)
Tynecastle High	McLeod Street	P/S (now S)	ESB (1912)
Victoria	Newhaven Main Street	P	LSB (1921)
Wardie	Granton Road	P	
Warrender Park	–	P	ESB (1883)
Westburn	Sighthill Road	P	
Wester Hailes Education Centre	Murrayburn Drive	S	
Yardheads	–	P	LSB (1921)

Key: Designation: P = Primary; S = Secondary

Opened By :

COSB   Colinton School Board
CSB   Cramond School Board

CTSB	Corstorphine School Board
DSB	Duddingston School Board
EAE	Education Authority for Edinburgh (1919-29)
ECED	Edinburgh Corporation Education Department.
EPS	Episcopal Schools transferred to Edinburgh.
ESB	Edinburgh School Board.
FPF	Formerly Privately Funded.
LRC	Lothian Regional Council.
LSB	Leith School Board.
MCC	Midlothian County Council.
PSB	Portobello School Board
RCS	Roman Catholic Schools tr. to Edinburgh.
STCB	St Cuthbert's & Dean School Board
WLC	West Lothian CC.

James Gillespie's handed over to it in 1904, when private funds proved inadequate.

The insignia of the respective boards for Edinburgh and Leith are still to be seen on older school buildings, Edinburgh's stern Boadicea contrasting with Leith's magnificent schooner under sail. (The best example of the latter still decorates the north-facing exterior wall at Bonnington Primary, dating from 1907). Within ten years of being established, the Leith board was administering nine schools, seven of them crowded beyond capacity, to a total of 5,284 pupils. By the start of the First World War, there were 15 Leith schools accommodating 14,520 pupils, taught by 298 teachers, plus 54 specialising in sewing, music, or swimming.

The Leith schools joined Portobello's (absorbed in 1902) in the new Edinburgh education authority in 1920, bringing such fine secondaries as Leith Academy and Trinity Academy into a unified system. Leith Academy can claim a history going back to the Reformation, but passed into local authority hands in 1848. It moved from its 1929 building on the edge of the Links (itself a replacement for a more impressive 18th century building) to a custom-built school just off Easter Road in 1991. (The 1929 building is now part of Queen Margaret College; *see* UNIVERSITIES AND COLLEGES). Trinity Academy dates from 1893, its building designed by the School Board architect, George Craig, in 'ambitious Renaissance' style, according to the *Buildings of Scotland* series.

Portobello had its own education authority until merged with Edinburgh in 1902, by which time its Burgh School was 26 years old. Within five years its roll had grown from 290 pupils to 700 with class sizes of up to 138! The *Third Statistical Account* records without comment that 'this grave overcrowding was reduced by poor attendance and epidemics'.

In 1918, 38 new county and city education authorities took over – and Edinburgh and Leith merged in 1920 – but in 1929 a new Education Act placed educational responsibilities on four cities and 31 counties in Scotland. Edinburgh

Corporation Education Department was the title to be seen on the familiar grey jotters for the next 46 years, and in 30 years after the end of the Second World War, no less than half of the city's existing primary schools were opened.

The newer secondaries include Craigroyston, Forrester's, Holy Rood (RC), St Augustine's (RC) and the unique Wester Hailes Education Centre, which includes wider community facilities. The principal loss of a secondary school in recent years has been the closure of Holy Cross Academy (RC) in Ferry Road, following the transfer of so many Leithers to new schemes on the west of the city. Holy Cross was held in particular reverence by other schools for the quality of the football players it seemed able to supply from the School 1st XI direct to Hibernian FC!

When local government reorganisation allocated education to the new Regional authorities in 1975, this represented their principal outlay, exceeding that on social work. In 1996 education returned to single-tier authorities, in Edinburgh's case to the modern equivalent of the ECED of 1929–75.

INDEPENDENT SCHOOLS

As already noted, Edinburgh has a major proportion of Scotland's private school population being educated within the city boundaries. Lothian Regional Council figures issued in October 1995 placed this at 25 per cent of the city's 68,000 population of school-age children (i.e. 17,000), although it should be noted that the capacity of the city's private schools is around 12,000, and this assumes maximum capacity. Possibly the LRC statistic includes those Edinburgh children attending boarding schools elsewhere in the United Kingdom, and the figures may be blurred even more by the numbers of children boarding at Edinburgh schools from outside the city (12 schools in the city offer just over 1,700 boarding places).

In 1995 those independently-run Edinburgh schools were as shown opposite.

Schools run independently of the local authority for children with special needs include the Royal Blind School and Donaldson's School for the Deaf (for information on these, *see* under HOSPITALS), Barnardo's at Blackford Brae, Rudolf Steiner, and Westerlea at Corstorphine.

History of private school education in Edinburgh

The history of private education in the city is closely linked to the care and schooling of the children of burgesses who had died or had become financially embarrassed. Indeed, until the 19th century, the High School (later Royal High) was seen as the school for the progeny of the well-to-do, and such institutions as Heriot's or George or John Watson's provided 'hospitals' in the sense of a charitable institution, although principally for children of deceased or financially-distressed burgesses.

George Heriot's school is situated where it was founded, just outside the Flodden Wall, but included in Telfer's later construction (*see* CITY WALLS). Boys were first admitted in 1659, benefitting from a legacy from Heriot, who died in 1624 having served James VI as goldsmith and jeweller. In 1886, Heriot's became a day

SCHOOL	ADDRESS	MAXIMUM ROLL	BOARDERS
Cargilfield	Barnton	228	92
Clifton Hall	Newbridge	110	125
Daniel Stewart's/ Melville College	Ravelston Dykes	2164★	45
Dunedin	Gilmerton Road	22	--
Edinburgh Academy	Henderson Row	1100	170
Fettes College	Carrington Road	605	455
George Heriot's	Lauriston Place	1570	--
George Watson's	Colinton Road	2240	80
Mannafields Christian	Easter Road	30	--
Mary Erskine	Ravelston Dykes	2000★	40
Merchiston Castle	Colinton	400	350
Regius School	South Clerk Street	20	--
St Denis/Cranley	Ettrick Road	250	110
St George's (Girls)	Garscube Terr.	930	105
St Margaret's (Girls)	East Suffolk Rd.	870	128
St Mary's Music School	Manor Place	65	30
St Serf's	Wester Coates Gdns.	270	--

★ 1,280 junior places are combined between Daniel Stewart's/Melville and Mary Erskine.

school, and three smaller schools were taken over by the Edinburgh School Board.

The daughters of the better-off were educated in Edinburgh from 1694, when the Merchant Maiden Hospital opened its doors. Its name changed in 1870 to the Educational Institution for Young Ladies, and for many years, *Mary Erskine's* (renamed in 1944) occupied a building at the east end of Queen Street, moving to Barnton in 1966.

George Watson's is one of the biggest private schools in the country, and since 1930 has an extensive campus style site off Colinton Road, complete with an excellent rugby ground just round the corner. George Watson was the Bank of

Scotland's first accountant, bequesting a foundation which allowed the opening of the school in 1741. There was a separate Ladies College from 1871, now integrated with the boys' at Colinton Road.

Edinburgh's other private schools nearly all date from the 19th century. In 1824, a number of citizens, including Lord Cockburn and Sir Walter Scott, were dissatisfied with the teaching of classics at the High School, and founded *Edinburgh Academy*. *Melville College* opened its doors some eight years later, although known initially as the Edinburgh Institution. By 1920 it has moved its base from George Street to Melville Street, adopting that name, but has since merged with *Daniel Stewart's*, whose Queensferry

315

Road 'pauper palace' was completed in 1848. **Fettes College** was another product of the move towards private education, opening in 1870 on a site of 200 acres left by Sir William Fettes. Its spire, designed by David Bryce, makes it the most striking school outline in the city.

With women pressing to enter university in the late 19th century, new schools sprang up to offer a more substantial education than the fare of dancing, sewing, and music deemed suitable for fashionable young ladies hitherto. **George Watson's Ladies' College** opened in George Square in 1871, later moving the primary school to St Alban's Road, but its work is now covered by that of George Watson's, mentioned above. **St George**'s opened in 1888, following an exchange of letters in *The Scotsman* concerning the need for more educational opportunities for the fair sex. Once based in Melville Street, the school is now located in the Ravelston area. **St Margaret's** is based in Newington, boasting a substantial campus east of Craigmillar Park. **St Denis's** (founded 1855) and **Cranley** are now united at the latter's Merchiston site.

Of the smaller schools, **Merchiston Castle School** was formed in 1833, and originally situated at the site of Napier's tower, now the centre of Napier University campus. The school moved to Colinton in 1930, and is usually credited with popularising rugby in Scotland (*see* RUGBY). **Cargilfield** was founded in 1873 in the Trinity area, but moved in 1899 to Barnton Park. It is a preparatory school, although no longer intended entirely for boarders.

One Edinburgh school with an unusual claim to fame was **St Trinnean's**, whose blameless existence from 1922 to 1946 – for most of that time at St Leonard's House, behind the Royal Commonwealth Pool – inspired writer Ronald Searle to create 'St Trinian's', the ultimate Girls School from Hell, featured in a number of British comedy films in the 1950s and 60s (*see* FILMS). This was purely a work of Searle's imagination intended to amuse young acquaintances, and should not be regarded as a comment on the standard of Edinburgh private-school education!

Sewerage

Lothian Regional Council were responsible for sewerage and drainage in and around Edinbrgh, from 1975 to April 1996, but since then this duty has been undertaken by the new East of Scotland Water Authority.

Edinburgh's disposal of effluent has hitherto earned the city less praise than its historic and highly effective water supply system. Even into the early 1970s, Scotland's capital was still dumping untreated sewage into the Forth close to shore, generating deserved criticism about a city putting on a beautiful face, but failing to observe basic toilet etiquette. An investment of £53 million in the 1970s has, however, eradicated the problem over the last two decades, with Edinburgh's sewage-treatment system now equalling any other in the world.

Edinburgh's principal sewage disposal facility is at Seafield, on a site east of Leith docks reclaimed from the sea. Serving Musselburgh as well as Edinburgh, the site processes effluent from around 125,000 homes. This is separated into liquid and solid constituents, the former being disposed of out to sea by means of a 2,884 yard (2,637 metre) pipeline, while the latter is pumped to Leith Docks where it is bulk-loaded on board the sludge-carrying vessel *Gardyloo* (2,695 tons deadweight), its name echoing the cry given by less than environmentally-conscious inhabitants of the Old Town. Sea disposal in two deepwater locations, in the area of the Bell Rock and north of St Abb's Head, will however have to cease when new EC regulations come into force by the end of 1998.

History

Until the 18th century the close-packed houses of the Old Town had no drainage system worthy of the name. Indeed, one of the reasons for the royal court's peripatetic nature was to leave behind the detritus of a season at any one palace or castle, so the problems facing ordinary citizens scarcely bear thinking about.

The habit of throwing slops from an upstairs window into the street below, with the cynical cry of 'Gardyloo' (*Gardez l'eau*, or 'look out – water'), turned the streets into sewers. Here grew the 'Flowers of Edinburgh', as a critic of the city described the resulting excrement. In the 18th century, the citizens were expected to eject their excreta from that day at ten o'clock, whereupon the city's taverns would burn paper tapers to overcome the resulting smell. A pedestrian still out-of-doors after that time would hire a cadie or caddie, a guide who would venture in front shouting 'haud your hand' to the households above. Tobias Smollett writes in his novel

Humphrey Clinker (1771) of walking through the dark city streets, when:

> the throwing up of a sash or otherwise opening of a window made me tremble, while behind and before me at some little distance fell the terrible shower.

Not surprisingly, plague and cholera were frequent visitors to Edinburgh, and by 1800 the Town Council had found action necessary. Three sewers were constructed from the Old Town to Holyrood Park – from the Nor' Loch and the north side of the Canongate, from the Cowgate eastwards, and from George Square. Their contents emptied into an open ditch near Meadowbank, known unsurprisingly as the Foulburn, flowing to a 250-acre (102.5 hectare) sewage farm area near Craigentinny. Remarkably, this drain remained open to the air until 1922, when both it, and the Craigentinny farm, were made redundant by a new sewer running from Clockmill Lane, near Piershill, to Seafield.

Other parts of the city were drained by the Water of Leith, with the result that, even as late as 1853, James Rendel, an engineer reporting to the Leith Dock Commissioners on future plans for the docks, commented on

> the injury which the Harbour is now sustaining from the sewage matter sent into it from Edinburgh and Leith . . . Not only is the quantity of solid matter become so considerable as to cause growing expense in dredging to maintain the proper navigable channel up to the new dock, but its less solid products are deposited in such increased

quantities as to have become an intolerable nuisance.

Legislation in 1854, 1864, and 1889 improved the city's sewage problem overall, but it was not until the last of these dates, some 34 years after Rendel made his report, that the Water of Leith came under the supervision of a board of Commissioners, with direct control passing to Edinburgh Corporation in 1920. This did not eradicate the problem of sea disposal, with the Craigentinny sewer a major part of an infrastructure which was in need of modernisation right up until the 1970s, taking sewage from Leith to the west and Portobello on the east. There was another outfall to the east at Joppa. Not surprisingly, the Forth's mussel colonies have been contaminated for many years, and bathing was recently prohibited at Portobello, supposedly the city's own seaside resort.

In 1971 a new interceptor sewer network was announced to concentrate primary treatment at a new works at Seafield, and this is now complete. Critics of the scheme suggested that it was over-elaborate, comprising both primary treatment and long-distance outfall discharge, but the network's designers in fact proved prescient, sufficient land being reclaimed to help bring Edinburgh's sewage treatment arrangements up to modern required standards.

(*see also* CLEANSING)

Shops

Edinburgh had 3,527 retail shops serving the public in 1986, according to the most recent figures available from Edinburgh District Council at the time of writing. Although Glasgow boasts the largest area of shop floorspace in Scotland, Edinburgh has the highest ratio per 1,000 customers – 1,527 square metres, in comparison with Aberdeen's 1,355, Dundee's 1,349, and Glasgow at 1,247 per 1,000.

Of these 3,527 shops, approximately 89 per cent were outside the city centre itself (i.e. a parallelogram of the New Town from the West End to Leith Street, including Princes and George Streets, and the Waverley Market). The largest category of retail units were those selling foodstuffs, with recreational products second, clothing third, and furniture in fourth place.

Pride of place in any discussion about Edinburgh's shopping venues must go to **Princes Street**. The earliest proprietors in what is often described as Britain's most beautiful thoroughfare, such as philosopher David Hume, would have been horrified if they could see it nowadays – as a commercialised city-centre street, as far removed from a residential area as is possible to imagine.

Princes Street is not uniformly successful; local citizens are becoming accustomed to seeing LEASE FOR SALE signs, as in shopping centres with less prestige, although a commercial survey published in 1995 reported that the street's rental values continued to rise with demand. One shop was reported to be paying £170 per square foot (in contrast, the highest reported rental in Glasgow's Argyle Street was some £30 lower). The most lucrative part of Princes Street in 1995 – the 'prime drag' – was believed to be the stretch between Hanover and Frederick Streets.

The best that can be said of Princes Street is that it is architecturally undistinguished; some critics have called it worse than that. Moray MacLaren described it as 'one of the most chaotically tasteless streets in the United Kingdom'; Compton Mackenzie believed it to be the finest street in Europe when he first saw it in 1907, its character now destroyed by chain-stores.

Like many hybrids, Princes Street lacks any perceptible unity of design. Originally designated for housing, it had to undergo a commercial metamorphosis within a century of its first construction, while 20th century shop units, although often attractive enough in their own right, sit uneasily in the street. Even conscientious efforts at commercial conservation seem unconvincing, as Debenham's found in the early 1980s when opening their Princes Street store within the shell of an existing building, only to find that some customers were perhaps less than appreciative – if they want to visit an ancient monument, that's what they'll do, whereas a store should *look* like a store!

Such well-known names as R.W. Forsyth, Darlings, and Binns, have vanished from the street, the first-named of these still remembered for their immaculate yellow and black delivery vans. One survivor is well into its second century as an Edinburgh institution. **_Jenners_** was listed in the business press in 1994 as Scotland's eighth most profitable retail business, and, with an estimated profit of £3.9 million, the most prosperous on a single site.

The shop was founded in 1838 by two young Englishmen who had been attracted to work in Edinburgh's retail trade, but who found themselves dismissed for attending the Musselburgh Races one afternoon. Nothing daunted, Messrs Kennington and Jenner opened their own haberdashery in a converted house at 47 Princes Street on 1 May that year, specialising in ladies' fashions and fancy goods. Renamed Jenners from 1868, the firm overcame a serious fire in 1892 – watched by up to 40,000 people who had no television to entertain them in those days – and went on to celebrate its centenary in 1938 with considerable aplomb. The present building, supposedly based on the design of Oxford's Bodleian Library, dates from 1895.

That Princes Street is catering for a different, perhaps less socially-elevated customer, than in past years, is unarguable. Shop units selling compact discs and videos, ice cream, or bargain books – all these are a world away from R.W. Forsyth and Greensmith Downes, former Princes Street traders who catered for a more gentrified clientele, and didn't care if you knew it. Marcus the Furrier and Melroses' teas were two famous specialist shops in the street, the former with its three stuffed black bears holding flagpoles above the shop, the latter with its shopful of exotic aromas. Yet Princes Street is not entirely in decline as a retail centre of excellence. The opening of two specialist bookshops (east and west Waterstone's) is a development to be welcomed.

George Street was always something of a shopping backwater compared to Princes Street, and contains to this day a large proportion of non-retail buildings; indeed, between the junctions with Hanover Street and St Andrew's Square, there are no retail shops at all. Bookshops figure largely in George Street – the city's first

Waterstone's was opened at the street's west end (it has since migrated to the next block eastwards), while the Edinburgh Bookshop is something of a national institution, now owned by James Thin's. The Church of Scotland has a busy bookshop here, and Reader's Digest settled on George Street for a while. Confirming the street's refined character was a film-maker's decision to employ the Blackwood's shop front at no. 45 George Street (now an insurance office) as a perfect exterior for the hidebound (fictional) textile firm ridiculed in the 1950s comedy *Battle of the Sexes* (see FILMS).

Few shopping malls have generated as much controversy as Edinburgh's **St James Centre**, immediately west of Leith Street, and forming such a visual stumbling block to the eye viewing the cityscape from the Calton Hill. Opened in 1970, the Centre was the first sheltered shopping area in the capital, which has always lacked the facilities offered to the pedestrian consumer by Glasgow's arcades or Carlisle's huge railway terminus-like indoor market.

The welcome introduction into Edinburgh of sheltered shopping, on the site of the former St James's Square, hardly compensated for the centre's fortress-style appearance, especially when viewed from the eastern side, where an urban motorway thankfully failed to make an appearance (*see* ROADS AND STREETS), but where an addition to John Lewis's premises has improved the building's eastern aspect. With one department store and 63 small units, the Centre has proved popular with the public over the years, doubtless helped by the provision of 1,300 parking spaces in multi-storey car parks nearby. The opening of the St James Centre has caused wholescale change in the range of shops at the east end of Princes Street (*see* below under History).

Waverley Market is no longer literally a market, having lasted exactly 100 years in that role. In 1984, after lying derelict for some time, the site was reopened as a shopping mall with 50 units on two levels, an atrium adding interest at the east and west ends of the development. Although undoubtedly attractive and well laid-out, the location of this mall in an area custom-designed for barrow traders seems to symbolise the final victory of the shopkeeper over the street-seller and hawker (*see also* MARKETS).

Smaller developments dating from the late 1960s and early 1970s, and appearing as the very latest fashion at that time, were opened at New Kirkgate in Leith, Asda near Portobello, and at Wester Hailes. The pioneering Asda development was unusual in that the store had to move half a mile to the south within 15 years of opening because of a new road infrastructure on the city's eastern boundary.

Three traditional shopping areas away from the citycentre were Leith Walk, Morningside Road, and Portobello High Street. In a 1990 survey, these thoroughfares were found to accommodate the following shopping areas – Leith Walk (350 shops occupying 46,548 square metres), Morningside Road (176, 20,104), and Portobello High Street (175, 18,990). So many of these premises nowadays are either vacant or given over to charity organisations, that the above figures should not be taken at their face value as indicating genuine retail units.

OUT OF TOWN SHOPPING DEVELOPMENTS

Edinburgh was slow to develop shopping areas away from the city centre, possibly because the car ownership figures were low compared to the national average (*see* ROADS AND STREETS). The introduction of two-tier local authorities in 1975 may have helped to speed the process by tying Edinburgh and the three other Lothian Districts, more closely together in planning facilities based on an improved roads infrastructure. Out of town facilities have resulted at Lady Road, Kinnaird Park, and South Gyle.

The first of these, *Cameron Toll* shopping centre at Lady Road, is of course not strictly out of town at all, but is in the southern suburbs roughly equidistant between Morningside and Niddrie. Built in the early 1980s on ground long left undeveloped, the proprietors soon discovered why, the new development proving vulnerable to flooding from the Braid Burn. With this natural obstacle overcome, the centre has gone on to provide a useful service for shoppers on the city's south side, combining two large stores with 47 small specialist units, totalling nearly 22,000 square metres of floorspace.

Kinnaird Park is situated on the extreme eastern boundary of the city built on the site of the former Newcraighall coalmine known familiarly as the 'Klondyke'. Kinnaird is well served by road, being close to the newly-instituted By-pass, improving its accessiblity to car-owning shoppers throughout the city and Lothians. Large shop units are formed around a courtyard car-park, with a bowling-alley and multi-screen cinema as additional attractions.

The Gyle is Edinburgh's biggest shopping development of them all. Stretching across 50 acres (20.5 hectares) west of Sighthill and Corstorphine, this £68 million shopping centre is a joint development between the District Council and two major retailers who are well represented at each end of an arcade running east and west. There are no fewer than 63 small retail units, some of them arranged as market stalls rather than as formal shops. There is a food court and bistro on a higher level.

With 2,600 free car parking spaces, the site is well equipped to handle the mass of shoppers it attracts, not only from the city, but also from the Lothians via the nearby By-pass, and West Lothian and Central Scotland from the A8. Car park users should remember to keep their heads down when walking to and from their cars – the centre has been built directly under the flight path to and from runway 13/31 at Edinburgh airport (*see* AIRPORTS). Another criticism concerns the lack of any entertainment facility – there is no multi-screen cinema or bowling facility here, as at Kinnaird Park, at the other end of Edinburgh's road by-pass system.

The *Co-operative* movement once held a strong grip on Edinburgh's retailing industry but today is less well-represented, and appears to have experienced difficulties in adjusting to changing customer habits. St Cuthbert's is no more, replaced by Scotmid and a small number of specialist brand-names. Scotmid owns two department stores in the city, at the former Leith Provident HQ, whose building still boasts a symbolic beehive in low-relief, and in Nicolson Street, but the store in Bread

Gyle shopping centre extends over 50 acres on the western edge of the city, and is a mecca for shoppers from all over the city and the Lothians. As this view proves, it is not necessary to depend on private transport to travel to and from the centre.

Street is now a hotel. There are 32 food stores trading in the city under the Scotmid banner, as well as undertakers, TV suppliers and travel agents. In 1960 it was all so different (*see* History of the Edinburgh Co-operative movement *below*).

History

The retail trade has had as much of an influence on Edinburgh's development as any of its basic manufacturing industries. With a long history of a population packed together in a restricted area, such as the Old Town, it was inevitable that the city would develop a tradition of self-sufficiency, of citizens making and trading, of buying and selling, amongst themselves.

A large number of baillies and provosts over the centuries were involved in the retail trade, and this may explain why street-trading has been less prominent in Edinburgh in the last 150 years than it has been in the recent history of other comparatively-sized British cities. Apart from the establishment of the Waverley Market in 1869, providing retail opportunities for hawkers and traders unable to pay for shop ownership or lease, there has been little encouragement for Edinburgh traders to operate, except through shops (*see also* MARKETS).

If there should be any doubt about the transformation in Edinburgh's retail shopping traditions, a glance at the difference over 35 years in the roll-call of shops in the first block of Princes Street itself, between Register House and South St Andrew's Street, will make the point.

Princes Street (1st Block, East to West); Numbering excluded. Shop positions not strictly aligned.

1960	1995
F.W. Woolworth	Burger King
Elliot's bookshop	(Unoccupied)
Montagu Burton	Evans (ladies' fashions)
(gents' tailoring)	Waterstone's (books)
	Principles (ladies' fashions)
	Walt Disney
Royal British Hotel	Royal British Hotel
John Collier (tailoring)	Birthday (card) Shop
H. Samuel (jeweller)	Owen & Robinson's
	(jewellers)
	Watches of Switzerland
R.W. Forsyth	Bally (shoes)
(gents' outfitters)	

So much of a prime site was this part of Princes Street that even the turnover of the popular Palace Cinema, between Woolworth's and Elliot's bookshop (the latter taken over a few years later by John Menzies), could not save it from being sold for retail space. Only hotels could generate sufficient revenue per square foot in Princes Street to prevent shops taking over the entire throughfare. For more information on this point, see CINEMAS. As observed in that section, nowadays a cinema in Princes Street might do very well, given the current recession in retail trading.

THE CO-OPERATIVE MOVEMENT IN EDINBURGH

In 1950, some 10 per cent of shops in Scotland were owned by retail co-operative societies (*Third Statistical Account*, 1966 – it is important to cite a source for this statistic, which seems almost unbelievable to a present-day shopper). Edinburgh had no fewer than three retail co-operative societies at one time – St Cuthbert's (by far the biggest, begun in 1859 with a capital of all of £30), Leith Provident and the Portobello. In 1923 St Cuthbert's was the most successful 'Co-op' in Britain; although only the fifth largest in the country, it enjoyed the highest turnover, and two years later opened a new bakery and dairy at Port Hamilton, between West Fountainbridge and Morrison Street.

By 1960, St Cuthbert's boasted 80 grocery outlets, 75 bakeries, 72 butchers (or 'Fleshing branches'), 28 fruit shops, nine tailoring, eight shoe shops, 17 'drug departments', along with (only) two fishmongers, two coal merchants, a dairy, firewood factory, undertakers, six laundries, and a farm at Gogar. In addition, there were 17 'County and Suburban' branches, including such city locations as Niddrie, Corstorphine, Craigentinny, and Davidson's Mains. The company's headquarters were (as Scotmid's are now) in East Fountainbridge, with the Bread Street side of the building being the main shop.

Leith Provident had its office in Junction Street with 27 grocery and bakery outlets stretching from Newhaven to Easter Road. There were seven fruit shops, 20 'fleshers' but, curiously, only one fish shop. The Provident even owned its own farm, at Kirknewton, near Midcalder.

The Portobello Society's office in the local High Street boasted a distinctive fish-scale tower (the latter is still there, although the Portobello store is no more). There were seven retail shops at one time, a Scotmid food store in Bath Street now replacing them.

These three societies were backed by their own Wholesale Association, complete with its own flour mills (Chancelot Mill originally sited just off Ferry Road), whose golden-tipped clock-tower brought such distinction to the Leith skyline.

In 1964 a 'Store' dividend guaranteed a shopper a return of sixteen pence (1s 4d) in the pound, equivalent to a present-day supermarket returning seven pence to the shopper for every pound he or she has just spent (adjusted, this could mean an effective 15 per cent discount to the regular shopper). The paperwork needed to process dividend payments was done in the years before computers were commonplace; perhaps the time of the 'co-op' could return? A 1995 discussion on retail shopping among a number of Edinburgh community councillors included an impromptu recitation of the 'Store' numbers held by every one of the group some three decades previously! There was nothing much wrong with a shopping movement which could inspire such brand loyalty!

Social Work

Responsibility for social work in Edinburgh lies with Edinburgh City Council since April 1996, taking over from the former Lothian Region. Headquarters for the city's Social Work department is sited at Shrubhill House, just off Leith Walk.

In 1995–6 23 per cent of the former Region's expenditure was budgeted on social work concerns, including home helps, residential homes for the disabled and disadvantaged, young person centres, and lunch clubs. Social work represented the second highest item of expenditure on the Council's list of functions, after education. There were 6,479 staff employed in social work activities in 1995-6, representing 28 per cent of the Council's staffing levels, again second only to education. These figures include data for Midlothian, East and West Lothian, as well as Edinburgh. Lothian was split into seven areas for administrative purposes, four of them in Edinburgh, dividing the city into north-west, south-west, north-east, and south-east, sectors.

In addition to the formal social work provisions made by the Regional authority, the city has a large number of voluntary bodies providing support services to those who need them. In 1992, Lothian Region signed a partnership agreement with the Edinburgh Voluntary Organisations Council, and in 1994/5 donated £18 million in grants to such bodies (including those in the Lothians outside Edinburgh), and provided relief from business rates where these organisations had rateable premises. Also in 1994/5 Edinburgh District Council donated £7 million to voluntary charities, although one social worker has pointed out that these figures can be inverted; in effect, the voluntary sector is currently providing £25 million-worth of social work services which the authority would otherwise have to carry out itself, almost certainly incurring higher staff costs.

Working to overcome *poverty* has been a local government responsibility since 1929, but it is the present District Council which administers hostels in the Grassmarket area, with assistance from the Region, while the

Salvation Army is also active in this area, as are a number of charitable organisations. As shown below, the number of lodging-type - accommodations has been reduced over the years, despite the unfortunate fact that the number of homeless appears to be increasing.

Lothian Region is now expected to work with the local Health authorities to implement the current Government's *Care in the Community policy*. This seeks to maximise those aspects of health and community care which can be centred on the home, and includes the running down of major institutional care centres for the psychiatrically ill wherever possible. This entails reducing the residential aspects of such centres as the Royal Edinburgh Hospital, and at Gogarburn. Whenever possible, patients are now being accommodated in small domestic units in residential areas, the homes concerned being run by charities part-funded by the Region.

A major problem for health and social work staff in recent years has been the increased availability of *drugs* on the streets, from amphetamines to heroin. The Region's Social Work Department and the Lothian Health Board have co-operated in setting up a number of projects to counteract the worst effects of drugs and to attempt to rehabilitate victims and offenders. An extra degree of urgency has been added by the evidence which shows that the spread of HIV and AIDS in Scotland has been largely associated with the sharing of hypodermics among drug users (*see also* CRIME). This has led to the introduction of schemes to supply needles to registered addicts, while those

individuals unfortunate enough to develop AIDS can be accommodated at Milestone House, Scotland's first AIDS hospice, located in the grounds of the City Hospital.

History

Edinburgh has a long history of help for the aged, the disabled, or disadvantaged. Both the Church and the Town Council have been active over the centuries in a social work capacity, long before the 1845 Act instituted a statutory requirement on local authorities to deal with poverty. In addition, medical services gradually became available from the opening of the Royal Infirmary in 1729 (*see* HOSPITALS).

It was only in the early years of the Victorian era that the Poor Law Act required local authorities to act to relieve poverty, although Edinburgh had already addressed the problem of providing care and education for impoverished or disowned children. In 1733 the Orphan's Hospital was set up, with support from the Church and the Society in Scotland for the Propagation of Christian Knowledge. Great stress was placed on the need for the children (54 soon after opening) to earn their keep by weaving and spinning. John Watson's School was established in the 1750s, also dedicated to the care of 'foundling' children.

A Charity Workhouse was opened in the city in 1743 by the order of the Town Council, with two more following in Canongate and West Kirk (St Cuthbert's) in 1761. Some education was given, but there should be no doubt about the arduousness of the workhouse regime for children, with a percentage death rate of more than three per cent for those in the Edinburgh establishment, and as much as ten per cent for those in the West Kirk workhouse, and 14 per cent in the Canongate. (Rates of infant mortality for even the children of well-off families were of course incredibly high by present-day standards).

In 1844, the year before the passing of Poor Law legislation, Edinburgh had just completed a century of running its own Charity Workhouse. This was situated at Greenlea, between Craiglockhart and Morningside, by then accommodating 600 adults and 480 children. In practice, children were accommodated separately from adults, as later required by legislation from 1934, there being six homes under city control, three in Colinton and three in Morningside, before local government reorganisation in 1975.

In 1948, responsibility for poor relief effectively passed to central government in the form of National Assistance (later, Social Security), following the legislation brought forward by Attlee's postwar Labour administration, although local authorities were still expected to care for the elderly, orphaned children, and those unfortunates who simply needed a bed for the night. In the last-named category of need, the City operated seven lodging houses at the end of the 1950s, six in the Grassmarket and Canongate area, and one in Leith. A women's hostel existed in Merchant Street.

Edinburgh has a tradition of **psychiatric care** going back nearly two centuries, mainly thanks to the efforts of Dr Andrew Duncan who agitated for the setting up of a proper facility for the care of those deemed to be suffering from mental illness. Before 1813, the psychiatrically ill in Edinburgh were condemned to be incarcerated in the Bedlam, in what was then the Bristo area of the city, where treatment was primitive or non-existent. Thanks to Duncan's efforts, a hospital was set up at Jordanburn, then outside the city to the south, and the site is now wholly occupied by the Royal Edinburgh Hospital, where one of its principal clinics, dealing with alcohol-related problems, is named after Duncan himself (*see also* HOSPITALS). For the care of the blind and deaf, *see* HOSPITALS.

Sports

Edinburgh is the base for the Scottish Sports Council, located at Caledonia House in the South Gyle area. This grant-making body supports, and helps to finance, most of the nation's sports. Its funds have, since 1994, been supplemented by revenue from the National Lottery.

The following sports are dealt with in this volume under their own headings:

Athletics, Boxing, Cricket, Football, Golf, Ice Sports, Racing, Rugby, Swimming, Tennis.

Of those sports facilities provided and maintained by Edinburgh District Council (until local government reorganisation in 1996), some 48 per cent of expenditure was met by user income, except for swimmers who contributed 37 per cent towards their facilities, while users of pitches and tracks contributed no less than 109 per cent of expenditure (1993/4 statistics).

Edinburgh's principal centre for track

and field sports is **Meadowbank Stadium**, built on the site of Old and New Meadowbank stadia. The Old was a football pitch off the now-vanished Clockmill Lane, home to Leith Athletic FC, and surrounded by a cinder track used for speedway meets. New Meadowbank, opened next door in 1934, is described under ATHLETICS, which it principally catered for, although football was also played here, the action perfectly visible to passengers on double-deck buses passing by, so modest was the terracing for spectators. At the end of the 1960s this was all swept away, the speedway to Powderhall, and the football to fields afar,

in preparation for the present stadium, giving athletics centre stage.

Opened by the former City Council in May 1970, and presently owned by Edinburgh District Council, the stadium is the largest and best-equipped of its kind in Scotland and, along with the city's Commonwealth Pool (*see* SWIMMING) provided the nucleus for the 9th and 13th **Commonwealth Games** in 1970 and 1986 respectively.

The 1970 event will be remembered for its atmosphere of good-natured rivalry, which led to it being dubbed 'The Friendly Games'. Scottish athletes excelled, particularly Ian Stewart in the 5,000 metres,

9th Commonwealth Games, 1970. The Scottish team enters the Meadowbank stadium during the opening ceremony in what became known as the 'Friendly Games', as successful as the 1986 Games (also held in Edinburgh) were disastrous, particularly in financial terms. (The Scotsman)

Lachie Stewart in the 10,000, Rosemary Stirling in the 800, and Rosemary Payne in the discus event. Unfortunately the 1986 Games were fraught with financial difficulties, being forced to survive without government support, and cursed by bad weather. Victories for Liz Lynch in the womens' 10,000 metres and Sally Gunnell in the 100 metres hurdles helped to launch their careers, but the 1986 Games were otherwise unmemorable, and the real drama was unfolded in the committee-rooms.

The posthumously-disgraced business tycoon Robert Maxwell had announced his support for the Games at the eleventh hour, although this did not run to the kind of financial support many contractors had been led to expect, and some of them were forced to write off their losses in an experience which the city of Edinburgh would rather not have had – and all because the Scottish capital had offered to take over the event when another venue had to withdraw!

From 1974–95, Meadowbank was rented as the home ground for Meadowbank Thistle FC, now playing at Livingston (*see also* FOOTBALL). The Meadowbank site has a cycling velodrome (for which a roof would be a welcome addition) and an events hall suitable for basketball and indoor hockey. On the other side of the city, Saughton Sports Centre provides much-needed facilities.

Craiglockhart Tennis and Sports Centre occupies the site known locally as 'Happy Valley', the Craiglockhart centre being purchased by the City Council in 1958 and converted into a sports facility in 1976. Extensive refurbishment and extensions in 1994/5 have produced one of the finest sports centres in the country, with six indoor tennis courts and eight clay courts outdoors (*see also* TENNIS). Other sports such as badminton and table tennis are catered for, as well as aerobics.

Powderhall Stadium closed on 6 October 1995 after 120 years of varied sporting activity. Most closely associated with greyhound racing in the years after 1922, the stadium hosted athletics events from 1871, when the famous Powderhall Sprint was first run at the riverside stadium, with amateur athletics championships being held there from 1883 (*see* ATHLETICS). The great Eric Liddell recalled training at Powderhall to the background noise of baying dogs, and both Leith Athletic and Edinburgh City football teams used the venue. In the final 19 years of service, Edinburgh Monarchs speedway team roared round the cinder track, having moved from Old Meadowbank. Their final contest against Glasgow Tigers was won without the loss of a single heat, but both teams have now been replaced by a Scottish Monarchs side, racing in Glasgow.

American football (which holds no similarity to association football) is a new addition to the Edinburgh sports scene, the Scottish Claymores team opening their campaign at Murrayfield rugby stadium in 1995. The team met with only limited success in its first season, but in its second, won the World Bowl Final at Murrayfield, being watched by a huge TV audience worldwide.

Statistical Accounts

The last of the three *Statistical Accounts* about Edinburgh was published in 1966, under the editorship of David Keir. As the frequent references to it throughout this book will show, the Third account volume was an encyclopedia about Edinburgh in all but title – an information source as reliable as it was fascinating.

The 1966 volume is arranged into eight parts – 'The Place and the People,' 'Capital City,' 'The Public Weal' (i.e. local government, politics, public health, housing etc), 'The Social Pattern,' 'Finance and Industry,' 'Education,' 'The Arts and Humanities,' and finally 'Nature.' It boasted no fewer than 200 contributors.

In this volume the narrative is much more self-conscious than in the two previous editions, although still highly informative, and supported by an excellent index. The unconscious testimony which the modern reader takes from the 1966 volume is the perceived homogeneity of Edinburgh society at that time – ethnic communities are treated by the *Account* as curiosities, a brief description of them tacked on to a fairly lengthy discourse about European groups in the city. Yet the British government was already trying to integrate Britain into Europe at that time, and the modern reader might find this to be an inverted sense of priorities in discussing the demography of the area.

The most curious feature of an otherwise much-prized volume (try writing a book about Edinburgh without referring to the *Third Statistical Account*!) is a chapter entitled 'Room at the Top', where a number of establishment figures of the 1960s, including Sir Compton Mackenzie, discuss such compelling matters as the politeness of Edinburgh taxi-drivers, while failing, in spite of the chapter heading, to address the egalitarianism, or otherwise, of Edinburgh society.

Below is a brief history of the *Statistical Accounts*. Before proceeding however, mention should be also made of other directories about Edinburgh which are useful to the historian. *A List of Neighbours and Inhabitants* was first printed in 1682 for the Canongate and Leith areas, but the most important of these early directories is *Williamson's Directory for Edinburgh, Canongate, Leith and Suburbs*. First published in 1773/4, by Peter Williamson, a remarkable individual who claimed to have been kidnapped, and forced to live with Red Indians in North America, Williamson's is a simple list of names and addresses arranged alphabetically.

The *Edinburgh and Leith Post Office Directory* began publication in 1807/8, and comprised alphabetical listings of householders and businesses, as well as a street-by-street directory, indicating who lived at each address. While essential to citizens at a time before phone books were available, this series, available on reference in most of the city's larger libraries, is invaluable to the historian.

From these volumes can be learned such facts as the number of printers operating in the city at any one time, the name and frequency of ships travelling to London – even a 'reverse' telephone directory in later years' volumes. The list was compiled by postmen visiting premises in the afternoons, persuading residents and businesses to update their existing details. Unfortunately, some postal staff were more diligent than others, and the books' details have to be treated with caution, often being out-of-date, particularly in the later volumes. The annual series ended with the 1974-75 volume, possibly the victim of changed industrial practices.

History of the Statistical Accounts

Published by the Scottish Council for Social Service, with assistance from Edinburgh University, the third Account differed from its two predecessors in not being arranged on a parish-by-parish basis, nor was it compiled by the incumbent ministers. The first account, arranged by Sir John Sinclair, and published from 1791 to 1798 was so arranged; indeed whenever a description of a parish was received at the editorial office, it was included in whatever volume was about to go to press, irrespective of geographical or alphabetical arrangement. An index was bound with the 20th volume in the series (but not in the final volume!), and an enterprising English publisher republished the series in postwar years with the parishes sensibly grouped into cities or counties.

The second account series was known as the *New Statistical Account* and appeared between 1834 and 1845, arranged by city or county. 'Edinburgh' is in fact Midlothian in this series, with such communities as Colinton, Corstorphine, and Duddingston included as parishes outside the city. Edinburgh itself is described in the words of ministers of 17 urban parishes.

The third series produced its Edinburgh volume with little delay while the work was in press. The same cannot be said of the Midlothian or West Lothian volumes – containing descriptions of some areas, such as Ratho, Kirkliston, and South Queensferry now considered to be in the Edinburgh municipality – but these volumes were respectively some 22 and 26 years in press, unfortunately. The Midlothian account is now largely of historical interest, despite its comparatively recent publication date (1977), while the West Lothian volume published in 1992 sensibly carries a modern postscript for each chapter.

All three editions have provided historians with a valuable, indeed invaluable, source of information about local communities, often in considerable detail. If there is a detectable difference in writing style, it lies in the more direct reporting approach of the first series, where the data seems more raw, making the unconscious testimony so much more valuable to the present-day research worker.

Swimming

Edinburgh's swimming pools administered by the District Council admitted more than a million bathers in the year 1993/4. Expenditure *per capita* of the city's population on swim centres (and other recreational facilities) came to over £30 in the same year. Just over one-third of expenditure on the city's pools is met directly from admission charges, and the average attendance per hour at pools is 56 – roughly one admission each minute during the hours of opening.

At the time of writing, swimming in the Firth of Forth is not encouraged, indeed it was recently banned altogether at Portobello, but citizens have a choice of a number of excellent indoor facilities – the Royal Commonwealth Pool, Ainslie Park Leisure Centre, Leith Waterworld, Wester Hailes Community Centre, Leith Victoria, Portobello, Infirmary Street, Warrender, Dalry, and Glenogle. All those below are the responsibility of Edinburgh District Council at the time of writing, with the exception of Wester Hailes Education Centre, run by Lothian Region, the authority also responsible for school pools.

Edinburgh citizens who have made their mark as outstanding swimmers include David Wilkie, Olympic breast-stroke gold medallist in 1976, and Portobello's W.E. (Ned) Barnie, one of the outstanding long-distance swimmers of his time who swam the English Channel both ways, and who swam from Fisherrow to Portobello while in his 70s. Sir Peter Heatly, for so long associated with the Commonwealth Games movement, made his name as the most prominent high-diver in the city's history, winning three successive Empire gold medals at the games held in 1950, 1954, and 1958.

INFIRMARY STREET BATHS
Edinburgh's oldest and most centrally-situated baths are to be found at Infirmary Street, just a belly flop away from South Bridge. Opened by the Town Council on 25 July 1887, they were intended to provide swimming and washing facilities – in the form of two pools and individual baths – for a population of 100,000 living without proper washing facilities within a quarter mile radius in the crowded closes of the Old Town.

Originally comprising two pools – it seemed essential to segregate male and female bathers in an earlier age, no matter how unrevealing swimwear was in those days – Infirmary Street baths were still heavily used until recently, although not to the extent of three-quarters of a million who swam or bathed there in 1943. Only one pool now survives, the ladies' having been destroyed by vandals in 1960, the shell of the building still standing. Closure was threatened in the late 1970s and again in the 1990s when the leaking swimming pool, losing 8,500 gallons a day, proved difficult to repair, but the crisis was averted by the use of special sealant, and Infirmary Street managed to remain open until 1996, when it finally closed its doors.

PORTOBELLO BATHS
No longer to be confused with the open air pool since the latter's demolition in 1987, Portobello's indoor baths are an architectural gem. Designed by City Architect Robert Morham, and opened in 1898, this is a Hispanic-style building, whose balconies overlook the Forth at the bottom of Bellfield Street. Inside are two pools, the larger, originally the mens', being overlooked by elaborate balconies now unfortunately hidden by a false ceiling. Even worse has been the change from salt to fresh water, the intending swimmer no longer being greeted by the distinctive smell of salt before even having a chance to cast a cloot. Saltwater also provided excellent buoyancy, particularly appreciated by the less experienced swimmer. Turkish and aerotone baths have long been a feature at Portobello, and the baths is a centre for Portobello Swimming Club and the Water Polo Club, both

POOL	YR. OPENED	MAIN POOL(ft)	2ND POOL(ft)	REMARKS
Infirmary St	1887	80 x 40	35 x 20	2nd pool closed 1960
Dalry	1895	75 x 35		
Leith Victoria	1898	75 x 35		Reopened 1995
Portobello	1898	75 x 35	50 x 25	
Glenogle	1900	75 x 35		
Warrender	1907	75 x 35		Private 1887–1906
Portobello (Outdoor)	1936	300 x 135		Closed 1978
Royal Commonwealth	1970	150 x 65	60 x 48	
Wester Hailes Education Centre		75 ft long		Plus diving & toddlers' pools
Ainslie Park	1989	75 x 38		
Leith Waterworld	1992			Irregular configuration

enjoying excellent reputations in competitions. Closed at the time of writing, Portobello baths are to benefit from a multi-million pound refurbishment scheduled for completion in 1997.

ROYAL COMMONWEALTH POOL

Opened for the Commonwealth Games in 1970, and also used for the 1986 Games, the 'Commonwealth' has established itself as an integral part of the Edinburgh, indeed Scottish, swimming scene. The main swimming area of more than 1,000 square metres is overlooked by a L-shaped viewing area as well as spectator accommodation along one side. Secondary pools exist for learning and for children, while the construction of a diving area, going down to a maximum depth of just over 16 feet, provides an excellent facility for divers, although its introduction has led to the removal of diving boards from all other city baths. It is perhaps no coincidence that the standard of diving among young swimmers is no longer what it once was, and the excellent diving facility at the Commonwealth pool has unfortunately failed to compensate.

WARRENDER BATHS

Unusual in that it began its existence as a private swimming pool, Warrender fell into public hands in 1906, when club membership subscriptions were insufficient to sustain it. Warrender has a pleasant atmosphere, with changing cubicles along each length of its single pool, but without the galleries which characterise Infirmary Street. There is a modern fitness room, but no refreshment facilities. Warrender club, which originally created the pool, is now thriving.

DALRY BATHS

Opened in 1895 in a congested area of the city, Dalry Baths were designed, like Portobello's, by City Architect Robert Morham, but with Italianate detail in a building enclosing the standard 75 x 35 feet (22.5 x 10.5 metres) pool.

GLENOGLE BATHS

Five years after the opening of Dalry Baths, Glenogle's opened, in the Water of Leith valley between Stockbridge and Canonmills. The architect was again Robert Morham, his building adapted from his Dalry design, with a standard sized pool.

LEITH VICTORIA

Opened in the same year as Portobello's indoor pool, the 'Viccy' is a popular swim centre just off Junction Place (and a few yards from Dr Bell's School, one of the first local authority schools in the Edinburgh area to have its own pool). A red sandstone building with a standard-sized pool, the 'Viccy' was threatened with closure when Leith Waterworld opened only about 600 yards away in 1992. Fortunately, the District Council accepted that the new facility was unsuitable for those requiring to swim for fitness, and made the happy decision to repair and reopen the older pool, in September 1995.

AINSLIE PARK

Opened in July 1989, its principal claim to fame is its new (1995) installation of an ultra-violet cleaning system which is unique in Scotland, but is believed likely to maintain pool hygiene as an alternative to chlorine.

Private baths exist off Belford Road at **Drumsheugh**, its pool building distinguished with Moorish columns. Opened in 1884, before the city afforded ordinary people the opportunity of indoor swimming, this facility was built on three levels. The main attraction is a 70 x 35 feet (21 x 10.5 metre) pool, with depth increasing from three to eight feet (0.9 to 2.4 metres). There are associated Turkish baths.

History

Before environmental laws became more stringent, bathing in the Firth of Forth was popular with Edinburgh citizens. Not just with city folk either – Portobello beach in particular echoed to Glaswegian accents for the second half of every July. There was precious little time for this before the 19th century, when bathing took on a formalised character, with the swimmer only emerging from his or her wheeled bathing machine once it had been trundled to the water's edge. Photographic views of Leith Sands show bathing machines still in use in the 1860s, and they were doubtless used at Portobello at that time as well.

The early history of indoor baths is almost entirely centred on therapeutic bathing, and not swimming in the athletic sense. Even individual baths were rare enough in the Old Town of Edinburgh – not least because the water supply was so unreliable – although commercial baths were open from the second half of the 18th century. The first Royal Infirmary placed great emphasis on bathing for hygiene and therapeutic reasons. Portobello had baths from 1804 and Seafield from 1813, but it was not until late in the 19th century that swimming indoors became popular.

The history of municipal provision of baths in Edinburgh begins with the opening of the Infirmary Street facility in 1887, and 'baths' was a literal description. Even today individual domestic-size baths are available for public hire, while the main attraction was the existence of two

Outdoor swimming was still popular in 1950s Portobello judging by this shot of the eastern terrace of the open air pool. Opened in 1936, when the Lord Provost's party had to flee the artificially-generated waves, the pool lost popularity in the 1960s and '70s, closing in 1978. (The Scotsman)

swimming-pools, one of which is no longer extant. The size of the main pool is 80 by 40 feet (24 x 12 metres), the ladies' pool having been 35 by 20 feet (10.5 x 6 metres). These sizes were slightly larger than the later pools constructed in the city, as can be seen from the table on page 332. Notice that Edinburgh had two Olympic-size pools between the years 1936-78, while Glasgow, despite its pioneering of public swimming baths (5 facilities by the time

Infirmary Street opened), has only just opened an Olympic-sized pool.

Edinburgh's swimmers are the poorer for the loss of the **Portobello Outdoor Pool**, an Olympic sized utility, with diving facilities, novelty features, a restaurant, capacity for 6,000 spectators, and lacking only one detail – a roof. It was situated between Portobello High Street and the Promenade, immediately to the west of the Figgate Burn.

Designed in cream and green concrete by Ian Warner of the City Engineer's department, the pool was opened on 30 May 1936. It occupied formerly derelict industrial land next to the power station, the latter supposedly supplying heat to warm the water to 68°F, although your hardy encyclopedia editor must, from personal experience, cast doubt on whether this worked properly! No less than 300 feet by 130 (90 x 39 metres, twice the area of the Royal Commonwealth pool), with depth varying from 12 to 78 inches (0.3 to 1.95 metres), the pool could cater for 1,284 bathers simultaneously, and boasted a 33 foot (9.9 metre) bathing tower over a 15 feet (4.5 metre) deep area.

Behind sinsister-looking grills at the deep end lurked wave-making equipment – four 24 feet-long (7.2 metre) 'plunger' pistons, whose power was badly underestimated on the opening day. Veteran Portobello swimmer Ethel Tweedie recalled the Lord Provost's official party in 1936 scattering from the steps of the shallow end as the machine was turned on and the waves suddenly bore down on them! In later years a siren had to be sounded before this feature was brought into operation.

Portobello's climate was really too cold for this to be a popular attraction postwar, and by 1978 the annual turnover of swimmers barely exceeded that of a prewar Saturday. Closure followed the following year, although demolition did not take place until 1987. Had a roof been provided, the city could have retained a swimming pool which was one of the biggest and finest in Europe. The site is now utilised for five-a-side football and a new indoor bowling facility.

Tennis

Lawn Tennis has been played in Edinburgh for over a century, and the capital is home to a number of long-established clubs, as well as the Scottish Lawn Tennis Association, based in the city's West End at Melville Crescent.

The recently upgraded Craiglockhart Tennis and Sports Centre offers exciting new facilities for the sport, with eight American fast-dry clay courts outdoors and six indoors. With up to 2,000 spectator capacity, the Centre hosted the World Doubles Cup in May 1995. While welcoming the investment in the new complex, some older tennis enthusiasts have regretted the loss of grass surfaces at Craiglockhart at the present time.

As well as Craiglockhart, Edinburgh City Council also runs a number of tennis courts throughout the city, and courts, rackets, and balls can be hired for a small fee.

The tennis clubs based in Edinburgh, and members of the East of Scotland District Association, associated to the SLTA, are as follows:

History
There were already a number of lawn tennis clubs in Edinburgh when, in June 1895, 19 enthusiasts met to form the Scottish Lawn Tennis Association in the offices of the Scottish Equitable Life Association in St Andrew's Square. (Now known as Scottish Equitable PLC, this company appropriately sponsored the centenary history of the Association in 1995, written by George Robertson.)

The first two office-bearers were both members of the city's Dyvours Club, the

NAME OF CLUB	ADDRESS	NO. COURTS	REMARKS
Abercorn	Abercorn Crescent	5	
Barnton Park	12 Barnton Park	4	Floodlights
Blackhall	Keith Terrace	3	F/lights
Braid	Cluny Gardens	3	F/lights proposed
Colinton	Westgarth Avenue	6	
Corstorphine	Belgrave Road	3	
Craigmillar Park	Cameron Toll	4	F/lights
Dean	Lennox Street	4	
Drummond	Scotland St Lane East	2	
Dyvours (Grange Club)	Raeburn Place	8	F/lights
Hatton	Burnwynd, Kirknewton	3	
Henderland Road	Henderland Road	2	
Lomond Park	Stirling Road	5	
Merchiston	Polwarth Terrace	3	
Moray House C.P.E.	Cramond Road N.	5	
Mortonhall	Pentland Terrace	5	F/lights proposed
Murrayfield	Corstorphine Road	4	
St Serfs	Clark Road	3	
Thistle	Paties Road	6	F/lights
University of Edinburgh	Peffermill	3	
Waverley	Suffolk Road	4	

oldest in the city and still going strong. It owes its unusual name to the term 'Dyvours hose', a legal requirement that, under Scots law, bankrupts were required to wear contrastingly-coloured hose or socks. This may have provided an analogy with the club's policy of playing summer and winter versions of the game (the latter indoors in what was described as the 'Tin Temple').

The Scottish Championships predated the establishment of the SLTA by some 18 years, and was played indoors in the Tin Temple for the first six years from 1878. The competiton did not leave Edinburgh as a venue until 1893, but was soon back again in the capital, at such locations as Corstorphine, Myreside, Inverleith, Craiglockhart, Powderhall, and Murrayfield.

Theatres

Edinburgh has six theatres in use for professionally-produced drama all the year round (in 1995), and five more which mount dramatic productions from time to time but also fulfil other functions. These are listed below, and their history summarised. Former theatres are listed in a separate table.

Theatrical venues less frequently used for drama, include the Church Hill Theatre in Morningside Road, the Assembly Hall, Assembly Rooms, and Adam House. Of the above, the Church Hill Theatre, opened in 1965, is a favourite with amateur groups, but often features professional drama at

NAME OF THEATRE	LOCATION	CAPACITY	1994 TURNOVER (£M)
Playhouse	Greenside Place	3,000	£9.0
Festival	Nicolson Street	1,900	£5.75 (Est.)
King's	Leven Street	1,300	£1.9
Royal Lyceum	Grindlay Street	773	£1.3
Traverse	Cambridge Street	350	£0.6
Theatre Workshop	Hamilton Place	143	£0.1

Festival time. The Playhouse comes into this category, and, although the biggest Edinburgh theatre in terms of capacity and earning-power, has become an almost permanent home nowadays to musicals and pop concerts, belying its early history as the capital's biggest cinema (*see* CINEMAS). The Assembly Hall is of course the main meeting-place of the Church of Scotland, who generously made it available for Festival productions from 1948, while the Assembly Rooms in George Street have become an important centre for Fringe drama, being ingeniously adapted with a number of temporary stages. Adam House, well-known to those undergoing written examinations over the years, contains a compact basement theatre popular with amateur groups.

The official Festival has also seen the utilisation of such unlikely theatre spaces as Murrayfield Ice Rink and the Cornmarket at Chesser. With around 180 venues being used at every Festival Fringe, it is almost impossible to list all the theatre spaces in Edinburgh, most of them improvisatory.

The Ross bandstand in Princes Street gardens is now officially entitled the Ross Theatre, although it can scarcely be adjudged a drama centre, and an open-air amphitheatre, somewhat underused, exists in Braidburn Valley Park, with the Braid Burn, and a path, separating the grassy stage from the tiers of grass 'seating'. Strangely perhaps, no attempt has so far been made in Edinburgh to follow Glasgow's example and convert former industrial premises into a theatre as the Tramway and The Shed have been so imaginatively created in that city, from a former transport depot and shipbuilding facility respectively.

FESTIVAL THEATRE

Formerly known as the Empire, this is the flagship of Edinburgh theatres. It stands in Nicolson Street almost opposite the Royal College of Surgeons, its exterior transformed in 1993 by the addition of a three-storey glass-faced atrium, although the auditorium seating and fittings are disappointingly traditional.

The theatre has a long history as a variety house, as the Empire Palace Theatre of Varieties from 1892, when part of the Moss chain of theatres. Previously, the Nicolson Street site was occupied by circuses and the Royal Amphitheatre. Variety occupied the new stage from the start, although the city's first cinema show took place here, in 1896. Fire severely damaged the original theatre in May 1911, causing 11 deaths, including that of Sigmund Neuberger, better known as the illusionist Lafayette (*see* FIRE FIGHTING). The house reopened in the following August, and in October 1928 re-

No longer Edinburgh's largest cinema, the Playhouse has been a theatre since 1987, and is seen in this 1995 picture in its role as an official Festival venue. Its survival is very much a matter for rejoicing; tenders for contractors to undertake its demolition were issued in 1984. (Frank Reid)

emerged from a year-long refurbishment with its auditorium very much as it is today. It boasted seating for 2,016 (since reduced) and a huge stage area of 900 square metres, particularly appreciated by ballet companies during the Festival. Despite these advantages, the theatre was sold to a leisure company for bingo in 1963.

In 1991, with no prospect of a custom-built opera house on the horizon, Edinburgh District Council were pleased to back the creation of a trust to purchase the theatre, and with the support of Lothian Region and Lothian and Edinburgh Enterprise, succeeded in refurbishing the building to the highest modern standards, being assisted by funding from Historic Scotland, the Scottish Arts Council and Scottish Tourist Board. The new Festival Theatre opened in June 1994, and 320,000 tickets were sold in the first nine months. Unfortunately, subsequent financial

With its attractive glass-fronted atrium, the Festival Theatre has brightened up Nicolson Street since 1994. Its pedigree goes back more than a century, even before the Empire Palace Theatre opened here in 1892, with Scotland's first film show taking place here four years later. (City of Edinburgh Council)

difficulties have slightly tarnished what has otherwise been a highly accomplished renovation.

KING'S

Possibly Edinburgh's best-known theatre, the King's was completed in December 1906, with its owners in financial difficulties. It conveniently fell into the hands of the Howard and Wyndham company (owners of the Royal Lyceum) who shrewdly put the building contractor on their Board. The new theatre opened with pantomime, with which it has long been identified, as well as touring musicals and plays, while providing the best that Edinburgh could offer as an extemporised opera house for the International Festival.

Originally seating 1,800, this total was reduced by 200 with the closure of the 'Gods' in 1951, and has lowered further to 1,300 subsequently. Its external appearance is described by Charles McKean as 'good, not brilliant, Edwardian baroque in red sandstone, rather Glaswegian', but its extensive wood and glass interiors do not inhibit a pleasant sense of cosiness.

Owned by Edinburgh District Council since the 1970s, the King's has seen much of its cultural programme transferred to the new Festival Theatre, with a corresponding increase in touring productions outwith Festival times. The pantos have never stopped.

ROYAL LYCEUM

Situated in Grindlay Street, with the Usher Hall as its closest neighbour, the Royal Lyceum is old enough to dispute the Empire's (Festival Theatre's) claim to be the city's oldest theatrical site. Opened in 1883 and used continuously for drama ever since, this is very much a Victorian architectural confection, which seated as many as 2,500 in the 1930s, and now boasts the addition of a glass entrance porch.

The Lyceum is the city's principal repertory theatre with a resident company dating from 1929, from which year the Masque, Brandon Thomas, and Wilson Barrett companies trod the boards here before the Second World War. As one of the Howard and Wyndham theatres in the city, the Lyceum tended to present a slightly upmarket image, while its owners' other houses, the King's and Theatre Royal, specialised in pantos and musicals, and music hall, respectively. In 1965 the Lyceum became the first repertory theatre in Scotland to receive local government support, the theatre company producing its first offering – *The Servant of Twa Maisters* – on 1 October of that year.

In the 1970s, the theatre was envisioned by many as the obvious home for a Scottish National Theatre Company, but despite the creative energies of Bill Bryden, who did much to give the Lyceum a highly innovative reputation, this failed to materialise. Taken over by Edinburgh District Council in 1977, the Theatre continues to offer new productions to the Edinburgh playgoer through the contributions of its own resident company. Its centenary was celebrated by the publication of a history by playwright Donald Campbell – *A Brighter Sunshine* (Polygon).

TRAVERSE

Synonymous with experimental theatre at its best, Edinburgh's Traverse has graduated from being an independent theatrical club in a rundown part of the Old Town, to the status of a subsidised public theatre in the most luxurious of quarters in the New.

The Traverse was founded in 1963 by a group of citizens, led by American Jim Haynes and the city's own Richard Demarco, who were determined that Edinburgh's intellectual life would not be restricted to the three weeks of the International Festival. Opening a theatre in what was virtually a living room in a James Court tenement in the Lawnmarket was a bold act in itself, and a succession of innovative directors ensured that a formidable reputation was built up. Premises in the Grassmarket were later utilised before the move to the New Town in 1992 was made possible with the support of Edinburgh District Council.

Now the Traverse is to be found

underneath a commercial building off Cambridge Street known familiarly as the Drum, offering new plays at remarkably low seat prices, and with good restaurant and bar facilities. Nevertheless, older theatre-goers may miss the unique atmosphere of the informal early days – when a rapt audience once watched as a young man in modern dress burst into the middle of a Greek tragedy and asked loudly and clearly 'Did someone order a taxi?'

THEATRE WORKSHOP

Founded in the early 1970s, Theatre Workshop began as an educational charity intended to introduce children in less affluent areas to the attractions of theatre. By 1973 the Workshop was looking for accommodation to replace its base in Hanover Street, and is now established in a former public hall in Hamilton Place, Stockbridge. With a theatre there seating around 150, it continues to be supported by the local authorities and the Scottish Arts Council. Programmes are no longer exclusively aimed at children, but there is an extensive extra-mural programme to encourage maximum participation by young people in theatre.

History

As with dancing, drama and theatrical activity were originally centred on the Court at Holyrood, where the indoor tennis court was used for plays, its manager in post-Restoration days being Thomas Sydserf, publisher of Scotland's first newspaper, the *Mercurius Caledonius* (*see* NEWSPAPERS). Holyrood was the venue for the first production of Shakespeare in Scotland – *Macbeth*, produced in 1672. Just over a century later, the tennis court was destroyed by fire, in 1774.

Even earlier than this, a performance of Sir David Lyndsay's *Ane Satyre of the Thrie Estaitis* was given before Marie of Guise in the open air at Greenside in August 1554, near the site of the present Playhouse theatre. In 1561 Town Council members decided to ban a dramatic performance of *Robin Hood*, only to find themselves chased by an angry mob of citizens, who besieged the provost and baillies in the Tolbooth until they rescinded their decision by a public retraction at the Mercat Cross.

By the 17th century, the city authorities still viewed drama with suspicion, although in 1670 permission was given for the erection of three booths for revels, and in 1682 a booth with a floor area of no less than 800 square feet was allowed to be built near Blackfriars' Wynd. The municipal appointment of Master of the Revels existed well into the 18th century in Edinburgh.

The 18th century saw travelling players reach the city in greater numbers, and with more professionalism; when actor-manager Anthony Aston brought drama to Skinner's Hall in 1727, he caused equal drama in court by challenging local complaints against structural problems in a neighbouring property, allegedly caused by audience overcrowding. The Town Council was clearly ill at ease with the idea of the citizens enjoying themselves, budgeting payment on this occasion for witnesses against the travelling show!

Nevertheless, Taylor's Hall, opened by a Signora Violante from Dublin, and a building in Carruber's Close, were used for theatrical entertainment in the 1730s and

CLOSED THEATRES

(arranged by last-known name).

NAME OF THEATRE	LOCATION	CLOSED	REMARKS
ADELPHI			
(*see* THEATRE ROYAL, Broughton Street)			
ALHAMBRA	Leith Walk	c1918	Later a cinema
ALHAMBRA			
(*see* GARRICK)			
AMPHITHEATRE	Leith Walk area	c1792	
CALEDONIAN			
(*see* THEATRE ROYAL, Broughton Street)			
CONCERT HALL	Canongate	1769	
CORRIE'S NEW ROOMS			
(*see* THEATRE ROYAL, Broughton Street)			
EDINBURGH	Castle Terrace	1877	Later Synod Hall & cinema
EMPIRE			
(*see* FESTIVAL in list of present-day theatres)			
FESTIVAL			
(*see* GAIETY)			
GAIETY	Leith Kirkgate	1956	Also a cinema
GARRICK	Grove Street	1921	Also a cinema
GATEWAY	Elm Row, Leith Walk	1965	Also a cinema
GRAND	St Stephen's Street	1909	Later circus & cinema
JUNCTION STREET THEATRE			
(*see* NEW THEATRE, Bangor Road)			
LEITH ROYAL MUSIC HALL	Tolbooth Wynd	1872	
LITTLE THEATRE	High School Yards	c1964	University Settlement
MARIONVILLE	Marionville Road	1790	Private, (*see* text)
NEW PAVILLION			
(*see* GARRICK)			
NEW PRINCESS			
(Kirkgate, *see* GAIETY)			
NEW THEATRE	Bangor Road, Leith	1888	Same as Junction St Theatre
NEW THEATRE CIRCUS			
(*see* THEATRE ROYAL, Broughton Street)			
NEW THEATRE ROYAL			
(*see* THEATRE ROYAL, Broughton Street)			
OPERETTA HOUSE	Chambers Street	1906	Later a cinema
OPERETTA HOUSE	Waterloo Place	c1878	
PALLADIUM	East Fountainbridge	1966	Also cinema, circus, & disco

PANTHEON			
(*see* THEATRE ROYAL, Broughton Street)			
PAVILLION			
(*see* GARRICK)			
PLAY HOUSE	Canongate	1747	
PRINCE OF WALES			
(*see* GARRICK)			
PRINCE OF WALES			
(*see* OPERETTA HOUSE, Waterloo Place)			
PRINCES	Shandwick Place	c1956	Founded by Edin. Play Club
PRINCESS	Nicolson Street	1881	Later a cinema
QUEEN'S			
(*see* SOUTHMINSTER)			
QUEEN'S			
(*see* THEATRE ROYAL, Broughton Street)			
ROYAL PRINCESS'S			
(*see* PRINCESS, Nicolson Street)			
SADDLER'S WELLS			
(*see* THEATRE ROYAL, Broughton Street)			
SOUTHMINSTER	Nicolson Street	1877	
THEATRE ROYAL			
(Canongate, *SEE* CONCERT HALL)			
THEATRE ROYAL	Broughton Street	1946	
THEATRE ROYAL	Shakespeare Sq.	1859	
(now GPO)			
TIVOLI			
(*see* GRAND)			

For those theatres which converted to cinemas, *see* CINEMAS.

1740s, the latter venue being financed by the poet Allan Ramsay, opening in November 1736 with *The Recruiting Officer* and *The Virgin Unmasked*. Only one year later, theatre was effectively banned in any part of Britain outside London unless a Royal warrant was obtained. To circumvent the regulation, drama was often advertised as an interlude in a programme of music 'but everyone knew that the concert was perfunctory and that the interlude was the real business of the evening', as historian A.J. Youngson recounts.

In 1747 a theatre known as the Concert Hall was built at the head of the Canongate, probably in the area of the present-day Old Playhouse Close at 196 High Street. Its manager at one time was West Digges, who had an unfortunate occasional tendency to forget to pay his actors, and he had to reside within the sanctuary of Holyrood at one time (*see* ABBEYS). The Canongate theatre was the venue in 1756 for the first performance of John Home's play *Douglas*, which, although it inspired the enthusiastic cry from a member of the audience of 'Whaur's your Shakespeare noo?', has failed to emulate the immortality of the Stratford Bard's works.

A performance of Ramsay's *Gentle Shepherd* in Leith in February 1767 is significant in being the earliest documented theatre event in the port. Billed as an interval entertainment in a programme of music, the play was performed in what historian J.S. Marshall has identified as the Ark in Cables Wynd.

Edinburgh's first custom-built theatre was the Theatre Royal in Shakespeare Square, where the Post Office building now stands on the north-east corner of North Bridge. This opened in 1769, three years before the North Bridge connected the Old Town with what was soon to become the New. The neighbouring bridge had in fact collapsed when still unfinished at the time of the theatre's opening, leaving the new building almost alone on the north side of the valley. Old Town residents had to approach via Leith Wynd or Halkerston's Wynd, the latter having to be liberally strewn with ashes on winter evenings to allow the bearers of sedan chairs a firm foothold.

The Theatre Royal overcame the problems caused by its initial inaccessibility, and, reports Edward Topham, was well-patronised. In 1784 the Kirk's General Assembly is reputed to have closed early enough to allow the ministers and elders time to see Sarah Siddons tread the boards at the Royal. Entertainment historian George Baird, to whom we owe so much

for our knowledge of the theatres and cinemas of Edinburgh (*see* BIBLIOGRAPHY, Leisure), believed that the theatre was very profitable when demolished after compulsory purchase to allow construction of the new General Post Office in 1859, after 90 years of entertainment, including a command performance of *Rob Roy* for George IV in 1822.

The second site in the city to accommodate a Theatre Royal was situated in a section of Broughton Street no longer extant, but approximately where the steps for St Mary's Metropolitan Cathedral now overlook the roundabout joining Picardy Place and Leith Street. This was best known as the Theatre Royal (obviously, after the closure of its predecessor in 1861), although it had a number of other names in its lengthy history. Remarkably, the building burned down in 1853 (when known as the Adelphi), 1865, 1875, 1884, and in 1946. The 1865 conflagration caused six deaths including that of the Dean of Guild, George Mortimer, who valiantly tried to rescue a victim buried under rubble, only to be killed himself. The last of these accidents, in 1946, proved to be the final curtain for the 1,500 seat venue, although the shell of the building remained visible more than 20 years later.

Other old-established theatres in Edinburgh shared their history with cinema entertainment – particularly the Princess Theatre in Nicolson Street, the Garrick in Grove Street, the Gaiety in Leith, and, above all, the Gateway in Elm Row. For this reason the theatre historian is recommended to refer to the work of Brendon Thomas in his

The Last Picture Shows, Edinburgh (see CINEMAS) as the written histories of the city's now extinct theatres, such as Dibdin's Annals of the Edinburgh Stage, are very dated, apart from those books dealing with individual theatres. The Third Statistical Account (1966) gives a detailed history of the Gateway, owned by the Chuch of Scotland. George Baird's unpublished records in Edinburgh City Libraries should certainly be consulted, as should Norma Armstrong's bibliography in manuscript form of the city's theatres from 1715 to 1820. A summary table of Edinburgh theatres gleaned from these works is listed on pages 342–3.

A fascinating footnote in Edinburgh's theatre history concerned the 150-seat Marionville theatre, built in the 1780s by James Macrae so that he, his wife, and their friends, could satisfy their urge to indulge in amateur dramatics. Tragedy struck in 1790, however, when Macrae became involved in an altercation with a servant over the hiring of a sedan chair for a lady leaving the Theatre Royal. Macrae felt it necessary to administer a beating to the servant, whose master, Sir George Ramsay, declined to dismiss him, implying that he disbelieved Macrae's account of the incident. Honour had then to be satisfied, astonished golfers at Musselburgh Links witnessing a pistol duel between Macrae and Ramsay one April morning. Sir George was killed, and Macrae had to flee to France, where he soon found himself in the Bastille. Although he survived until 1820, his life and career were ruined, and the theatre's subsequent history is unknown.

Tourism

'Thy sons, Edina, social, kind,
  with open arms the Stranger hail'. . .(Burns)

Ever since Thomas Cook organised the first package tour to Edinburgh back in the 1850s, the Scottish capital has been recognised as the motor which drives the nation's tourist industry. In 1992 the city was visited by 1.92 million people, spending £338 million, although that does not include visitors staying with local people, or day-trippers. Unofficial sources put the figure as high as 8,000,000 visitors annually. The number of tourist-linked jobs in the city was estimated at 20,000 in a 1993 survey by the District Council.

With such attractions as the Castle, the Palace of Holyroodhouse, and the International Festival, it is obvious that the city has a lot to offer the visitor. However, complacency should not be allowed to affect the resident's perception of the city's attractiveness. A 1989 report called the Edinburgh Tourism Review found that, although the city has a central area and setting of world significance, confirmed in 1995 by the award of World Heritage status by UNESCO, the first such award to any site on the Scottish mainland, nevertheless, there were problems to be considered.

These were perceived as traffic congestion, with inadequate provision for pedestrian movement, and an inappropriate number of car and coach parking facilities, lack of training for staff in tourist-related jobs, and poor presentation and marketing of the city, particularly in countering an image of sedateness.

As a result of the Review, an organisation called Edinburgh Marketing was set up, its tourist-orientated functions since taken over by the Edinburgh Tourist Board, which is working with the two local authorities and Local Enterprise Edinburgh and Lothian (LEEL) in the Edinburgh Tourism Initiative. Its purposes are to improve Edinburgh's position in an industry becoming increasingly competitive, and in particular to maximise the tourist potential of the Old Town.

ATTRACTIONS

The most popular attractions for visitors in Edinburgh are as follows (1992 Scottish Tourist Board figures unless otherwise indicated):

Edinburgh Castle	992,078 (1994)
Royal Botanic Garden	662,459
Edinburgh Zoo	526,438 (1994)
Royal Museum Scotland (Chambers Street)	474,024 (1994)
Royal Scots Regimental Museum	400,000 (Est.)
National Gallery of Scotland	358,235
Scottish United Services Museum	343,096
Palace of Holyroodhouse	252,343 (1994)
Scottish National Portrait Gallery	239,155 (1994)
Museum of Childhood	234,808

The city's festivals are an obvious attraction for visitors – although perhaps an exaggerated one; it is not unknown for visitors to the city in August to express surprise at finding some sort of Festival going on! At least, they knew enough about Edinburgh to know that it was worth visiting in the first place!

A recent boost to the capital's tourist industry is the long-overdue opening of the *Edinburgh International Conference Centre*. Situated in the city's West End, overlooking the Western Approach Road, but entered from Morrison Street, this drum-like building opened for business on 17 September 1995. Its main auditorium seats 1,200 in a raked configuration, the space being divisible by moving partitions into areas of 600 seats and two smaller areas of 300 each. The stage is 200 metres square and there are secondary stages of 20 square metres each. A banqueting or exhibition hall of 1,200 square metres completes the very impressive facilities, although one minor criticism is the labelling of the different suites with place names foreign to the Edinburgh area – Strathblaine, Fintry, Galloway etc.

When it is considered that the Foreign Office reportedly refused to bring a European Community 'summit' to Edinburgh in the 1980s because of a perceived lack of a conference hall, a decision only overcome for reasons of political expediency by 1992, it is obvious that the city's conference centre is a much-needed boost for an area of the tourist trade which peaks outside the usual period of July and August.

ACCOMMODATION

In 1993 the number of hotel and guest rooms available for visitors to Edinburgh totalled 7,162, providing 14,479 beds. 569 self-catering units were available, and four camping parks. Hostels and educational premises making bed spaces available at holiday times comprised 2,964 in 2,537 bedrooms. (Scottish Tourist Board figures). According to Edinburgh District Council

Edinburgh's International Conference Centre opened in 1995, providing a long-overdue venue for meetings for up to 1,200 delegates. The main auditorium can be divided up by moving curved partitions to create three separate meeting places. (City of Edinburgh Council)

figures, there were 162 hotels in the capital in 1992/3, offering 5,661 rooms and 11,185 bedspaces, (*see also* HOTELS).

TRANSPORT LINKS

Obviously, good transport links will always be an important factor in enhancing an area's attractiveness to visitors. Edinburgh, in that case, is an enigma. It is one of the few cities in Britain with no motorway – or even dual-carriageway – link to London, it has no airport providing regular flights to and from North American destinations, and comparatively few to Europe, and no fast rail link from airport to the city centre. The city's principal railway station is stuck at the bottom of a valley with no escalators for pedestrians, despite a newspaper call for escalator provision as far back as 1925, (*see*

also AIRPORTS, RAILWAYS, ROADS AND STREETS).

Edinburgh is a place the tourist really has to *want* to visit! No wonder more and more cruise ships are coming to Leith – it's probably the easiest way to get here!

DISADVANTAGES OF TOURISM

A local councillor once remarked that a community's desire to stimulate tourism in its area was a sure sign that residents didn't know just what tourists can be like. Any inhabitant of York or the Lake District could agree with that adage, as thousands of uninvited visitors block the streets, clog up public transport, and increase pressure on cleansing and sewerage systems never intended to cope with such increased numbers. When it is considered that the population of Edinburgh can increase by something like 25 per cent on a single summer day, the scale of the problem can be appreciated.

One subtle change that tourists have brought to Edinburgh over the last 40 years is an enforced reduction in the Edinburgh citizen's natural hospitality, of the kind Burns wrote about in his 'Address to Edinburgh'. Improved air connections, and the spread of 'backpack' tourism, has led to a huge increase in the number of visitors to Edinburgh who may have difficulties with the English language (or the Edinburgh version of it), to the extent that a local person can no longer offer directions to tourists obviously lost in the street, *unless* the tourist asks for these first. Helpful local people, rebuffed by tourists staring at upside-down maps, should remember that these visitors may come from cities where people approaching them in the street are threatening violence, begging, or selling something. Edinburgh folk must put their natural helpfulness on 'hold'. Tourists seem to prefer asking other tourists for directions anyway!

Trams

Edinburgh's last tram ran on 16 November 1956. When it reached its depot at Shrubhill (Leith Walk) for the last time – shorn of many of its fittings by screwdriver-wielding souvenir hunters *en route* – it brought to an end 85 years of tram operations in Scotland's capital, using three forms of motive-power – horse, cable, and electricity.

In contrast to many British cities, trolleybuses never operated in Edinburgh.

History

Edinburgh's first trams were horse-powered and operated from 6 November 1871 by Edinburgh Street Tramways, a commercial concern, between Haymarket and Bernard Street in Leith. The system's construction was contracted to Sir James Gowans, the route from Leith reaching Princes Street by alternative lines up Leith Street or along York Place and St Andrew's Street. So difficult were the inclines for the unfortunate horses, that 'trace' or auxiliary horses had to be employed where the incline was steepest. North Bridge was crossed by tram line in 1872 and a circle route was soon offered to the public, in both directions, via Marchmont and Church Hill back to the West End.

It appears that bad management made the city authorities take an interest in acquiring the system themselves, as they were permitted by law to do, while cable operation began to sound appealing, particularly for a city with so many hills. In cable car operation, a wire rope cable was quite literally wound through the streets in a narrow open conduit between the tram tracks. When the tram driver wished to stop his vehicle he simply retracted the gripper mechanism attaching his tram to the cable, reapplying it when he wished to restart his vehicle. A short section of track can still be seen today in Waterloo Place, the third 'rail' (in fact, the open conduit) still visible.

Meanwhile in 1888, another commercial tram company introduced cable cars to the city, running between Hanover Street and Goldenacre on a 3.5 inch (8.5 cms) wire rope cable operated by stationary steam engines at a depot in Henderson Row.

Owned by the Edinburgh Northern Tramways Company, a five-minute frequency was offered, and tracks extended from Frederick Street down to Comely Bank via Stockbridge.

The cable system was considerably extended in June 1888 with the opening of the Edinburgh and District Tramways Company, effectively a commercial adjunct to the Town Council. The legal and financial ramifications of the municipal takeover were highly complicated, and are best recounted in D.L.G. Hunter's book on Edinburgh's transport (*see* BIBLIOGRAPHY, Transport). The principal city cable was operated from Shrubhill, with auxiliary cables operated by smaller power stations at Tollcross and Portobello.

While Edinburgh invested in cable operations, the reorganisation of the transport authorities resulted in Leith Town Council taking over the trams and buses in the Port from 1904. Very farsightedly, the Council decided to convert its trams to electric operation, (as did Musselburgh) and from August 1905, Leith's trams liveried in Munich Lake and Ivory, and taking their power from overhead wires, started running between the foot of Leith Walk and Bonnington Terrace, and Pilrig and Stanley Road. Pilrig rapidly became an unwanted obstacle between the Leith and Edinburgh systems at the junction of Pilrig Street and Leith Walk.

For around a quarter of a century it was impossible for a citizen to make an uninterrupted journey up or down Leith Walk. After Leith had electrified in 1905, shaming its neighbour up the Walk, passengers had to alight from one car and get into another which would take them on to their destination. The 'Pilrig Muddle' became famous, and Leith Central station made rapid inroads into travelling revenue after its opening in 1903.

Edinburgh had preferred cable cars to electric because it was felt that an overhead catenary would be unacceptable to public opinion, particularly in Princes Street or on the Mound. But within 20 years, the Edinburgh system became an anachronism. San Francisco's little cable cars may have climbed half-way to the stars, but Edinburgh's 200 cars on 25 route miles – the fifth largest cable system in the world – were a stock-in-trade for every music hall comedian of the time.

Edinburgh and Leith amalgamated in 1920, although to no immediate effect in eradicating the 'Muddle'. It was not until 20 June 1923 that an electric tram was able to voyage from Leith into the great unknown – South Bridge – where the dignatories on board were bombarded with flour by students. A new line built westwards from Ardmillan to Slateford in 1910 had been electrified from the start, but that line was unique in Edinburgh, and converting the existing system was a substantial operation. Princes Street was converted from cable to electric traction overnight in October 1922, and the last cable car ran to Portobello on 23 June 1923. Tram travel all the way to Port Seton was now possible until 1928 and Musselburgh until 1954.

Edinburgh's electric trams operated from four depots – Gorgie, Leith Walk, Portobello, and Tollcross, with Shrubhill the main engineering centre. The vehicles themselves were home-made or came from various manufacturers, or in some cases

Withdrawal of tram services in the city was looming when this 1930s 'streamlined' vehicle was pictured outside Morningside Road railway station on the 11 service to Stanley Road, Trinity. This service lasted to September 1956, and Edinburgh's last trams ran in November of that year. Morningside's railway station closed in 1962. (W.S. Sellar)

were second-hand from other systems. An example of the first of these categories is preserved tramcar 35, built at Shrubhill in 1948. Perhaps the most interesting of Edinburgh trams was the 'streamlined' class, delivered by English Electric and other builders in 1935. Even to postwar eyes, these trams exuded a certain glamour; trams *de luxe*.

Many transport historians believe that Edinburgh's tram system was dismantled without sufficient thought being given to future conditions. With their tracks running in the middle of city-centre thoroughfares, and with some increased reserved areas on major arterial roads, they could have provided, assuming investment in new vehicles, the very kind of rapid

transport system being so expensively considered for the city nowadays. As it was, nearly 48 route-miles (77 kilometres) of the network was brought to the point of oblivion in less than five years.

Edinburgh-born author and TV personality Ludovic Kennedy recalled the city's tram network in his autobiography when he wrote 'I loved the Edinburgh trams, the yellow slatted wooden seats, the whine and rattle as they gathered speed, the driver's low-pitched bell to shoo people out of the way'.

ELECTRIC TRAM ROUTES IN EDINBURGH

(Based on information in J.L. Stevenson's book *The Last Trams*, Edinburgh 1986, currently out of print). The colours listed below refer to the lamps displayed on the front upper body of the tram to identify it at night.

The last tram was given an unusually sensitive farewell party by the Corporation on 16 November 1956. After a day in which specially white-liveried car no 224 had toured what was left of the system, a farewell parade of ten trams departed Braids terminus at 7.45 pm for Shrubhill. The last car of all, 217, dropped behind at the Mound, from where, with 224, it made its way to the depot preceded by a preserved horse bus. Thousands watched this tribute to 85 years of tram transport.

ROUTE		COLOURS	CLOSURE DATE
1	Liberton-Corstorphine	Red/Blue	27 March 1954
2	Stenhouse-Granton	Blue/Blue	13 December 1952
3	Newington Stn-Stenhouse	Blue/White	28 March 1953
4	Piershill-Slateford	White/Blue	2 May 1953
5	Piershill-Morningside	Red/Green	30 October 1954
6	Marchmont Circle	White/Red	26 May 1956
7	Stanley Road-Liberton	Red/Red	11 March 1956
8	Granton-Newington Stn	Red/Yellow	2 April 1955
9	Colinton-Granton	Yellow/Yellow	22 October 1955
10	Bernard St-Colinton	White/Yellow	22 October 1955
11	Stanley Rd-Fairmilehead	Red/White	11 September 1956
12	Corstorphine-Joppa	Yellow/Blue	10 July 1956
13	Churchhill-Granton Circular	White/Green	16 June 1956
14	Churchhill-Granton Circular	Yellow/Green	16 June 1956
15	King's Road-Fairmilehead	Green/White	18 September 1954
16	Fairmilehead-Granton	Green/Green	11 September 1956
17	Newington Stn/Granton	White/White	10 March 1956
18	Waverley-Liberton Dams	Yellow/White	25 March 1950
19	Craigentinny Avenue-Tollcross	Green/Red	26 May 1956
20	Post Office-Joppa	Red/Red	13 November 1954
21	Post Office-Levenhall	Green/Green	13 November 1954
22	Stenhouse-North Junction St	Blue/Blue	13 December 1952
	(Previously Post Office-Musselburgh until 1939)		
23	Granton Rd Stn-Morningside	Green/Yellow	16 November 1956
24	Waverley-Comely Bank	Red/Red	31 May 1952
25	Craigentinny Ave-Drum Brae	Blue/Yellow	10 July 1954
26	Piershill-Drum Brae South	Blue/Red	10 July 1954
27	Granton Rd Stn-Firrhill	Yellow/Red	6 August 1955
28	Stanley Road-Braids	Blue/Green	16 November 1956

Twinning

Edinburgh is twinned with eight other cities worldwide, and these are listed below. This entry also deals with other 'Edinburghs' throughout the world, even although there are no formal twinning links with any of them.

The twinned cities are arranged in chronological order of an agreement being signed:

CITY	YEAR WHEN AGREED	POPULATION
Munich (Germany)	1954	1.3 million
Nice (France)	1958	331,000
Florence (Italy)	1964	453,000
Dunedin (NZ)	1974	105,600
San Diego (USA)	1977	1.9 million
Vancouver (Canada)	1977	1.26 million
Xi'an (China)	1985	5.9 million
Kiev (Ukraine)	1989	2.6 million

The twinning of communities in different countries began in Europe after the Second World War, and was originally designed to establish links which might help prevent a third conflagration. The arrangement involves the exchange of visits by youth and school groups, the sharing of exhibitions, and the swapping of technical information on projects of shared interest.

As can be seen from the list above, Edinburgh's twinned cities are now also to be found beyond Europe's shores. The largest is Xi'an in north-west China, and this twinned status enabled Edinburgh residents to enjoy a District Council Museums' exhibition of the Terracotta Army in 1988. All four of the latest cities to twin with Scotland's capital are considerably bigger than Edinburgh, but curiously, Edinburgh's status as a national capital does not seem to weigh heavily in this equation – not one of the eight twinned cities was also a capital when the twinning agreement was drawn up, although Kiev is now. Xi'an is proving to be a controversial twin. In 1994 a number of District councillors argued against renewing a twinning arrangement with Xi'an in view of the Chinese government's appalling human rights record, and the twinning is currently suspended.

In addition to the official twinning arrangement between the cities, there is also an Edinburgh-San Diego Twin City Association promoting a range of mutual activities between the cities. In the case of Munich, a miniature version of the twinning treaty between Edinburgh and the Bavarian capital was signed in December 1992 between the city communities of Wester Hailes and Neuperlach (Munich), formalising 13 years of community links between the two suburbs.

Lothian Region had an informal partnership arrangement with the Danish city of Alborg, and, at the close of its working life in 1995, was arranging informal links with the Japanese city of Kyoto.

OTHER 'EDINBURGHS'

Communities also known as 'Edinburgh', or something very similar, can be found in the states of Illinois, Indiana, Missouri, New Jersey, North Dakota, and Virginia in the United States of America. There is an

'Edinburg' in Texas, an 'Edinboro' in Pennsylvania (shades of the original Edinburgh's delineation in Bradshaw's British railway timetables!), as well as a Mount Edinburgh in Australia's Queensland.

In addition to all these, the principal settlement in the mid-Atlantic volcanic island of Tristan da Cunha is called Edinburgh. Perhaps the biggest of all these communities is the south Texan city of Edinburg, founded by an Edinburgh-born settler called John Young. The original settlement no longer exists and the present city decided to drop its final 'h' in 1911. A university town of around 29,000 inhabitants in 1990, Edinburg is the capital of Hidalgo county, in the Lower Rio Grande valley.

Universities and Colleges

Edinburgh has three universities and a sustantial number of further education colleges. As a result, the student population of the city was no less than 32,068 present on the day of the 1991 Census, or designated as 'absent residents'. Of these, 4,923 had been born outside the United Kingdom.

The three universities are: **Edinburgh**, **Heriot-Watt** and **Napier**. The Open University has its Scottish headquarters in Edinburgh, its Scottish student body totalling 11,771 in 1993.

EDINBURGH UNIVERSITY

Founded in 1583, Edinburgh University is the youngest of Scotland's first four establishments of learning dating from post-Reformation times. Its principal centres in the city are the Old College on South Bridge, the complex (including Medical School, Library, and Theatre) based on Bristo Place and George Square, and King's Buildings, where a science campus is located near the foot of Liberton Brae.

The University is traditionally famous for its legal department and its medical school, the latter being situated next door to the Royal Infirmary, where, until 1948, senior university staff and students worked unpaid (*see* HOSPITALS). A strong teaching connection still exists, although changes in educational techniques have allowed the Infirmary's planned move to Little France to cause no inconvenience. The Dental Hospital also has strong links with the University.

The governing body is the University Court, composed of delegates from the *Senatus Academicus* – responsible for teaching and discipline in the university – as well as representatives of the General Council of Graduates, the Principal, the Chancellor's Assessor, and the Rector. The last-named is elected by the student body triennially, and in Edinburgh a tradition has sprung up of a student rector being elected, as opposed to the usual comedian or actor so frequently chosen elsewhere. Both *Senatus* and University Court meet six times annually.

The university's buildings interiors are among the most imposing in central Edinburgh, particularly the Upper Library and New Senate Room, while the McEwan Hall is described by the *Buildings of Scotland* volume as a 'magnificent

353

Edinburgh has lost many of its farms over the second half of the 20th century, but cattle still graze within the city's boundaries. This 1995 view looks over pasture land to King's Buildings with the Edinburgh School of Agriculture to the left of the picture.

petrified blancmange with a shallow ribbed dome and lantern'. It is the venue for the university's degree-awarding ceremonies. More utilitarian is the 86 acre (35 hectares) campus at King's Buildings at West Mains Road and Mayfield Road, dating from 1920.

History

Scotland already had three universities when Edinburgh's was established as the 'Tounis College' by the city council in 1582. Mary of Guise had commissioned lectures on canon law and Greek at the city's Magdalen Chapel some 25 years before, so an element of a teaching tradition already existed, and the new college inherited part of a legacy from the Bishop of Orkney to help establish a college of law. Degrees were awarded from the outset, although these had no strictly legal validity until James VI granted an Act of Parliament

sanctionising this in 1621 – in return for which he required the new seat of learning to be known as King James's College for all time thereafter.

It has not been so known, and the university's constitution has changed over the centuries, the connection with the Town Council becoming a matter of some friction, being legally broken in 1858.

HERIOT-WATT UNIVERSITY

The city's second oldest university, Heriot-Watt was promulgated in 1966 from the college of the same name. In 1989 it abandoned its city-centre bases – in Chambers Street, where the Sheriff Courts now take its place, and the Mountbatten building in the Grassmarket – to occupy a new campus at Riccarton, near Currie. Its syllabus has always leaned to the technical, with engineering and scientific subjects prominent, but has included brewing science from 1905 and mining engineering from 1913. Off-shore engineering is another area of study highly relevant in modern times.

History

Initially established as a night school for 'mechanicals', the university was known as the Watt Institute, and occupied a number of addresses in the city before amalgamating in 1879 with part of George Heriot's Hospital (i.e. school). The new Heriot-Watt college became a central institution in 1902, and enjoyed a very central site, complete with a statue of James Watt famous for its unfinished appearance (the protractors Watt was supposed to be holding were missing).

NAPIER UNIVERSITY

This is the newest of the city's centres of learning, having been formed from a technical college established in 1964. It currently has 9,300 students, taught by 1,500 staff. Napier is based around three principal campuses, the oldest being at Merchiston, where the tower building belonging to John Napier (of logarithms fame) is the centrepiece for an imaginative development. There are newer campuses at Sighthill, at Craiglockhart, and at Craighouse, near Morningside. There is also a smaller centre in Morningside Road, formerly the parish church.

The University has four faculties – Applied Arts, Engineering, Science, and the Business School.

EDINBURGH COLLEGE OF ART

Opened in 1907, Edinburgh's art college enjoys a worldwide reputation. Its syllabus covers such practical aspects of arts as design, architecture, and planning, but the traditional skills are well represented, and the college, based at Lauriston Place has a fine sculpture court as its centrepiece.

Some of its alumni are known as the 'Edinburgh School', and although perhaps less well-known than the Glasgow Boys, the work of Gillies, MacTaggart and Redpath still command respect through the art world. Their use in the 1920s and '30s of bold colouring and semi-abstract expression of local landscapes and topical portraiture is still recognisable.

QUEEN MARGARET COLLEGE

Based on four campus sites, 'QMC' is fast becoming recognised as a potential university in the making. The college specialises in modern arts and sciences, based in such fields as communications, domestic economy, and tourism management. It has four campuses, the main one on a 24 acre (10 hectares) site at Clerwood Terrace, north of Corstorphine. The Gateway theatre was recently acquired from Scottish Television for drama instruction, as well as the former Leith Academy building on the edge of Leith Links. There is also a Business Development Centre in Drumsheugh House in the city's west end.

History

The college's roots lay in the founding of the Edinburgh School of Cookery in 1875, renamed the Edinburgh College of Domestic Science in 1930, and known as 'Atholl Crescent' for nearly all that time. The college was particularly active in the Second World War in nominating its brightest graduates for canteen management as the spread of munition and other factories overwhelmed commercial catering firms. In 1959 the college was designated a centre for higher learning, and in 1971 changed its name to the more euphonius Queen Margaret College, since its range of subjects now stretched far beyond catering.

MORAY HOUSE COLLEGE

One of the oldest colleges in the city, Moray House began training teachers as far back as 1835, although its modern curriculum is now much wider. It has occupied the Moray House building between Canongate and Cowgate since 1848, but has now spread to a second campus, the former Dunfermline College of Physical Education at Cramond. In 1991 Moray House became the Institute of Education of Heriot-Watt University, and continues its fine tradition of educational and vocational training.

STEVENSON COLLEGE

Founded in 1970, Stevenson College is situated adjacent to South Gyle Business Park, and is active in a wide range of educational disciplines, from engineering to social work. The college is named for Robert Stevenson, the Scottish civil engineer and lighthouse builder who was the grandfather of Robert Louis Stevenson.

TELFORD COLLEGE

Founded in 1968, Telford College has three campuses in the city – all of them in the Crewe Toll area – and no fewer than 15,000 students, of whom 2,500 are full-time. Subjects taught range from building to hairdressing.

JEWEL AND ESK COLLEGE

With one of its three campuses situated within the city – on Milton Road East – this college carries on a strong tradition of vocational and technical education. It has taken on the former teaching activities of Leith Nautical College, which explains why its Edinburgh building has a ship's superstructure for training purposes, completed in 1977. (The 'Jewel' was a lucrative coal seam *see* DISTRICTS: NIDDRIE)

Villages

Edinburgh contains a number of almost self-contained communities which deserve the generic description of villages, and are all worthy of a visit. They are, in purely alphabetical order – Cramond, Dean, Duddingston, Newcraighall, and Swanston. The edges of such formerly distinct communities of Colinton, Corstorphine, Davidson's Mains, Joppa, Morningside, Restalrig, Stockbridge and Newhaven, have become blurred as the 'gaps' between districts have been filled in to produce an almost homogeneous conurbation (*see* DISTRICTS). The history of the city's villages has been extensively recorded by historian Malcolm Cant, and the reader is referred to his works listed in the BIBLIOGRAPHY, under Districts.

CRAMOND

Recent excavations suggest that the Romans built a fort at the mouth of the Almond as far back as AD 142, but the community at Cramond has made light of what, for many others, would be a powerful tourist attraction to exploit. Cramond villagers obviously believe that their community is attractive enough as it is, and they would be difficult to argue with on that score.

The whitewashed, red-roofed cottages make up one of Edinburgh's most beautiful areas, yet the village was a hive of industry in the 18th and early 19th centuries. A number of mills on the river produced iron implements, from nails to anchors, but water power from the river proved to be too unreliable to make Cramond competitive in the increasingly industrialised world, particularly since coal had to be brought specially to the area.

Oyster fishing was another occupation for the villagers at one time, but now Cramond is very much residential. Its residents may be the most prosperous in the city; no less than three-fifths of the houses contain six or more rooms, three times the city average. Car-owning statistics show that Cramond had 1.37 cars per family (city average 0.69), with nearly 5 per cent of Cramond motorists owning three or more cars each.

For more information about its maritime history, *see* PORTS. (*see also* FERRIES and BRIDGES)

DEAN VILLAGE

Just half a mile from the city's West End, the Dean Village nestles in the valley of the Water of Leith, with Telford's great bridge brooding above (*see* BRIDGES). Originally called the Village of the Water of Leith, this self-contained community was famous for meal-milling and bakery products. Now it is a highly attractive residential area, its

centrepiece 19th century quadrangle called Well Court, accommodating artisans' houses and a hall. New housing has blurred the edges of the old village, but it is still one of Edinburgh's most interesting districts.

DUDDINGSTON

A linear village at the south-eastern entrance to the Queen's Park, (although the parish extended to Easter Duddingston, nowadays Joppa), Duddingston is one of the oldest-inhabited parts of Edinburgh. The earliest inhabitants were lake-dwellers living in stilt-supported crannogs, but the terrestrial village grew from the siting of the Kirk, founded in the 12th century and still characterised by a fine Norman arch. Although most of the buildings here date from the 19th century, the village was part of the Holyrood debtors' sanctuary at one time, and it was here that James Tytler wrote much of the *Encyclopaedia Britannica*, where Raeburn pictured the skating minister of the Canongate, and where Edinburgh's oldest pub was established, possibly as early as the 15th century. Well worth visiting! (*see also* LOCHS and PUBS.)

NEWCRAIGHALL

Probably the most distinctive of the city's villages, Newcraighall is situated on Edinburgh's north-eastern frontier. It is a former mining village, similar to hundreds once common in coalfields all over Britain, with its rows of single-storey terraces once overlooked by the lift-tower of the colliery which gave the settlement its *raison d'être*. Although coal had been dug here for many centuries it was the opening of the 'Klondyke' seam in 1897, a year after a gold rush in Canada (which gave the new mine its name) that saw the village reach its peak as a mining centre.

By the 1920s, 1,000 men were producing a quarter of a million tons of coal a year, some of the underground galleries reaching out under the Forth. However, geological problems forced the pit's closure in 1968, and the nearby Kinnaird retail park nowadays offers less dangerous employment for local people. Their community has made its impact on the silver screen, the 1972 film *My Childhood* launching the tragically all-too brief career of local film director Bill Douglas (*see* FILMS).

SWANSTON

Separated from the rest of Edinburgh by the new by-pass (*see* ROADS AND STREETS), Swanston village shelters under the Pentland Hills, and is forever associated with Robert Louis Stevenson. The village itself consists of eight whitewashed 19th century cottages, which must be among the few in southern Scotland to be thatched (with reeds from the Tay). The village was well restored by the local authority in 1964 and is one of the city's most attractive locations, although the lack of a focal point may disappoint some visitors. Stevenson summered here from 1867 to 1880, the village featuring in his novel *St Ives*.

Water Supply

From April 1996, responsibility for the provision of water and sewerage services (*see also* SEWERAGE) has been undertaken by East of Scotland Water, one of the three new Scottish utilities taking over from the former regional authorities, in Edinburgh's case, from Lothian Region Water and Sewerage Department.

In 1993 Lothian was responsible for 17 supply reservoirs, 92 service, and seven compensation reservoirs, the last named being used to 'top up' the region's rivers and streams to statutorily stipulated levels. The supply reservoir closest to Edinburgh is Torduff, just above Colinton (the nearby Bonaly reservoir no longer serves such a function), and the largest is the new Megget reservoir in Borders Region. The latter provides a daily water yield of 102.3 megalitres, Talla 81.8, and Fruid 52.3. Torduff in contrast currently provides 0.9 megalitres daily. Water is also taken from the Central Scotland Water Board's supply from Loch Lomond (68.8 megalitres daily), and the capital is nowadays spared the problem of drought which was so regularly a feature of summers after the Second World War.

The city is divided into 12 supply zones – four based on Alnwickhill, four at Firrhill, two at Fairmilehead, and one each at Hillend and Torduff, supplying a total population of 400,000 with fresh water, which, since 1990 has been the subject of stringent European standards regarding quality. This has increased the cost of an industry that Edinburgh people have tended to take for granted, and which has a strong historic legacy.

Water is still freely available to the Scottish consumer on an unmetered basis (although meters can be made available on request). A recent English visitor to Edinburgh expressed astonishment at this fact, enquiring 'how on earth is the water industry paid for up here?' The answer is – through a water rate added to the Council

Tax and levied (for a commission) by the local authorities on behalf of the new water utility.

History

Edinburgh was one of the first British cities to have its own conduited fresh-water supply. In 1616 a Town Council committee led by the Provost, and including James Henrysoun the city's pioneering Medical Officer (*see* PUBLIC HEALTH), visited Comiston, on what we would now call a 'fact-finding' mission to view the springs there, although no actual improvements in water supply appear to have resulted until 1676. The delay is thought to have been caused by public reluctance to pay a levy on fireplaces to fund what historian William Maitland called 'so necessary and desirable a work'.

Up to that time Edinburgh's drinking and household water was taken from the lochs to north and south, the Nor' and Burgh Loch respectively, unless the citizen was lucky enough to have access to the wells in the castle or Cowgate, or two city draw-wells. One of these, the Muse Well in the Grassmarket, had a pendulum pump fitted to it, but by 1747 was so heavily used by the brewers, despite their having their own well, that the Town Council had to ensure that the well was locked at night. In the 16th century a commercial service of water-bearers sprang up, even although their services seem to have been frowned upon by the Council, which in 1580 banned female water-bearers outright. Such a ban was probably difficult, if not impossible, to enforce, and male carriers (Caddies, who also acted as guides after dark) were long a part of the city scene.

Edinburgh Castle had two wells, the Forewell, which can be seen near the Half Moon Battery and is 110 feet (33 metres) deep, and the Back Draw Well, located in the former barrack area. There was also a well immediately to the north of, and underneath the overhang of, the Castle Rock, sometimes referred to as St Margaret's Well, although it should not be confused with the outlet of that name once located in Restalrig. The well-head for the latter was ceremonially 'moved' to the Queen's Park in the 1840s. The Cowgate had one well of such capacity, (77 feet/23 metres shaft with 125 feet/37.5 metres of water permanently available) that the brewing industry in the city prospered on its supply.

By the 17th century, demand for water was beginning to outrun supply, and carriers were having to bring water from the Wells of Wearie in Holyrood Park. Drought was particularly bad in 1653–4, increasing the need for action to supplement the Council's avowed intentions of procuring a piped supply.

In 1676, nearly 60 years after the Town Council had received legal permission to proceed with the project (funding the project proved unwelcome to city ratepayers at that time), a start was made on bringing water into the city from Comiston Springs. These still exist, housed in a small, lightly graffitied, building above Oxgangs Avenue bearing no official plaque denoting its original purpose. Although no longer used for drinking water, the springs empty into cisterns once decorated by lead figurines of a hare, tod (fox), swan, and peewit, denoting the springs' names, some of

A conduited water supply reached Edinburgh's street wells from the nearby Pentlands from 1676. It was to be another two centuries before every house had a domestic supply as a matter of course. (Edinburgh City Libraries)

which are now transferred to the area's avenues of suburban bungalows.

From this cistern, a Dutch engineer named Peter Bruschi or Breusch, laid a 3 inch (7.6 cms) conduit made of lead into the city at a cost of £2,900, with Bruce (as he became known) receiving a bonus of £50. This was a highly significant gratuity – Bruce, a Roman Catholic, suffered considerable religious persecution and had to bring court action against his tormentors who damaged his mills and threw his wife into a pond (*see* INDUSTRY: PRINTING).

Bruce's supply was driven three miles into Edinburgh by gravity, the difference in height being 60 feet (18 metres), 60,000 gallons being conducted per day. The city's supply reservoir was built on Castlehill (replaced by a more modern 1.7 million gallon capacity tank in the 1840s, the latter being in continuous use for nearly 150 years). From here, water flowed to five public wells in the city, nine additional outlets having to be brought into use soon afterwards. From 1945, this historic source of water has drained to the Braid Burn, and the figurines are preserved in Huntly House Museum.

Five of the original 1680s wells can still be seen. The most prominent and decorative of these is the Bow Foot Well, which still stands at the foot of Victoria Street at the east end of the Grassmarket. It was designed in its present form in 1681, complete with the town's seal, by Sir William Browne, the work involved being carried out by Robert Milne, the King's Mason. Less dramatic is the rather plain structure opposite the old Sheriff Court building, immediately west of St Giles. The others are located at the pavement's edge at the head of Old Assembly Close, above the Netherbow at Mowbray House, and at the foot of the Canongate near the west entrance to Queensberry House. The last of these has ironwork dating from a later period (1817). Unfortunately, the well built in the High Street opposite the top of Niddry Street has been removed since being illustrated in A.J. Youngson's 1966 history *The Making of Classical Edinburgh*, (*see* BIBLIOGRAPHY, Buildings).

From 1760 a second supply fed in from Swanston, but demand began to increase yet again with the construction of the New Town at the end of the 18th century, and by 1819 a private company bought the existing waterworks from the city for £30,000. The Edinburgh Water Company set about constructing a new reservoir at Glencorse and securing a new supply from Crawley Springs. By 1821 Edinburgh was receiving 2.5 million gallons daily, with the first house supply being offered at this time. (Leith appears to have enjoyed a house supply on a limited basis in the 1790s – *see* LEITH.) Water supply to all houses was made compulsory by a Police Act of 1862, but this was not fulfilled for some years.

Further investment became necessary as the Industrial Revolution, although mild in Edinburgh compared to other cities, swelled the population figures. In 1869 the Edinburgh and District Water Trust, consisting of representatives from the city, as well as the independent burghs of Leith and Portobello, was constituted, and tackled the problem of seeking water sources even farther to the south. The creation of the Talla reservoir was an epic in itself, the work not being complete until 1905, and requiring conduiting over a distance of 38 miles to the city outskirts, including 22 miles (35.2 kilometres) of specially-constructed aqueduct.

A spectre which has haunted the history of Edinburgh's water supply was the proposal to turn the picturesque St Mary's Loch, in the Yarrow valley, into a reservoir. This was a continuing debate in Town Council circles for much of the second half of the 19th century, finally being rejected on economic grounds, although the second stage of the Megget scheme will allow the pumping of water from the loch to the Megget utility when need arises.

In 1949 the then Edinburgh Corporation became the water authority for both the city and the county of Midlothian, on the basis that city consumers comprised 85 per cent of the total served. The principal post-war works undertaken to cater for the city's ever-increasing demand for water have been the Fruid, Megget, and Loch Lomond schemes. Starting in 1949, water from the Fruid and Manzion burns was diverted by weir and tunnel through the hills to the existing Talla reservoir near Tweedsmuir, with a reservoir constructed at Fruid itself in the 1960s. The Megget reservoir was finished in 1983 after seven years of work, involving the construction of Scotland's highest embankment dam (181 feet high) and one-third of a mile wide. 28 miles of tunnel, pipelines, and aqueducts had to be constructed, and three miles of public road relaid higher in the valley.

In 1973 water came on stream from Loch Lomond through long-distance pipeline, and none too soon, the winter of 1972-3 having seen the first water shortage at that time of year in living memory. Summer shortages were only too prevalent in Edinburgh in the 1950s and '60s, but post-war investment in Edinburgh's water supply infrastructure has had the desired effect of eradicating shortages.

NATURAL AND THERAPEUTIC WELLS

Edinburgh still has a number of naturally-occuring wells, some of whose waters are claimed to have medicinal properties. In Holyrood Park, the Bonnie Wells o' Wearie are bonny no more, having dried up when the railway was built through a tunnel from here to St Leonard's around 1830. On the other side of the park, St Anthony's Well rises close to the ruined chapel overlooking St Margaret's Loch, although it is not thought to have any particular properties. Not far away, at road level, is St Margaret's Well, moved, as previously mentioned, from Meadowbank when the North British Railway works were built in the 1840s. The Gothic cell containing the water source is believed to be modelled on St Triduana's.

St Triduana's in Restalrig is named after a saint who is reputed to have plucked out her own eyes and sent them to an unwelcome, and doubtless unnerved, admirer rather than submit to his advances. The well's waters were supposed to heal ocular problems and were still in use up to 1900. St Katherine's, or the Balm Well, near Liberton, produced minerals in suspension rumoured to benefit the skin. It was protected by James VI, damaged by Cromwell's supporters and rebuilt during the Restoration.

St Bernard's Well stands on the Water of Leith, between Stockbridge and the Dean Village, although it no longer produces sulphurous waters. It is tastefully enshrined in a mock-Roman temple in 1788 (by Alexander Nasmyth to the commission of Lord Gardenstone), and enjoyed a reputation as an all-round health-giver, attested to by Lord Gardenstone himself. The authors of a book on Scotland's medicinal wells, warn fellow well-enthusiasts that not all of the nation's natural water sources are as dignified as St Bernard's, with its marble statue dedicated to Hygeia. (see *Scottish Healing Wells* by Ruth and Frank Morris, 1982.) Nearby is St George's Well, built in 1810 by the Water of Leith, close to where the gorge is straddled by the Dean Bridge.

ARTESIAN WELLS

Edinburgh's brewing industry has flourished largely on its own water supply, but to supplement natural springs in the Cowgate, Holyrood and Duddingston

St Bernard's Well no longer produces its sulphurous waters for those who may believe in its therapeutic powers. This is the most attractively decorated well in Scotland.

areas, an artesian well was sunk by William Younger in the Grange area in 1889, and was in use until 1985. An artesian well is driven down into water-bearing strata originating at a greater height than the well's location, thus forcing water upwards as it seeks its own level. The Grange site was marked by the construction of a massive 22,300-gallon capacity tank building opposite Carlton cricket ground. From here, two pipes ran to the Holyrood and Dumbiedykes areas. (*see also* INDUSTRY: BREWING). The site is now given over to housing.

363

Cloud shadow sweeps across the Edinburgh cityscape as seen from Blackford Hill in this 1995 shot.
The Castle is to the left of the picture.

Weather

It was Edinburgh's own Robert Louis Stevenson who wrote of his home city's weather:

> raw and boisterous in winter, shifty and ungenial in summer, and a downright meteorological purgatory in the spring . . . there could scarcely be found a more unhomely and harassing place of residence.

More succinctly, the modern British playwright Tom Stoppard, who owes much to the city for the early championing of his work, has ungratefully called Edinburgh 'the Reykjavik of the south'.

Neither description is justified. East central Scotland is much drier than the west of the country, and it is not unusual to have winters entirely free of snow in Edinburgh. Perhaps the winds are the city's undoing; one historian, Hugo Arnot, believed that the 'great violence of the winds' ensured that the smell of the Old Town's plumbing, or lack of it, was widely dispersed, possibly resulting in Edinburgh attaching less priority to proper sewerage arrangements than should have been the case in years gone by. The statistics listed below hardly suggest any kind of purgatorial weather regime, when compared with, for example, Glasgow.

Daily temperatures (degrees Celsius):

	1992	1951-80 (Averaged)
Edinburgh	8.9	8.5
Glasgow	8.8	8.6

Daily sunshine (hours):

	1992(Av)	June 92	1951-80 (Av)
Edinburgh	3.6	5.3	3.7
Glasgow	3.3	6.3	3.6

Total rainfall (millimetres)

	1992	1951-80 (Av)
Edinburgh	676	646
Glasgow	1,224	951

Days with snow lying at 0900 GMT.

	1992	1989-91 (Av)
Edinburgh	5	0
Glasgow	3	8

Source : *Scottish Abstract of Statistics.*

The most recent data about Edinburgh's weather was recorded at the Royal Botanic Garden, but until 1992, measurements were taken from the Royal Observatory on Blackford Hill at a height of 441 feet (132 metres) above sea level, in comparison with Glasgow's at Abbotsinch at a height of 18 feet (5.4 metres). Whether this gave the latter an advantage in such matters as winter temperatures is not admitted to by officialdom! Certainly Edinburgh's January and February readings in 1992 were higher (i.e. warmer) than in the previous year, and also higher than the average figure for the years 1951 to 1980.

The city has a branch of the Meteorological Office, situated in Broomhouse Drive, Saughton. This co-ordinates measurements and readings from a variety of locations in the city and its outskirts. Readings are taken daily at the Royal Botanic Garden, as already mentioned, as well as at Edinburgh Airport,

Bush Estate, Penicuik (two different stations), East Craigs scientific station, Leith Harbour (wind measurements), and the Royal Observatory (whose records go back to 1896). This is, however, essentially a *recording* service; Edinburgh's weather *predictions* come from the Meteorological Office in Glasgow, and there is presently something of a weather 'blind spot' in the south-east of Scotland and north-east England, where no radar utility exists to track weather systems. Edinburgh's citizens have more cause than most to treat weather forecasting as something of an inexact science.

A feature of Edinburgh weather which residents and visitors have to endure, is haar. Known to meteorologists as advection fog, this onshore mist is the product of warm air travelling over a cold surface, such as the sea, and then rolling into the city, irrespective of season, on about ten days a year. Opinion towards this phenomenon seems polarised, some citizens enjoying the extraordinary change in perspective where the outline of buildings is softened and the horizon blanked out, while others regard it without affection.

History shows that Edinburgh's mist is no recent feature of local weather conditions. In 1561 Mary Stewart landed at Leith in a haar to claim her throne, her ship not seen by shore watchers, and the city and ports' dignatories caught by surprise. An unusual weather watcher on that occasion was John Knox who took the meteorological conditions as an omen:

In the memorie of man, that day of the year, was never seyn a more dolorous face of the heavin, than was at her arrival, which two days after did so continue; for besides the surfett weat, and corruption of the air, the myst was so thick and so dark, that skairse mycht any man espy ane other the length of two pair of buttis.

History of weather observations

Edinburgh holds an important place in the development of meteorological science. Measurements of air pressure, temperature, rainfall, and wind, were being made by an unknown doctor in the St Giles area in the years 1731-36, with a network of amateur weather-watchers springing up from 1764. In 1855 the Scottish Meteorological Society was founded in Edinburgh, but observing a much wider area. The Society's observers benefitted from the use of the Stevenson Screen, a louvred box devised by Edinburgh's Thomas Stevenson (1818-87), father of RLS, to allow temperature readings unaffected by direct sunshine, and this has become standard equipment for the modern meteorologist.

From 1860 to 1907, the Society's leading light was Alexander Buchan FRS, who came to Edinburgh from Kinross, unable to pursue a teaching career because of a throat illness. Such was his interest in meteorology that within seven years he was demonstrating weather systems on the world's first charts showing isobars, at the Society's then headquarters at 10 St Andrew's Square. He was also responsible for the theory of travelling weather systems, a concept which is now familiar to watchers of daily·television weather forecasts. More's the pity that Edinburgh has not continued in the forefront of weather forecasting!

Wildlife

Edinburgh is rich in wildlife. Covering 100 square miles (26,080 hectares), this is Scotland's biggest city in terms of area, with a comparatively low ratio of people per acre (*see* POPULATION). Inevitably, this creates living opportunities for wildlife in the parkland, gardens, and gap sites which make up such a large proportion of the capital. The variety of terrain also guarantees an assortment of fauna and flora adapted to environments ranging from the 1,500 feet (450 metres) hill contour down to the marine littoral.

Even to the author of this Encyclopedia, by no means a particularly eagle-eyed observer, such delights as kingfishers, foxes, woodpeckers, hares, and shrews have shown themselves in the city, while to see an osprey over Morningside definitely rates a special mention!

The Lothian Biological Records Centre reports that in summer 1995, the following numbers of species of wild creatures could be found in the Edinburgh District area (totals given below are approximate):

The lowest number of species of any of the animal classes listed above is of course that of reptiles, whose sole city representative is the common lizard. No record exists of snakes having been found recently in Edinburgh, although biologists agree that at least one of the city's hills offers suitable conditions for the adder, Britain's only poisonous snake which is not dangerous, indeed is timid, provided it is not approached. The *Third Statistical Account*, published in 1966, comments that 'slow-worms which used to live on Blackford Hill have evidently disappeared'. Any observation of a reptile species inside the city should certainly be communicated as soon as possible to the Scottish Wildlife Trust.

At the time of writing (July 1995), there are three Local Nature Reserves (LNRs) in the city, administered by Edinburgh District Council. These are at Straiton Pond, the first to be declared (*see* LOCHS), the Hermitage of Braid/Blackford Park (*see* PARKS), and Corstorphine Hill (*see* HILLS). There are no National Nature Reserves, the latter being designated by the national authority on nature conservation, Scottish Natural Heritage (SNH).

Mammals	30	species
Birds	230	(inc. non-nesting visitors)
Amphibia	6	(Toad, frog, & four species of newt)
Reptiles	1	(common lizard)
Arachnida (spiders)	150	species
Insecta	12	Orders found, including:
Beetles	500	species minimum
Flies	1,000	species minimum
Butterflies/Moths	700	species
Flowering plants/Ferns	1,000	(inc. 'garden escapes')
Mosses/Liverworts	200	species

There are, however, a number of SSSIs (Sites of Special Scientific Interest) as designated by SNH; these include quite small areas, often with geological as opposed to wildlife interest – such as the Agassiz Rock at Blackford (see HILLS), but almost the entire Forth shoreline of Edinburgh is an SSSI. The largest site so designated in Edinburgh is the Queen's Park, now administered by Historic Scotland.

A proposal to establish a regional park centering on the Pentland Hills has already passed through a consultative stage, although its implementation may be delayed by the reorganisation of local government. In addition, the District Council has also identified the following 28 sites in the city area as being of considerable wildlife importance, the more interesting examples of which are listed:

Braid Burn Corridor	(Semi-natural woodland, roe deer, fox, badger, dipper etc).
Braidburn Valley Park	(Meadowsweet, Water Crowsfoot).
Braid Hills/Mortonhall	(Scrub/heathland plants and birds).
Brunstane Burn	(Variety of aquatic life and small mammals).
Bruntsfield Golf Course (Barnton)	(Little Grebe, roe deer, fox, badger)
Calton Hill & Regent Gardens.	(Woodland, scrub)
Coastline	(Wildfowl, waders, common seals).
Craiglockhart Hills	(Rare grass species, exotic trees, marsh flora, wildfowl at pond. An excellent Nature Trail has been laid out by local volunteers).
Craigmillar Hills & Hawkhill Wood	(Naturally regenerated woodland, scrub, Pipistrelle bats).
The Dells – Colinton, Craiglockhart, and Woodhall Mains	(Semi-natural woodland, Kingfisher, Dipper).
Disused Railway Network	(Mature woodlands, mammals).
Drum Wood	(Ornamental planting, also wetland).
Duddingston Golf Course	(Mature woodland, aquatic fauna).
Duddingston Loch & Bawsinch	(Wildfowl, mature woodland, ground flora).
Edmonstone	(Wooded area, ground flora).
Figgate Burn Park	(Wildfowl, woodland birds).
Gogar Burn	(Kingfishers, invertebrates).
Granton Pond	(Fish, wildfowl – no public access).
Holyrood Park and Meadowfield Park	(Largest unimproved grassland area in Lothians. 350 species of higher plants found here. Some rare invertebrates, also scrub flora).
Lochend Park	(Wildfowl, willows).
Niddrie Burn complex	(Aquatic flora, semi-natural woodland, unimproved grassland flora, Pipistrelle bats).
Redford Brae & Laverockdale	(Native tree species, diverse ground flora).
River Almond	(Water and woodland bird species).
Royal Botanic Garden	(Obviously, floral interest, also large bird and grey squirrel populations).
Silverknowes	(Wading birds, wildfowl).

Union Canal	(Wildfowl, aquatic fauna).
Warriston Cemetery	(Diverse tree varieties, mammals).
Water of Leith	(Fish and invertebrate populations, aquatic birds, including Kingfisher).

The following organisations dedicated to wildlife have offices in Edinburgh (consult the telephone directory for current address and phone number):

Scottish Natural Heritage, Scottish Wildlife Trust, Royal Society for the Protection of Birds, Scottish Ornithologists Club, Countryside Ranger Service (Edinburgh City Council), Scottish Society for the Prevention of Cruelty to Animals (contact this organisation concerning injured animals and birds), Edinburgh Natural History Society, Botanical Society of Edinburgh.

Zoos

Scotland's national zoological park is situated in the Corstorphine area of Edinburgh, three miles west of the city centre. Set in 80 acres (32.8 hectares) on the south side of Corstorphine Hill, the Zoo is the largest in Scotland, and one of the three largest in the United Kingdom. The collection comprises 63 different species of mammals, 64 of birds, 27 of reptiles, 6 of amphibians, and 5 of invertebrates, totalling over 1,400 specimens. Staffed by 120 people, the park is open 365 days a year, and attracted 526,438 visitors in 1994. Its excellent

breeding programme and high curatorial standards have ensured that Edinburgh's zoo has escaped the criticisms which have been heaped on many less well-run establishments.

The park is owned and operated by the Royal Zoological Society of Scotland (RZSS), a learned society dedicated to the study and care of wild animals. The membership is no less than 13,000 strong, and the Society operates an active educational policy at the park.

Edinburgh Zoo, or to be more accurate Scotland's Zoo, is particularly noted for its collection of polar fauna. Since 1914, penguins have been a major part of the zoo's collection, thanks to the membership of the Salvesen shipping family in the RZSS. For decades, the denizens of the penguin colony have provided one of the city's best-loved traditions by going for a walk through the park grounds at two o'clock each day. In 1994 a new penguin enclosure was opened, accommodating 184 of these delightful birds – Britain's largest colony at the time of writing (1995).

History

Corstorphine is not the first site for a zoological garden in the capital. An earlier version of the zoo occupied an area known formerly as Broughton Park, off East Claremont Street, from 1839 to 1857. The collection included an elephant, bears, and the large cats. It is not entirely clear why it closed down; possibly the proprietor's policy of promoting firework displays and the re-enactment of Crimean battles within the park in its later years fatally stressed the animals to the point that the collection dwindled in numbers. Financial problems were probably not the reason for closure, as a substantial sum of money found its way from the former concern into the coffers of the newly-formed Zoological Society of Scotland when it began to actively campaign for a new zoological centre from 1909.

The Zoological Society of Scotland (Royal from 1947) began entirely as an amateur association which successfully persuaded the City Council to take over an estate on the south side of Corstorphine Hill and lease it to the embryonic society. Thus, the Zoo has always received strong municipal backing, and from the opening in 1913 – when animals were temporarily borrowed from a private zoo in Kent – the Edinburgh public has shown extraordinary interest and support. Much of the park was laid out by pioneering conservationists Patrick Geddes and Frank Mears, who successfully adapted the hillside's quarries to form natural-looking enclosures. The Zoo's first director, Tom Gillespie, overcame the site's limited natural water sources by installing a pumped supply, and this has

undoubtedly provided one of the keystones of the Zoo's success.

Despite the onset of the First World War within a year of opening, and the privations of the second conflict in 1939-45, the Zoo established itself very successfully, enjoying breeding success with species previously unable to reproduce in captivity, beginning with king penguins and orang-outangs, while white rhinoceros and Siberian tigers are recent products of the breeding programme. The Zoo has been particularly lucky in the high proportion of specimens gifted to it; often from the Salvesen family, but also from aristocratic, and indeed royal, sources. One disappointment has been the enforced closure of the Carnegie Aquarium, opened in 1927, but whose running costs proved to be too much of a burden for the Zoo in recent years.

The Zoo has had only four Directors – Tom Gillespie (1913–1950), Donald Bowles (1950–55), Gilbert Fisher (1956–1973), and Roger Wheater (1973–), and their work has contributed enormously to the success story of one of the world's finest zoos.

Bibliography

GENERAL

Catford, E.F. *Edinburgh: The story of a city*. Hutchinson, 1975.

City of Edinburgh District Council. Census 91, Edinburgh Topic Sheets.

Keay, J. and Keay, J. *Collins Encyclopaedia of Scotland*. Collins, 1994.

Lothian Regional Council. Structure Plan 1994.

McKean, C. *Edinburgh : Portrait of a City*. Century, 1991.

Rae, W. *Edinburgh: The New Official Guide*. Mainstream, 1994.

Statistical Accounts. (1st, New, and Third). Edinburgh.

ARTS

City of Edinburgh Museums and Galleries. *A Picture of Edinburgh : a celebration of the city and its countryside*. 1995.

Edinburgh Galleries Association. *The Edinburgh Gallery Guide*.

Royle, T. *Precipitous City*: *The Story of Literary Edinburgh*. Mainstream, 1980.

BUILDINGS

Berry, E. *The writing on the walls*. Cockburn Association, 1990.

Bunyan, I.T. *Building Stones of Edinburgh*. Edinburgh Geological Society, 1987.

Dunlop, A.I. *The Kirks of Edinburgh, 1560-1984*. Scottish Record Society, 1989.

Gifford, J. et al. *Edinburgh (Buildings of Scotland)*. Penguin, 1984.

McIvor, I. *Edinburgh Castle*. Batsford/Historic Scotland, 1993.

McKean, C. *Edinburgh: An Illustrated Architectural Guide*. Royal Incorporation of Architects in Scotland, 1992.

McKean, C. T*he Scottish Thirties*. Scottish Academic Press, 1987.

McWilliam, *C. Lothian, except Edinburgh (Buildings of Scotland)*. Penguin, 1978.

Richardson, J.S. *The Abbey and Palace of Holyroodhouse*. HMSO, 1978.

Tranter, N. *The Fortified House in Scotland*. Vol. 1. Edinburgh: Oliver & Boyd, 1962.

Wallace, J.M. *Historic Houses of Edinburgh*. John Donald, 1987.

Youngson, A.J. *The Making of Classical Edinburgh*. EUP, 1966.

DISTRICTS

Baird, W. *Annals of Duddingston and Portobello*. Elliot, 1898.

Cant, M. *Edinburgh: Sciennes and the Grange*. John Donald, 1990.

Cant. M. *Villages of Edinburgh*. (2 vols). John Donald, 1986-7.

Easton, D. (ed.). *By Three Great Roads: A history of Tollcro*ss .... Aberdeen University Press, 1988.

McGowran, T. *Newhaven-on-Forth: Port of Grace*. John Donald, 1985.

Statistical Accounts. (1st, New, and Third). Edinburgh.

EDUCATION AND SCIENCE

Anderson, R.D. *Education and the Scottish People 1750-1918*. Oxford, 1995.

Birse, R.M. *Science at the University of Edinburgh 1583-1983*. Edinburgh University, 1994.

Bown, D. *Four Gardens in One*. HMSO, 1992.

Bruck, H.A. *The Story of Astronomy in Edinburgh*. EUP, 1983.

Edinburgh School Board. *Yearbooks* (various years).

Stevenson, S. and Morrison-Low, A.D. *Scottish Photography: A Bibliography*, 1839-1989. Mainstream, 1990.

ENVIRONMENT

City of Edinburgh Museums and Galleries. *A Picture of Edinburgh: a celebration of the city and its countryside.* 1995.

Edinburgh District Council Planning Department. *An urban nature conservation strategy for Edinburgh: urban wildlife site descriptions.* [No date, received 1995].

Edinburgh Natural History Society. *A Guide to Edinburgh's Countryside.* Macdonald, 1982.

McAdam, A.D. and Clarkson, E.N.K. *Lothian Geology: an excursion guide.* Scottish Academic Press, 1986.

Nimmo, I., *Edinburgh's green heritage*, City Council, 1996

FAIRS AND FESTIVALS

Dale, M. *Sore Throats and Overdrafts.* Precedent Publications, 1988.

Hardy, F. *Slightly Mad and Full of Dangers.* Ramsay Head, 1992.

McNeill, F.M. *The Silver Bough.* Vols. 1-4. Maclellan, 1968.

Scottish Tourist Board. *Edinburgh Festivals Study.* STB, 1992.

GENERAL HISTORY

Dingwall, H.M. *Late seventeenth-century Edinburgh : a demographic study.* Scolar Press, 1994.

Graham, H.G. *The Social Life of Scotland in the Eighteenth Century.* Black, 1899.

Jeffrey, A. *This Present Emergency.* Mainstream, 1992.

Robertson, D. and Wood, M. *Castle and Town: Chapters in the history of the Royal Burgh of Edinburgh.* Oliver & Boyd, 1928.

GOVERNMENT/LOCAL GOVERNMENT.

Armet, H. (Ed.) *Extracts from the Records of the Burgh of Edinburgh.* Oliver & Boyd, 1967.

Cousland, C.J. *Honoured in Scotland's Capital.* 1946.

Craig, F.W.S. *British Parliamentary Election Results.* Macmillan, 1977.

Gray, J.G. *City Not Forsaken.* Edina Press, 1981.

Rait, R.S. *The Parliaments of Scotland.* Maclehose, 1924.

Scottish Burgh Records Society. *Extracts from the Records of the Burgh of Edinburgh.* (1528-57),(1557-71),(1589-1603).

Williams, J.C. *Edinburgh Politics, 1832-1852.* PhD. Thesis, Edinburgh University, 1972.

Young, M.D. *The Parliaments of Scotland: Burgh and Shire Commissioners.* Scottish Academic Press, 1993.

INDUSTRY

Checkland, S.G. *Scottish Banking, a History, 1695-1973.* Collins, 1975.

Cramb, G.E. *History of the Biscuit Makers of Edinburgh.* (Unpublished MS, Edinburgh City Libraries, 1983).

Donnachie, I. *A History of the Brewing Industry in Scotland.* John Donald, 1979.

Halliday, Robert S. *The Disappearing Scottish Colliery.* Scottish Academic Press, 1990.

Munn, C.W. 'The Emergence of Edinburgh as a Financial Centre', in *Industry, Business and Society in Scotland since 1700.* (Cummings, A.J.G., and Devine, T.M. eds). John Donald, 1994.

Third Statistical Account, 1966.

Woodward, H.W. *The Story of Edinburgh Crystal.* Dema Glass, 1984.

LEISURE

Baird, G. *Edinburgh Theatres, Cinemas, and Circuses, 1820-1963.* (Unpublished MS, Edinburgh City Libraries, 1963).

Casciani, E. *Oh How We Danced!* Mercat, 1994.

Scottish Film Council. *Scottish Screen Data Digest* 1994.

Stuart, M. W. *Old Edinburgh Taverns*. Hale, 1952.

Thomas, B. *The Last Picture Shows, Edinburgh*. Moorfoot, 1984.

LEITH

Leith School Board. *Yearbooks* (various years).

Marshall, J.S. *The Life and Times of Leith*. John Donald, 1986.

Marshall, J.S. *Old Leith at Leisure*. Edina Press, 1976.

Mowat, S. *The Port of Leith: its History and its People*. Forth Ports PLC/John Donald. [no date].

PERSONAL VIEWS/REMINISCENCES

Appleby, L. *A medical tour through the whole of Great Britain*. Faber, 1994.

Carlyle, Alexander. *Autobiography*. Foulis, 1910 reprint.

Chambers, Robert. *Traditions of Edinburgh*. Chambers, 1967 (first published in 1824).

Stevenson, R.L. *Edinburgh: Picturesque Notes*. 1878.

PUBLIC SERVICES

Cameron, J. *Prisons and Punishment in Scotland from the Middle Ages to the Present*. Canongate, 1983.

Edinburgh City Libraries. *Lum Hats in Paradise: Edinburgh's Public Library 1890-1990*. 1990.

Reid, A. *Aye Ready! The History of the Edinburgh Fire Brigade, the oldest municipal brigade in Britain*. 1974.

Robertson, D. *A History of the High Constables of Edinburgh*. 1925.

Scottish Office. *A Report on Her Majesty's Inspectorate of Constabulary, Lothian and Borders Police*. 1992.

Tait, H.P. *A Doctor and two Policemen: the history of Edinburgh Health Department, 1862-1974*. [no publisher], 1974.

SPORT

Donald, B. *The Fight Game in Scotland*. Mainstream, 1988.

Mackay, J.R. *The Hibees: The story of Hibernian Football Club*. John Donald, 1986.

McConnell, T. *The Tartan Turf: Scottish Racing, its horses and heroes*. Mainstream, 1988.

Robertson, G. *Tennis in Scotland: 100 years of the Scottish Lawn Tennis Association, 1895-1995*. SLTA, 1995.

Twydell, D. *Rejected F.C. of Scotland, Vol. 1*. Yore Books, 1992.

TRANSPORT

Booth, G. *Edinburgh's Trams and Buses*. Bus Enthusiast, 1988.

Brodie, I *Steamers of the Forth*. David & Charles, 1976.

Hunter, D.L.G. *Edinburgh's Transport*. 2nd Edn. Mercat Press, 1992.

Lloyd's Ports of the World. Colchester, 1994.

Mullay, A.J. *Rail Centres, Edinburgh*. Ian Allan, 1990.

Pooley's Flight Guide: United Kingdom and Ireland, 1994.

Index